International Trade and Economic Development

International Trade and Economic Development

Rajat Acharyya

and

Saibal Kar

Great Clarendon Street, Oxford, OX2 6DP,
United Kingdom

Oxford University Press is a department of the University of Oxford.
It furthers the University's objective of excellence in research, scholarship,
and education by publishing worldwide. Oxford is a registered trade mark of
Oxford University Press in the UK and in certain other countries

First Edition published in 2014

Impression: 1

Published in the United States of America by Oxford University Press
198 Madison Avenue, New York, NY 10016, United States of America

British Library Cataloguing in Publication Data
Data available

Library of Congress Control Number: 2014932449

ISBN 978-0-19-967285-1

Printed and bound in Great Britain by
Clays Ltd, St Ives plc

■ PREFACE

With considerable interest and not necessarily the best expertise, we endured a mutual feeling for the last few years that despite sifting through a lot of resources in the subject, there seems to be a dearth of Masters-level textbooks in International Trade and Economic Development which bring together the entire gamut of issues that should be staple reading for a student opting for this course. Several disparate studies in various areas of trade and development are available in academic journals and as contributions in edited volumes, which we realized could be put together in a systematic and coherent manner to constitute a good stock of course materials for postgraduate course work. At the same time, we observed that issues like trade and labour market, trade and labour migration, standards and copyrights, and outsourcing or offshoring, to name a few, despite their critical importance in view of contemporary experiences in the developing countries, do not receive adequate emphasis in available books. Thus, our ambitious project began. While writing different chapters of the book, we set our goal to offer the most advanced and contemporary readings in trade and development with obvious references to developing countries. In the end, we hope that we have been able to provide our readers a systematic account of the progress of the relevant and important topics on which future research in trade and development shall be built.

We expect that the book should cater best to Masters-level students in Economics interested in international economics broadly defined, and influence critical research questions in related areas. It may also be useful, in parts, for advanced undergraduate students, who have studied basic international economics and mathematical tools commonly used in economics as the prerequisites.

In the course of writing this book, we made debts with many people. First of all, we are deeply indebted to two anonymous reviewers of the book proposal for invaluable suggestions to do with the contents and overall directions. Second, we owe our intellectual debts to friends and colleagues who shaped our scattered ideas during discussions, through critiques in seminars and conferences and via informal interactions in the past. Special mention must be made of Kaushik Basu, Hamid Beladi, Gerrit Faber, Maria D.C. Garcia-Alonso, Kausik Gupta, Basudeb Guha-Khasnobis, Ronald W. Jones, Eliakim Katz, Sugata Marjit, Devashish Mitra, Late Kalyan K. Sanyal, George Slotsve and Thomas Straubhaar for offering valuable suggestions and lending support as mentors, co-authors, and friends. We have undoubtedly learnt a lot more from the colleagues and the students at the various places we visited and been affiliated to, such as the Amsterdam School of Economics; Calcutta University; Centre for Studies in Social Sciences, Calcutta; HWWI, Hamburg; IZA, Bonn;

Jadavpur University; University of Burdwan; University of Kent; University of Rochester; UNU-WIDER; Utrecht University, etc. We remain indebted to Adam Swallow and Aimee Wright for bearing with us during the course of writing this book. Saibal Kar would also like to thank his daughter Ujjayini, now 10 years old, for reading and appreciating the introduction to this book.

The writing of the book borrowed precious time from our families, which they have endured and yet, indulged us at the same time. We express our heartfelt thanks to them.

November 2013
Rajat Acharyya and Saibal Kar

■ CONTENTS

■ LIST OF FIGURES

■ LIST OF TABLES

■ LIST OF ABBREVIATIONS

ASEAN	Association of South East Asian Nations
BENELUX	Belgium, The Netherlands, and Luxembourg
BOP	balance of payments
BPO	business process outsourcing
CAC	capital account convertibility
CARICOM	Caribbean Community and Common Market
CGE	general equilibrium model
CM	Common Market
CU	Customs Union
DAC	Development Assistance Committee
ECB	European Central Bank
ECSC	European Coal and Steel Community
EDT	total outstanding debt
EEC	European Economic Community
EFSF	European Financial Stability Facility
EKC	Environment Kuznets Curve
EMU	Economic and Monetary Union
EPZ	export processing zone
ERM	Exchange Rate Mechanism
EU	European Union
FDI	foreign direct investments
FII	foreign institutional investments
FTA	Free Trade Area
GCC	Gulf Cooperation Council
GDP	gross domestic product
HOS	Heckscher-Ohlin-Samuelson
ILO	International Labour Organization
IMF	International Monetary Fund
IPR	Intellectual Property Rights
IR	individual rationality
IT	information technology
ITeS	IT-enabled services
LDCs	less-developed countries
LHS	left hand side
LTRO	Long Term Refinancing Option
MBD	market-based (price) discrimination
MERCOSUR	Mercado COMUN DEL Sur (Spanish) / Southern Common Market
MFN	most-favoured nation
MNC	Multi-National Corporation
MNE	multinational enterprise
NAFTA	North American Free Trade Agreement

NICS	Newly Industrialized Countries
NTPC	National Thermal Power Corporation of India
OBM	own brand manufacturing
ODA	Official Development Assistance
ODM	original design manufacturing
OECD	Organization for Economic Cooperation and Development
OEM	original equipment manufacturing
OPEC	Organization of the Petroleum Exporting Countries
PPF	production possibility frontier
PTA	preferential trading arrangement
R&D	research and development
RHS	right hand side
RTA	regional trading arrangements
RTB	regional trade blocs
SACU	South African Customs Union
SDT	short-term debt
SEZ	special economic zone
SMSA	Standard Metropolitan Statistical Area
TA	teaching assistant
TAA	Trade Adjustment Assistance
TFP	total factor productivity
TIC	trade indifference curve
TOT	terms of trade
TRIPS	trade related intellectual property rights
UNCTAD	United Nations Conference on Trade and Development
UNESCO	United Nations Educational, Scientific and Cultural Organization
UNHCR	UN High Commission for Refugees

Introduction: The Scope and Coverage of Trade and Development

The history of international trade in commodities chronicled over the last two millennia is as rich and complex as the epics of *Iliad* and *Odyssey* and the *Mahabharata*, which spread over 8 to 4 BCE. In fact, the perceived timings of when the underlying storylines of these epics were taking shape and the period when ancient trade was reaching its new heights are not historically anachronous. Powerful archaeological and textual evidence suggests that at the peak of ancient civilizations, breakthrough techniques in agriculture, brewing, metalwork, weaving, and cattle rearing had become the appurtenances of political and economic power. Strange as it might seem in view of the escalating cost we associate with international trade in goods and services even today, autarky was not the natural choice for traders in 10000 BCE. Various luxury items, stone beads, gold, silver, silk, and seeds were regularly traded between the early-urban settlements in lowland Mesopotamia. By 8000 BCE, trade routes throughout Asia, Africa, and Europe were already in place. Cross-country transport of wheat and grains, dried meat, fish and fruits, liquor etc. were treated as the blue-chip goods that comprised the caravan consignments of the time. City states of Mesopotamia, Eastern Mediterranean, lower Nile Valley, Indus Valley, and countries like China controlled the ancient trade in olive oil, spices, incense, opium, wool, textiles, copper, iron, enamelled mosaics, celadon pottery, cedar timber, silver inlay, carved ivory, precious gemstones, honey, wine, raisins, livestock, and horses.

About a century prior to the birth of Jesus of Nazareth, these trade routes across the East and the West were bustling with activities. Major trade took place along the Incense Route, the Spice Route, the Silk Route and through shorter passages epitomizing perhaps the first wave of globalization. The epics distinctively name and recount the locations, the characteristics, and the interactions between the most important agents of that world order. If the reader judiciously discounts the supernatural excesses of the time, these epics and numerous other religious accounts provide evidence of strong bilateral and multilateral trade, at least exchanges, in goods between the pockets of civilizations. Interestingly, and as a justification for this paraphernalia as motivation for our book, these pockets of civilization both in the East and in the Middle

East, Asia Minor, Egypt, Rome, Athens, and the Horn of Africa were substantially more advanced technologically, and were richer settlements compared to places where much of the wealth has accumulated over the last four centuries.

The pattern continued through the Middle Ages, with Catholic Crusades, expansion of dominion by Muslim conquests, and by the Mongols. The sea routes started getting greater prominence at the time, along with firmly settled trade relationships between cities in Europe, the Middle East, China, India, and the Far East. The trade interactions took truly biblical proportions over the next few centuries provoking the European fortune-seekers, usually with the help of state patronization, to venture into lands of flowing milk, honey, and spices on the one hand and to the land of gold, access to which would allow them to buy all of these, on the other. The fall of the Aztecs in the hands of the Spanish conquerors (1521 CE) and a decade later the similar fate of the Incas (1532 CE) actually began an era of 'fortune reversals'. The El Dorado remained as hidden as ever (even the last hope of finding it, Indiana Jones, seems to have retired—but of course, who can be sure of hidden cards in Hollywood!) and did not help in recovering the lost fortune. Trade and outflow of resources by that time had largely become a one-way traffic to Europe. It is also well-known that once the prosperous trade routes of yesteryears, both land and sea, brought in economic and political aggressors with guns, horses, syphilis, and strong business acumen, the pockets of prosperity started growing big holes in them through which resources drained out thick and fast (Diamond, 1997 had provided strong arguments in favour of 'longitudinal' expansion). By the time the Mercantilists shaped the modern forms of international trade (of course, they believed only in trade surpluses), accumulations and growth in the manner the world recognizes these aspects now, the tables had turned and the odds that trade brings prosperity and peace were largely in favour of the colonial rulers on four corners of the earth. While we witnessed brief turnabouts during the two World Wars, pushing the richer nations in Europe to 'man-made' distresses (fortunately, almost nobody talked about environment at the time), the general direction that the study of international trade and economic development would adopt had found a structure. In other words except for a few unanticipated occurrences, such as the 'transfer paradox'—an outcome of the reparations sent to war devastated Europe, Japan, and the US, the developing countries started drawing the full attention of the subject of trade and economic development. Such attention may have intellectually compensated for the reversal of fortune. The reversals of fortunes for the poor countries have recently been studied from the point of view of institutional reversals in the colonies of Europe (Acemoglu, Johnson, and Robinson, 2002). However, long before that, observed patterns of trade between the developed and the developing countries served as the progenitor of the celebrated Singer-Prebisch hypothesis (1950) and subsequently, the 'subject' of international trade and economic development. In a different way, the reversal according to this thesis occurred owing to the falling terms of trade for the colonies specializing in the export of primary products and importing the costlier manufacturing goods from the colonizers. We devote due attention to this hypothesis in Chapter 1, graduating into several interesting sub-domains in the area. These include further discussion on the problems of trade in primary commodities in Chapter 2, of interactions between international trade, domestic markets for factors, and implications for economic growth in Chapter 3, and the considerably debated role of FDI and MNC activities in developing countries in Chapter 4. Some of these issues, as it is well known to the reader, constitute the core debates in this subject area. As pointed out earlier, we intend to cover the available and time-tested wisdom in the field with some of the less-traversed and yet compelling issues. These include the rich, but textbook-wise under-emphasized, relationship between trade and factor mobility.

We realize that any attempt to cover the length and breadth of topics related to factor mobility, literally speaking, is clearly beyond the scope of a couple of chapters, and for that matter a couple of oversized books. So essentially, we focused on a few interesting issues ranging from well-known graphical treatments by Bhagwati (in Chapter 5) to more modern observations on the complex dynamics involving labour, capital, and technology. The role of asymmetric information between source and destination of the mobile factors of production is the subject matter of Chapter 6. Since money as the form of capital is supposed to be monochrome and speaks the same language no matter where it is deployed, the onus of discrimination, of information black-out, and of considerable social tension is borne, often disproportionately, by the mobile labour. Evidently, the impact of labour mobility is non-trivial for both the source and the host countries. The impact, as this literature claims, depends crucially on how the productivity of mobile labour is interpreted across countries. It simultaneously determines the choice of location made by labour and capital, the occupational categories for labour, the pattern of inward remittances, and of investments in physical and human capital in the context of North-South models of international economics. We offered a few interesting observations on these matters outside the traditional domain of international trade.

Subsequently, the book discusses foreign aid (Chapter 7), dealing with conventional as well as contemporary treatments in the economics of trade and development. The flow of foreign aid is a deeply researched topic and quite dispersed across a number of sources—books, journals, and cross-country development reports. While much of the interest in the interaction between foreign aid and development is reflected in the simple and elegant structures available in Basu (1998), the important ramifications on the theory of aid and on the methodological and empirical studies on aid are briefly touched upon to apprise the student of its scope and coverage. Tracing such topics chronologically may be important at a time when there seems to be a general bias against reviewing older literature beyond a decade or so from the present time, to the extent that the incidence of proving and re-proving the Hechscher-Ohlin-Samuelson theorem gets quite pervasive in the field. We continue to discuss important references on which newer ideas are built. In the later part of the book, we begin with a chapter on economic welfare and poverty. It is also a well-researched topic with numerous contributions available in the literature. We made use of the most comprehensive and commanding surveys in this area to motivate and explore the trade-poverty links with the help of simple models (Chapter 8). Further, Chapter 8 argues that since the main resistance to trade liberalization in most countries comes from import competing industries where it directly leads to job losses, the trepidation about economic reforms turns itself into heated political debates. Compensation schemes (generally termed as Trade Adjustment Assistance or TAA) for those who lose jobs due to trade liberalization, are available only in a few advanced countries. None of the developing and transition countries practice TAA schemes. Moreover, the majority of developing countries do not 'functionally' offer unemployment benefit or other social security safeguards. However, any intervention such as unemployment benefit creates further distortions, particularly when unemployment is frictional and not structural. The solution is a second-best in comparison to a market-driven first best outcome. This chapter derives a second-best policy of trade adjustment assistance, with implications for group inequality in a developing society.

The issues about economic integration (Chapter 9), despite seeming aberrations from much more challenging free trade regimes, cannot be set aside in view of development and welfare implications entrenched in it. Chapter 10 discusses the role of TRIPS, the debates about trade standards and of industrial strategies as part of very recent literature in this area. It also accommodates the relations between international trade and the endogenous growth theories of more recent origins. Chapter 11 deals with outsourcing, offshoring, and industrial strategies at the destination as an example of the recent industrial organization-centric developments in international economics.

The choice of topics to be included in this book has not been easy. The subject is extremely rich with contributions from the best in the field. Consequently, we relied partly on our experiences with teaching postgraduate courses in trade and development where the slow build-up to the topics of current interest have been generally accepted and appreciated by the students. The course material we have chosen is also influenced by the contents and references adopted by specialists in the subject. Consequently, each chapter discusses the relevant literature and then provides detailed analytical structures that closely capture the core elements of the topic in hand. The theoretical applications duly supported and motivated by empirical evidence have been drawn mainly from papers published in leading journals and therefore, might be construed as a useful compilation of somewhat dispersed teaching materials. We nevertheless acknowledge that despite our best efforts, we may not have done justice to many interesting questions in trade and inequality; on the impact of international trade on land as an important input; about trade and entrepreneurship; or trade and redistribution etc. These currently remain as vibrant subjects of research. Chapter 12 summarizes findings from each chapter, preceded by a non-technical discussion on international financial contagion. The conclusion further highlights our shortcomings, both owing to constraints in time, space, and our incapability of comprehending the subject more than we could grasp in this attempt. If the students and teachers of international trade and economic development consider this book to be a useful source of information, it will give us the right kind of incentive to work further in the area.

■ REFERENCES

Acemoglu, D., Johnson, S., and Robinson, J. A. (2002). 'Reversal of Fortune: Geography and Institutions in the Making of the Modern World Income Distribution'. *The Quarterly Journal of Economics* 117 (4): 1231–1294.

Basu, K. (1998). *Analytical Development Economics: The Less Developed Economy Revisited*. Cambridge, MA: The MIT Press.

Diamond, J. (1997). *Guns, Germs and Steel: The Fates of Human Societies*. New York: W.W. Norton.

Prebisch, R. (1950). 'The Economic Development of Latin America and its Principal Problems'. Reprinted in *Economic Bulletin for Latin America* 7 (1), 1962.

Singer, H. (1950). 'US Foreign Investment in Underdeveloped Areas: The Distribution of Gains Between Investing and Borrowing Countries'. *American Economic Review*, Papers and Proceedings, 40: 473–485.

1 International Trade and Development Paradigms

Interaction between international trade and the process of development is a complex one. The importance of international trade as a development strategy dates back to the writings in seventeenth- and eighteenth-century Europe, known as the 'mercantilist ideas'. It was viewed as a means of acquiring wealth by maintaining a trade surplus. This idea, however, was criticized by Hume (1752) who argued that a trade surplus is only a temporary phenomenon, as the changes in prices and money supply consequent upon a trade surplus would lead to an automatic adjustment towards a balance of payments (BOP) equilibrium. Since then, the role of international trade in promoting development and growth of countries has been debated by economists as well as policy-makers. Such debates essentially evolve around costs and benefits of free trade vis-à-vis those of protectionism. Even in the writings of ancient Greek philosophers, just as among the present-day economists, the dual role of international trade was apparent: recognition of the benefits of international exchange along with the concern that certain domestic industries and economic agents would be harmed by foreign competition.

This chapter reflects upon these debates. We begin with the mercantilist idea of trade promotion as a development strategy, and its critique by Smith (1776). The development debates around free trade versus protectionism are discussed thereafter.

1.1 Mercantilist Theory of Trade and Development

Mercantilism was a school of thought on international trade policy that emerged in the seventeenth and eighteenth centuries. Two distinct ideas associated with the mercantilists shaped much of the public policy of that time. First was that countries should maintain a trade surplus through export promotion and import protection, since this is the only alternative to war to acquire precious metals, known as specie. This idea was severely criticized by Hume in the eighteenth century. A country acquiring specie through a trade surplus will experience a rise in its purchasing power. Consequent increased spending will raise prices of domestic goods, which will induce the domestic consumers to switch to consumption of foreign goods. Imports thus increase. On the other hand, higher prices of domestic goods erode their competitiveness in the foreign markets and exports thus decrease. That is, rising prices leads to a trade deficit and a consequent out-flow of species. This is known as Hume's price-specie flow mechanism and constitutes the starting point of the monetarist approach (see later) that postulated balance of payments imbalances as a purely monetary, and more importantly, temporary phenomenon.

The second idea associated with mercantilism was that a nation should pro-mote exports of manufactured goods and imports of raw materials essential for such manufacturing exports. This selective trade promotion and protec-tion was motivated by better employment opportunity in manufacturing pro-duction than in mining or extracting raw materials from the earth. There was also the idea of building up industries to strengthen the domestic economy and national defence. In achieving these trade promotion and restriction poli-cies, the mercantilists advocated export subsidies and tariff protection for do-mestic manufacturing firms.

Smith, in his Wealth of Nations (1776), criticized this idea by asserting that if certain trade is not profitable for private merchants *without subsidies*, then it would be unlikely to be profitable for the nation. He essentially was talking about the costs of export subsidies. Smith also did not subscribe to tariff pro-tection, as he viewed such a policy as eliminating competition and encour-aging domestic producers to exercise their market power. To Smith, monopoly was inefficient and thus wasteful. Accordingly he refuted the idea of trade pro-tection and instead advocated that free trade is good by developing his pro-ductivity and vent for surplus theories.

1.2 Classical Political Economists on Trade and Growth

Smith, Ricardo, and Malthus were among the classical political economists who had some well-articulated arguments on the relationship between international trade and growth of nations. However, their arguments were mostly on the supply-side constraints on output growth. Most of the clas-sical political economists were pessimistic about long run growth pros-pects of the industrialized countries. They believed that these countries would reach a point of stagnation much earlier than the resource-rich, primary goods-exporting countries. In this perspective, Ricardo viewed international trade as a way of delaying the stationary state. Through his doctrine of comparative advantage he demonstrated two important results. First, all trading nations will experience welfare gains when they trade according to their comparative advantage. Even a country that is inferior in all lines of production relative to other nations will benefit if it exports goods in which its inferiority is least, and thus in which it has comparative advantages. The consequent increase in the rate of profit and efficient reallocation of resources through production specialization will step up the rate of capital accumulation and hence the rate of growth. Malthus, on the other hand, viewed reallocation of resources from agriculture to the manufacturing made possible by international trade as a way of offsetting diminishing returns in agriculture. With growing population, agriculture is over-cultivated, which in turn lowers yield per acre by the law of diminishing returns. International trade allows imports of food and releases the pressure on agriculture. To Malthus, trade also had a favourable effect on output growth through increase in labour supply. As international trade expands the set of consumables, the people will perceive the opportunity cost of leisure rising and thus will work harder and for longer hours than in absence of international trade and such increased consumption opportunities.

Smith perceived the two ways in which international trade promotes growth. First, by widening the extent of the market, international trade makes possible large scale production and consequently creates scope for further division of labour, which in turn improves the level of productivity and thus growth. This was his Productivity Theory, which in contrast to Ricardo's static gains from trade, looked upon international trade as a dynamic force. To Smith, large scale production also enables firms to reap the benefits of economies of scale and would encourage them to innovate. In Ricardo's argument, production specialization meant allocation of resources and was a reversible process. But in Smith's argument, specialization involves adopting and reshaping production structure of the economy to meet export demand, which is an irreversible process.

As Myint (1958) observed, in late nineteenth-century Europe, this productivity theory was pushed into an export-drive argument, which has been seen by many as the precursor to the subsequent export-led growth argument. It was believed that since international trade raises productivity and growth, so the state should *promote* trade instead of adopting a laissez faire policy. This often led to exploitation of the colonies by their European rulers to step up their exports.

The second contribution of international trade perceived by Smith was providing a vent for surplus productive capacity of the economy. To Smith, surplus land in an economy isolated from international trade arises because of the narrowness of the domestic market. He also talked about surplus labour, which was linked to his concept of *unproductive* labour. So essentially, low productivity according to him was the cause of actual output falling short of the potential output in nineteenth-century Europe. Thus, according to Myint, Smithian argument of surplus productive capacity was a supply-side argument rather than the effective demand argument of Keynes and Kalecki in the early twentieth century. In such a context, a surplus productive capacity suitable for export markets was virtually a costless way of acquiring imports and expanding domestic production.

Later, Findlay (1970) put Myint's interpretation of the Smithian vent for surplus argument into a formal analysis, which is illustrated in Figure 1.1. The negatively sloped straight line DC reflects the production possibility frontier (PPF) of a country producing handicrafts and food. The constant slope indicates the constant opportunity cost of expanding food production in terms of handicrafts. Initially, the economy was operating at a point A well within the PPF, which is a reflection of surplus land as well as surplus labour. Low productivity of labour in food sectors implied low food-wages. This meant that labour enjoys leisure, since the opportunity cost of leisure is low. Now suppose the food price relative to handicraft price is higher in the world market as shown by the steeper line p^*. When this economy opens up for international trade, larger quantities of handicrafts exchange for one unit of food. This raises the opportunity cost of leisure and results in an increase in labour supply. Food output thus shifts to point B on the PPF. Note that, due to initial surplus land and labour, expansion of food production did not require handicraft production to contract. But once international trade pushes the economy on to its PPF indicating that all surplus land and labour have now been fully utilized, further expansion of the food production (along the PPF) would now require a contraction of handicraft production to release land and labour to sustain additional food

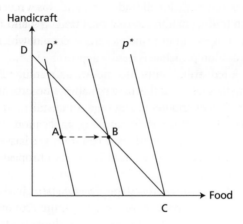

Figure 1.1 International Trade and Vent for Surplus

production. Now the Ricardian phase starts. The economy, having a comparative advantage in food production, moves down along the PPF until it is completely specialized in food production, and is importing all its requirement of handicraft. The entire process, Smithian adjustment followed by Ricardian complete specialization, leads to a gain for the economy as its consumption possibility frontier (indicated by the $p*C$ line) now expands beyond the PPF.

1.3 The Post-World War II Debate: Free Trade vs. Trade Protection

The current debate on international trade as a development strategy largely focuses on costs and benefits of free trade vis-à-vis trade protection. Whereas there is often a two-way relationship between pattern of trade and a country's stage of development in the existing theory, the country experiences regarding the role of international trade in a country's development and growth process are mixed. There are both success and failure stories, and more recent evidence indicates that rather than international trade per se, it is perhaps the composition and quality-content of a country's export basket that matters most (Hausman, et al., 2007; Agosin, 2007). Moreover, an export-led growth may not always be desirable because the terms of trade may deteriorate so much so that the initial favourable welfare effect of growth may actually be reversed; a phenomenon, demonstrated by Bhagwati (1958), which is known as the *immiserizing growth*.

Even the perceived static benefits of free international trade are grounded on some restrictive assumptions, which may not always be satisfied. Actual gains may, therefore, remain far below the potential. The gains from trade theorem, the oft-quoted benefit of free international trade, which postulates that international trade is a positive-sum game for all trading nations, loses much of its appeal because within each trading nation international trade creates winners and losers. Thus, without a compensation principle, trade does not benefit all economic agents. A compensation principle is hardly applied by trading nations, and thus what emerges is a redistribution of income within trading nations (along with across the trading nations), and this may not always be in the desired direction. For example, if trade redistributes income against unskilled workers, as has been observed in recent times, this has far-reaching implications for the poor, since most of the poor are unskilled workers. Even if we set aside such distribution issues, the gains from trade theorem itself is far from realized when markets do not function properly in the sense that the market prices fail to reflect a country's actual line of comparative advantage. The typical examples of such market failures are externalities in production and consumption. This does not mean that trade should be prohibited or restricted, but the crux of the matter is that without necessary corrective actions, such market failures may actually lead to a fall in welfare when a nation opens up for trade.

The primary argument for trade protection, in the present context, on the other hand, is to protect infant industries of a nation in its early stages of development. Mill made a strong argument in favour of promoting infant industries as early as in 1848, which subsequently has been a critical element in discussions and design of the development strategy of a nation. Unfortunately, the infant industry argument has often been misunderstood, misperceived, and misused. Infant industry protection does not call for once and for all tariff protection. Protecting industries that can withstand foreign competition will only encourage inefficient production specialization and inefficient resource allocation. Moreover, there are some obvious costs of protection, which should be weighed against the long run benefits that infant industry protection may generate. What is even worse, trade protection generates rents for certain economic agents, which might encourage them to undertake wasteful lobbying activities in order to influence the government policy in actually protecting the domestic industries. Krueger (1974) and Bhagwati (1982) were the leading researchers to point out such losses of trade protection. Resources used in lobbying to influence trade policy choice mean that the economy produces and consumes less than its endowments would have allowed. The developing country experiences do support the existence of such lobbying or rent-seeking activities and costs thereof.

On the other hand, Metzler (1949) demonstrated that for a large trading nation, an import tariff may not protect its domestic, import-competing industries. At the initial world relative price of imports, an import tariff raises the domestic relative price of imports. This in turn lowers the demand for the country's imports in the world market and thus lowers the world relative price of imports. If this subsequent terms of trade (TOT) improvement is large enough to outweigh the initial effect of the tariff, the domestic relative price of imports declines. This paradoxical result, known as the *Metzler Paradox* in the trade literature, arises when the exporting country's import demand elasticity is smaller than the importing country's marginal propensity to consume its export goods.[1] In such a paradoxical situation, an import tariff fails to protect the domestic industry.

1.4 Export Pessimism and Legacy of Inward-Looking Development Strategy

The infant industry argument, the theory of optimum tariff and above all the writings of Lewis (1954), Rosenstein-Rodan (1943), Prebisch (1950), Singer (1950), and Hirschman (1982) on export pessimism and North-South debate

---

[1] For derivation of this condition see Caves, Frankel, and Jones (2006).

contributed towards shaping development policies of many countries and the adoption of inward-looking development strategies by a large number of less-developed countries in the immediate post-World War II period. The export pessimism grew out of the observations on defaults on international debt for a large number of countries, suggesting that the external environment was not as conducive as it was during pre-World War I times to promote growth. It was contended that the rich dividends that countries received by promoting trade during the golden years of booming world trade prior to 1914 were unlikely in the post-World War II period, because the world trade had not boomed since 1914. The cornerstone of the export pessimism was, however, the Prebisch-Singer hypothesis that primary goods-exporting poor countries will experience secular deterioration of their TOT vis-à-vis the manufacturing-exporting rich nations. They shared the view that the trade relation between rich and poor nations is a kind of *Centre-Periphery* relation, a term coined first by Lewis (1954), in which the advanced Centre, or the rich nations, generates the momentum of capital accumulation and innovation, and the backward Periphery, or the poor nations, responds more or less passively to the parameters set by the Centre. This trade relation leads to perpetuation of the role of poor nations as producers of primary goods and buyers of manufacturing goods. Moreover, as we will elaborate in Chapter 2, whatever technical progress that international trade ushers in results in falling prices of the primary exports (or further worsening of the TOT) to the benefit of the Centre. That is, the productivity gains in the Periphery are actually exported away to the Centre. These observations led Prebisch (1950) to conclude that '...industrialization is the only means by which the Latin American countries may fully obtain the advantages of technical progress'. A few years later, Nurkse (1959), in his Wicksell lecture, put forward his export lag thesis in which he contended that the exports of primary goods-producing countries tend to lag behind the rate of increase in world trade and that of the manufacturing-exporting countries. The common idea shared by all these economists advocating export pessimism is that the demand for primary goods is income inelastic, so that as the per capita income grows the demand for primary goods rise less than proportionately. These writings on export pessimism and secular deterioration of TOT for the primary goods-exporting countries, despite a great deal of subsequent criticisms of the hypotheses, had a tremendous influence on the policy-makers in the less-developed countries (LDCs) in adopting a protectionist and inward-looking import-substituting development strategy.

At the same time, Bhagwati (1958) published his immiserizing growth thesis by which he argued that if export demand is price inelastic, an export-biased growth that worsens the country's TOT may actually make the country worse off as the TOT in such a case may worsen so much so to outweigh the initial benefits conferred by growth. Though Bhagwati himself strongly advocated free trade policy and export promotion as the most appropriate development strategies, his immiserizing growth thesis had its influence on the adoption of import-substitution development strategies. However, subsequent analysis by Johnson (1967) demonstrated that similar immiserizing possibility may arise even when a small country grows under tariff protection. Thus, a protectionist development strategy may not insulate a country from immiserization.

The inward-looking development strategies got further support from the unequal exchange thesis of Emmanuel (1969). The cornerstone of the unequal exchange thesis, as we will elaborate in Chapter 2, is that low prices of exports from the Periphery, consequent upon low wages or undervaluation of labour there, contribute to the high standard of living in the Centre. The wage differences across the Centre and Periphery, not commensurate with productivity differences, underlie the undervaluation of exports and the unequal exchange that international trade implies for the Periphery. This caused further apprehension for the perceived static and dynamic gains that international trade ushers in.

But, during the late 1960s and 1970s, many LDCs found it difficult to maintain the momentum of growth and development when they experienced deteriorating balance of payments and depleting foreign exchange reserves. Of course, a major reason for this was the adoption of pegged exchange rate regimes that required interventions in the foreign exchange market by selling or buying foreign currencies whenever external shocks puts pressure on the pegged exchange rate.[2] But, tariff protections also distorted export and production compositions of the LDCs by shifting resources from the export sectors to the import-competing sectors. This lowered export earnings significantly and made it difficult for most of the LDCs to pay for the import bill for necessary imports of capital and intermediate goods to sustain their industrialization processes. A new orthodoxy of export promotion development strategy thus emerged, reiterating ideas of the classical political economists on dynamic gains from free trade, on the one hand, and offering new theoretical arguments based on economies of scale and product innovations, on the other hand.

However, as Bhagwati (1988) argues, whether a protectionist import-substitution strategy or an export promotion strategy will be appropriate for a country depends to a large extent on its level of development itself. The argument that an import-substitution development strategy will promote industrialization and growth is perhaps more relevant for more primitive countries that have little industrial base and are dependent heavily on primary and agricultural goods, such as the African countries. But for semi-industrialized countries like India, and many other Asian and Latin American countries at present levels of development, for which manufacturing constitutes a sizeable

---

[2] See Krugman (1979) for a formal analysis of how a BOP crisis may emerge under a pegged exchange rate regime and Acharyya (2013) for similar arguments in the context of India's BOP crisis in the early 1990s.

proportion of total exports, import-substitution development strategy is more likely to impede development and growth by encouraging inefficiencies.

1.5 Development Crises and Globalization as a Universal Development Strategy

We presently live in a world that is characterized by substantial complexity in both economic and social fronts. In the post-world war decades, overshadowed by a long spell of cold war, most countries were essentially circumspect about the actions of other countries. However, once the IT revolution and the slow but unmistakable capture of globalization swept the nations since the early 1980s, it became quite impossible to insulate individual countries from various changes that followed considerable homogenization of economic and social spheres. This undoubtedly has favourable and adverse implications for countries all around, and in general interactions between most countries would be increasingly difficult to strategize under the circumstances. There are too many independent players with incentives and disincentives nested in a complex maze of activities. Available evidence suggests that countries that have so far fended off adverse impacts of globalization may not have done so by virtue of premeditated domestic planning, but may have benefited from the presence of many other idiosyncratic factors that could well generate other forms of crises at a different point in time. This situation is distinctly different from much more conservative, self-reliant, closed-door, non-integrated countries of yesteryears, which interacted with others mainly via international trade in commodities and through international political relations. However, since 2008 as it would be agreed upon even by the most liberal of economists, there is a relentless supply of crisis globally, and that it has significantly outweighed the positive impacts of globalization. It is undoubtedly important to check five years hence, whether the end of the dark tunnel is at all visible or not, despite the fact that many countries that are collateral damages of the blazing wildfire will not have the instruments to contain it independently. The damages caused by these crises meant huge loss of economic resources and activities everywhere the crisis took significant proportions, led to unemployment as high as 25% in many developed countries, and lowered growth and redistribution remarkably. India, fortunately, has not been seriously affected by the ongoing crisis, although very recently the macroeconomic calculations had to be readjusted to a growth rate of 6%, the lowest in a decade. This is blamed on the so-called *eurozone crisis*.

The newest in the series of crises is the European debt crisis, the eurozone crisis represents Europe's struggle to pay the debts it has built up in recent decades. Five of the region's countries—Greece, Portugal, Ireland, Italy, and Spain—have, to varying degrees, failed to generate enough economic growth to make their ability to pay back bondholders the guarantee that publicly-issued bonds directly carry. The five countries were seen as being the countries in imminent danger of a possible default. But surely the global integration does not allow individual countries to operate in isolation any longer? Thus, the crisis has far-reaching consequences that extend beyond their borders to the world as a whole. In fact, the head of the Bank of England, Sir Mervyn King referred to it as 'the most serious financial crisis at least since the 1930s, if not ever'(October 2011).[3] Under the circumstances, it is probably important to enquire if India would be able to avoid spillover effects of this crisis completely. We will discuss some of the opinions and predictions of the highest authorities in this country in this regard, preceded by a brief description of what constitutes the core of the crisis in Europe.

1.5.1 THE BEGINNING OF THE CRISIS

The global economy has experienced slow growth since the US financial crisis of 2008–2009, which has exposed the unsustainable fiscal policies of countries in Europe and around the globe. Greece, which spent heartily for years and failed to undertake fiscal reforms, was one of the first to feel the burden of weaker growth. When growth slows down, the tax revenue falls, and the budget deficits soar to the extent that it pushes the entire economy to an unstable quarter. In this regard, one must not forget that the macroeconomic condition of a country, which is now part of a complex monetary union, can no longer be treated in isolation. The unavoidable transactions between members of a monetary union would immediately lead to the spread of the impact in the territories of its members, both via capital and labour mobility. Whether by falsification of national accounts or by the compulsion of generous redistributive practices common in Europe, Greece's debts were larger than the size of the nation's entire economy, and the country could no longer hide the problem.

Investors responded by demanding higher yields on Greece's bonds, which raised the cost of the country's debt burden and necessitated a series of bailouts by the European Union and European Central Bank (ECB). The markets also began driving up bond yields in the other heavily indebted countries in the region, anticipating problems similar to what occurred in Greece. As investors contemplate that the debtor could soon become insolvent (with some possibility that they might also bounce back to normalcy), the investments are driven into

---

[3] See: http://www.telegraph.co.uk/finance/financialcrisis/8812260/World-facing-worst-financial-crisis-in-history-Bank-of-England-Governor-says.html.

high-risk zones and must require high compensation. If the indebted countries turn around then the investors make huge returns, but in case the countries falter, the entire system takes a nosedive along with the investors begetting a global crisis. Characteristically speaking, this is somewhat different from the burst of the real estate bubble. Boldrin and Levine comment that in the real estate crisis, the transfer of monitoring responsibility from the public authorities to individual private banks was the root of the crisis.[4] The imprudent private banking system in the US as a whole failed miserably in checking the credentials of the borrowers and pushed loans where it did not belong in the first place. The real estate market was destined to suffer because people borrowed much more than they could ever pay back. In addition, financial engineering by big lenders such as Fannie Mae or Lehman Brothers spread the risk of holding unstable mortgages to many other subsidiaries and financial institutions globally. On a good state of nature, this financial jugglery to raise quick capital and continue with production and service in seamless manners could generate fortunes. On a bad spell of events it leads to a global crisis where millions lose jobs and homes and wait for the governments to pull them out of misery. Compared to the housing crisis, the European crisis is much grander. This has to do with national governments of five different countries that acted much more irresponsibly, despite the presence of such a supra-national authority as the European Union. The major reason for the lack of monitoring, it is argued, lies in the lack of fiscal coordination between EU member countries. EU is, after all, a monetary and currency union with fiscal decisions still controlled exclusively by individual countries with intermittent cautions from the ECB to retain the fiscal deficit within manageable limits, such as 3–4% of the country's gross domestic product (GDP). The lack of fiscal prudence on the part of five major countries led to a vicious cycle. As country risks of investment went up, institutional and individual investors in publicly-issued bonds demand higher yields and this equates to higher borrowing costs for the country in crisis. To meet debt servicing, the countries will need to borrow again in a short while and the entire mechanism may blow up within a visible time frame. Worse still, the effect of high borrowing cost by countries in distress will spill over as a contagion effect to other countries that are also in need of external and internal borrowing.

1.5.2 COMBATING THE CRISIS IN EUROPE

The European Union has taken action, but it has moved slowly since it requires the consent of all nations in the union. The primary course of action thus far has been a series of bailouts for Europe's troubled economies. In spring 2010, the European Union and International Monetary Fund (IMF) disbursed 110

---

[4] (www.dklevine.com/general/crisis_and_bailout.pdf).

billion euros (the equivalent of $163 billion) to Greece. Greece required a second bailout in mid-2011, this time worth about $157 billion. On March 9, 2012, Greece and its creditors agreed to a debt restructuring that set the stage for another round of bailout funds. Ireland and Portugal also received bailouts, in November 2010 and May 2011, respectively. The eurozone member states also created the European Financial Stability Facility (EFSF) to provide emergency lending to countries in financial difficulty.

The European Central Bank (ECB) had to be involved in the process simultaneously. It is expected in most such situations that the central bank of a country, in this case the ECB for the whole of Europe, consented in purchasing government bonds via an announcement made in August 2011. In other words, it is still the backdoor policy to sustain fiscal stability of a region and bail out the worst hit countries by pledging guarantee and support on behalf of individual institutional and other investors. This may be a way out in the short run, but does not guarantee that the countries will be normalized soon, given that the debt-to-GDP ratio for these countries is more than 100%. In December 2011, the ECB made €489 billion ($639 billion) in credit available to the region's troubled banks at ultra-low rates, then followed with a second round in February 2012. The name of this programme was the Long Term Refinancing Operation (LTRO). Numerous financial institutions had debt maturing in 2012, causing them to hold on to their reserves rather than extend loans. Slower loan growth, in turn, could weigh on economic growth and make the crisis worse. As a result, the ECB sought to boost the banks' balance sheets to help forestall this potential issue. The problems are manifold with such short-term approaches, typically because these do not provide directions for turnaround and there is no optimal bailout rule as yet established for countries varying in size significantly. Notwithstanding, in 2012, President of the ECB Mario Draghi announced that the ECB would do 'whatever it takes' to keep the eurozone together.[5] In the same way as favourable budgetary announcements turn around the drooping share markets from time to time, the bond market also reacted favourably and investors started settling for lower yields during the second half of the year. While Draghi's statement didn't solve the problem, it made investors more comfortable buying bonds of the region's smaller nations. Lower yields, in turn, have bought time for the high-debt countries to address their broader issues. Unless the country really turns around based on such favourable investment climate, the central bank, which holds a large part of the country debt, will plunge in turn. Banks are required to keep a certain amount of assets on their balance sheets relative to the amount of debt they hold. If a country defaults on its debt, the value of its bonds will plunge. For banks, this could mean a sharp reduction in the amount of assets on their balance sheet—and possible insolvency. Due to the

[5] http://www.telegraph.co.uk/finance/financialcrisis/9428894/Debt-crisis-Mario-Draghi-pledges-to-do-whatever-it-takes-to-save-euro.html.

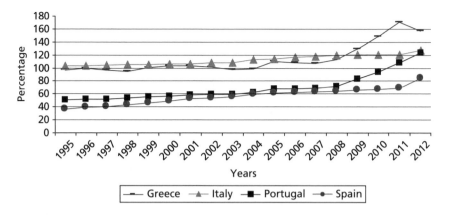

Figure 1.2 Public Debt as a Percentage of GDP in Select European Countries
Source: European Central Bank: Data Warehouse.

growing interconnectedness of the global financial system, a bank failure doesn't happen in a vacuum. Instead, there is the possibility that a series of bank failures will spiral into a more destructive 'contagion' or 'domino effect'. Figure 1.2 clearly shows that for more than 15 years, since 1995, Greece and Italy were facing a level of public debt of about 100% of their respective GDPs. By 2011, the level of debt for Greece (rising to 170% of GDP) is quite remarkable, despite a general rise for all the other countries, namely, Italy, Portugal, and Spain that are presently in a state of unsustainable debt-burden jeopardizing the stability of the eurozone as a whole. The present sub-section deliberated on the effect of such external shocks on the state of development for the developing countries.

The political implications of the crisis were enormous. In the affected nations, the push toward austerity—or cutting expenses to reduce the gap between revenues and outlays—led to public protests in Greece and Spain and in the removal of the party in power in both Italy and Portugal. On a national level, the crisis led to tensions between the fiscally-sound countries, such as Germany, and the higher-debt countries such as Greece. Germany pushed for Greece and other affected countries to reform the budgets as a condition of providing aid, leading to elevated tensions within the European Union. After a great deal of debate, Greece ultimately agreed to cut spending and raise taxes. However, an important obstacle to addressing the crisis was Germany's unwillingness to agree to a region-wide solution, since it would have to foot a disproportionate percentage of the bill.

The tension created the possibility that one or more European countries would eventually abandon the euro (the region's common currency). On one hand, leaving the euro would allow a country to pursue its own independent policy rather than being subject to the common policy for the 17 nations using the currency. But on the other, it would be an event of unprecedented magnitude for the global economy and financial markets. This concern contributed to periodic weakness in the euro, relative to other major global currencies during the crisis period.

1.5.3 WHAT IS IN STORE FOR DEVELOPING COUNTRIES?

The economic advisory wing of the Government of India notes that the eurozone crisis has been moving from one peripheral economy to the next, and more recently, is affecting the core economies in the eurozone. The EU accounts for close to 26% of the world GDP (at market exchange rates) and the eurozone 19.4%. The Euro area accounts for about 10% of the global equity markets turnover and the euro accounts for 26% of the allocated global holding of reserves. Thus the significance of this crisis is not merely that it comes in the aftermath of the global crisis, but more importantly, it threatens the pace of recovery of the global economy especially because the EU, and within that the eurozone, is a significant market for rest of the world.

In its 'spillover' report on the effects of eurozone policies on other major economies, the IMF observed that an intensification of the Euro area debt crisis, especially if stress were to spread to the core economies, could have major global consequences. In particular, if the eurozone core economies were to be affected, banks throughout the eurozone immediately require more and higher quality capital. While capital raising and recapitalizing banks is needed, the report observes that in the short run, this may lead to contraction of country-wise GDP and growth.

It is inevitable that the developed countries still reeling from the US Financial crisis, except a few Organization for Economic Cooperation and Development (OECD) countries, will share the greater burden of another crisis of the type discussed so far. However, the developing giants such as India and China would not be totally exempt for straightforward reasons. For both China and India, Europe and the eurozone is the destination of a large share of exportable goods and services. India in particular, suffered from a drop of 25% in the last quarter for some of the services it has been exporting to Europe and USA. The European Union alone accounts for as much as 20.2% of India's exports (in 2009–2010) and 13.3% of India's imports. European Union countries imported roughly €33.1 billion worth of agriculture products, fuel and mining products, machinery and transport equipment, chemicals, semi-manufactured products, textile and clothing products in 2010 from India. The EU exports to India amounted to €34.8 billion, the majority of which was machinery, chemical products, and semi-manufactured items (which was almost 2.6% of EU exports). Bilateral trade between the two has grown on average 9.6% during 2006–2010. EU services exports to India during 2010 totalled €9.8 billion and EU imports from India totalled €8.1 billion. That apart, the total foreign domestic investment (FDI) from the EU during 2010 amounted to €3.0 billion, while India also invested about €0.6 billion in the EU. All these statistics taken together offers a clear picture of how interconnected these markets are, and how much they would have expected to grow in a few more years. This is undoubtedly threatened by the crisis, and will take quite long to recuperate and get back to the growth path. This is not in sight at present. Since a slowdown in the eurozone is likely to have a major adverse impact on India's exports, India probably needs to look for markets elsewhere, although it is reasonable to argue that close replacements seem distant and infeasible. China, on the other hand seems to be at the negotiating table with better bargaining terms simply because they retain large portions of the US treasury bills and other countries' sovereign debts. While this raises more fundamental questions about the criticality of financial trading with a country's sovereign debt to be debated currently, the situation will not get reversed within a reasonable time.

Apart from the bilateral and multilateral trade relations that India enjoys with the European countries, the financial interlinkages between the countries are put under serious threat. The global financial crisis directly bears testimony to the fact that the bank and non-bank financial systems played a crucial role in transmitting the crisis from the advanced economies to various parts of the world, including the emerging markets. In this regard, there is also an ongoing debate on how the foreign banks should operate in developing and transition countries so that they do not easily transmit recession from the developed sources. Overall, therefore, it is expected that while India may not be severely hit by the crisis, it cannot completely bypass the negative effects of global slump and therefore reconsider its internal adjustments much more seriously than it is undertaking at this point. To put it simply, India needs to be managed better. The resources that the country has in stock are significantly under-utilized and neglected, typically owing to coordination failure in the loose federal structure that we endure. The revenue collection and redistribution mechanisms must work in a better way to garner largely untapped resource within the country—a process which may easily begin with reformulations of certain laws and regulations within the country.

1.6 International Trade, Pollution, and Sustainable Development

Another major concern for free international trade as a development strategy is the adverse effect of trade on the local, national, and global pollution levels. This has opened up a debate over optimal policy for *sustainable* development that links between environmental protection and development at large. In general, sustainable development concerns a pattern of resource use that aims to meet human needs while preserving the environment.

International trade affects the environment in more than one way. In the short run, however, trade shifts pollution load from one country to the other. The direction of such shifts depend on the nature of pollution, whether it is a production pollution or a consumption pollution, and on the pattern of comparative advantage of nations. To explain, suppose goods degrades the environment while they are being produced. Goods, however, degrade the environment in varying degrees and thus can be ranked according to their pollution emissions per unit of output, or what can be called pollution intensities. The countries, which have a comparative advantage in producing goods that are high in the ranking in terms of pollution intensities, will specialize in and export these goods after trade opens up. The countries importing these goods (that is, the countries which have comparative disadvantage in producing these goods) will specialize in goods which are low in the pollution intensity ranking, shifting resources from the import-competing goods. Thus, international trade, according to comparative advantage of nations, lowers the national pollution level in the latter group of countries but raises it in the former group of countries exporting the *dirtier* goods. That is, international trade is not necessarily bad for all trading nations in so far as the environmental degradation through international trade is concerned.

Of course, the comparative advantage of nations in dirtier goods itself can be the outcome of a *deliberate* policy action by the governments of these nations. Nations that do not implement environmental regulations strictly in their countries devalue the environment and encourage their local producers to price their products below the social marginal costs. Note that the pollution generated while producing a good is a classic case of negative production externality, in which case the private marginal cost is an underestimation of the social marginal cost of production. Such undervaluation and consequent pricing below the social marginal cost by some countries establishes a comparative advantage for these countries in dirtier goods, given that the fundamentals (like factor endowment, technology, and consumer preferences) are more or less similar to the rest of the countries. This dimension of policy *inaction*, observed to be more prevalent in the developing countries, has led to a recent debate of *ecological dumping* and unfair trade practices by these countries. Moreover, it is often contended that such policy inaction making these countries *pollution havens* attracts capital inflow and leads to migration of dirty industries from the developed to the developing countries. The developing countries also compete among themselves to deliberately keep their environmental standards below those of their competitors to attract foreign capital. This leads to a race-to-the-bottom and degradation of the environment all around.

These issues have given rise to a policy debate in which the developed countries are in favour of imposing uniform standards across countries so that genuine competitiveness, according to the fundamentals, can determine the pattern of trade. But the developing countries perceive such policy actions as nothing but an attempt to use the environmental issues as rationalization for non-tariff barriers for protecting the domestic markets in the developed countries from foreign competition. Their logic rests on the fact that their revealed comparative advantage often reflects the cost advantage that these countries enjoy in terms of abundant cheap labour. Thus, the comparative advantage would anyway have been there, even if environmental standards were strictly implemented forcing their local producers to produce at the social marginal cost. Moreover, a uniform environmental standard across the globe loses much of its appeal since pollution load is shifted from the importing country to the exporting country. This is relevant only when the production pollution is trans-boundary in nature, in which case the environment in the importing country is also affected if it is a downstream country in the context of water pollution, or is global in nature such as CO_2 emission by industrial activities. The acid rain in the European countries, on the other hand, exemplifies the need for policy coordination in case of global pollution and global negative externality.

Similarly, there is no prima facie evidence on direct foreign investment in these countries flowing primarily into the dirty industries. As argued in Acharyya (2013), 'it is true that the Asian countries, particularly the East Asian countries, have competed among themselves since 1990s to attract FDI under the notion that it is a necessary precondition for faster growth. Such competition has mostly been reflected in large unilateral tariff reductions to signal the external world about their more open trade and investment regimes. It is not clear, however, to what extent they competed in terms of lowering environmental regulations and taxes.'

On the other hand, if pollution is emitted while a good being consumed instead of while it is being produced, then international trade shifts the pollution load from the countries having comparative advantage and exporting dirtier goods to those nations that import these goods. In such cases, of course, the developed countries' demand for environmental protection through imposition of environmental standards and tariffs on imports from the developing countries makes some sense. Yet, such a case does not call for trade protection as an optimal policy. This being a case of consumption externality, the celebrated works of Bhagwati, Srinivasan, and Johnson among others on optimal intervention in the presence of externalities during 1970s and 1980s, suggest that domestic consumption should be taxed instead of international trade being restricted or prohibited. Tariffs themselves create distortions in the production sector of the economy which then has to be weighed against the gain in pollution emission that tariffs generate by restricting consumption of imports.

International trade also affects the environment of nations through its growth effect. It had been observed by Grossman and Krueger (1993) and Selden and Song (1994) that per capita income growth initially raises the national pollution levels, but as it grows larger and larger, pollution levels start declining. This U-shaped relationship between pollution level and income per capita is known as the Environment Kuznets Curve (EKC) as Kuznets (1955) had observed similar relationship between per capita income and income inequality within a nation. To the extent to which international trade causes per capita income growth, it has a long run effect on the environment, which is however ambiguous in the sense that whether the growth effect of trade raises or lowers the pollution level depends on the level of per capita growth of the nation itself, as the EKC suggests. There are several explanations for EKC (see Copeland and Taylor, 2003 and Stern, 1998). One explanation is the interactions between supply of pollution and demand for pollution. At low levels of growth, the demand for higher environmental quality is low and economic agents as well as the government put more weight on income growth itself rather than on its adverse environmental implications. Thus, the scale and composition effects on the supply side raise the national pollution levels. When the country achieves a high growth path and per capita income level rises to a high level, consumers become more conscious about quality of the environment and quality of life in general. The preference then switches to consumption of more eco-friendly goods. This shift in preferences shifts the composition of goods produced as well, in favour of cleaner goods. The pollution level thus falls as per capita income grows further. The crucial element in this argument is that the cleaner goods are income elastic in demand whereas the dirtier goods are income inelastic in demand.

What follows from this EKC argument is that trade as a sustainable development strategy appears to be reasonable for countries that have already achieved a high growth path and thus on the right side of the turning point. There is, however, also the argument that a very fast growth (like the case of China) can make a country move to the right side of the turning point faster and thus making international trade a sustainable development strategy even within a relatively short period of time.

■ REFERENCES

Acharyya, R. (2013). *Trade and Environment*. Oxford India Short Introduction Series, New Delhi: OUP.

Agosin, M. R. (2007). 'Export Diversification and Growth in Emerging Economies'. Working Paper No. 233, Departamento de Economía, Universidad de Chile.

Bhagwati, J. N. (1958). 'Immiserizing Growth: A Geometric Note'. *Review of Economic Studies* 25: 201–205.

Bhagwati, J. N. (1982). 'Directly-Unproductive Profit-Seeking (DUP) Activities'. *Journal of Political Economy* 90: 988–1002.

Bhagwati, J. N. (1988). 'Export-Promoting Trade Strategy: Issues and Evidence', *World Bank Research Observer*, Vol. 3 (1): 27–57. Reprinted in: J. Bhagwati, *Political Economy and International Economics*, edited by D. Irwin. MIT Press: Cambridge, 1991.

Caves, R. E., Frankel, J. A., and Jones, R.W. (2006). *World Trade and Payments: An Introduction.* New Jersey: Prentice Hall.

Copeland, B. R. and Taylor, M. S. (2003). 'Trade, Growth and the Environment'. NBER Working Paper No. 9823, National Bureau of Economic Research, Cambridge, MA.

Emmanuel, A. (1969). *L'échange inégal: Essais sur les antagonismes dans les rapports économiques internationaux*. Paris: François Maspero. Translated by B. Pearce (1972), *Unequal Exchange: A Study of the Imperialism of Trade*. New York and London: Monthly Review Press.

Findlay, R. (1970). *International Trade and Development Theory*. Columbia: Columbia University Press.

Grossman, G. M. and Krueger, A. B. (1993). 'Environmental Impacts of a North American Free Trade Agreement'. In: P. Garber, (ed), *The US-Mexico Free Trade Agreement*. Cambridge, MA: MIT Press.

Hausman, R., Hwang, J., and Rodrik, D. (2007). 'What You Export Matters'. *Journal of Economic Growth* 12(1): 1–25.

Hirschman, A. O. (1982). 'The Rise and Decline of Development Economics'. In: C. F. Diaz-Alejandro, G. Ranis, M. R. Rosenzweig, and M. Gersovitz (eds). *The Theory and Experience of Economic Development: Essays in Honor of Sir W. Arthur Lewis*, pp. 372–390. London: Allen & Unwin.

Hume, D. (1752). *Political Discourses*. Edinburgh: A. Kincaid and A. Donaldson.

Johnson, H. G. (1967). 'Economic Expansion and International Trade'. *Manchester School of Economic and Social Studies* 23: 95–112.

Krueger, A. O. (1974). 'The Political Economy of the Rent-Seeking Society'. *American Economic Review* 64: 291–303.

Krugman, P. (1979). 'A Model of Balance-of-Payments Crises'. *Journal of Money, Credit and Banking* 11(3): 311–325.

Kuznets, S. (1955). 'Economic Growth and Income Inequality'. *American Economic Review* 45: 1–28.

Lewis, W. A. (1954). 'Economic Development with Unlimited Supplies of Labour'. *Manchester School of Economic and Social Studies* 22: 139–191.

Metzler, L. A. (1949). 'Tariffs, the Terms of Trade, and the Distribution of National Income'. *Journal of Political Economy* 57 (1): 1–29.

Myint, H. (1958). 'The Classical Theory of International Trade and the Underdeveloped Countries'. *The Economic Journal* 68 (270): 317–337.

Nurkse, R. (1959). 'Patterns of Trade and Development'. Wicksell Lectures, Stockholm: Almqvist & Wicksell.

Prebisch, R. (1950). 'The Economic Development of Latin America and its Principal Problems'. Reprinted in: *Economic Bulletin for Latin America* 7 (1), 1962.

Rosenstein-Rodan, P. N. (1943). 'Problems of Industrialisation of Eastern and South-Eastern Europe'. *The Economic Journal* 53: 202–211. Reprinted in A. N. Agarwala and S. P. Singh, (eds) *The Economics of Underdevelopm*ent. Bombay: Oxford University Press (1958).

Selden, T. M. and Song, D. (1994). 'Environmental Quality and Development: Is There a Kuznets Curve for Air Pollution Emissions?'. *Journal of Environmental Economics and Management* 27: 147–162.

Singer, H. (1950). 'US Foreign Investment in Underdeveloped Areas: The Distribution of Gains Between Investing and Borrowing Countries'. *American Economic Review*, Papers and Proceedings 40: 473–485.

Smith, A. (1776). *An Inquiry into the Nature and Causes of the Wealth of Nations*. London: W. Strahan.

Stern, D. I. (1998). 'Progress on the environmental Kuznets curve?' *Environment and Development Economics*, 3: 173–196.

2 Problems of Trade in Primary Commodities

Ricardo's Doctrine of Comparative Cost Advantage postulates that static gains can be realized for all countries regardless of what they export, as long as such exports conform with their respective comparative cost advantages. But, Prebisch (1950) and Singer (1950) observed a secular deterioration of the terms of trade (TOT) for the countries that exports primary goods vis-à-vis the countries that export manufacturing goods. This means, in the long run, the distribution of gains from international trade will be increasingly in favour of the advanced industrialized countries. Consequently, international trade is not a positive sum game in the long run. Thus, free trade as a development strategy works better for only a particular type of commodity-composition of export baskets of nations. Comparative advantage in primary goods may bring initial static gains when trade opens up, but subsequently adverse terms of trade movement and price instability associated with growth in exports of primary goods makes nations heavily dependent on such exports worse off. Sub-Saharan African countries, most of which were dependent on three or fewer primary commodities for more than half of their export earnings during the 1990s, are the glaring examples in this regard.

The observations by Prebisch (1950) and Singer (1950), known as the Prebisch-Singer hypothesis,[1] led to subsequent analyses of unequal exchange between countries, with most significant contributions made by Emmanuel (1972). Myrdal (1965) also strongly put forward his argument that international trade operated as a mechanism of international inequality. All these arguments of unequal distribution of gains from international trade for the developing countries laid the foundation for inward-looking import-substitution development strategy adopted by many developing countries during the 1960s and 1970s. This chapter discusses these arguments and their critiques.

---

[1] See Singer (1964; 1998) for collections of these papers and related discussion. Further, see Sarkar and Singer (1991) for an example of the several cross-country empirical verifications that were conducted since about 1980s.

2.1 Prebisch-Singer Hypothesis of Unequal Distribution of Gains

To both Prebisch and Singer, the unequal distribution of gains from trade across the developed and the developing countries, which they termed as Centre and Periphery respectively, arose because of three factors: export of primary goods by the Periphery countries, a relatively slow rate of innovation in the primary good producing industries, and a secular deterioration of the commodity TOT against the primary commodities. These factors are essentially intertwined. Productivity gain in the primary export good lowers its world price and thus worsens the TOT for the Periphery. The Centre benefits from such cheaper imports. Thus, productivity gains in export sectors in the Periphery are exported away through TOT deterioration, causing an uneven distribution of gains from trade. In support of his hypothesis, Prebisch (1950) observed that the relative price of the primary goods declined during 1876–1947. He considered the inverse of UK's barter TOT as a proxy for the price of primary goods relative to the price of manufacturing goods, which, however, drew a good deal of criticism as we will discuss later. Thus, concerned with the development experiences of the Latin American countries, Prebisch argued that it is not through trade with other regions but through industrialization that these countries can fully reap the benefits of technical progress.

But Prebisch (1950) and Singer (1950) differ in their explanations for the secular deterioration of the commodity terms of trade for the primary good exporting Periphery countries. Singer found his explanation in income inelastic demand for primary goods. Despite relatively faster technical progress in manufacturing, which should have lowered its relative price vis-à-vis primary goods through supply shocks, the relative price actually increased. To him, this was because real income gains from technical progress raised the demand for manufacturing more than the demand for primary goods due to differences in the income elasticity of the two types of goods. And this (relative) demand shock must have been stronger than the (relative) supply shock to cause a rise in the relative price of manufacturing goods or a worsening of the TOT for the primary good exporting Periphery countries. Low price elasticity for primary goods can also explain an adverse trend in the TOT. With the demand for primary products less responsive to prices, a *ceteris paribus* technical improvement in primary goods production (or a structural oversupply) causes the world prices to decline by a larger extent than if demands were more responsive to prices. Consequent loss in their export earnings in face of falling prices induces the developing countries, or peripheries, to export larger volumes of primary goods. This in turn depresses down the prices and worsens the TOT further.

Prebisch, on the other hand, argued that higher wages in the Centre, because of stronger trade unions there relative to those in the Periphery, was the main driving force of the secular deterioration of the TOT against the Periphery. He further related his argument to the business cycles of nations. Stronger trade unions protect money wages in downswings and the consequent labour retrenchment situation from falling too much, and real wages during upswings and the corresponding price inflation by ensuring higher money wages for workers. But relatively weaker labour unions in the primary good exporting developing countries fail to manage the same wage increase during the upswings and prevent large wage cuts during the downswings and deflation. Thus, the wage cost in the Periphery rises less during upswings and declines more during downswings relative to that in the Centre, so that the relative cost of primary goods declines in both downswings and upswings, resulting in lower relative prices through competitive pressures.

More than fifty years since these seminal contributions, it seems that the debate continues to find its relevance even in the current policy dialogues. Ocampo (2001a, 27) suggests that the international economy is also marked by basic imperfections which are of a 'systemic' rather than a 'Centre-Periphery' nature. The first of these, according to Ocampo (2001) is the contrast between the rapid development of markets and the sluggishness in building global governance in developing countries, which has led to a sub-optimal supply of 'global public goods' (Kaul, Grunberg, and Stern, 1999). The second, Ocampo continues to explain, is the enormous difference between the rapid globalization of some markets and the 'flagrant absence of a true international social agenda or, more precisely, the lack of effective international instruments to ensure the fulfilment of the development goals which are periodically reiterated, most recently in the United Nations Millennium Declaration'. Finally, the incompleteness of the international agenda, which also has, to some extent, 'Centre-Periphery' dimensions, in view of the absence of issues of great interest to the developing countries, such as international mobility of labour or the more rapid opening-up by the developed countries of markets which are of great interest to the developing nations (see also Prebisch, 1976). These are aspects, which the reader will find, are of prime concern for the subsequent chapters in this book.

2.2 Critique of Secular Deterioration of TOT

While the theoretical explanations offered by Prebisch and Singer were appealing, the appropriateness of data and methodology used by Prebisch in demonstrating secular deterioration of TOT were questioned by many researchers. First, it was pointed out by Kindleberger, Johnson, Lipsey and Meier, and Baldwin among others, that during the period of study, the trend in UK's net barter TOT was not a true representation of the industrialized countries of the world. Thus, the inverse of UK's net barter TOT could not be taken as a proxy for TOT of primary goods vis-à-vis manufactured goods. There was also the criticism of not distinguishing between primary goods exported by the developed countries and by the developing countries [Meier and Baldwin (1957)]. However, consideration of the subset of primary goods produced and exported by the developing countries did not make any significant difference in the deteriorating trend in the TOT for the primary products. Second, exports were valued at *fob* prices whereas imports were valued at *cif* prices. The difference between a *fob* price and the *cif* price is usually accounted for by the transport costs. Thus, the movement in the net barter TOT may well have reflected movements in the transport costs.

The other objections concern whether changes in net barter TOT can be a true indicator of the gains from trade, and accordingly the claim by Prebisch and Singer that secular deterioration of TOT for primary goods implied an unequal distribution of gains from trade among the Centre and the Periphery. The main criticism was that the commodity TOT (or the relative commodity price index) is not a true indicator of the productivity gains that international trade may usher in. To overcome this problem, Viner (1937) suggested an index of Double Factoral Terms of Trade, which is the commodity TOT adjusted for relative productivities in the primary goods and in manufacturing goods:

$$P = p\frac{\pi_o}{\pi_M} \tag{2.1}$$

where, P denotes the Double Factoral Terms of Trade, p is the price index of primary exports relative to that of the manufacturing imports or the commodity TOT, π_o is the productivity index in primary good export sector, which is measured as the cost in terms of quantity of domestic factors of production used per unit of export, and π_M is the productivity of *foreign* factors in the manufacturing imports by the developing countries, which is measured as cost in terms of quantity of foreign factors of production employed per unit of imports. That this Double Factoral Terms of Trade provide a better guide to the gains from trade than the commodity terms of trade index is evident from taking the percentage change in both sides of (2.1):

$$\hat{P} = \hat{p} + \hat{\pi}_o - \hat{\pi}_M. \tag{2.2}$$

Given that productivity improvements mean $\hat{\pi}_o < 0$ and $\hat{\pi}_M < 0$, an adverse commodity TOT, $\hat{p} < 0$, does not necessarily mean that the Double Factoral Terms of Trade worsens for the developing countries and thus the gains from trade are unevenly distributed. If international trade raises the productivity of foreign factors of production in manufacturing imports by the developing countries faster than it raises the productivity of the domestic factors of production in primary exports, the developing countries *may* gain from primary exports even when the commodity TOT worsens.

2.3 **Unequal Exchanges**

Emmanuel (1972) in his thesis of unequal exchange articulated that the advanced industrialized countries, or the Centre, exploit the Third World countries, or the Periphery countries, through commodity trade, because the wage differences between the regions are much higher than the perceived differences in labour productivity in export goods that these regions produce. The unequal exchange arises from undervaluation of labour in the Periphery, reflected in low wages there compared to institutionally-determined high wages in the Centre. This undervaluation of labour translates into a low price of goods that the Periphery countries produce. Thus, through international trade, there is essentially a transfer of value from the Periphery to the Centre in the advantage of the latter group of countries. That is, low prices of exports from Periphery contribute to the high standard of living in the Centre. To Emmanuel, wages are more a reflection of the bargaining power of trade unions vis-à-vis that of the employers and State regulations such as minimum wage laws. On the other hand, absence of an international market for labour, because of high degree of immobility in physical movement of labour across countries and regions, makes wage differences across countries persist. These wage differences, not commensurate with productivity differences, underlie undervaluation of exports and the unequal exchange that international trade implies for the Periphery.

The subsequent literature on Centre-Periphery or North-South trade relations emphasizes that the advanced Centre or North generates the momentum of capital accumulation and innovation, and the backward Periphery or South responds more or less passively to the parameters set by the North. Accordingly, North and South are linked with each other as unequal trade partners.

The unequal exchange thesis of Emmanuel has evoked huge debates and critiques. Jedlicki (2007) summarizes some of these debates and critiques. Whereas among the Marxists, unequal exchange constituted part of their broad critique of capitalist accumulation and commercial imperialism through trade and globalization, the neoclassical economists, and in particular the advocates of free trade, found Emmanuel's thesis unnecessarily apprehensive of the static and dynamic gains that international trade ushers in. But, while the static gains due to comparative advantages are not to be denied, one may still cast serious doubts in developing countries gaining much in the long run through exports of raw materials and other primary products. Despite the claims of the celebrated Factor Price Equalization theorem of international trade (Samuelson, 1948), that the convergence of commodity prices through free trade will lead to convergence of factor prices notwithstanding the immobility of factors of production, wage differences persists and in many cases have in fact widened even in the present age of globalization in which trade barriers all around are falling, and the volume of world trade has increased manifold compared to that in the 1980s. Moreover, there is more recent evidence on the deterioration of the TOT of the developing countries supporting the observation by Prebisch. For example, a recent study reveals that the price-ratio of the basket of goods produced by the developing countries (the Periphery) relative to the basket of goods imported by these countries from the developed countries declined from an index of 100 in 1980 to 48 in 1992. To the extent the returns to factors are determined by the prices of goods that they produce, the adverse TOT should mean lower income and wages for labour in the developing countries. As Emmanuel and his followers would argue, herein lies the fallacy of gains from trade. Jedlicki (2007) cites a more recent example of cocoa producing and exporting countries of Sub-Saharan Africa. The low and often falling world prices of cocoa, due to structural over-supply and productivity gains, remunerate the small African farmers barely above the subsistence level. But its transformation into chocolates commands a high enough price and remunerates the workers in Switzerland with the highest wages in the world. Despite cocoa being the essential raw materials for chocolates, the high price of chocolates does not confer any benefit to the African farmers because the transformation takes place not in Africa, but through trade in Switzerland. High demand for chocolates does not raise the price of cocoa and consequently wages in African countries producing and exporting cocoa. Rather low wages there and the low price of cocoa benefits producers of chocolate in Europe and workers engaged in such production in the face of high demand for chocolates.

Bacha (1978) provided a formal analysis of Emanuel's unequal exchange due to the TOT effect of equalization of profit rates through trade, and linked it with the secular deterioration of TOT and, more importantly, an immiserizing possibility for workers in the Periphery observed by Prebisch (1950) and Singer (1950) in the context of Centre-Periphery trade relations. He also linked these issues to the surplus labour analysis of Lewis (1954). Lewis' main focus was on the reallocation of labour between agriculture and the industry, which he perceived as dynamic and expanding, and draws the surplus labour from agriculture. In his 'Economic Development with Unlimited Supplies of Labour' paper (1954), he discussed the dynamics of how a dualistic economy transforms into a fully commercialized economy.

To formalize his argument, Bacha considered a simple Ricardian two-goods Centre-Periphery framework with labour as the only factor of production. Centre was assumed to be completely specialized in manufacturing the good (M) and the Periphery in the primary good (O). The manufacturing good exported by the Centre is taken as the numeraire. Capitalists control all production activities and pay wages to workers in each country. All workers are fully-employed in the Centre, but surplus labour exists in the Periphery at the institutionally-given wage there. Let a_{LO} and a^*_{LM} denote respectively per unit labour requirement in producing the primary good in the Periphery and the manufacturing good in the Centre. Profits are earned as a mark-up over wages paid. Denoting the wages and rates of profits in the Centre and Periphery by w and w^*, and R^* and R respectively, the post trade equilibrium prices of the two goods are given as,

$$p = a_{LO}(1+R)w \qquad (2.3)$$

$$1 = a^*_{LM}(1+R^*)w^* \qquad (2.4)$$

where, p is the price of the primary good relative to the price of the manufacturing good or the TOT of the Periphery.

Let $M(a_{LO}, 1/p)$ and $M^*(a^*_{LM}, p)$ denote the per capita import demand in the Periphery and Centre respectively. Note that apart from the TOT, p or $1/p$, import demands depend on the productivity because its inverse captures the per capita output or income. A smaller value of a_{LO} means a higher labour productivity and consequently higher per capita output or income in the Periphery. This raises the demand for the manufacturing good imported from the Centre: $\partial M / \partial a_{LO} < 0$. Similarly, an increase in labour productivity in the Centre raises the import demand for the primary good exported by the Periphery: $\partial M^* / \partial a^*_{LM} < 0$. On the other hand, import demands respond adversely to a rise in the relative price of the imported good: $(\partial M / \partial(1/p)) < 0$, $\partial M^* / \partial p < 0$. Normalizing the labour force in the Centre to unity and denoting the total employment in the Periphery by L_e, the trade balance condition can be written as,

$$L_e M\left(a_{LO}, \frac{1}{p}\right) = pM^*(a^*_{LM}, p). \qquad (2.5)$$

Given the productivity parameters and the TOT, the trade balance condition determines the employment level in the Periphery. Thus, the equilibrium level of employment in the Periphery can be written as an implicit function:

$$L_e = L\left(p, a_{LO}, a_{LM}^*\right) \tag{2.6}$$

The factor price frontier in (2.4) for the Centre gives us a unique inverse relationship between w^* and R^*. That is, given one factor price, the other can be determined. On the other hand, once the rate of profit in the Periphery, R, is determined, the TOT and the equilibrium level of employment in the Periphery, L_e, are determined.

Bacha (1978) considered two cases. The first, which he labelled as the Prebisch-Singer case, is the one where R is the profit-maximizing profit rate in the primary export industry of the Periphery. Given that the total output in the Periphery is L_e / a_{Lo}, and taking the inverse function of (2.6) to express the (relative) price of the primary good as $p\left(L_e, a_{LO}, a_{LM}^*\right)$, the profit function is written as,

$$V = p\left(L_e, a_{LO}, a_{LM}^*\right)\frac{L_e}{a_{LO}} - wL_e. \tag{2.7}$$

Hence, profit-maximization implies,

$$\frac{\partial V}{\partial L} = \left[\frac{\partial p}{\partial L}L_e + p\right]\frac{1}{a_{LO}} - w = 0 \Rightarrow \left[\frac{1}{\dfrac{p}{L_e}\dfrac{\partial L_e}{\partial p}} + 1\right]\frac{p}{a_{LO}} = w \Rightarrow p = \left[\frac{1}{1 - \dfrac{1}{e}}\right]a_{LO}w \tag{2.8}$$

where, e is the absolute price elasticity of demand for labour in the Periphery. From the trade balance condition (2.5) it is easy to check that this price elasticity of labour demand equals the sum of (per capita) absolute price elasticities of import demands minus one (see Appendix: Proof):

$$e = \varepsilon + \varepsilon^* - 1. \tag{2.9}$$

By the Marshall-Lerner condition for stability of the equilibrium TOT, $\varepsilon + \varepsilon^* > 1$, so that $e > 0$.

From (2.3) and (2.8) it is apparent that,

$$1+R=\left[\dfrac{1}{1-\dfrac{1}{e}}\right].$$

(2.10)

Thus, given w^*, for example, the rate of profit in the Centre, R^*, the rate of profit and aggregate employment in the Periphery, R and L_e, and the TOT for the Periphery, p, are determined from (2.4), (2.5), (2.8), and (2.10). Bacha then examined how changes in productivity and wages affect the TOT of the Periphery and the level of employment there. First of all, an increase in the labour productivity in the Centre raises its import demand for the primary good and thus raises production and employment in the Periphery. This is evident from the trade balance condition (2.5). Second, an exogenous wage increase in the Periphery raises the relative price of its primary exports or improves its TOT, though less than proportionate to the wage increase. With no change in the productivity parameter, log differentiation of (2.8) yields,

$$\hat{p} = \hat{\delta} + \hat{w}$$

(2.11)

where, $\delta = 1 + R$, and hat over a variable denotes proportional change, e.g., $\hat{\delta} = d\delta / \delta$. Note that by definition, $\hat{\delta} = [dR/(1+R)] = [R/(1+R)] \, (dR/R) = \varphi \hat{R} < \hat{R}$. Now since an increase in wage raises the cost of production, the firms raise their price which lowers the demand, and since at the initial profit-maximizing equilibrium the demand was elastic, so the total revenue falls. This means that the rate of profit in the Periphery declines: $\hat{\delta} = \varphi \hat{R} < 0$. Hence, $\hat{p} < \hat{w}$. But, despite the TOT improvement for the Periphery, the aggregate employment as well as the total wage bill declines. That the aggregate employment declines can be worked out from the trade balance condition as shown in the Appendix: Proof section:

$$\hat{L}_e = \left[1 - (\varepsilon + \varepsilon^*)\right]\hat{p}.$$

(2.12)

Given the Marshall-Lerner stability condition, a TOT improvement for the Periphery thus lowers the aggregate employment there. On the other hand, the wage bill declines because at the initial profit-maximizing equilibrium the elasticity of labour demand, which equals e, was necessarily larger than one, so that the decline in the labour demand and employment is larger than the wage increase. Therefore, an exogenous wage increase actually makes the workers as a whole worse off.

An increase in labour productivity in the Periphery has a direct effect and an indirect effect. From the trade balance condition, by the direct effect, aggregate employment rises. The productivity increase raises output and income per capita in the Periphery and consequently its import demand by the income elasticity, η. At the initial TOT there is no change in the import demand for exports of the Periphery. Thus, the import value of the Periphery must come down to the initial level of its export earnings to maintain the trade balance. This necessitates a proportionate decline in aggregate employment *at the initial TOT*. But, the productivity increase in the Periphery lowers the cost of producing exports and hence the relative price of such exports. The TOT of the Periphery now worsens, which by (2.12) raises the aggregate employment by $e = \varepsilon + \varepsilon^* - 1$ at the margin. A productivity increase thus lowers aggregate employment if the direct effect is stronger than the indirect effect: $\eta > e$. This is known as the Johnson impoverishment condition. Algebraically,

$$\hat{L}_e = [\eta - e]\hat{a}_{Lo},\tag{2.13}$$

since a productivity increase means $\hat{a}_{Lo} < 0$, so $\hat{L}_e < 0$ if $\eta > e$. As pointed out by Bacha, it was the presumption of Prebisch and Singer that the income elasticity of the Periphery demand for the manufacturing good exported by the Centre is quite high, whereas the price elasticities are sufficiently low to meet the Johnson impoverishment condition. Consequently, productivity increase in the primary good export sector in the Periphery goes against the interest of its workers.

In contrast to the Prebisch-Singer case of the profit-maximizing rate of profit in the Periphery, Emmanuel often talked about equalization of the rate of profits through movement of capital from the Centre to the Periphery. Note that higher wages in the Centre relative to those in the Periphery, the key argument in the Prebisch-Singer-Emmanuel analysis, implies a higher rate of profit in the Periphery for any given TOT. Thus, in the aforementioned context, Emmanuel's case can be represented by the following condition if capital mobility is unrestricted and capital everywhere is homogeneous or perfect substitutes:

$$R = R^*.\tag{2.14}$$

Now (2.3), (2.4), (2.5), and (2.14) together determine R, R^*, p, and L_e, given the wage in the Centre. Two comparative static results deserve attention. First, an increase in the wage in the Centre reduces the rate of profit there and through capital flow the rate of profit in the Periphery must fall as well, until the rates are equalized, as in (2.14). Given the wage rate in the Periphery, this causes the TOT to worsen. This was a major concern of Emmanuel. But, the adverse

TOT means larger employment in the Periphery as evident from (2.12). Thus, as Bacha (1978) observes, the TOT deterioration that the increase in the wage rate in the Centre implies actually makes workers in the Periphery better off, and thus 'there is international solidarity of the working class movement' implicit in Emmanuel's argument.

Second, consider a technical progress in the Centre with its benefits being entirely appropriated by the capitalist class. Thus, the wage rate in the Centre remains the same but the rate of profit there goes up. Reverse capital flow now raises the rate of profit in the Periphery as well, and with it the TOT now improves. But this lowers aggregate employment. This is the indirect effect. On the other hand, higher income per capita in the Centre raises the demand for imports from the Periphery and consequently employment there through the income effect η^*. If this income effect is weaker than the price effect, captured through the price elasticity of labour demand, $\eta^* < e$, overall the employment in the Periphery declines.

◼ Appendix: Proof

Total differentiation of the trade balance condition (2.5) yields,

$$M dL_e + L_e \left[\frac{\partial M}{\partial a_{Lo}} da_{Lo} + \frac{\partial M}{\partial (1/p)} \left(-\frac{1}{p^2} \right) dp \right] = M^* dp + p \left[\frac{\partial M^*}{\partial a_{LM}^*} da_{LM}^* + \frac{\partial M^*}{\partial p} dp \right]$$

$$\Rightarrow$$

$$M L_e \hat{L}_e + M L_e \left[\frac{a_{Lo}}{M} \frac{\partial M}{\partial a_{Lo}} \hat{a}_{Lo} - \frac{(1/p)}{M} \frac{\partial M}{\partial (1/p)} \hat{p} \right] = p M^* \hat{p} + p M^*$$

$$\left[\frac{a_{LM}^*}{M^*} \frac{\partial M^*}{\partial a_{LM}^*} \hat{a}_{LM}^* + \frac{p}{M^*} \frac{\partial M^*}{\partial p} \hat{p} \right]$$

Using the initial balanced trade condition, this boils down to,

$$\Rightarrow \hat{L}_e + \left[-\eta \hat{a}_{Lo} + \varepsilon \hat{p} \right] = \hat{p} + \left[-\eta^* \hat{a}_{LM}^* - \varepsilon^* \hat{p} \right]$$

$$\Rightarrow \hat{L}_e = \eta \hat{a}_{Lo} - \eta^* \hat{a}_{LM}^* + \left[1 - (\varepsilon + \varepsilon)^* \right] \hat{p} \qquad (A.2.1)$$

From (A.2.1), the price elasticity of labour demand, e, can be obtained by putting $\hat{a}_{Lo} = \hat{a}_{LM}^* = 0$:

$$e \equiv -\frac{\hat{L}_e}{\hat{p}} = \left[\varepsilon + \varepsilon^* - 1 \right] \qquad (A.2.2)$$

Thus, using (A.2.2), we can rewrite (A.2.1) as,

$$\Rightarrow \hat{L}_e = \eta \hat{a}_{Lo} - \eta^* \hat{a}_{LM}^* - e\hat{p} \tag{A.2.3}$$

Now log differentiation of (2.3) yields,

$$\hat{p} = \hat{a}_{Lo} + \hat{\delta} + \hat{w} \tag{A.2.4}$$

Given the wage rate and the rate of profit in the Periphery, the relative price thus falls proportionately with the improvement in labour productivity: $\hat{p} = \hat{a}_{Lo} < 0$. Hence, putting $\hat{a}_{LM}^* = 0$ in (A.2.3), we obtain the Johnson impoverishment condition for an improvement in labour productivity in the Periphery as in (2.13) in the text:

$$\hat{L}_e = (\eta - e)\hat{a}_{Lo}$$

On the other hand, under Emmanuel's case of equalization of the rates of profit, for any given w', from (2.4) we get,

$$\hat{a}_{LM}^* = -\hat{\delta}^* \tag{A.2.5}$$

Since $\hat{R} = \hat{R}^* \Rightarrow \hat{\delta} = \hat{\delta}^*$, so using (A.2.5) we get the change in TOT for a give w and a_{Lo} as:

$$\hat{p} = -\hat{a}_{LM}^* \tag{A.2.6}$$

Substitution of (A.2.6) in (A.2.3) for $\hat{a}_{Lo} = 0$ yields,

$$\hat{L}_e = (e - \eta^*)\hat{a}_{LM}^* \tag{A.2.7}$$

Thus, productivity improvement in the Centre, which does not change the wage rate there but only the rate of profit proportionately, lowers the employment in the Periphery if $\eta^* < e$ as mentioned in the text.

■ REFERENCES

Bacha, E. (1978). 'An Interpretation of Unequal Exchange from Prebisch-Singer to Emmanuel'. *Journal of Development Economics* 5 (4): 319–330.

Emmanuel, A. (1972). *Unequal Exchange: A Study of the Imperialism of Trade*, Translation by B. Pearce. New York & London: Monthly Review Press.

Jedlicki, C. (2007). 'Unequal Exchange', 'Sustainable Human Development'. TJSGA/TL WNSI BRIEF/SD (B006) September.

Kaul, I., Grunberg, I., and Stern, M. A. (eds) (1999). *Global Public Goods: International Cooperation in the 21st Century*. New York: United Nations Development Programme (UNDP).

Lewis, W. A. (1954). 'Economic Development with Unlimited Supplies of Labour'. *Manchester School of Economic and Social Studies* 22: 139–191.

Meier, G. M. and Baldwin, R. E. (1957). *Economic Development: Theory, History, Policy*. NY: John Wiley and Sons.

Myrdal, G. (1965). *An International Economy*. New York: Harper and Row.

Ocampo, J. A. (2001). 'The Development Agenda Revisited'. *CEPAL Review* 74, LC/G.2135-P. Santiago, Chile: ECLAC.

Ocampo, J. A. (2001a). 'Raúl Prebisch and the Development Agenda at the Dawn of the Twenty-First Century'. *CEPAL Review* 75, December.

Prebisch, R. (1976). 'A Critique of Peripheral Capitalism'. *CEPAL Review* 1, E.76.II.G.2, Santiago, Chile: ECLAC.

Prebisch, R. (1950). *The Economic Development of Latin America and Its Principal Problems*. New York: United Nations.

Samuelson, P. A. (1948). *Economics*. New York: McGraw-Hill.

Sarkar, P. and Singer, H. W. (1991). 'Manufactured Exports of Developing Countries and Their Terms of Trade Since 1965'. *World Development* 19 (4): 333.

Singer, H. W. (1950). 'The Distribution of Gains Between Investing and Borrowing Countries'. *American Economic Review*, Papers & Proceedings 40: 478.

Singer, H. W. (1964). *International Development: Growth and Change*. New York: McGraw-Hill.

Singer, H. W. (1998). *Growth, Development and Trade: Selected Essays of Hans W. Singer*. Cheltenham: Edward Elgar.

Viner, J. (1937). *Studies in the Theory of International Trade*. London: George Allen & Unwin Ltd.

3 Terms of Trade and Growth

In Chapter 1, we discussed the trade-growth relationship as perceived by the classical political economists. Smith's trade as vent for surplus productive capacity of an economy and Ricardo's trade as a way of delaying the stationary state were the two cornerstones of such discussions. On the other hand, the export-led growth argument that was implicit in Smith's productivity theory was later articulated by Robertson (1940) in his trade as an engine of growth argument. The post-World War II development in the trade-growth relationship, however, focused on the TOT issue and consequent welfare implications of trade-induced growth, the relationship between income inequality and growth, and on product innovation and *endogenous* growth.

On trade-induced growth, TOT, and national welfare, Bhagwati (1953) demonstrated, similar in spirit to the Prebisch-Singer hypothesis, that an export-biased growth may be immiserizing for a large country because it worsens the country's TOT. Later, Johnson (1967) argued that growth may be immiserizing even for a small open economy when trade is restricted by an import tariff. In his case, it is not the TOT deterioration which is the source of immiserization because for a small country (as long as it remains small even after growth) there is no change in the TOT. Immiserization possibility arises because the tariff creates a pure distortion for the small country, which is accentuated through growth in factors of production and consequently in the aggregate value of output. Similar immiserization possibility was demonstrated by Brecher and Alejandro (1977) in the context of foreign capital inflow-led growth of a small open economy. These immiserization results put serious doubts on the export-led growth arguments and contribute much to the legacy of inward-looking, impost-substitution development strategy, often beyond the imagination of these authors themselves.

International trade augmenting growth through redistribution of income within a nation, on the other hand, rests on the assumption that the marginal propensity to save varies across the income classes. This idea can be traced back to the arguments of Keynes (1920), Kaldor (1957), and Kalecki (1971), who viewed that income inequality has a favourable effect on economic growth. All these economists shared the idea that the marginal propensity to save increases with wealth, so that growing income inequality means redistribution of incomes and wealth in favour of individuals whose marginal propensity to save is higher.[1] This raises the economy's aggregate savings, capital accumulation, and its rate of output growth. The relevance of international trade in this context is that it redistributes income and thus changes wealth or income inequality within trading nations. Opening up an economy to international trade raises the domestic relative price of exports in a country and consequently raises the rate of return to capital more than proportionately, and lowers the money wage if exports are relatively capital intensive and import-competing production is relatively labour intensive. This is the well-known price magnification effect à la Jones (1965). Similar effect can be generated through reduction of import tariffs (or quotas), if restricted (but non-prohibitive) trade was the initial state.[2] This redistribution of factor incomes causes the workers to save less and the capital owners to save more. But since capitalists usually have a higher marginal propensity to save than the wage earners, the aggregate savings of the economy rises. There will consequently be a higher rate of capital accumulation and growth. At the same time, trade liberalization will lower aggregate savings and the rate of capital accumulation, and consequently will lower the rate of growth in a country which imports relatively capital intensive goods. That is, international trade is expected to have an asymmetric income redistribution effect in the trading nations and hence contrasting effects on their growth rates. A slightly different argument was put forward by Corden (1971) in his factor-weight approach. Under constant returns to scale technology, the rate of growth in output is a weighted average of the rates of capital accumulation and the growth in labour force. The weights being the shares of national income of labour and capital, international trade affects the rate of growth of output by altering these weights through its redistribution effect. That is, the effect of income inequality on growth is measured by factor shares of income growth. But again, the trade-induced growth rates should be asymmetric across trading nations.

However, there are two caveats to the link between trade and growth. First, the wages of skilled workers relative to the wages of unskilled workers have risen over the last two decades in most parts of the globe.[3] This growing wage inequality means that aggregate savings by workers, skilled and unskilled

---

[1] Rosenstein-Rodan (1943) and Lewis (1954), on the other hand, argue that a distribution of income from the agricultural sector is critical for industrialization.

[2] Stolper and Samuelson (1941) were the first to demonstrate that an increase in tariff will raise the real return to the scarce factor and reduce the real return to the abundant factor of production. By the Heckscher-Ohlin theorem of pattern of trade, a country exports goods which intensively uses its abundant factor and imports goods which intensively use its scarce factor. This means tariff reductions will redistribute income in favour of capitalists in a capital abundant country and thus will augment the country's output growth.

[3] See Marjit and Acharyya (2003) for a documentation of this growing wage inequality and the debate over trade versus technological change as a plausible cause. Though empirical estimates are not overwhelmingly in favour of international trade causing such inequalities, the role of trade cannot be denied either. Recent developments in trade theory demonstrate that it is possible to have symmetric

together, should rise everywhere. If non-wage income rises too, or falls only marginally, aggregate savings of trading nations rises. Thus, it is possible to have a symmetric growth effect of trade in most of the trading nations. Second, as observed by Rodriguez (1999), 'whether one uses factor shares or normatively more desirable indicators of income inequality such as the Gini index, there is very little evidence that inequality is good for growth'. Alesina and Rodrik (1994), Persson and Tabellini (1994), and Pineda and Rodríguez (1999) all find a negative impact of inequality on growth in cross-country regression analysis using different measures of inequality such as the Gini coefficient and share of the median voters in GDP. But, in a panel data estimation, Forbes (2000) and Li and Zou (1993), and Barro (1999) found inequality having a positive effect on growth in the short run, which is, however, reversed in the long run.

Trade and development literature in the post-World War II period also brought manufacturing industry and effective demand constraint on growth to the centre-stage, along the Keynesian line of argument. In this context, Kaldor's Growth Laws, which were presented at his Inaugural Lecture in Cambridge in 1966 on the causes of the UK's slow growth rate, have attracted much attention as well as criticism. Among the series of assertions, Kaldor (1967) postulated that, due to economies of scale, a faster rate of growth of manufacturing output will bring in a higher rate of growth of labour prod-uctivity in manufacturing. The growth of manufacturing output is, however, constrained by demand from agriculture in the early stage of development and exports in the later stages. A faster rate of growth in export demand will lead to a virtuous circle of output growth and productivity growth. At the same time, Kaldor postulated a divergence of growth in the sense that lower costs of pro-duction in fast growing industries, due to economies of scale as well as tech-nological improvements, make it difficult for newly industrialized countries to gain world market shares and grow fast.

The other relevant theories of trade and growth are the North-South models of trade and growth. A dominant sub-group of these theories is the structuralist growth model, which has its roots in Keynes (1936), Kalecki (1971), Harrod (1937), Domar (1946), and Robinson (1956). The dual role of investment, both as a component of aggregate demand and as a flow that augments the stock of capital, holds the key in this tradition. The basic struc-turalist model perceives that if in an economy the capital constraint, deter-mined by the level of investment, does not bind, then excess capacity will prevail. The other possibility is that at any given point in time, an economy may experience involuntary unemployment. In some situations, as in the typical Keynesian effective demand determined equilibrium, both excess capacity and involuntary unemployment may persist. In such a situation,

relative wage movements in *all* trading nations together [Acharyya (2010), Feenstra and Hanson (2001), Davis (1996), Marjit and Acharyya (2003), Marjit and Kar (2005), Zhu and Trefler (2005)].

where essentially neither the capital constraints nor the labour constraint binds, investment becomes the key variable bringing about changes in the capacity utilization and output as it generates both demand and the change in the capital stock. Depending on the relative strength of investment to create demand or capacity, the capacity utilization—the ratio of effective demand to the level of capacity—rises or falls in the transient state. However, the level of investment itself depends on capacity utilization; when it is high, investment accelerates to generate more capacity though raises demand only proportionately so that an explosive cycle may emerge. The basic structuralist model has been extended by McKinnon (1964), Taylor (1933, 2004), and Dutt (1984) among others, to study growth under foreign exchange constraints and human capital formation.

A different variant of the North-South trade model has been used by Findlay (1980) to examine the two-way relationship between TOT and growth. In contrast to output growth being determined by exogenous growth in the labour force and steady state properties as in Solow (1956) considered by Findlay, more recent theories of trade and growth focus on an endogenous growth process through product innovation in the North, as in Grossman and Helpman (1991). An interesting study in such a context is how the product growth rate (or the rate of innovation) in the North is determined by the rate of imitation of products traded in the South (Helpman, 1993). The cornerstone of all these endogenous growth models, which have their roots in influential works by Lucas (1988), Romer (1990), and Rebelo (1992), is the allocation of resources across the research and development sector (R&D) and the manufacturing production sector of a trading nation. International trade reallocates labour as well as alters the returns from R&D.

This chapter, however, discusses only those theories that are relevant in the context of North-South trade, such as the immiserization theories of Bhagwati-Johnson-Alejandro, Findlay's two-way causation in TOT and growth relationship, and the structuralist discussion of the trade-growth relationship. The trade and product-growth analysis of Grossman and Helpman (1991) and Helpman (1993) will be discussed in Chapter 10, in the context of TRIPS and its implications for product innovation. The empirical estimates of the trade-growth relationship and the emerging dimensions of the trade-growth relationship in the present era of globalization are discussed in the latter part of this chapter.

3.1 Trade, Factor Mobility, and Immiserizing Growth

In a closed economy, exogenous growth in factors of production is always beneficial, since it shifts the production frontier (or expands the production set). Larger availability of domestic factors enables the economy to produce goods in larger quantities. The aggregate value of output and income thus increases. Even if prices of goods change as a consequence of changes in the production and supply of goods, real income gains are redistributed among economic agents within the economy—amongst producers and consumers and amongst factor owners through changes in factor prices consequent upon the commodity price changes. But in an open economy, larger output and consequent price changes have altogether different implications. If growth is export-biased in the sense that the increase in production of the export good is more than proportionate to that of the import-competing good, and the country is large enough to influence the world prices of its exports and imports, the world relative price of its exports will fall. This benefits the consumers abroad as well. That is, a part of the real income gain from growth is now exported away by the country. What Bhagwati (1953) demonstrated is that if this fall in the world relative price of exports (or deterioration of the TOT) of a country experiencing growth is large, the subsequent real income loss is far too high to outweigh initial real income gains prior to the price changes. That is, the country exports away more than it gains. Growth is thus immiserizing in such a case. If the growing economy had not been engaged in trade with the external world, the fruits of the price fall consequent upon the growth itself that would have been enjoyed by its domestic consumers only, would have just compensated for lower incomes for its domestic producers. But this is not the case for growth in an open economy. Similar argument holds when there is technical progress that augments production of export goods more than that of the import-competing good. The benefits of technical progress are exported away and in the end, the country *may* be worse off compared to its position before the technical progress. This is very much similar to the unequal distribution of gains from trade or unequal exchange arguments of Prebisch, Singer, and Emmanuel discussed in Chapter 2. The only difference is that such a possibility of immiserization was perceived to be a self-enforcing proposition for a country exporting primary goods. In contrast, Bhagwati's immiserization possibility may arise even for manufacturing exports, and is not a self-enforcing proposition in the sense that certain conditions have to be met for growth to be welfare-reducing for a large, open economy.

To explain in more concrete terms, consider a large trading economy producing two goods, Bicycle (B) and Carpet (C), with two factors of productions, labour (L) and capital (K), under constant returns to scale technology. Perfect competition prevails everywhere and both labour and capital are sectorally mobile and fully employed. Suppose carpet is relatively labour intensive and bicycle is relatively capital intensive for *all* relevant wage-rental ratios. The country under consideration, say, India, exports carpet to, say, China and imports bicycles from there.[4] Tastes of Indian and Chinese consumers are assumed to be identical and homothetic. Homothetic tastes make the relative demand for carpets and bicycles depend only on the relative price. Finally, suppose these are the only two countries in the world.

Now consider an exogenous growth in labour in India *ceteris paribus*. By the output magnification effect, or Rybczynski theorem, this raises the production of carpet more than proportionate to the growth in the labour force and lowers the production of bicycles in India at the initial world relative price of carpets, p^w (see the 'Fundamental Theorems and Proofs' section):

$$\hat{X}_C > \hat{L} > 0 = \hat{K} > \hat{X}_B \tag{3.1}$$

where, $\hat{X}_j = dX_j / X_j$ denotes the proportional change in the output (or level of production) of good-j ($j = B, C$).

At the initial world equilibrium relative price of carpets and corresponding demands for carpet and bicycles by the Indian consumers, this change in the composition of output raises the volume of India's exports of carpets and imports of bicycles. These changes in volume of trade lowers the world relative price of carpets, which is a deterioration of the TOT for India (and improvement for China) as India sells carpets and buys bicycles in the world market. There will thus be a consequent welfare loss for India. Algebraically, as shown in the 'Fundamental Theorems and Proofs' section, India's change in welfare, or real income, can be obtained as,

$$dy = -Mdp^w + (p^w dX_B + dX_C). \tag{3.2}$$

The first term on the right hand side captures the TOT effect. An improvement in the TOT, $dp^W < 0$, raises the real income of the home country. The second term captures the growth effect—the increase in the aggregate value of production evaluated at the world relative price or the TOT—which also raises the real income.

To derive the effect of growth and corresponding increase in aggregate expenditure (at initial TOT), $dg \equiv (p^w dX_B + dX_C)$, on the country's TOT, consider the following trade balance condition:

$$p^W M(p^W, g) = M^*(p^W) \tag{3.3}$$

---

[4] This pattern of trade between India and China may arise from relative factor abundance of these two countries as in Heckscher (1949) and Ohlin (1933). For example, if India is assumed to be a relatively labour abundant country and China relatively capital abundant, then by the well-known Heckscher-Ohlin theory, India will export the relatively labour intensive carpet and China will export the relatively capital intensive bicycle.

where, $g \equiv (p^W X_B + X_C)$ is the aggregate value of production or expenditure at the initial TOT. Total differentiation of this trade balance condition yields,

$$Mdp^W + p^W \left[\frac{\partial M}{\partial p^W} dp^W + \frac{\partial M}{\partial g} dg \right] = \frac{\partial M^*}{\partial p^W} dp^W$$

$$\Rightarrow M \left[1 + \frac{p^W}{M} \frac{\partial M}{\partial p^W} - \frac{1}{M} \frac{\partial M^*}{\partial p^W} \right] dp^W = -mdg \qquad (3.4)$$

where, $m \equiv (p^W \partial M / \partial g)$ is the marginal propensity to import.

Using $1/M = p^W / M^*$ from (3.3), and the absolute values of import demand elasticities $\varepsilon \equiv [(-p^W / M)(\partial M / \partial p^W)]$ and $\varepsilon^* \equiv [(p^W / M^*)(\partial M^* / \partial p)^W]$, from (3.4) we obtain the effect of growth in India's aggregate expenditure and income on its TOT as,

$$\frac{dp^W}{dg} = \frac{m}{M \left[\varepsilon + \varepsilon^* - 1 \right]} \qquad (3.5)$$

Denoting the marginal propensity to consume carpets in India by c, and the marginal propensity to produce carpets in India by δ, by definition $m \equiv c - \delta$. Hence, (3.5) can alternatively be written as,

$$\frac{dp^W}{dg} = \frac{c - \delta}{M \left[\varepsilon + \varepsilon^* - 1 \right]}. \qquad (3.6)$$

Note that by the Marshall-Lerner condition for stability of international equilibrium specified in (3.3), $\varepsilon + \varepsilon^* > 1$. Walrasian stability requires the excess demand in the world market for India's import good (bicycles) must fall as its world relative price rises, $\partial [M(p^W, g) - X^*(p^W)] / \partial p^W < 0$, which in turn by the trade balance condition for China, $X^*(p^W) = [(1/p^W)M^*(p^W)]$, requires $\partial [p^W M(p^W, g) - M^*(p^W)] / \partial p^W < 0$. Proceeding as before, it is straightforward to check that this condition is satisfied if $\varepsilon + \varepsilon^* > 1$.

Given this stability condition, from (3.6) it is apparent that a sufficient condition for TOT deterioration, $\partial p^W / \partial g > 0$, is that δ should be negative. Under the assumption that bicycles are relatively capital intensive, by the Rybczynski result (3.1), an exogenous growth in labour force (and corresponding growth in aggregate value of production and expenditure) lowers the import-competing production of bicycles in India and hence $\delta < 0$. Growth here is export-biased. However, if there had been capital accumulation without any growth in labour force, the import-competing production of bicycles would have risen and hence $\delta > 0$. Growth here is import-biased. TOT would then deteriorate only if $c > \delta$ so that despite the increase in production of bicycles, India's import demand rises. That is, an export-biased growth necessarily worsens India's TOT.[5]

Using $dg \equiv (p^w dX_C + dX_B)$ and (3.6), the change in welfare or real income of India following growth (in production and expenditure) as specified in (3.2) boils down to:

$$\frac{dy}{dg} = \frac{\delta - c}{\varepsilon + \varepsilon^* - 1} + 1 = \frac{\left(\varepsilon - c\right) + \left(\varepsilon^* - 1\right) + \delta}{\varepsilon + \varepsilon^* - 1}.$$

But, given that $\varepsilon \equiv \tilde{\varepsilon} + c$, where $\tilde{\varepsilon} > 0$ is the compensated price elasticity of demand for bicycles in India, the change in India's welfare boils down to,

$$\frac{dy}{dg} = \frac{\tilde{\varepsilon} + \left(\varepsilon^* - 1\right) + \delta}{\varepsilon + \varepsilon^* - 1}. \tag{3.7}$$

Hence, if China's import demand for carpets is elastic (or unitary elastic) $\varepsilon^* > (=)1$, a *necessary*, though not sufficient, condition for growth to be immiserizing, $dy / dg < 0$, is that $\delta < 0$. From the earlier discussions, this means that growth has to be export-biased. If China's import demand for carpets is inelastic, $\varepsilon^* < 1$, then the immiserization possibility is reinforced, but the point to remember is that this is not a necessary condition. That is, for Bhagwati's immiserizing growth, the pre-growth international equilibrium need not be at the backward bending (or inelastic) segment of China's offer curve.

What is evident from the argument is that growth may be immiserizing for a large country if it is export-biased, because the TOT in such a case worsens for the growing country and this constitutes a source of welfare loss. It may therefore seem logical to argue that for a small trading nation, growth must always be beneficial because the TOT for such a trading nation does not change. But Johnson (1967) argued on the contrary that even for a small country, growth may be immiserizing if there is a tariff in place on its imports. His case can be derived in the set up as follows. Suppose India is a small country and is growing under tariff protection. If $0 < t < 1$ denotes its *ad-valorem* tariff imposed on imports of bicycles from China, then the change in India's

---

[5] In case of both labour force growth and capital accumulation, with the former being faster than the latter, the output of carpets increases more than proportionate to the growth in labour force as in (3.1), but now the import-competing production of bicycles *may* rise as well: $\hat{X}_C > \hat{L} > \hat{K} > \hat{X}_B > 0$. In such a case, $\delta > 0$, and thus despite growth being export (sector) biased in the sense that $\hat{X}_C > \hat{X}_B > 0$, the TOT worsens only if $c > \delta$. However, even if the import-competing production of bicycles rises, it will not be large enough so that it is more likely that the (positive) value of δ will be small and the TOT will worsen.

welfare consists of the growth effect and the volume of trade effect (see the 'Fundamental Theorems and Proofs' section):

$$\frac{dy}{dg} = tp^w \frac{dM}{dg} + 1 \Rightarrow \frac{dy}{dg} = tp^w m + 1 \Rightarrow \frac{dy}{dg} = tp^w (c - \delta) + 1. \qquad (3.8)$$

Now a necessary condition for growth to be immiserizing is that $\delta > 0$, i.e., the import-competing production of bicycles must increase. This is obvious. A tariff creates a distortion by protecting the inefficient domestic producers of the import-competing good, if pattern of trade is consistent with the pattern of comparative advantage of India and China. Growth that raises the production of the import-competing good essentially magnifies the distortion and consequently lowers the welfare. Thus, distortion created by import tariffs for a small open economy is the source of immiserizing growth. As spelled out earlier, again the Rybczynski result indicates when this immiserization possibility arises. If India's growth in aggregate value of production and expenditure under tariff protection is caused by an exogenous growth in its labour force, then immiserization in the Johnson case cannot arise because in such a case inefficient import-competing production of bicycles in India falls and growth is export-biased. But if growth is caused by domestic capital accumulation, Johnson's immiserization possibility arises.

Immiserization may also arise for a small country if growth is caused by capital inflow instead of domestic capital accumulation. This was demonstrated by Brecher and Alejandro (1977). In case of foreign capital inflow-led growth, the repatriation of returns to foreign capital constitutes an additional source of welfare loss. This is evident from the following expression for change in India's welfare when there is finitely large inflow of foreign capital (K_f)[6]:

$$dy = tp^w dM + (p^w dX_B + dX_C) - (rdK_f + K_f dr). \qquad (3.9)$$

The foreign capital is paid its value of marginal product under competitive conditions, which is repatriated back to the origin country. This payment to the foreign capital is thus a loss to the host country. However, if the rate of return to capital declines as the foreign capital flows in, the foreign capital takes away less than its value of marginal product, and there will be a positive net growth effect on the welfare of the host country. But if factor prices do not

---

[6] Under capital inflow, the value of GDP of India equals the total domestic factor income and returns to foreign capital: $wL + rK + rK_f = X_C + pX_B$. But if returns to foreign capital are fully repatriated, then India's aggregate value of consumption or expenditure must be less than its aggregate value of production (or GDP) by this magnitude: $D_C + pD_B = X_C + pX_B - rK_f$. Total differentiation of this national budget constraint and proceeding in the same way as shown in the Appendix for derivation of (3.2), we can obtain (3.9).

change, the competitive return to foreign capital will leave the host country with no gain from output growth as the foreign capital takes all that it contributes. Whether the rate of return to capital declines or remains unchanged depends on the magnitude of capital inflow.

To explain, first of all, note that there will be no distributional consequences of small and moderately large capital inflows that increase the total availability of capital in India but still keeps its overall labour-capital availability ratio within the Chipman-McKenzie cone of diversification, so that India continues to produce both carpets and bicycles domestically. Capital inflow changes the commodity composition of the production basket of India as more bicycles and fewer carpets will be produced, and with it changes its volume of trade. But as long India is a small country, such a change in its volume of trade will not affect the world prices for its exports of carpets and imports of bicycles. Accordingly, there shall not be any change in the wage rate (W) and rate of return to capital (r) in India. This is apparent from the following pair of zero profit conditions that reflect perfectly competitive domestic markets:

$$P_C^W = a_{LC}W + a_{KC}r \tag{3.10}$$

$$(1+t)P_B^W = a_{LB}W + a_{KB}r. \tag{3.11}$$

Thus, as long as labour and capital are homogeneous and mobile across the two sectors and earn the same wage and rate of return wherever they are employed in India, and both carpets and bicycles are produced in India, the factor prices are solely and uniquely determined by the world prices of carpets and bicycles. Thus, small and moderately large capital inflows that shift India's labour-capital availability ratio within the Chipman-McKenzie cone of diversification and keeps it incompletely specialized, factor prices do not change. This means that $K^* dr = 0$. On the other hand, competitive return to foreign capital means that it is paid its value of marginal product. That is, it takes away all the gains in the aggregate value of production such that $(p^W dX_B + dX_C) - rdK^* = 0$. Hence, the change in welfare in (3.9) now boils down to:

$$dy = tp^W dM. \tag{3.12}$$

Therefore, by the Rybczynski result, foreign-capital inflow-led growth is necessarily immiserizing if bicycles are capital-intensive, since in that case India's volume of imports of bicycles declines.

Again the Brecher-Alejandro case of immiserization arises for reasons similar to the Johnson case. Capital inflow-led growth magnifies the distortion (or inefficiency) caused by tariff if such inflow raises the production of import-competing bicycles. Note that if trade had been unrestricted ($t = 0$), there would have been no change in India's welfare since the repatriation of returns to foreign capital would completely wash out the initial growth effect.

For capital inflows that shifts India's overall labour-capital availability ratio outside the Chipman-McKenzie cone of diversification, India is completely specialized in the production of capital-intensive bicycles. The zero profit condition (3.10) drops out and factor prices are no longer determined solely and uniquely by the world prices of bicycles. These now depend on factor supplies or availability and corresponding marginal productivities of labour and capital. Diminishing return to (foreign) capital then causes the rate of return to capital to decline as more foreign capital flows in. Thus, foreign capital is now paid less than it contributes. Hence, under free trade, India unambiguously gains from growth caused by *large* foreign capital flow.

3.2 Structuralist Theories: Foreign Exchange, Savings, and Growth

During the 1960s emerged a debate over how to augment the growth rates of the developing economies by breaking their small-savings-small-growth vicious circles. The idea that was floated was much in the tradition of trade as an engine of growth. Foreign exchange earned by exporting goods enables an economy to finance its import of capital goods. This means that scarce domestic resources no longer need to be withdrawn from production of consumer goods for production of domestic capital goods. Alternatively, the country can import consumer goods and devote larger domestic resources to production of domestic capital goods. In either case, investment can be raised, and the growth rate can be augmented without reducing present consumption. In other words, foreign exchange earned through exports can supplement low levels of savings in the developing countries and resolve (at least temporarily) the trade-off between the present consumption and future consumption (or growth). At the same time, however, it has been recognized that such augmentation of growth rate is constrained by the availability of foreign exchange earned through exports, and the consequent import of capital goods for investment. That is, an open economy faces a foreign exchange gap (or foreign exchange constraint) in addition to a savings gap (or savings constraint) for its growth. Of course, this foreign exchange gap is relevant only for a large country, because a small country can export any amount (and earn corresponding foreign exchange) without depressing the world price of its exports. The foremost discussions and formalizations of these two gaps were by Chenery and Bruno (1962), McKinnon (1964), and Chenery and Strout (1966). These two-gap models, as they are commonly referred to, originate from the post-Keynesian growth models of Harrod (1939) and Domar (1946).

Thus, in contrast to the normative dimension of trade and growth—whether international trade leads to unequal exchange and whether growth is immiserizing—these two-gap models are concerned about the constraints on growth of the developing (or Southern) countries where domestic savings is typically low and export capacity is limited. What emerges as the resolution of these two gaps from writings of this post-Keynesian tradition is that foreign aid and external loans or debts can bridge these gaps. To exemplify, we discuss the formulation of the two gaps by McKinnon (1964).

Let K_d and K_f denote respectively the units of domestic and foreign capital available. Assume that b units of domestic capital produce one unit of output (Y) and c units of foreign capital produce one unit of domestic output. These capital-output ratios are assumed to be constant so that an addition to the capital stock, either domestic or foreign, proportionately raises the level of output. In the Keynesian tradition, all prices are assumed to be constant and normalized to unity. Thus, Y denotes the physical output as well as the value of the output. The domestic and foreign capitals are measured in the same physical unit so that the total stock of capital in the economy under consideration is $K = K_d + K_f$. Therefore, the overall capital-output ratio when both domestic and foreign capitals are available is given by,

$$\frac{K}{Y} = \frac{K_d + K_f}{Y} = b + c. \tag{3.13}$$

Noting that $dK = I$, where I denotes total investment in the economy, the change in output can be written as,

$$dY = \frac{1}{b+c} dK = vI. \tag{3.14}$$

But, the total investment in the economy cannot exceed savings (S) by the domestic citizens and external loans or debt or aid (A), because these are the only ways to finance investment:

$$I \leq S + A. \tag{3.15}$$

Let income earners save a constant fraction s of their incomes, and a denotes the aid-output ratio. Hence, using (3.14) and (3.15) we can write the savings gap or savings constraint on growth of output, $g = dY/Y$, as,

$$g \leq v(s + a). \tag{3.16}$$

But import of foreign capital K_f cannot exceed the availability of foreign exchange earned through net exports of consumer goods and acquired through loans, aids, or debts (A). Thus, foreign investment is constrained as follows:

$$I_f \leq (X - M) + A \tag{3.17}$$

where, X denotes the (value of) export of consumer goods and M denotes the (value of) import of consumer goods, $(X - M)$ is the trade balance of the country. The right-hand side represents the availability of foreign exchange to finance the import of foreign capital, assuming that there is no foreign exchange reserve.

Let us assume a constant fraction m of national income is spent on the imported consumer goods and a constant fraction e of income is exported. Then proceeding as before, if the increase in output is achieved only through additional import of foreign capital (i.e., through foreign investment), then the growth of output will be constrained by the following condition (the foreign exchange gap):

$$g \leq v_f \left[(e-m) + a \right] \tag{3.18}$$

where, $v_f = 1/c$.

The actual growth rate of output for the economy is given by either the savings gap (3.16) or the foreign exchange gap (3.18), whichever is binding. This is illustrated in Figure 3.1. The curve SS' represents the savings gap (or constraint) and the curve FF' represents the foreign exchange gap (or constraint). For both constraints, strictly positive growth rates when no loans or aids flow in (i.e., $a = 0$) are ensured through the assumptions of strictly positive marginal propensity to save (s) and an export surplus (which in this formulation means $e - m > 0$). These are self-explanatory from (3.16) and (3.18). It is also easy to check that the locus of foreign exchange gap is steeper than the locus of savings gap because by definition $v_f \equiv 1/c > 1/b + c \equiv v$. However, what is not obvious is that the vertical intercept of the SS' locus, vs, is larger than that of the FF' locus, $v_f(e - m)$. For $a = 0$, by the static equilibrium condition that $X - M = S - I$, which given the specifications just covered means $(e - m) - s = -I/Y$, it follows that $(e - m) < s$. Yet it is plausible that $v_f(e - m) > vs$, in which

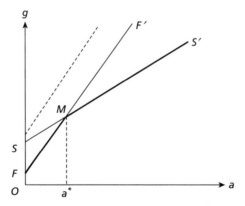

Figure 3.1 Savings and Foreign Exchange Constraints on Growth

case the *FF'* locus lies wholly above the SS' locus (as shown by the broken line in Figure 3.1). In such a case we have only the savings constraint binding for all values of the loan-GDP or the aid-GDP ratio. The two gaps essentially reduce to one gap, and the analysis adds little value as we are back in the world of Harrod-Domar. Yet the importance of loans or aids remains, as the positive slope of the savings constraint (as well as the foreign exchange constraint) reflects that larger flows of loans or aids augments growth by bridging the savings (or foreign exchange) gap.

The more interesting case is the one in which the two constraints cross each other, as shown in Figure 3.1 by the solid lines. For low levels of aid flow, the foreign exchange constraint is binding so that aids essentially bridge the foreign exchange gap. The economy then grows at the rate specified in (3.18). Beyond a threshold level of aid flow, the savings constraint becomes binding and then further aid flows bridge the savings gap. The economy now grows at the rate as specified in (3.16). In general, the two-gap analysis suggests that the economy will grow along the lower envelope *FMS'*. Algebraically,

$$g = min\left[\left\{v_f\left(e-m\right)+a\right\}, v\left(s+a\right)\right].\tag{3.19}$$

The two-gap model also has some interesting implications for the usual policy prescriptions for augmenting growth. First, an increase in savings propensity shifts the savings constraint upward, but this augments growth only for a loan-GDP or an aid-GDP ratio larger than a^*, because the savings gap matters only for such ratios. Second, augmenting growth through larger net exports, $X - M$, as suggested by Keynes (1939) and Kalecki (1970) in their effective demand approaches, matters only when the foreign exchange constraint is binding, as in the case of aid flows smaller than a^*.

Despite its simplicity and appealing policy conclusions, the rigid assumptions of the two-gap models have drawn a lot of criticism that raises doubts about applicability of these models to explain long run growth dynamics of developing countries. Not only the assumption of fixed capital-output ratios is an unrealistic representation of productivity of capital, the complete neglect of optimal allocation of wealth and savings by individuals has made these models less relevant in the context of increasing access of developing country wealth-holders in the fast-integrating asset markets.

3.3 North-South Trade, TOT, and Growth

Motivated by the Lewis-Prebisch-Singer-Emmanuel arguments of unequal exchange and uneven development of North and South through international trade, a new class of growth model was developed during the 1980s in the context of trade between Northern and Southern countries. The primary feature of this class of growth model was the assumed differences in the production structures and consequent growth processes in the North and the South. In most cases, North is a producer of manufacturing goods, used both for consumption and investment, under perfectly competitive market conditions with fully-employed labour. Output growth in such a situation is caused by exogenous growth in the Northern labour force and steady state capital accumulation like that in Solow (1956). The South, on the other hand, is characterized as a Lewisian economy with surplus labour and fixed real wages, producing and exporting primary goods. The Southern growth rate is thus caused by its employment growth, which in turn depends on the Northern growth rate. The primary objective of these North-South growth models was to demonstrate the possibility of unbalanced growth in the North and South.

Two models of North-South trade and growth are discussed here. One is Darity's (1982) formalization of balanced growth strategy by the LDC's advocated by Lewis (1954) and Nurkse (1961). The other is Findlay's (1980) model of TOT and growth.

3.3.1 LEWIS-NURKSE GROWTH PROCESS AND ECONOMIC DEPENDENCE

The purpose of the formalization of the Lewis-Nurkse balanced growth process by Darity (1982) was to examine the consequences of it for the income of the Southern countries relative to that of the Northern countries, and whether or not growth in Lewis-Nurkse fashion must mean persistent poverty for the Southern countries.

Let y^N and y^S denote respectively per capita Northern output of manufacturing good and per capita Southern output of primary good and $g^N \equiv \dot{y}^N / y^N$ and $g^S \equiv \dot{y}^S / y^S$ denote respectively rate of growth in per capita Northern output and Southern output. The Northern growth rate depends on industrial investment (i) there, which in turn depends on the per capita Northern output and the Northern real wage rate (w^N):

$$g^N = g^N \ (i), \ \frac{\partial g^N}{\partial i} > 0 \tag{3.20}$$

$$i = i(y^N, w^N), \frac{\partial i}{\partial y^N} > 0, \frac{\partial i}{\partial w^N} < 0. \tag{3.21}$$

The increase in per capita output has a *stimulating* effect on Northern investment for various reasons. The typical Keynesian line of argument is that a rise in per capita output generates optimism about future growth prospect and consequently encourages further investment. On the other hand, a rise in Northern real wage rate has a *dampening* effect because it means a redistribution of income away from the capitalists.

The wage rate on the other hand varies positively with the per capita output level, which reflects the competitive pressure on wages as the economy expands its production:

$$w^N = w^N(y^N), \frac{\partial w^N}{\partial y^N} > 0. \tag{3.22}$$

Substitution of (3.21) and (3.22) in (3.20) yields the Northern growth rate as function of the per capita Northern output:

$$g^N = f(y^N, w^N(y^N,)), \frac{\partial f}{\partial y^N} > 0, \frac{\partial f}{\partial w^N} < 0. \tag{3.23}$$

Thus, there is a *direct* effect of increase in per capita output on growth through increase in investment and an *indirect* effect on growth through an increase in wage rate and corresponding decline in the investment. For small per capita output (or income) levels, it is more likely that the indirect effect is weaker, so that the Northern growth rate increases with the increase in per capita output levels. But as per capita output grows, the indirect effect gets stronger so that

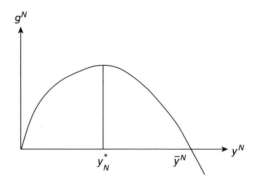

Figure 3.2 Per Capita Growth Rate in the North

the growth rate increases at a decreasing rate, and declines beyond a threshold level of per capita output as shown in Figure 3.2. Let y_N^* denote this threshold level and $\bar{y}^N$ denote the per capita output level for which $g^N = 0$, i.e., for which North reaches its steady state. Note that the Northern growth rate is independent of the per capita output level in the South. This is evident from (3.23).

For the South, suppose trade acts as an engine of growth: An increase in the Northern growth rate expands the export market for the primary good produced by the South and correspondingly raises its growth rate. On the other hand, a rise in its own per capita output only retards its growth rate. Primary goods cannot be used for investment. Thus, Southern investment is dependent on imports of manufacturing goods from the North. As an increase in South's per capita income level raises the real wage there, beyond the Lewisian turning point (where most of the surplus labour from agriculture is drawn to the industry), it discourages investment through imports of manufacturing goods.

Thus, the Southern growth rate varies inversely with per capita Southern output and positively with the Northern growth rate:

$$g^s = h(y^s, g^N), \frac{\partial h}{\partial y^s} < 0, \frac{\partial h}{\partial g^N} > 0. \tag{3.24}$$

At steady state, $\dot{y}^S = 0$ or $g^s = 0$. Using (3.24), the relationship between the Southern and Northern per capita income levels at steady state can be obtained as:

$$\left. \frac{dy^s}{dy^N} \right|_{g^s = 0} = -\frac{(\partial h / \partial g^N)(\partial g^N / \partial y^N)}{\partial h / \partial y^s}. \tag{3.25}$$

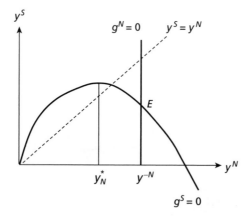

Figure 3.3 Balanced Growth and Persistent Poverty of the South

Since, $\partial g^N / \partial y^N > 0 \; \forall \; y^N < y_N^*$ and $\partial g^N / \partial y^N < 0 \; \forall \; y^N < y_N^*$, so using the signs of partial derivatives in (3.24) we have,

$$\left.\frac{dy^S}{dy^N}\right|_{g^S=0} \begin{cases} >0 \; \forall \; y^N < y_N^* \\ <0 \; \forall \; y^N > y_N^* \end{cases}. \tag{3.26}$$

Thus at steady state, the Southern per capita income first rises with the Northern per capita income and then declines beyond the threshold level of Northern per capita income, y_N^*. The $g^S = 0$ locus capturing this relationship at steady state for the South is thus an inverted-U shape, as shown in Figure 3.3. On the other hand, since $g^N(\bar{y}^N) = 0$ and the Northern growth rate is independent of the per capita income level in the South, so at the steady state for the North, $y^N = \bar{y}^N$ regardless of the level of y^S. Thus, $g^N = 0$ locus is vertical at $y^N = \bar{y}^N$.

The point of intersection, E, between these $g^N = 0$ and $g^S = 0$ loci represent the long run Lewis-Nurkse balanced growth equilibrium. This equilibrium, being below the 45° line (along which $y^S = y^N$), has the significance that if the South begins with a relatively low income level (and corresponding poverty), balanced growth essentially means that it remains poor forever. Thus, persistent income inequality between the North and the South can be a steady state condition.[7] Though initially growth in Northern per capita income raises the Southern growth rate through international trade, as the Northern growth itself decelerates in the long run, so does the Southern growth rate. This causes

---

[7] The other possibility is that the steady state balanced growth equilibrium E lies above the line, in which case the South, beginning with a relatively lower income level, eventually overtakes the North in the long run, and become permanently affluent.

initial inequality to persist and often to accentuate. This persistence, or even worse, accentuation, of the initial income gap and poverty does not arise due to TOT deterioration for the South as had typically been argued by Prebisch, Singer, and Emmanuel, rather it reflects the economic dependence of the South on the North through imports of manufacturing goods. The Lewis-Nurkse balanced growth proposal was that of supporting growth in Southern per capita income through its own *internal* engine of growth rather than through trade as an external engine of growth. This essentially shifts up the declining part of the $g^S = 0$ locus in Figure 3.3, and narrows the income gap.

3.3.2 LONG RUN TOT AND GROWTH

The common element in the Lewis-Nurkse-Prebisch-Singer hypotheses of unequal distribution of gains from trade and income, Emmanuel's thesis of unequal exchange and Bhagwati's case of immiserizing growth, was the deterioration of the TOT that growth results in. That is, the causality had been assumed to be running from growth to TOT. But, changes in the TOT also influence growth rates. That is, there is actually a two-way causation. Findlay's (1980) formalization of North-South trade and growth was to examine the implications of such two-way causation.

In the tradition of the North-South trade literature, Findlay also characterized the South as a Lewisian economy with surplus labour, fixed real wages, and export of primary goods. Its growth process is Lewisian in nature in the sense that output growth draws upon the surplus labour pool of the economy at constant real wages until the turning point is reached. On the other hand, the North, the exporter of manufacturing goods, experiences growth through an exogenous growth in a fully-employed labour force. It is a Solow-type growth process, with the domestic capital accumulation matching the growth in labour force in the steady state.

Goods in each country are produced with constant returns to scale (CRS) technology using labour and domestic capital under perfectly competitive conditions. Both countries are completely specialized in their respective export goods. By the property of the CRS production function, per capita output (q^N) in the North increases at a decreasing rate with the increase in the capital-labour ratio (k^N):

$$q^N = f\left(k^N\right), f' > 0, f'' < 0. \tag{3.27}$$

Taking the manufacturing good as the numeraire (so that $p^N = 1$), the factors are paid according to their marginal productivities:

$$r^N = f'(k^N) \tag{3.28}$$

$$w^N = f(k^N) - k^N f'(k^N). \tag{3.29}$$

For the South, we have similar conditions:

$$q^S = h(k^S), h' > 0, h'' < 0 \tag{3.30}$$

$$r^S = p^S h'(k^S) \tag{3.31}$$

$$\bar{w}^s = h(k^S) - k^S h'(k^S)q \tag{3.32}$$

where, w^{-S} is the fixed real wage in the South and k^S is the ratio of Southern capital stock to the number of workers *employed* (L_e^S).

Note that by (3.32), k^S is fixed so that $\overset{\bullet}{k}{}^S = 0$. This means that the level of employment in the South increases proportionately with the rate of domestic capital accumulation: $\overset{\bullet}{L}_e^S = \overset{\bullet}{K}{}^S$. Findlay assumed that workers in the South do not save. So capital accumulation and investment is financed by savings out of returns to capitalists:

$$I^S = \overset{\bullet}{K}{}^S = s^S r^S K^S \tag{3.33}$$

where, s^S is the marginal propensity to save by the Southern capitalists.

Since the primary good is used only for consumption, this investment (and corresponding capital accumulation) is realized in the South through imports of manufacturing good from the North.

In the North, the manufacturing good is used both for consumption and investment. With workers also saving, and workers and capitalists having the same marginal propensity to save (s^N), we have,

$$I^N = \overset{\bullet}{K}{}^N = s^N f(k^N)L^N. \tag{3.34}$$

Since, $\dot{k}^N / k^N = \dot{K}^N / K^N - \dot{L}^N / L^N$, so using (3.26) we arrive at the Solow transitional growth path for the North:

$$\dot{k}^N = s^N f(k^N) - g^N k^N \qquad (3.35)$$

where, $g^N = \dot{L}^N / L^N$ is the exogenous rate of growth in labour force in the North.

At any point of time, global equilibrium requires that the trade between the North and the South must be balanced. Let m and μ denote respectively the per capita consumption import demand in the North and in the South, which depend on the TOT and the per capita consumption levels in the two countries:

$$m = m(p^s, (1 - s^N) f(k^N)) \qquad (3.36)$$

$$\mu = \mu \left(\frac{1}{p^s}, \overline{w}^s + (1 - s^s) k^s \frac{r^s}{p^s} \right). \qquad (3.37)$$

Note that since workers in the South do not save, so they spend all their incomes on consumption of primary and manufacturing goods.

The import demand for primary good in the North is meant only for consumption, so that its total import demand for primary good equals,

$$M^N = m L^N = m(p^s, (1 - s^N) f(k^N)) L^N. \qquad (3.38)$$

But, Southern import demand for manufacturing good is the sum of consumption demand (as specified in (3.37) in per capita terms) and investment demand (as specified in (3.33)). Hence,

$$M^S = \left[\mu \left(\frac{1}{p^s}, \overline{w}^s + (1 - s^s) k^s \frac{r^s}{p^s} \right) + s^s r^s k^s \right] L_e^S. \qquad (3.39)$$

The trade balance condition requires

$$p^s M^N = M^S \qquad (3.40)$$

which defines the TOT at any point of time consistent with balanced trade and corresponding equilibrium:

$$p^S = \lambda \left[\frac{\mu(.) + s^S r^S k^S}{m(.)} \right] \tag{3.41}$$

where, $\lambda = L_e^S / L^N$.

Equation (3.41) shows that the TOT depends on the growth rates of the regions—employment growth in the South and labour force growth in the North. At the same time, relative growth depends on the TOT as evident from the following:

$$\frac{\dot{\lambda}}{\lambda} = \frac{\dot{L}_e^S}{L_e^S} - \frac{\dot{L}^N}{L^N} = \frac{\dot{K}^S}{K^S} - g^N$$

Using (3.31) and (3.33) this boils down to:

$$\dot{\lambda} = \left[s^S p^S h'\left(k^S\right) - g^N \right] \lambda. \tag{3.42}$$

The steady state growth of the region is characterized by $\dot{k}^N = 0$ and $\dot{\lambda} = 0$. This is illustrated in Figure 3.4. Note that $\dot{k}^N = 0$ for $k_e^N = k^N(s^N, g^N)$. That is, the steady state capital-labour ratio k_e^N in the North is determined independent of the value of λ. But, by (3.33) and (3.41), $p^S = p^S(k^N, \lambda)$, and so the steady state level of employment in the South relative to the labour force in the North depends on the capital-labour ratio k^N in the North. Total differentiation of (3.42) for $\dot{\lambda} = 0$ yields,

$$s^S h'(k^S) \left[\frac{\partial p^S}{\partial \lambda} d\lambda + \frac{\partial p^S}{\partial k^N} dk^N \right] = 0$$

$$\Rightarrow \frac{d\lambda}{dk^N} \bigg|_{\dot{\lambda}=0} = -\frac{\partial p^S / \partial k^N}{\partial p^S / \partial \lambda}. \tag{3.43}$$

As shown in the 'Fundamental Theorems and Proofs' section, $\partial p^S / \partial k^N > 0$ and $\partial p^S / \partial \lambda < 0$ by the Marshall-Lerner stability condition mentioned earlier. Hence, the $\dot{\lambda} = 0$ locus is positively sloped in the (k^N, λ) space. These signs of the partial derivatives also mean that $\dot{\lambda} < 0$ for all pairs of (k^N, λ) in the region above the $\dot{\lambda} = 0$ locus, and $\dot{\lambda} > 0$ in the region below the $\dot{\lambda} = 0$ locus. On the other hand, it is easy to check that $\partial \dot{k}^N / \partial k^N < 0$ so that $\dot{k}^N > 0$ for

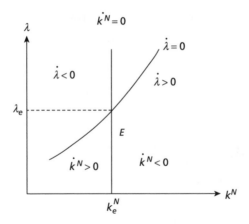

Figure 3.4 Steady State Southern Employment

all $k^N < k_e^N$ and $\overset{\bullet}{k}{}^N < 0$ for all $k^N > k_e^N$. The equilibrium steady state level of employment, consistent with balanced trade, is given by λ_e in Figure 3.4. Thus, again, corresponding output growth in the South is dependent on the output growth in the North, reflecting the economic dependence of the South on the North through imports of manufacturing goods for investment and growth in employment and output. The equilibrium TOT is then determined from (3.41) given these steady state values (k_e^N, λ_e). This is, however, the short run value of the TOT. Its long run value is given by the one obtained at the steady state equilibrium of the world economy, with balanced growth of the North and the South. This is determined as follows.

By definition,

$$\frac{\overset{\bullet}{k}{}^S}{k^S} = \frac{\overset{\bullet}{K}{}^S}{K^S} - \frac{\overset{\bullet}{L}{}_e^S}{L_e^S}.$$

Using $g^S = \overset{\bullet}{L}{}_e^S / L_e^S$ and (3.33), this boils down to,

$$\overset{\bullet}{k}{}^S = s^S r^S k^S - g^S k^S \tag{3.44}$$

$$\overset{\bullet}{k}{}^N = 0$$

But by the fixed real wage in the South, $\overset{\bullet}{k}^{S} = 0$. Hence, given (3.24), the long run equilibrium value of the TOT is determined from (3.44) as,

$$\overline{p}^{S} = \frac{g^{N}}{s^{S}h'(k^{S})} = F(g^{N}, s^{S}, \overline{w}^{S}). \tag{3.45}$$

In the long run, as the TOT attains this steady state balanced growth equilibrium value, the trade balance condition (3.41) determines the unique steady state value of λ given the steady state value k_{e}^{N} as shown in Figure 3.4. What is to be noted is that the long run value of the TOT depends *only* on the exogenous growth of the labour force in the North, savings propensity in the South, and the real wage there. Changes in other parameters will bring in temporary changes in the TOT (as indicated by (3.41)), but eventually the TOT must converge to its long run value given by (3.45) through changes in the steady state values (k_{e}^{N}, λ_{e}).

To illustrate, consider a shift in the Northern demand for primary goods. This means an increase in m at the initial (long run) value of the TOT, $\overline{p}^{S}$. This shift in demand will cause an excess demand for the primary good in the world market, which by the Marshall-Lerner stability condition for short run balanced trade equilibrium condition necessitates that the TOT must improve for the South (see the 'Fundamental Theorems and Proofs' section). This raises the rate of return to capital, and consequently the rate of capital accumulation and the rate of growth (in employment) in the South in the short run, as evident from (3.31) and (3.33). The increase in primary goods production and export supply by the South worsens its TOT until it converges back towards its long run balanced growth value specified in (3.45). Thus, at the long run equilibrium with steady state and balanced growth, a shift in import demand of the North proportionately raises only the rate of growth in the South relative to the exogenous growth in the Northern labour force as indicated by the trade balance condition (3.41) for $\overset{\bullet}{p}^{S} = \overline{p}^{S}$. To see how the relative incomes change, let Y^{S} and Y^{N} denote respectively the national income (or value of output) in the South and the North. Let y denote the relative income of the South:

$$\gamma \equiv \frac{Y^{S}}{Y^{N}} = \frac{\overline{p}^{S}h\left[k^{S}(\overline{w}^{S})\right]}{f(k_{e}^{N})}\lambda_{e}. \tag{3.46}$$

From the earlier discussion then, it follows that the South gains proportionately with the increase in λ_{e}:

$$\hat{Y}^{S} - \hat{Y}^{N} = \hat{\lambda}_{e} > 0, \tag{3.47}$$

These results reveal trade as an engine of growth for the South and increase in its income relative to that of the North.

However, international trade may not always facilitate an improved position for the South, as there may be conflicts between changes in its TOT and the growth. Consider for example the following two exogenous shocks. First is a shock originating in the North, such as an increase in its natural growth rate, g^N. This shifts the $\dot{k}^N = 0$ locus to the left (see eq. (3.35)) and reduces k_e^N. This must lower λ_e. On the other hand, as evident from (3.46), the long run value of the TOT improves proportionately. Thus, there is a permanent improvement in the South's TOT coupled with a fall in its (employment) growth rate. The change in relative income of the South now equals,

$$\widehat{Y}^S - \widehat{Y}^N = \widehat{p}^S + \widehat{\lambda}_e = \widehat{g}^N + \widehat{\lambda}_e$$

Thus, the South's relative income increases only if the decline in its (relative) employment is less than proportionate to the increase in North's natural growth rate. This depends on the curvature property of the $\dot{\lambda} = 0$ locus.

The second shock we consider is the one that originates in the South itself such as an increase in the fixed real wage. This raises the capital-labour ratio in the South and reduces the marginal productivity of capital there. The long run value of the TOT again rises (now proportionate to the fall in the marginal productivity of capital). But a higher real wage lowers employment there so that λ_e falls again. Thus, a higher real wage enables the South to improve its TOT permanently, but at the cost of a fall in the relative employment and its growth rate. Again, South's income relative to North's income may rise or fall.

These cases imply that growth rates may be retarded, despite improvement in the TOT. At the same time, it is *possible* to increase the South's share of global income.

3.4 **Country Experiences**

Recent empirical estimates of export-led growth suggest that rather than how much a country exports, it is more important *what it exports*. This observation is consistent with the new growth theories developed by Lucas, Romer, and Rebelo during the late 1980s and early 1990s, which emphasize product differentiation and quality improvement attained through R&D as the sources of growth. Thus, the source of growth is *endogenous* rather than exogenous. In these endogenous or new growth theories, the variable of concern is the product growth rate rather than output growth rate. For an open economy, these new growth theories imply that faster growth of exports of manufacturing goods per se does not matter for augmenting growth. Rather, a country's ability to produce newer varieties and improving quality of its export products is an important factor behind faster growth.

At the same time, it is important for a country to have a diversified export basket rather than relying on fewer commodities for most of a its export earnings to sustain its growth momentum. In Chapter 2 we discussed arguments and empirical evidence that exports of primary goods and a narrow line of comparative advantage are not conducive for growth, and that these particular growth process may actually hurt the country. The same holds for countries that have a low-value addition and unskilled labour intensive manufacturing export base.

A diversified export basket smooths out fluctuations in export earnings of a country, and consequently its value of output, caused by asymmetric price shocks. Export diversification, thus, helps in stabilizing export earnings in the long run and its sustained impact on output growth of an economy. On the other hand, exports of a country can have strong linkages in the economy in terms of skill formation, productivity increase and product diversification when the shares of high-value addition activities, like high-technology exports, are high in the total export of a country.

Empirical estimates of the growth impact of export diversification have been quite conclusive. The foremost evidence has been provided by Lederman and Maloney (2007) in a cross-country analysis. They observed that export concentration was negatively related to growth during 1975–1999. Agosin (2007) found similar evidence of significant impact of export diversification on per capita GDP growth in Asia and Latin America over the period 1930–2003. Hesse (2008), however, observed a non-linear relationship between export diversification and economic growth for the period 1962–2000. The developing countries benefit from diversifying their exports whereas the advanced countries perform better with export specialization. Thus, the level of growth itself may be important for diversification to matter for augmenting output growth. A dynamic panel study by Aditya and Acharyya (2013) for 65 countries for the period 1965–2005 reconfirms such a non-linear relationship. However, the effect of export diversification is observed to be stronger when export of a country is greater than the world average export. In a sense, this supports the idea that the *level* of exports may matter as well.

Rodrik (2006) and Hausman, Hwang and Rodrik (2006), on the other hand, provide evidence that composition of exports matter for faster growth. The growth in exports of high-technology goods and services, such as aerospace, chemicals, pharmaceuticals, scientific instruments, machineries, and data processing and office equipment, seems to be one major source of export-led growth. The success of China in maintaining high and sustained growth over the last two decades has largely been due to its diversified as well as sophisticated and high-technology intensive skill-based manufacturing exports.

To some extent, the growth momentum of India during the late 1990s and early 2000, on the other hand, had been due to its growth in service exports. A more general evidence is provided by Hausman, Hwang, and Rodrik (2007) who observed that a productivity measure of a country's export basket significantly and positively affect economic growth. Thus, the countries that produce high-productivity goods experience faster growth than the countries that produce low-productivity goods. Aditya and Acharyya (2013) also found that the higher the share of high-technology exports in manufacturing exports of a country, the larger is its aggregate value of output.

■ Appendix: Fundamental Theorems and Proofs

I. Rybczynski Theorem

Consider the following full employment conditions for labour and capital used in bicycle and carpet productions in India:

$$L = a_{LB}X_B + a_{LC}X_C \tag{A.3.1}$$

$$K = a_{KB}X_B + a_{KC}X_C \tag{A.3.2}$$

where X_B and X_C are output levels of computers and textiles respectively produced in the home country; and a_{ij} denotes per unit requirement of the i-th factor in j-th production. Consider now the effect of a change in factor endowments at a given set of world prices of bicycles and carpet. By the property of one-to-one correspondence under the standard assumptions of a Heckscher-Ohlin model, the factor prices and corresponding least-cost input choices do not change. Total differentiation of these full employment conditions then yields the following expressions:

$$dL = a_{LB}dX_B + a_{LC}X_C \tag{A.3.3}$$

$$dK = a_{KB}dX_B + a_{KC}X_C. \tag{A.3.4}$$

Dividing (A.3.3) throughout by L and little manipulations yield:

$$\frac{dL}{L} = \frac{a_{LB}X_B}{L}\frac{dX_B}{X_B} + \frac{a_{LC}X_C}{X_C}\frac{dX_C}{X_C}$$

$$\Rightarrow \hat{L} = \lambda_{LB}\hat{X}_B + \lambda_{LC}\hat{X}_C \tag{A.3.5}$$

where, $\lambda_{Lj} \equiv (a_{Lj} X_j / L)$, $j = B, C$, is the share of sector-j in total labour employment. Proceeding similarly, (A.3.4) boils down to:

$$\widehat{K} = \lambda_{KB} \widehat{X}_B + \lambda_{KC} \widehat{X}_C \tag{A.3.6}$$

where $\lambda_{Kj} \equiv a_{Kj} X_j / K$, $j = B, C$, is the share of sector-j in total capital employment. Subtracting (A.3.6) from (A.3.5) yields:

$$\widehat{L} - \widehat{K} = (\lambda_{LB} - \lambda_{KB}) \widehat{X}_B + (\lambda_{LC} - \lambda_{KC}) \widehat{X}_C. \tag{A.3.7}$$

By definition:

$$\lambda_{LB} + \lambda_{LC} = 1 \tag{A.3.3a}$$

$$\lambda_{KB} + \lambda_{KC} = 1. \tag{A.3.3b}$$

Now the determinant of the employment share matrix is given by

$$|\lambda| = \lambda_{LB} \lambda_{KC} - \lambda_{KB} \lambda_{LC} \tag{A.3.9}$$

such that $|\lambda| > 0$ if

$$\lambda_{LB} \lambda_{KC} > \lambda_{KB} \lambda_{LC} \Rightarrow \frac{a_{LB}}{a_{KB}} > \frac{a_{LC}}{a_{KC}}. \tag{A.3.10}$$

That is, $|\lambda| > 0$ is positive if bicycles are labour intensive relative to carpets. Alternatively, $|\lambda| < 0$ is positive if bicycles are capital intensive relative to carpets. Using (A.3.3a) and (A.3.3b), the expression in (A.3.9) can be rewritten as:

$$|\lambda| = \lambda_{LB} - \lambda_{KB} \tag{A.3.11}$$

$$= \lambda_{KC} - \lambda_{LC}. \tag{A.3.12}$$

Therefore, substitution of these values in (A.3.7) yields,

$$(\widehat{X}_C - \widehat{X}_B) = -\frac{\widehat{L} - \widehat{K}}{|\lambda|}. \tag{A.3.13}$$

Thus, an increase in the relative endowment of labour in India, $\hat{L} > \hat{K} > 0$, raises the relative supply of carpets, i.e., $\hat{X}_C > \hat{X}_B$, if bicycles are relatively capital intensive (or carpets are relatively labour intensive), $|\lambda| < 0$.

On the other hand, since the absolute value of $|\lambda|$ is less than one, so (A.3.13) implies an output magnification effect:

$$\hat{X}_C - \hat{X}_B > \hat{L} - \hat{K} \Rightarrow \hat{X}_C > \hat{L} > \hat{K} > \hat{X}_B.$$

If there is no capital accumulation, this output magnification effect implies that the production of bicycles in India contracts as specified in (3.1) in the text.

Similar logic shows that if $|\lambda| > 0$, i.e. if bicycles are relative labour intensive, then

$$\hat{X}_B > \hat{L} > \hat{K} > \hat{X}_C.$$

II. Change in the Real Income of India

Define the social welfare function for India as:

$$U = U\left(D_B, D_C\right)$$

where D_B and D_C are the total consumption of bicycles and carpets respectively by the Indian consumers. Total differentiation of the social welfare function yields,

$$dU = \frac{\partial U}{\partial D_B} dD_B + \frac{\partial U}{\partial D_C} dD_C \Rightarrow \frac{dU}{\partial U / \partial D_C} = \frac{\partial U / \partial D_B}{\partial U / \partial D_C} dD_B + dD_C. \quad \text{(A.3.14)}$$

The left hand side expression in the equation can be interpreted as the change in welfare measured in terms of the export good (carpets), or the change in the *real income* for India, denoted by *dy*. Now, with p_d being the relative price of bicycles that the Indian consumers face, utility maximization means, $\partial U / \partial D_B / \partial U / \partial D_C = p_d$. Note that under free trade $p_d = p^W$. But, p_d is greater than or less than p^W when trade is restricted through an import tariff. Thus, (A.3.14) boils down to,

$$dy = dD_C + p_d dD_B. \quad \text{(A.3.14a)}$$

But, any change in welfare or real income (thus measured in terms of the export good) must be consistent with the balanced trade for the country evaluated at the equilibrium TOT or the equilibrium relative price of India imports:

$$p^W M = X.$$

Note that, as discussed earlier, the trade balance condition essentially means that the national budget constraint evaluated at the equilibrium TOT is satisfied: $p^W D_B + D_C = p^W X_B + X_C$.

Total differentiation of the balanced trade condition yields,

$$p^W dM + M dp^W = dX. \tag{A.3.15}$$

Using $M = D_B - X_B$ and $X = X_C - D_C$, this boils down to,

$$dD_C + p^W dD_B = -M dp^W + (dX_C + p^W dX_B).$$

Under free trade, since $p_d = p^W$, so

$$\Rightarrow dy = -M dp^W + (dX_C + p^W dX_B). \tag{A.3.16}$$

The first term on the right hand side captures the TOT effect. An improvement in the TOT, $dp^W < 0$, raises the real income of the home country. The second term captures the growth effect—the increase in the aggregate value of production evaluated at the world relative price or the TOT—which also raises the real income.

Under tariff, however, we have a volume of trade effect as well. To see this, rewrite (A.3) as,

$$\left(p^W - p_d\right) dM + M dp^W = dX - p_d dM.$$

Using $M = D_B - X_B$ and $X = X_C - D_C$, this boils down to,

$$dD_C + p_d dD_B = -M dp^W + (p_d - p^W) dM + (dX_C + p_d dX_B)$$
$$\Rightarrow dy = -M dp^W + (p_d - p^W) dM + (dX_C + p_d dX_B). \tag{A.3.17}$$

III. Long Run TOT and Growth: Slope of the $\dot{\lambda} = 0$ locus

Recall the per capita import demands from the text reproduced here:

$$m = m(p^S, (1 - s^N) f(k^N))$$

$$m^S = \left[\mu\left(\frac{1}{p^S}, \overset{-s}{w} + (1 - s^S) k^S h'(k^S) \right) + s^S p^S h'(k^S) k^S \right].$$

Let us denote $s^S p^S h'(k^S) k^S$ by δ, $(1 - s^N) f(k^N)$ by β and the per capita Southern consumption expenditure $w^S + (1 - s^S) k^S h'(k^S)$ by α. Thus, using these notations, the trade balance condition $p^S = \lambda[\mu(.) + s^S r^S k^S / m(.)]$, as in (3.41) in the text, can be written as,

$$p^S m(p^S, \beta) = \lambda[\mu(1/p^S, \alpha) + \delta]. \tag{A.3.18}$$

Noting that α is constant, total differentiation of (A.3.13) yields,

$$m dp^S + p^S \frac{\partial m}{\partial p^S} dp^S + p^S \frac{\partial m}{\partial \beta}(1 - s^N)f'(k^N)dk^N$$

$$= \{\mu + \delta\}d\lambda + \lambda \left[\frac{\partial \mu}{\partial(1/p^S)}\left(-\frac{1}{\left(p^S\right)^2} \right) + s^S h'(k^S)k^S \right]dp^S$$

$$\Rightarrow \left[m + p^S \frac{\partial m}{\partial p^S} + \frac{\lambda}{\left(p^S\right)^2} \frac{\partial m}{\partial(1/p^S)} - \lambda s^S h'(k^S)k^S \right]dp^S$$

$$= \{\mu + \delta\}d\lambda - p^S \frac{\partial m}{\partial \beta}(1 - s^N)f'(k^N)dk^N. \tag{A.3.19}$$

Now consider the coefficient of dp^S denoted by C:

$$C = \left[m + p^S \frac{\partial m}{\partial p^S} + \frac{\lambda}{\left(p^S\right)^2} \frac{\partial \mu}{\partial(1/p^S)} + \lambda s^S h'(k^S)k^S \right] = \left[m - \frac{\lambda \delta}{p^S} - m\varepsilon^N - \frac{\lambda \mu}{p^S} \varepsilon^S \right]$$

where, $\varepsilon^N \equiv (-p^S/m)(\partial m/\partial p^S)$ is the absolute price elasticity of (consumption) import demand by North and $\varepsilon^S = (-(1/p^S)/\mu)(\partial \mu/\partial(1/p^S))$ is the absolute price elasticity of (consumption) import demand by South.

Now taking out $m - (\lambda \delta/p^S)$ from the right hand side and using (A.3.13) the coefficient of dp^S can be simplified to,

$$C = \left(m - \frac{\lambda \delta}{p^S} \right) \left[1 - \frac{m}{\left(m - \frac{\lambda \delta}{p^S} \right)} \varepsilon^N - \frac{\lambda \mu}{p^S \left(m - \frac{\lambda \delta}{p^S} \right)} \varepsilon^S \right] = \frac{\lambda \mu}{p^S} \left[1 - \frac{p^S m}{\lambda \mu} \varepsilon^N - \varepsilon^S \right].$$

$$\tag{A.3.20}$$

The Marshall-Lerner stability condition in this set up implies $[(p^S m/\lambda \mu)(\varepsilon^N + \varepsilon^S)] > 1$ so that $C < 0$. Hence, from (A.3.19) we get the signs of the partial derivatives of the $p^S = p^S(k^N, \lambda)$ function as:

$$\frac{\partial p^S}{\partial k^N} = \frac{1}{C}\left[-p^S \frac{\partial m}{\partial \beta}(1 - s^N)f'(k^N) \right] > 0 \tag{A.3.21}$$

since an increase in Northern per capita consumption expenditure raises its per capita import demand, and

$$\frac{\partial p^S}{\partial \lambda} = \frac{1}{C}\left[\mu(.) + s^S p^S h'(k^S)k^S\right] < 0 \tag{A.3.22}$$

as specified in the text.

IV. Comparative Static: Short Run TOT Improvement for the South

A shift in the Northern demand for primary goods may arise due to a fall in the marginal propensity to save, s^N. To see how this changes the short TOT, given the steady state values (k_e^N, λ_e), differentiating the trade balance condition as before we get,

$$\frac{\partial p^S}{\partial s^N} = \frac{1}{C}\left[p^S \frac{\partial m}{\partial \beta} f(k^N)\right] < 0 \tag{A.3.23}$$

since $C < 0$ by the stability condition as discussed. Hence, an increase in consumption expenditure and corresponding demand for import of primary goods by the North due to a fall in the marginal propensity to save there raises the price of the primary good exported by the South at the steady state values (k_e^N, λ_e).

■ REFERENCES

Acharyya, R. (2010). 'Successive Trade Liberalization and Wage Inequality'. *Keio Economic Studies* 46, 29–42.

Aditya, A. and Acharyya, R. (2013). 'Export Diversification, Composition and Economic Growth: Evidence From Cross-Country Analysis'. *Journal of International Trade and Economic Development* 22 (7): 959–992.

Agosin, M.R (2007). 'Export Diversification and Growth in Emerging Economies'. Working Paper 233, Departamento de Economía, Universidad de Chile.

Alesina A. and Rodrik D. (1994). 'Distributive Politics and Economic Growth'. *Quarterly Journal of Economics* 109 (2): 65–90.

Barro, R. J. (1999). 'Inequality, Growth and Investment'. NBER Working Paper 703.

Barro, R. J. (2000). 'Inequality and Growth in a Panel of Countries'. *Journal of Economic Growth* 5(1): 5–32.

Bhagwati, J. N. (1953). 'Immiserizing Growth: A Geometric Note'. *Review of Economic Studies* 25: 201–205.

Brecher, R. and Alejandro, C. D. (1977). 'Tariffs, Foreign Capital, and Immiserizing Growth'. *Journal of International Economics* 7: 3017–3022.

Chenery, H. B. and Bruno, M. (1962). 'Development Alternatives in an Open Economy: The Case of Israel'. *Economic Journal* 72: 79–103.

Chenery, H. B. and Strout, A. M. (1966). 'Foreign Assistance and Economic Development'. *American Economic Review* 56: 679–733.

Corden, M. (1971). *The Theory of Protection*. Oxford: Clarendon Press.

Darity, W. (1982). 'On the long run outcome of the Lewis-Nurkse international growth process', *Journal of Development Economics* 10(3): 271–278.

Davis, D. (1996). 'Trade Liberalization and Income Distribution'. NBER Working Paper 5693.

Domar, E. D. (1946). 'Capital Expansion, Rate of Growth, and Employment'. *Econometrica* 14: 137–147.

Dutt, A. K. (1984). 'Stagnation, Income Distribution, and Monopoly Power'. *Cambridge Journal of Economics* 3: 25–40.

Feenstra, R. and Hanson, G. (2001). 'Global Production Sharing and Rising Inequality: A Survey of Trade and Wages'. NBER Working Paper No. 8372.

Findlay, R. (1980). 'The Terms of Trade and Equilibrium Growth in the World Economy'. *American Economic Review* 70 (3): 291–299.

Forbes, J. K. (2000). 'A Reassessment of the Relationship between Inequality and Growth'. *American Economic Review* 90(4): 869–887.

Grossman, G. and Helpman, E. (1991). *Innovation and Growth in the Global Economy*. MIT Press: Cambridge.

Harrod, R. (1937). 'An Essay in Dynamic Theory'. *Economic Journal* 49: 14–33.

Harrod, R. (1939). 'An Essay in Dynamic Theory'. *The Economic Journal* 49 (193): 14–33.

Hausman, R., Hwang, J., and Rodrik, D. (2006). 'What You Export Matters'. *Journal of Economic Growth* 12: 1–25.

Heckscher, E. (1949). 'The Effect of Foreign Trade on the Distribution of Income'. In: H. S. Ellis and L. A. Metzler (eds). *Readings in the Theory of International Trade*, pp. 272-300. Philadelphia: Blakiston.

Helpman, E. (1993). 'Innovation, Imitation, and Intellectual Property Rights'. *Econometrica* 61(6): 1247–1280.

Hesse, H. (2008). 'Export Diversification and Economic Growth'. Working Paper No. 21, Commission on Growth and Development, World Bank, Washington, DC.

Johnson, H. G. (1967). 'Economic Expansion and International Trade'. *Manchester School of Economic and Social Studies* 23: 95–112.

Jones, R. W. (1965). 'The Structure of Simple General Equilibrium'. *Journal of Political Economy* 73: 557–572.

Kaldor, N. (1957). 'A Model of Economic Growth'. *The Economic Journal* 67 (263): 591–624.

Kaldor, N. (1967). *Strategic Factors in Economic Development*. Ithaca: Cornell University Press.

Kaldor, N. (1955). 'Alternative Theories of Distribution'. *Review of Economic Studies* 23 (2): 33–100.

Kalecki, M. (1970). 'Problems of Financing Economic Development in a Mixed Economy'. In: M. Eltis et al. (eds), *Induction, Growth and Trade: Essays in Honour of Sir Roy Harrod*. Oxford: Oxford University Press.

Kalecki, M. (1971). *Selected Essays on the Dynamics of the Capitalist Economy*. Cambridge: Cambridge University Press.

Keynes, J. M. (1920). *The Economic Consequences of the Peace*. London: Macmillan.

Keynes, J. M. (1936). *The General Theory of Employment, Interest and Money*. London: Macmillan.

Keynes, J. M. (1939). 'Relative movements of real wages and output'. *Economic Journal* 49: 34–51.

Kuznets, S. (1955). 'Economic Growth and Income Equality'. *American Economic Review* 45 (1): 1–23.

Lederman, D. and W. F. (2007). *Natural Resources: Neither Curse nor Destiny*. World Bank Publications, The World Bank, number 7183, January.

Lewis, W.A. (1954). 'Economic Development with Unlimited Supplies of Labour', The Manchester School, 22(2): 139-191.

Li, H. and Zou, H. (1993). 'Income Inequality Is Not Harmful for Growth: Theory and Evidence'. *Review of Development Economics* 2 (3): 313–334.

Lucas, R. (1933). 'On the Mechanics of Economic Development'. *Journal of Monetary Economics* 22: 3–42.

McKinnon, R. I. (1964). 'Foreign Exchange Constraints in Economic Development and Efficient Aid Allocation'. *Economic Journal* 74: 333–409.

Marjit, S. and Acharyya, R. (2003). *International Trade, Wage Inequality, and the Developing Countries: A General Equilibrium Approach*. Heidelberg: Physica/Springer Verlag.

Marjit, S. and Kar, S. (2005). 'Emigration and Wage Inequality'. *Economics Letters* 88 (1): 141–145.

Nurkse, R. (1952). 'Some International Aspects of the Problem of Economic Development'. *American Economic Review*, Papers and Proceedings 42: 571–582.

Nurkse, R. (1961). *Problems of Capital Formation in Underdeveloped Countries*. New York: Oxford University Press.

Ohlin, B. (1933). *Interregional and International Trade*. Cambridge: Harvard University Press.

Pineda, J. and Rodríguez, F. (1999). 'The Political Economy of Human Capital Accumulation'. Mimeo, Department of Economics, University of Maryland.

Persson, T. and Tabellini, G. (1994). 'Is Inequality Harmful for Growth?'. *American Economic Review* 34 (3): 600–621.

Rebelo, S. T. (1991). 'Long-Run Policy Analysis and Long-Run Growth'. *Journal of Political Economy* 99 (3): 500–521.

Rebelo, S. (1992). 'Growth in Open Economies'. *Carnegie–Rochester Conference Series on Public Policy* 36: 5–46.

Robertson, D. (1940). 'Mr. Keynes and the Rate of Interest'. In: *Essays in Monetary Theory*, Staples Press Ltd (Reprinted 1956).

Robinson, J. (1956). *The Accumulation of Capital*. London: Macmillan.

Rodríguez, F. (1999). 'Does Inequality Lead to Redistribution? Evidence from the United States'. *Economics & Politics* 11: 2.

Rodrik, D. (2006). 'What's So Special About China's Exports?'. *NBER Working Paper* 11947, Cambridge, MA: MIT Press.

Romer, P. M. (1990). 'Endogenous Technological Change'. *Journal of Political Economy* 93: 71–102.

Rosenstein-Rodan, P. N. (1943). 'Problems of Industrialization of Eastern and South-Eastern Europe'. *Economic Journal* 53 (210-211): 202–211.

Solow, R. (1956). 'A Contribution to the Theory of Economic Growth'. *The Quarterly Journal of Economics* 70 (1): 65–94.

Stolper, W. and Samuelson, P. A. (1941). 'Protection and Real Wages'. *Review of Economic Studies* 9: 53–73.

Taylor, L. (1933). *Structuralist Macroeconomics: Applicable Models for the Third World*. New York: Basic Books.

Taylor, L. (2004). *Reconstructing Macroeconomics: Structuralist Proposals and Critiques of the Mainstream*. Cambridge, MA: Harvard University Press.

Zhu, S. and Trefler, D. (2005). 'Trade and Inequality in Developing Countries: A General Equilibrium Analysis'. *Journal of International Economics* January: 21–43.

4 Foreign Direct Investment and Multinational Firms

4.1 Introduction

Over the last two decades, official aid to developing countries has been increasingly replaced by movements of private capital, mainly in the form of foreign direct investment (FDI) by multinational enterprises (MNEs). The capacious literature on FDI reveals that among many other important issues, growth and welfare implications for the developing countries in general have perhaps taken a focal point and have attracted considerable attention from researchers and policy-makers alike. A number of studies which consider this issue in adequate detail include—although not limited to—those by Jones (1984), Beladi and Marjit (1992), Chao and Yu (1994, a, b), Olarreaga (1996), Marjit and Beladi (1996), Marjit et al. (1997), and Chaudhuri (2003 a, b). These studies show that the growth and welfare related implications of FDI would be different depending on the importance of factors such as capital gains repatriation, technology transfer, productivity, wage and export spill overs, the depths of political and economic involvements of MNEs, and the often invoked political question of 'threats to national sovereignty'.

These studies, however, circumnavigate a more central issue: the role of MNEs in proliferating FDI flows and subsequently affecting growth and welfare. The discussion propagates along various dimensions with virtually unlimited contributions in each, for example, on the *choice between exports and FDI* at the firm level (Helpman, Melitz, and Yeaple (2004) show that the least productive firms serve domestic markets, relatively more productive firms export, and the most productive firms engage in FDI); on *technology transfer* (Blomstrom, Kokko, and Zejan, 1994; Marjit and Beladi, 1999; Xu, 2000; Chaudhuri, 2003a; Driffield and Taylor, 2002; Kabiraj and Marjit, 2003; and many others); effects of *productivity, wage, and export spill overs* (Aitken et al.,1997; Blomstrom and Kokko, 2003a, b; Blomstrom and Sjoholm, 1999; Aitken and Harrison, 1999; Fosfuri et al., 2001, Gorg and Strobl, 2001, and Gorg and Greenaway, 2004, for an exhaustive survey); on the *economic and political importance of MNEs* (Bhagwati, 1972; Datta, 1979; Vernon, 1993; Eden and Potter, 1993); *MNE activities in regime of economic reforms* in the poor countries and its implications on economic growth (Batra, 1986; Yu, 1982; Chao and Yu, 1994, 1995; Beladi and Marjit, 1999; Graham and Wada, 2001; Kohpaiboon, 2003; Nunnekamp and Spatz, 2003), etc.

Many of the aforementioned topics have been substantially covered in Feenstra (2004, Chapter 11) and provide the crucial analytical background for venturing further into the effects of FDI via activities of MNCs in developing countries. In this regard, one could think of several implications of MNC activities on the growth, development, and welfare of the developing and transition countries around the world. We will begin with the question of where the foreign capital should ideally locate itself in a typical developing country. Section 4.2 will cover the analysis of an exogenous inflow of foreign capital in a model of international trade in the presence of unemployment in the host country. We use a few compelling studies to offer a comparison of the implications of such capital inflow to the intermediate goods sector vis-à-vis the final goods sector of the recipient country. The entire developing world, as it seems in the present context, is struggling with the question of where, how much, and when to accommodate foreign capital in the matrix of its domestic economy. It has been argued previously that foreign investments could help to bridge the savings-investment gaps for the poor countries. However, with newer modes of financial practices, complex investment climate, and the onset of strong multilateral negotiations, the direct mechanisms as suggested in those studies appear less convincing to the researchers and the policy-makers alike. Albeit the regimes of strong resistance to foreign capital has been substantially relaxed since around the 1980s in almost every developing country of the world, some embracing freer investment climate earlier and some a little later, the location choice and the welfare implications are still quite fuzzy. Marjit, Broll, and Mitra (1997) offered an important study in this direction, where the inherent contradiction associated with the efficacy of foreign investment in a country with trade distorting protection in place and the location choice of possible investments are formally modelled. Subsequently, we draw on available research to shed light on the welfare implications of foreign capital inflow in targeted sectors. Interestingly, even with full repatriation of capital income, it is possible to register higher welfare levels in an economy depending on the level of intersectoral links and the existence of a tariff-protected sector.

Section 4.3 discusses possible links between foreign capital inflow and the labour market interactions for a developing country, with subsequent sections elaborating on a general equilibrium model and policy implications following from the proposed structure.

4.2 **Targeting Sectors for Foreign Capital Inflow and Welfare Implications**

Using Marjit, Broll, and Mitra (1997), we construct a tariff-distorted unemployment-ridden economy producing two final goods, X and Y, and an intermediate good, M. The typical developing economy produces X in the rural sector and Y and M in the urban sector, such that M is used as an intermediate input in the production of Y. X and Y both use labour (earning a wage premium, $\overline{w}$) and a capital of type 1 ($\overline{K}_1$ earning r_1 as the return from the capital market), whereas M uses labour and specific capital of type 2 ($\overline{K}_2$ earning r_2). The rural wage rate adjusts to the labour market when the urban wage premium rations job in the economy. The labour market equilibrium via movement of workers between the urban and rural production, as in the well-known Harris and Todaro (1970) structure, is maintained in the following way: $\overline{w}(a_{LY}Y + a_{LM}M) = w\overline{L} - wa_{LX}X$, where $\overline{L}$ is the total stock of labour in the country. The goods are traded at world prices (all normalized to 1) with Y and M protected by tariffs at the rates T and t, respectively. Note that this structure does not need to invoke the trade balance conditions presently, with Y and M as import goods and X as the export good. We will assume that the country in question has low endowment of the specific capital of type 2 and produces an insufficient amount of M, despite price protection. Consequently, M^F amount of the intermediate good has to be imported and we are particularly interested in looking at the endowment augmenting effects of foreign capital inflow on $(\overline{K}_1, \overline{K}_2)1$ while allowing for full repatriation of capital income. Define $M^F = a_{MY}Y - M$. The general equilibrium model takes the following form:

$$a_{LX}w + a_{KX}r_1 = 1 \tag{4.1}$$

$$a_{LY}\overline{w} + a_{K_1Y}r_1 + a_{MY}(1+t) = (1+T) \tag{4.2}$$

$$a_{LM}\overline{w} + a_{K_2M}r_2 = 1+t \tag{4.3}$$

$$a_{K_1X}X + a_{K_1Y}Y = \overline{K}_1 \tag{4.4}$$

$$a_{K_2M}M = \overline{K}_2 \tag{4.5}$$

$$(a_{LY}Y + a_{LM}M) = \frac{w}{\overline{w}}[\overline{L} - a_{LX}X]. \tag{4.6}$$

The six equations are split into competitive price conditions (4.1–4.3) and the full-employment conditions (4.4–4.6). As already mentioned, we consider a capital inflow in the final goods sectors X and Y. While Y is an import substitute, X may be considered as a mining product directly exported from the country. We assume the choice of sector for allowing capital inflow in such a way that, $[(dK_1 / K_1 = \beta) > (0 = dK_2 / K_2)]$. Henceforth, we will represent all $dZ / Z = \hat{Z}$. Since our purpose here is to explore the welfare implications of choosing the final goods sector as the target for capital inflow, we first obtain the welfare condition accommodating possible changes in parameters and variables of the system. The specific factor model comprising of equations (4.1–4.6) solves uniquely for the six variables $[X, Y, M, r_1, r_2, w]$ given the negotiated urban wage, the exogenous tariff rates, and the factor endowments. Y is capital-intensive in production.

The welfare condition is a change that accommodates (i) variable wage and capital income bills, (ii) the tariff revenue from the import of final good, and (iii) the tariff revenue from the import of the intermediate good.

$$d\Omega = dW^A + d(r_1\bar{K}_1) + d(r_2\bar{K}_2) + T(dD_Y - dY) + t(dD_M - M) \qquad (4.7)$$

where, $d\Omega$ = change in the level of welfare; (D_Y, D_M) = demand for Y and M; W^A = aggregate wage bill in the economy.

Since the equilibrium attained through the mobility of labour across sectors ensures that the total wage bill does not change and that the other factor prices are also not amenable to changes in endowments in this structure, equation (4.7) modifies to:

$$d\Omega = \dfrac{(r_1 d\bar{K}_1) + (r_2 d\bar{K}_2) - TdY + tdM^F}{1 - \dfrac{Tm_Y}{1+T}} \qquad (4.8)$$

where, $r_1 d\bar{K}_1$ is repatriated; m_Y ($0 < m_Y < 1$) is the marginal propensity to consume Y out of Ω; we simplify (4.8) to (4.9) as,

$$d\Omega = \dfrac{-TY}{1 - \dfrac{Tm_Y}{1+T}} \hat{Y} + \dfrac{tM^F}{1 - \dfrac{Tm_Y}{1+T}} \hat{M}^F. \qquad (4.9)$$

It is also apparent from equations (4.4) and (4.6) that

$$\lambda_{K_1 X} X + \lambda_{K_1 Y} Y = \bar{K}_1 = \beta \qquad (4.10)$$

$$\frac{w}{\overline{w}} \lambda_{LY} \hat{Y} + \lambda_{LX} \hat{X} = 0. \tag{4.11}$$

These solve for $\hat{Y} = \lambda_{LX} \beta / |\lambda| > 0$, where, $|\lambda| = [\lambda_{KY} \lambda_{LX} - \lambda_{KX} \overline{w} / w \, \lambda_{LY}] > 0$ and,

$$\widehat{M}^{F} = \frac{\lambda_{LX} \beta}{|\lambda| \lambda m^{F}}, \quad \text{where,} \quad \lambda m^{F} = \frac{M^{F}}{a_{MY}}.$$

Using these changes, we compute the transformation in welfare as,

$$d\Omega > 0 \quad \text{iff} \quad t M^{F} \widehat{M}^{F} - T Y \hat{Y} > 0. \tag{4.12}$$

This reduces to: $d\Omega > 0$ *iff* $(t / T) > (1 / a_{MY})$.

In other words, the derivation shows that an inflow of capital to the final goods sector raises overall welfare in the economy if the ratio of protection for the intermediate and the final goods sector strictly exceeds the inverse of the factor share of the intermediate good in the production of Y. This condition further suggests that the government policy should be in favour of retaining and raising the tariff on the intermediate good and lowering the same on the final import good. The inflow of capital with full repatriation facility must reduce welfare if it promotes the not-so-competitive good. In fact, a rise in the imported intermediate good may perhaps help to make commodity Y competitive over time while promoting the export good in the first place. This is undoubtedly a move towards avoiding trade-related distortions and the policy should therefore lead to greater economic welfare.

Will it be similar, if instead capital flows into the intermediate goods sector? Foreign capital inflow into the intermediate goods sector with full repatriation facility assumes that $[dK_1 / K_1 = 0 < dK_2 / K_2 = \beta]$. Using the same procedures as before, $\hat{Y} = \lambda_{LM} \lambda_{KX} \widehat{M} / |\lambda|$, whereas, $\widehat{M}^{F} = \hat{Y} - \lambda m / \lambda m^{F} \widehat{M}$. Reorganizing we get,

$$d\Omega > 0 \quad \text{iff} \quad \frac{t}{T} \frac{\left(\lambda_{LM} \lambda_{KX} - |\lambda| \lambda m \right)}{\lambda_{LM} \lambda_{KX}} > \frac{1}{a_{MY}}. \tag{4.13}$$

Clearly, (4.12) and (4.13) are largely similar conditions, except that the inflow of capital with full repatriation in the intermediate sector will violate (4.13) and therefore lead to loss of welfare, if $(\lambda_{LM} \lambda_{KX} / |\lambda| - \lambda m) < 0$. The intuition is as follows. A rise in the output of M following an inflow of capital in the sector draws labour and raises the expected wage rate in the system. Consequently, X contracts and Y expands and in turn requires more M to meet the expansion in supply. However, since production of M already expanded the import share, M^{F} may rise or fall. Therefore, the negative welfare effect of a rise in Y domestically may not be countered by a rise in M^F, unlike in the previous case. Still, if $t = 0$ and $T > 0$, the foreign capital inflow in the intermediate sector is unambiguously immiserizing. However, if $t > 0$ and $T = 0$, condition in (4.13) is upheld as long as $(\lambda_{LM}\lambda_{KX}/|\lambda| - \lambda m) > 0$. The present condition is a comparison of the ratio of labour use in L compared to M. If it exceeds a critical value, then capital inflow into the intermediate goods sector is welfare-improving for the economy. The results lend useful insight into a policy problem that many developing countries continue to struggle with. In fact, in terms of intersectoral linkage, it can further be shown that the foreign capital-induced growth in the sector that supplies intermediate goods to the rural sectors can be welfare-improving even if the intermediate sector is protected (Marjit and Beladi 1999). Consider fertilizers as an intermediate input into the production of agricultural commodities. If foreign capital comes into the production of fertilizers, it will draw workers from other sectors in order to sustain the production growth. If there are no other sectors in this economy, it is expected that labour will have to be drawn from the rural farms. Consequently, that rural sector which uses labour intensively will find it difficult to continue producing at the previous level and must contract. The other rural sectors that might be using land intensively would then use the released land component to expand on the level of production. This might require more intermediate inputs from the fertilizer industry and in turn raise the demand for imported inputs. Since, the intermediate good is protected and therefore distortionary for the economy, more imports in the sector should raise welfare. This is the basic intuition behind this result and falls in line with the previous model. Overall, therefore, the well-known immiserizing impact of foreign capital inflow does not hold under such cases. Still there could be adverse results, which are compelling according to a number of other considerations.

4.2.1 FDI IN RETAIL

The sweeping effect of globalization and capital flows has retail FDI as one major element and may be deemed as a major policy-shock for most developing and transition countries where the latest waves of retail expansion have registered serious proportions. The impact on welfare of the host countries has, however, not undergone major theoretical and empirical analyses. Studies on production reorganization and welfare implications need to find stronger place in this literature. Presently, we too would settle for discussion on the subject from a cross-country perspective, to apprise the reader of its importance, at least.

Retail chains in South America, Central America, East Asia, South Asia, and countries in Africa has grown meteorically since the mid-1990s (Reardon and Hopkins, 2006). It seems that just in terms of food retail, a meagre 5% share in South America, Central America and Mexico, and South-East Asia (except China) went up to 50% between 1990 and 2012. However, several studies show that the urban consumers in Latin America, South-East Asia, and Africa tend to consume more of the staples and processed food (usually, but not necessarily from the supermarket alone) and depend on traditional retailers for fresh produce. In terms of pricing also, for the countries where retail superstores have entered via later waves, the processed food is cheaper in the modern sector but the results for the fresh food is mixed. However, for the countries where the retail sector expanded in the first wave, such as in the US and the UK (but not with foreign capital), even the fresh food segment charges lower than the traditional farmers' market, wet markets, etc. This is primarily a result of better supply chain management and related scale efficiency. The supply chain, it is argued, is another important matter that lies at the core of the global debate that earlier witnessed vehement protests and political chaos in countries like Argentina or potential ones in India. Beginning with local procurement, the supermarkets slowly expand their chains to regions, to other parts of the country, and at an advanced stage to the cheaper sources, globally. For example, a recent (Minten, Reardon, and Sutradhar, 2010) study of the expansion of superstores in Delhi, India shows that modern retailers sell 41% imported apples vis-à-vis 16% by traditional stores. However, the survey also showed, somewhat unexpectedly, that the traditional stores are more careful about selling apples, potatoes, or onions without rotten spots or cut-marks and put up a strong case for local reputation and trust against formidable brand names. Perhaps, it is not so unexpected in countries with late-wave retail expansion where huge informal and logistically convenient presence of the retail sector still draws millions on a day-to-day basis rather than once-a-week shopping and refrigeration practice now commonplace in developed countries. Note that the choice between local convenience stores and supermarkets has also to do with the opportunity cost of time and individual preferences. If the outside option available to an individual engaged in the production of home goods *à la* Gary Becker goes up, then preferences regarding choice of shopping is likely to respond to it. The employment of women in particular, for developing countries in general, in which some of the East Asian countries show huge improvement in participation, could lead to certain convergence in the preference patterns, such that superstores and food chains find reinforcement with the help of its own dynamics.

Not surprisingly, therefore, Reardon and Hopkins (2006) argued that the spread of supermarkets significantly lowered the presence of traditional retail sectors in countries like Argentina, Chile, and Indonesia during the1990s. This paper outlines that the sector which suffered most within the domain of the traditional sectors includes small general stores selling broad lines, and processed foods and dairy products. However, according to their descriptions, fresh produce shops and wet-markets selling fish and other perishable consumer goods held out longer. The paper draws on the experiences of urban Argentina following the entry of an FDI-sponsored retail sector (Gutman, 2002), where, between 1984 and 1993 as the supermarket revolution took off, the number of small food shops declined from 209,000 to 145,000. This secular decline by 30%, and in terms of number nearly 64,000 stores, naturally had a large effect on urban employment and self-employment figures within a decade. Fortunately, the impact was not symmetric and some of the more specialized outlets, as Rodriguez et al. (2002) note, in particular bakeries, fresh fish, and meat, as well as fruit and vegetable shops, disappeared less quickly. For Indonesia, Natawidjaja et al. (2006) reports that while sales in the supermarkets rose 15% a year, those of traditional retail declined at 2% a year and within 15 years, the share of market captured by superstores went up to 30%, accounting for 30% of the food and allied production. Moreover, in Chile, 15,777 small shops in Santiago disappeared between 1991 and 1995 (Faiguenbaum et al., 2002).

However, once again the pattern was not uniform everywhere, as the East Asian countries and China both had domestic retail shops upgraded to the level of shopping malls that compete quite well with foreign multi-brand chains.

This is notwithstanding the fact that the number of varieties available in supermarkets is multiple times compared to that available in traditional retail stores and it even includes varieties of staples such as rice, flour, or corn. There should be little doubt that utility must increase with choice, suggesting that on some grounds at least the superstores may be more welfare-inducing compared to the traditional outlets. In this regard, one may recall the ingenious contribution by Akerlof (1970), where the traditional rice market in Delhi played a significant role. Every time that Akerlof visited the retail shops for purchasing rice (he also received similar information from other consumers), he found that the supposedly same variety and grade of rice turned out to be different on every occasion. The temporal and cross-sectional variation in 'quality' was large enough to preclude any element of standardization and the assurance of quality easily enjoyed by the western consumer. The gap in information between the buyers and sellers regarding the quality of commodities, despite attaining critical levels, did not reflect very well in the price. It offered one of the foundations of the celebrated theory and applications of 'asymmetric information'. Sellers hoarding and dominating the information front tend to dispose of bad quality products at the price of a good quality item. The loss of welfare turns substantial for the consumers and it arises directly from the lack of access to crucial information.

Arguably therefore, in developing countries the advent of 'formal' retailers is expected to provide sufficient quality assurance for fresh and processed food compared to that sold in informal markets. The modern retail stores are exposed to considerable monitoring and policing unlike the traditional retail outlets and could attract consumers whose utility is enhanced if hygiene or environmental priorities are given due emphasis. It should be reflected in the price also. The spread of bird flu or swine flu drove many consumers to modern retail stores in Thailand. It should be noted that compliance with global forces does not mean that the country cannot implement rules and checks such as enforcement of competition policy, restriction on monopolization, import controls, adherence to labour laws, safety regulations, zoning and hours for superstores, prevention of price undercutting or predatory sales, preventing unregulated expansion, etc. The government can restrict modern retailers from issue of credit cards that ties up consumers and further impose state-specific tax rates to control invasive practices, just like it happened in the US and UK, which are the first-wave retail supermarket countries. The government may also mandate modern retailers to pay its suppliers immediately and not use the suppliers' credit to support expansion without own direct investments, which large retailers are infamous for doing. These positive and normative questions may be taken up in future for providing important trade-welfare links in relation to mobility of capital under the auspices of retail FDI.

Subsequently, we look into what the foreign capital inflow can offer to the question of skill formation in developing countries.

4.3 **Foreign Capital and Skill Formation**

Compared to the categories discussed in the introduction, the interaction between FDI flows and the labour markets of the recipient countries is a relatively new area of research, although its crucial connections with economic growth have been immediately observed (see, Greenaway and Nelson, 2001).[1] In fact, a number of recent studies go on to discuss the impact of foreign capital on the demand for skill in the recipient countries, e.g., Berman et al. (1994, 1998), Head and Ries (2002), Pavcnik (2003). These, and some of the other findings, suggest that countries that are well-endowed with a human capital to

---

[1] This paper provides an elegant and comprehensive discussion of the large literature concerning foreign capital inflow in the developing countries. Section VI in particular, provides an intriguing note on the labour market consequences of FDI in the developing countries, and discusses the trade-related wage gap debate at length. However, Baldwin (1995), Feenstra and Hanson (1996, 1998), Markusen and Venables (1997), Davis (1998), Das (2002), and Acemoglu (2003) also contribute to the FDI-related wage gap debate.

start with, foreign capital flows in to use this stock, eventually bringing about skill-biased adjustments in sector-wise capital-labour ratios. Borensztein et al. (1998), Xu (2000), Noorbaksh et al. (2001), Yussof and Ismail (2002), Das (2002), Darrat et al. (2002), Miyamoto (2002) and others further conclude that FDI is positively associated with growth, but only where human capital is sufficiently high or is above a critical level to absorb technology diffusions.

Furthermore, Slaughter (2002) refers to empirical evidence on the positive relationship between FDI and the demand for skill, indicating that the process works mainly within the MNEs rather than through knowledge spill overs to domestic firms (see Kathuria, 2000 for empirical evidence on India broadly in accord with this hypothesis). In a nutshell, therefore, most studies in this genre account for the changes in demand for skill at the workplace when foreign capital flows in.

On the other hand, however, there seems to be little understanding of how inward FDI influences the supply of human capital in the developing countries (Slaughter, 2002; Ritchie, 2002). Inclusion of a structured theoretical analysis in this regard should contribute towards a more comprehensive knowledge on the subject.

Our motivation to include this section on how foreign capital might influence the supply of skill in a poor country has been further strengthened by suggestions in Slaughter (2002). It hints at two different modes by which MNEs can positively contribute towards investment in human capital. One is the short-term firm level activity whereby the host country's labour force acquires skill from within the foreign firm, or through support extended by such firms to local educational institutions. MNEs can directly affect the supply of skilled labour as their transferred knowledge might boost the skills of their own employees and of others in the domestic firms via spill overs.[2] The other method is the creation of a long-term macro environment to the extent that MNEs and their affiliates raise the demand for and wages of skilled workers through technology transfer and capital investments, which in turn provides positive incentives for skill formation. Finally, if foreign firms grow, and if that yields larger tax revenue for the government, then state-funded education may benefit.[3]

Consequently, this section focuses exclusively on the possible interactions between foreign capital inflow and skill formation when a poor country initiates a regime of economic reforms. Interestingly, the demand for foreign capital is endogenous in our model and is determined simultaneously with

---

[2] Hanson (2000) reports that Intel Corporation established a large assembly and testing facility in Costa Rica to expand high school training in electronics and English under a mutual agreement with the government there.

[3] Also see Dollar and Kraay (2000) for empirical findings along this line. However, both long-term and short-term prospects of skill acquisition driven by foreign capital inflow, as discussed here, may face insurmountable problems. While the short-term prospect is undoubtedly laden with standard problems of 'free-riding' associated with on-the-job training facilities and thus may not be a viable strategy for any firm to undertake, the long-term plan may face more severe difficulties. It is well

the level of skill formation, so that the degree of complementarity between the two is suitably accounted for. Furthermore, observing that the debate on skilled-to-unskilled wage gap in the poor countries is rather inconclusive in nature, we reflect on the issue as a natural derivative of the central question.

In a regime of economic reforms, trade liberalization often takes centre stage and broadly includes tariff reduction in the manufacturing sector, agricultural trade liberalization, and a realignment of the national currency (which usually takes the form of currency devaluation). We address three specific questions when such a reform package is instrumented: first, does *trade liberalization* promote skill formation and boost inflow of foreign capital in the economy? Second, how do incentives offered to foreign capital affect skill formation and skilled-unskilled wage inequality? Finally, is an increase in agricultural export price counterproductive for skill formation and foreign capital inflow? In Section 4.3.1 we present a model to explore the relations between tariff reform, skill formation, and wage inequality. Given this structure, Section 4.3.2 provides results from comparative static experiments and Section 4.4 concludes the chapter with inferences drawn from the three different models we could accommodate presently. Algebraic proofs in support of our main findings are relegated to the appendices

4.3.1 THE MODEL

A representative economy comprises a traditional heavy import-competing sector X, an export sector Y that uses foreign capital, a skill formation sector S in which unskilled workers are trained to become skilled workers, and an agricultural export sector, Z.[4] Factor inputs are sector specific (an extension of Jones, 1971), in that X uses skilled labour and domestic capital, Y uses skilled labour and foreign capital, S uses unskilled labour and domestic capital, while Z uses unskilled labour and land. Unlike in the previous section, we now consider Y denoted as the 'New Technology' sector to be intensive in human capital (compared to X), more broadly defined as 'skill' in this section.

The symbols are standard, as in the previous section, but in order to redefine the new ones, the following set shall be useful.

a_{ij} = Input output ratio in sector j, j = X, Y, S, Z.

w_S = Skilled wage; $\quad\quad\quad\quad$ w = Unskilled wage
r, r^* = Rate of return on domestic and foreign capital respectively

---

known that MNEs employ various tools to avoid paying local taxes and to ensure full repatriation of capital gains, thus jeopardizing the prospects of tax-led development financing in the host country.

[4] It is considered a poor country, because it has a lower capital-labour ratio compared to the rest of the world. This further implies that it may be willing to offer a high premium per unit of foreign capital, as we have assumed.

π = Premium on foreign capital; $\quad\tau$ = Rate of return on land

P_j^* = World price of jth good; $\quad t$ = Tariff rate on sector X

$\bar{U}, \bar{T}, \bar{K}$ = Stock of unskilled workers, land, and domestic capital

K^* = Foreign capital; $\quad\quad\quad\quad S$ = Skilled labour

and, '^' = Proportionate change

The competitive (zero-profit, per unit cost equals per unit price) and full-employment conditions of this economy are as follows.

$$a_{SX}w_S + a_{KX}r = P_X^*(1+t) \tag{4.14}$$

$$a_{SY}w_S + a_{K^*Y}r^* = P_Y^* \tag{4.15}$$

$$a_{US}w + a_{KS}r = w_S \tag{4.16}$$

$$a_{UZ}w + a_{TZ}\tau = P_Z^* \tag{4.17}$$

$$a_{SX}X + a_{SY}Y = S \tag{4.18}$$

$$a_{US}S + a_{UZ}Z = \bar{U} \tag{4.19}$$

$$a_{KX}X + a_{KS}S = \bar{K} \tag{4.20}$$

$$a_{K^*Y}Y = K^* \tag{4.21}$$

$$a_{TZ}Z = \bar{T} \tag{4.22}$$

The description of this model is an extension of the previous types described earlier. The capital-scarce country offers a risk premium to every unit of foreign capital that flows into the country. We assume that the government offers πr return to every unit of foreign capital, either directly or as subsidy to firms which attracts foreign capital, where $\pi > 1$.[5] For example, foreign capital in the

---

[5] Committing to an $r^* > r$ is standard practice for capital scarce developing countries, at least in the short run. Essentially, even if r^* is set equal to the domestic market-determined interest rate, favourable tax policy towards foreign capital—or similar other policies—may ensure real (net of tax) $r^* > r$. Alternatively, interpret the return on foreign capital as $r = r + \pi$, with $\pi > 0$ as the risk premium for every unit of foreign capital invested in the country. Interestingly, even if $\pi < 0$, (equivalent to $\pi < 1$ in the other case), it implies that government imposes a tax on each unit of foreign capital and yet foreign capital may flow in, since the limiting case for foreign capital inflow is $r^* < r_w$, where r_w is the guaranteed outside option for the foreign capital. Therefore, even if $\pi < 0$, inflow of foreign capital is possible as long as, $r^* \geq r_w$.

power sector in India demands a 16% post-tax return in dollar terms, while NTPC (National Thermal Power Corporation of India) does not get any guaranteed rate (Kumar, 1999, page 1002). Thus, if domestic capital gets a return of 8% then the government sets $\pi = 2$ per unit of foreign capital. A higher return offered to foreign capital may also be driven by another important factor, often used in related analyses, that foreign capital and domestic capital are not homogeneous in characteristics. If foreign capital brings with it advanced technology specifically needed for the sector, then π can be reinterpreted as the technology premium offered to foreign capital. In other words, this implies imperfect substitutability between domestic and foreign capital and is a direct manifestation of Jones (1971), where capital is similarly assumed to be sector specific, while labour homogeneous and freely mobile.

The exact magnitude of π may be decided by negotiations between the government and the foreign investors. In practice, the magnitude of π negotiated may depend on the investor's bargaining power and the host country's rank in the risk index formulated by credit rating agencies (viz. Moody's) and sometimes those by the World Bank and the IMF. In the initial stage of attracting foreign capital, countries usually offer a high π and over time, with sufficient inflow of capital, they tend to reduce their offers. In this short-run model, π is however, unique and exogenous.[6] Substituting $r^* = \pi r$ (or, $r^* = r + \pi$) in equation (4.15) not only helps to determine the system, but also provides an added instrument, which the policy-maker might choose to manipulate when the interest rate is endogenous.

The nine equations solve for nine input price and quantity output variables (w_S, w, r, τ and X, Y, Z, S, K^*). Input coefficients, i.e., a_{ij}'s are functions of factor prices and are determined once the factor prices are obtained. This is a full-employment model with perfectly competitive markets. Production functions follow standard neoclassical assumptions, such as, constant returns to scale and diminishing returns to factor inputs. Thus, given π and commodity prices, determine w_S and r, simultaneously from equations (4.14) and (4.15). Substituting r and w_S in (4.16) determines w. Finally from (4.17) obtain, τ.

On the production side, equation (4.22) determines Z, given the total land resources available. As the stock of unskilled labour is also given exogenously, the equilibrium level of skill formation, S, is known from equation (4.19).[7]

---

[6] It is quite possible that π is a function of the critical level of risk determined endogenously when production takes place. This requires modelling the risk component of production explicitly and may be considered as a possible extension. In this case, however, the foreign investors and the government negotiate on an *ex-ante* level of risk and determine π.

[7] One could think of a system of lottery for allocating unskilled workers between the skill formation sector and the agricultural production sector. In India, for example, state run secondary schools operate a system of lottery for entry at the basic level. Obviously, those who cannot override the system by going to private facilities must wait for their turn. Thus, skill formation in this model is not the outcome

Now, when S is determined, X is obtained from (4.20) and subsequently, Y from (4.18). Finally, equation (4.21) determines K^* as a function of the level of output in Y, factor prices, and technological coefficients.

4.3.2 CHANGES IN POLICY

Let us suppose, three mutually exclusive policy instruments are implemented in this economy. These include a tariff cut on the import-competing sector, an increment in π, and a rise in the price of the agricultural export good, by order of appearance in sub-sections *a*, *b*, and *c*. Sub-section *d* additionally incorporates the policy of currency devaluation along with a tariff cut and an increment in π.

a. Tariff reduction in the protected sector

Proposition 4.1: *A tariff cut in the import-competing sector unambiguously promotes skill formation, induces greater inflow of foreign capital, and reduces wage inequality between the skilled and the unskilled.*

Proof: An intuitive explanation is provided here while detailed technical derivations are available in Appendix 1.

Suppose the government introduces trade liberalization in the form of a lower tariff rate on the protected sector, such that, $\hat{t} < 0$, which immediately contracts output and employment in X. As sector X shrinks and return to domestic capital falls in this sector, capital moves on to sector S and skilled labour to sector Y.[8] Consequently, unskilled wage increases and the return to land falls. Both output and employment falls in the agricultural sector and unskilled labour is released to join the skill formation sector. As skill turnouts from S increases, skill employment and output in sector Y increases and demand for foreign capital increases. Thus, although the return to skill does not change, the wage gap between the skilled and the unskilled falls.

Essentially, therefore, a tariff cut in the import-competing sector lowers the wage inequality between the skilled and the unskilled, promotes skill formation, and mobilizes greater flow of foreign capital into the economy. Interestingly, none of these results depend on the factor intensity assumption across sectors, and should therefore be considered fairly general.

---

of an individual's optimization decision. Slaughter (2002) provides further discussion on incentives for skill formation.

[8] This is broadly in agreement with the empirical evidences in many post-reform economies, where the traditional import-competing sectors have contracted. Moreover, the financial institutions in the post-reform decades have started offering substantial amounts of higher education related loans that were not available earlier.

b. Increase in r^* ($\hat{\pi} > 0$)

Proposition 4.2: *A ceteris paribus increase in the interest rate offered to foreign capital reduces the rate of skill formation, lowers the rate of foreign capital inflow and lowers the wage gap, if sector Y is more skill-intensive compared to sector X.*

Proof: An intuitive explanation is given here. See Appendix 2 for algebraic proof.

Suppose, due to lobbying by the MNEs or believing that this would attract more investments, the government upwardly revises the negotiated interest rate offered to foreign capital. This in practice can be a decision in favour of longer tax holidays offered, exemption from meeting social obligations (foreign banks in most developing countries are exempt from priority sector lending obligations), etc. that effectively increases the return to foreign capital. To provide a tractable analysis, we use $\hat{\pi} > 0$ as reflecting such renegotiation.

Interestingly, this generates a number of counterproductive results, under the assumption that sector Y is more skill-intensive compared to sector X. An increase in π lowers the return to skill in sector Y at an unchanged price level. Skilled workers relocate themselves in the traditional import-competing sector, where w_s falls consequently, and r rises. Domestic capital from sector S finds it more rewarding to relocate in sector X, leading to an increase in the equilibrium r in S. Under competitive conditions, this implies a fall in w, such that unskilled labour moves back to sector Z causing an expansion in employment and output there. Therefore, an upward revision of π increases output and employment in X and Z at the cost of both the new technology sector and the skill formation sector. Consequently, the demand for foreign capital falls in the economy.

The moral of the story is that by offering higher incentives to per unit foreign capital, the policy actually penalizes sector Y. The contraction of output in sector Y lowers the demand for foreign capital into the country—an outcome contrary to expectations and often not internalized when policies yield to lobbying pressures.

c. Increase in the world price of the agricultural commodity—A rise in P_z^*

Proposition 4.3: *A ceteris paribus increase in the export price of agricultural good causes a drop in skill formation and lowers the rate of inflow of foreign capital into the country.*

Proof: Details of the proof is available in Appendix 3.

A rise in the world price of agricultural good (due to, say, liberalization of trade in agriculture in the poor countries or the removal of farm subsidy in the OECD countries) will neither favour skill formation in the economy, nor reduce the existing wage gap between the skilled and the unskilled. Since return to land alone increases and agricultural output grows, skill turnout must suffer. Thus capital is released from this sector and relocates in sector X, which expands by drawing labour away from Y. Consequently, output falls in this sector and the rate of foreign capital inflow must also fall. However, the state of existing wage inequality between the skilled and the unskilled does not change.

d. A Generalized Result with Exchange Rate Devaluation

Proposition 4.4: *If sector Y is relatively skill-intensive compared to sector X, then the proposed rate of currency devaluation must lie within two critical bounds for positive skill formation, larger foreign capital inflows, and lower wage inequality in the country:*

$$\frac{\theta_{SY}}{\theta_{SX} - \theta_{SY}} \left[\alpha \hat{t} + \frac{\theta_{SX}}{\theta_{SY}} \theta_{K \cdot Y} \hat{\pi} \right] < \hat{e} < \frac{\theta_{K \cdot Y}}{\theta_{KX} - \theta_{K \cdot Y}} \left[\alpha \hat{t} + \theta_{KX} \hat{\pi} \right].$$

Proof: Details of the proof is available in Appendix 4. An intuitive explanation is offered here.

Since most economic reforms, at least in the recent past, have been undertaken as a package where more than one instrument of change has been implemented simultaneously, we offer a similar experiment, where the representative country lowers the tariff rate ($\hat{t} < 0$), offers higher incentive to foreign capital ($\hat{\pi} > 0$) and performs a currency devaluation at the same time. In order to accommodate these simultaneous changes, a partial reformulation of the general equilibrium set of equations is required, in that all international prices are expressed in domestic terms, where, $P_j = eP_j^*$, with e as the exchange rate between international and domestic currencies. The exchange rate devaluation implies $\hat{e} > 0$.

If the proposed rate of currency devaluation lies within two critical bounds characterized by a linear combination of $\hat{t} < 0$ and $\hat{\pi} > 0$, then this unambiguously leads to an increase in the skilled wage, a fall in the domestic interest rate, a relatively greater increase in unskilled wage, and a fall in the return to land. Consequently, a contraction in the agricultural sector would be followed by an increase in the level of skill formation, a contraction in X, and finally an increase in Y. The demand for foreign capital would eventually increase in the economy. The interesting implication of the result (which can be further enriched by bringing in liberalization of agricultural trade) is that the outcomes may be quite different if the rate of devaluation lies outside the critical bounds. This further indicates that unless the decisions are strongly centralized and perfect coordination between different policy-making units exist, the outcomes may easily bypass the target.

4.4 **Concluding Remarks**

This chapter explored the link between foreign capital inflow and skill formation in a small open economy as the mainstay, when the beginning of the chapter was devoted to an emergent question of where the foreign capital should locate itself in order to generate welfare for the entire system. Generally speaking, this chapter aids understanding of the degree of complementarity between foreign capital inflow and welfare, of which aggregate skill formation at the economy-wide level is an important component. The exogenous changes we have accounted for include liberalizing industrial imports, offering higher incentives to foreign capital for promoting exports, and liberalizing agricultural trade in addition to sector choice made by foreign capital in the presence of protection from international trade. We also considered the policy of currency devaluation, which many developing countries have used in the recent past and might resort to in future, as part of a reform package.

The main findings of this chapter also offer interesting policy implications for the developing countries that experiment with various forms of reform from time to time. Once the welfare implications of foreign capital locating to the final goods sector or the intermediate goods sector is duly appreciated, the rest of the chapter showed that skill formation—a necessary instrument for fostering growth in economies at the middle stage of development—increases output in the new-technology sector with improved prospect for exports, and creates greater demand for foreign capital. On the other hand, a *ceteris paribus* increment in the rate of return to foreign capital proves counterproductive in the sense that it actually contracts the export sector and lowers the demand for foreign capital. Furthermore, growth in the agricultural exports may also hurt the modern export sector. A growing agricultural sector employs more unskilled labour, reduces the level of skill formation, and causes capital to relocate away from S to the protected import-competing sector. As more capital flows into sector X, it draws skilled workers away from the modern export sector. Finally, the country is assumed to implement currency devaluation as a policy alongside trade liberalization. We obtain a critical bound within which the rate of currency devaluation must exist, in order for the country to experience higher skill formation, higher export growth, and lower wage inequality. A part of the chapter has additionally tried to emphasize the effect of foreign capital inflow and skill formation on the level of skilled-to-unskilled wage inequality. We showed that import liberalization as a policy can easily be treated as the best, not only because of its positive impacts on skill formation and export growth, but also because of its unambiguous role in lowering wage inequality. However, wage inequality may still be lower when foreign capital receives a higher negotiated return, only if the 'new' export sector is more skill-intensive compared to the import-competing sector. Agricultural trade liberalization leaves the state of wage inequality unchanged, while currency devaluation can lower wage inequality, but only under very restrictive conditions.

However, none of these results have any further normative implications associated with them, except that on wage inequality. We believe that a full-fledged welfare analysis of the present exercise should be of considerable importance to concerned institutions. It is also of little doubt that skill formation, being essentially a dynamic concept, would methodologically be better dealt with in a model with continuous time. Extending this concept along these lines might be a fairer treatment of the problem, although the basic outcomes may not be much different.

■ Appendix 1: Proof of Tariff Reduction and Skill Formation

Notations and derivations follow Jones (1965). Applying *Envelope Theorem* on equations *(1)* – *(4)*, we obtain the following changes, with $\theta_{ij} = a_{ij} w_i / P_j$ i.e., the income share of ith factor in j^{th} sector, and $\lambda_{ij} = a_{ij} X_j / L_i$, i.e., input share of jth commodity in i^{th} factor.

From (4.14), $\theta_{SX}\widehat{w}_S + \theta_{KX}\widehat{r} = \alpha\widehat{t} < 0$, where, $\alpha = \dfrac{t}{1+t}$.

From (4.15), $\theta_{SY}\widehat{w}_S = 0$.

From (4.16), $\theta_{US}\widehat{w} + \theta_{KS}\widehat{r} = \widehat{w}_S$.

From (4.17), $\theta_{UZ}\widehat{w} + \theta_{TZ}\widehat{t} = 0$.

These solve for the factor prices:

$$[\widehat{w}_S = 0]; [\widehat{r} = (\alpha\widehat{t}/\theta_{KX}) < 0]; [(\widehat{w} = -\dfrac{\theta_{KS}}{\theta_{US}\theta_{KX}}\alpha\widehat{t}) > 0];$$

$$[(\widehat{t} = \dfrac{\theta_{UZ}}{\theta_{TZ}}\dfrac{\theta_{KS}}{\theta_{US}\theta_{KX}}\alpha\widehat{t}) < 0] \text{ as, } \widehat{t} < 0. \tag{4AI.1}$$

Evidently, $(\widehat{w}_S - \widehat{w}) < 0$.
 Differentiating (4.22) and using relations in (4AI.1),

$$\widehat{Z} = -\widehat{a}_{TZ} = [-\sigma_Z\theta_{UZ}(\widehat{w} - \widehat{t})] < 0.$$

Thus production in the agricultural sector falls and employment in that sector falls as well, $\widehat{U}_Z < 0$. Thus more unskilled labour can be accommodated in the skill formation sector, especially when capital also flows in from the contracting import competing sector. So, using equation (4.19),

$$\widehat{S} = \left[-\dfrac{\lambda_{UZ}}{\lambda_{US}}\widehat{Z} + \sigma_s\theta_{KS}(\widehat{w} - \widehat{r}) + \dfrac{\lambda_{UZ}}{\lambda_{US}}\sigma_Z\theta_{TZ}(\widehat{w} - \widehat{t}) \right] > 0.$$

Again, from (4.20), $\widehat{X} = \{-\lambda_{KS} / \lambda_{KX}[\widehat{S} + \sigma_s \theta_{US}(\widehat{w} - \widehat{r})] - \sigma_X \theta_{SX}(-\widehat{r}) < 0$ and $\widehat{S}_X < 0$.

Now, using equation (4.18), $\widehat{Y} = \{1/\lambda_{SY} \widehat{S} - \lambda_{SX} / \lambda_{SY}[\widehat{X} - \sigma_X \theta_{KX}(-\widehat{r})]\} > 0$.

Expansion of sector Y would now initiate greater flow of foreign capital into the economy.

$$\widehat{K}^* = \lambda_{K \cdot Y}[\sigma_Y \theta_{SY}(\widehat{w}_S - \widehat{r}^*) + \widehat{Y}] = \lambda_{K \cdot Y} \widehat{Y} > 0 \quad \text{QED.}$$

■ Appendix 2: Proof of Interest Rate Rise and Skill Formation

Suppose we rewrite equation (4.15) as,

$$a_{SY} w_S + a_{K \cdot Y}(r + \pi) = P_Y^* \tag{4.15}.$$

and $\widehat{\pi} > 0$, implies:

$$\widehat{r}^* = \widehat{r} + \widehat{\pi}.$$

Thus from (4.15), $\qquad \theta_{SY} \widehat{w}_S + \theta_{K \cdot Y}(\widehat{r} + \widehat{\pi}) = 0.$

Also, from (4.14), $\qquad \theta_{SX} \widehat{w}_S + \theta_{KX} \widehat{r} = 0.$

From (4.16), $\qquad \theta_{US} \widehat{w} + \theta_{KS} \widehat{r} = \widehat{w}_S.$

From (4.17), $\qquad \theta_{UZ} \widehat{w} + \theta_{TZ} \widehat{t} = 0.$

Using (4.14) and (4.15), and applying Cramer's rule,

$$\begin{bmatrix} \theta_{SY} & \theta_{K \cdot Y} \\ \theta_{SX} & \theta_{KX} \end{bmatrix} \begin{bmatrix} \widehat{w}_S \\ \widecheck{r} \end{bmatrix} = \begin{bmatrix} -\theta_{K \cdot Y} \widehat{\pi} \\ 0 \end{bmatrix}$$

solves for $\widehat{r}$ *and* $\widehat{w}_S$.

$\widehat{w}_S = -\theta_{K \cdot Y} \theta_{KX} \widehat{\pi} / \Delta < 0$, where $\Delta = (\theta_{SY} \theta_{KX} - \theta_{SX} \theta_{K \cdot Y}) > 0$, which measures the difference between skill-to-capital shares between sectors X and Y. Sector Y has a larger skill-to-capital share by assumption.

Similarly, $\widehat{r} = \theta_{K \cdot Y} \widehat{\pi} / \Delta > 0$.

Using equation (4.16), $\widehat{w} = -\theta_{K \cdot Y} \widehat{\pi} / \theta_{US} \Delta(\theta_{KX} + \theta_{KS}) < 0$.

Thus, $\widehat{w} / \widehat{w}_S > 1$, *iff*, $1/\theta_{US}[1 + \theta_{KS} / \theta_{KX}] > 1$.

Reformulating, $[1 + \theta_{KS} / \theta_{KX}] > \theta_{US}$, with, $\theta_{US} \leq 1, \theta_{KS} / \theta_{KX} > 0$ and the condition is always satisfied, such that, wage inequality must fall.

Finally, $\hat{\tau} > 0$.

Following the earlier procedure, the changes in output for sectors X, Y, S, and Z follow

$$\hat{Z} > 0, \hat{S} < 0, \hat{X} > 0, \hat{Y} < 0, \hat{K}^* < 0. \qquad \text{(AII.1) QED}$$

■ Appendix 3: Proof of Export Price Rise and Skill Formation

In this particular case, the only beneficiary is the specific factor in the agricultural sector:

$$[\hat{w}_S = 0]; [\hat{r} = 0]; [\hat{r}^* = 0]; [\hat{w} = 0]; [(\hat{\tau} = \frac{\hat{P}_Z^*}{\theta_{TZ}}) > 0].$$

On the other hand, sectors Z and X benefit from a higher agricultural price level, while Y and S suffer unambiguously:

$$\hat{Z} > 0, \hat{S} < 0, \hat{X} > 0, \hat{Y} < 0, \hat{K}^* < 0 \qquad \text{(AIII.1) QED}.$$

■ Appendix 4: Proof of Currency Devaluation and Skill Formation

From (4.14),
$$\theta_{SX} \hat{w}_S + \theta_{KX} \hat{r} = \hat{e} + \alpha \hat{t}.$$

From (4.15),
$$\theta_{SY} \hat{w}_S + \theta_{K^*Y} (\hat{r} + \hat{\pi}) = \hat{e}.$$

From (4.16),
$$\theta_{US} \hat{w} + \theta_{KS} \hat{r} = \hat{w}_S.$$

From (4.17),
$$\theta_{UZ} \hat{w} + \theta_{TZ} \hat{\tau} = \hat{e}.$$

Using (4.14) and (4.15), applying Cramer's rule,

$$\begin{bmatrix} \theta_{SX} & \theta_{KX} \\ \theta_{SY} & \theta_{K^*Y} \end{bmatrix} \begin{bmatrix} \hat{w}_S \\ \hat{r} \end{bmatrix} = \begin{bmatrix} \hat{e} + \alpha \hat{t} \\ \hat{e} - \hat{\pi} \theta_{K^*Y} \end{bmatrix}$$

solves for $\widehat{w}_S$ *and* $\hat{r}$, *as,*

$$\widehat{w}_S = \frac{\theta_{K^*Y}(\hat{e} + \alpha\hat{t}) - \theta_{KX}(\hat{e} - \theta_{K^*Y}\hat{\pi})}{\Delta}, \text{ where } \Delta = (\theta_{SX}\theta_{K^*Y} - \theta_{SY}\theta_{KX}) < 0 \text{ and}$$

$$\hat{r} = \frac{-\theta_{SY}(\hat{e} + \alpha\hat{t}) + \theta_{SX}(\hat{e} - \theta_{K^*Y}\hat{\pi})}{\Delta}.$$

Thus,

$$\widehat{w}_S > 0 \text{ and } \hat{r} < 0, \text{ iff}, \frac{\theta_{SY}}{\theta_{SX} - \theta_{SY}}\left[\alpha\hat{t} + \frac{\theta_{SX}}{\theta_{SY}}\theta_{K^*Y}\hat{\pi}\right] < \hat{e} < \frac{\theta_{K^*Y}}{\theta_{KX} - \theta_{K^*Y}}\left[\alpha\hat{t} + \theta_{KX}\hat{\pi}\right]$$

$$\text{(AIV.1)},$$

where, $\hat{e} > 0, \hat{t} < 0, \hat{\pi} > 0$.

Subject to fulfilment of condition (AIII.1) above, $\widehat{w}_S > 0, \hat{r} < 0, \hat{w} > 0, \hat{t} < 0$. Consequently, $\hat{Z} < 0, \hat{S} > 0, \hat{X} < 0, \hat{Y} > 0$ *and* $\hat{K}^* > 0$.

■ REFERENCES

Acemoglu, D. (2003). 'Patterns of Skill Premia'. *Review of Economic Studies* 70 (2): 199–230.

Aitken, B. and Harrison, A. (1999). 'Do Domestic Firms Benefit from Direct Foreign Investments?'. *American Economic Review* 89 (3): 605–618.

Aitken, B., Hanson, G., and Harrison, A. (1997). 'Spillovers, Foreign Investment, and Export Behavior'. *Journal of International Economics* 43 (1/2): 103–132.

Akerlof, G. A. (1970). 'The Market for "Lemons": Quality Uncertainty and the Market Mechanism'. *The Quarterly Journal of Economics* 84 (3): 488–500.

Baldwin, R. (1995). 'The Effect of Trade and Foreign Direct Investment on Employment and Relative Wages'. *OECD Economic Studies* 23: 7–54.

Batra, R. N. (1986). 'A General Equilibrium Model of Multinational Corporations in Developing Countries'. *Oxford Economic Papers* 38: 342–353.

Beladi, H. and Marjit, S. (1992). 'Foreign Capital and Protectionism'. *Canadian Journal of Economics* 25 (1): 233–238.

Beladi, H. and Marjit, S. (1999). 'Foreign Capital Inflows, the Non-Traded Sector and Welfare'. *Development Policy Review* 17 (1): 77–84.

Beladi, H. and Marjit, S. (1999). 'A General Equilibrium Analysis of Foreign Investment and Intersectoral Linkage'. *Journal of International Trade and Economic Development* 9 (2): 213–218.

Berman, E., Bound, J., and Griliches, Z. (1994). 'Changes in the Demand for Skilled Labour within US Manufacturing: Evidence from the Annual Survey of Manufactures'. *Quarterly Journal of Economics* 109 (2): 367–397.

Berman, E., Bound, J., and Machin, S. (1998). 'Implications of Skill-Biased Technological Change: International Evidence'. *Quarterly Journal of Economics* 113 (4): 1245–1280.

Bhagwati, J. (1972). 'Review of Sovereignty at Bay: The Multinational Spread of US Enterprises—Raymond Vernon'. *Journal of International Economics* 2: 455–459.

Blomström, M. and Kokko, A. (2003a). 'The Economics of Foreign Direct Investment Incentives'. *NBER Working Paper 9489*.

Blomström, M. and Kokko, A. (2003b). ' Mutinational Corporations and Spillovers'. *Journal of Economic Surveys* 12 (3): 247–277.

Blomström, M. and Sjoholm, F. (1999). 'Technological Transfer and Spillover: Does Local Participation with Multinationals Matter?'. *European Economic Review* 43 (4-6): 915–923.

Blomström, M., Kokko, A., and Zejan, M. (1994). 'Host Country Competition and Technology Transfer by Multinationals'. *Weltwirtschaftliches Archiv*, Band 130: 521–533.

Borensztein, E., Gregorio, J., and Lee, W. (1998). 'How Does Foreign Direct Investment Affect Economic Growth?'. *Journal of International Economics* 45 (1):115–135.

Chao, C. and Yu, E. (1994a). 'Foreign Capital Inflows and Welfare in an Economy with Imperfect Competition'. *Journal of Development Economics* 45 (1): 141–154.

Chao, C. and Yu, E. (1994b). 'Export Share Requirements and Welfare in LDCs: A Three-Sector General Equilibrium Analysis'. *The Journal of International Trade and Development* 3: 33–50.

Chaudhuri, S. (2003a). 'Foreign Capital Inflow, Technology Transfer, and National Income'. *Pakistan Development Review* 40 (1): 49–56.

Chaudhuri, S. (2003b). 'Foreign Capital Inflow, Non-Traded Intermediary, Urban Unemployment, and Welfare in a Small Pen Economy: A Theoretical Analysis'. *Pakistan Development Review* 40 (3): 225–235.

Darrat, A., Hsu, M., and Zhong, M. (2002). 'Foreign Trade, Human Capital, and Economic Growth in Taiwan: A Re-Examination'. *Studies in Economics and Finance* 20 (1): 85–94.

Das, S. P. (2002). 'Foreign Direct Investment and the Relative Wage in a Developing Economy'. *Journal of Development Economics* 67 (1): 55–77.

Das, G. (2002). 'Trade, Technology, and Human Capital: Stylised Facts and Quantitative Evidence'. *The World Economy* 25: 2.

Datta, A. K. (1979). 'The Impact of Multinationals on Economic Sovereignty of Less Developed Countries'. *Economic Affair* 24 (1-4): 17–25.

Davis, D. (1998). 'Technology, Unemployment, and Relative Wages in a Global Economy'. *European Economic Review* 42 (9): 1613–1633.

Dollar, D. and Kraay, A. (2000). '*Growth is Good for the Poor*'. Development Research Group, Washington, DC: World Bank.

Driffield, N. and Taylor, K. (2002). 'Spillovers from FDI and Skill Structures of Host-Country Firms'. Discussion Paper 02/4, Department of Economics, University of Leicester.

Dunning, J. H. (1981). *International Production and the Multinational Enterprise*. London: Allen & Unwin.

Eden, L. and Potter, E. (1993). *Multinationals in the Global Political Economy*. New York: St. Martin's Press. London: Macmillan.

Faiguenbaum, S., Berdegué, J. A., and Reardon, T. (2002). 'The Rise of Supermarkets in Chile: Effects on Producers in the Horticulture, Dairy, and Beef Chains'. *Development Policy Review* 20 (4): 459–471.

Feenstra, R. and Hanson, G. (1996). 'Foreign Investment, Outsourcing, and Relative Wages'. In: R. Feenstra, G. Grossman, and D. Irwin, (eds). *The Political Economy of Trade Policy*, pp. 89–127. Cambridge: MIT.

Feenstra, R. and Hanson, G. (1998). 'Foreign Direct Investment and Relative Wages: Evidence from Mexico's Maquiladoras'. *Journal of International Economics* 42 (3/4): 371–393.

Fosfuri, A., Motta, M., and Ronde, T. (2001). 'Foreign Direct Investments and Spillovers Through Workers' Mobility'. *Journal of International Economics* 53 (1): 205–222.

Gorg, H. and Greenaway, D. (2004). 'Much Ado about Nothing? Do Domestic Firms Really Benefit from Foreign Direct Investment?'. *The World Bank Research Observer* 19 (2): 171–197.

Gorg, H. and Strobl, E. (2001). 'Multinational Companies and Productivity Spillovers: A Meta Analysis'. *Economic Journal* 111, 473: F723–739.

Graham, E. M. and Wada, E. (2003). 'Foreign Direct Investment in China: Effects on Growth and Economic Performance'. Institute for International Economics Working Paper 01-03.

Greenaway, D. and Nelson, D. (2001). 'Globalization and Labour Markets: Literature Review and Synthesis'. Research Paper 2001/29, Research Paper Series, Globalization and Labour Markets Programme, University of Nottingham.

Gutman, G. (2002). 'Impacts of the Rapid Rise of Supermarkets on Dairy Products Systems in Argentina'. *Development Policy Review* 20 (4): 409–427.

Hanson, G. H. (2000). 'Should Countries Promote Foreign Direct Investment?' G24 Paper Series, 09, UNCTAD, New York and Geneva.

Harris, J. and Todaro, M. (1970). 'Migration, Unemployment and Development: A Two-Sector Analysis'. *American Economic Review* 60 (1): 126–142.

Head, K. and Ries, J. (2002). 'Offshore Production and Skill Upgrading by Japanese Manufacturing Firms'. *Journal of International Economics* 58 (1): 81–105.

Helpman, E., Melitz, M., and Yeaple, D. (2004). 'Exports versus FDI with Heterogeneous Firms'. *American Economic Review* 94 (1): 300–316.

Jones, R. (1971). 'A Three Factor Model in Theory, Trade, and History'. In: Bhagwati, Jones, Mundell, and Vanek (eds.), *Trade, Balance of Payments and Growth, Papers in International Economics in Honor of Charles P. Kindleberger*, pp. 3–21. Amsterdam: North-Holland.

Jones, R. W. (1984). 'Protection and the Harmful Effects of Endogenous Capital Flows'. *Economics Letters* 15: 325–330.

Jones, R. W. (1965). 'The Structure of Simple General Equilibrium Models'. *Journal of Political Economy* 73: 6.

Kabiraj, T. and Marjit, S. (2003). 'Protecting Consumers through Protection: The Role of Tariff-Induced Technology Transfer'. *European Economic Review* 47 (1): 113–124.

Kathuria, V. (2000). 'Productivity Spillovers from Technology Transfer to Indian Manufacturing Firms'. *Journal of International Development* 12: 343–369.

Kohpaiboon, A. (2003). '*Foreign Trade Regime and FDI-Growth Nexus: A Case Study of Thailand*'. mimeo, Australian National University, Canberra.

Kumar, A. (1999). 'Trade, Technology, and Employment Generation in India'. *The Indian Journal of Labour Economics* 42: 1001–1007.

Marjit, S. and Beladi, H. (1996). 'Protection and the Gainful Effects of Foreign Capital', *Economics Letters* 53 (3): 311–316.

Marjit, S., Broll, U., and Mitra, S. (1997). 'Targeting Sectors for Foreign Capital Inflow in a Small Developing Economy'. *Review of International Economics* 5 (1): 101–106.

Marjit, S. and Beladi, H. (1999). 'Technology Adoption and LDC Firms'. *Research in Economics* 53 (4): 421–429.

Markusen, J. and Venables, A. (1997). 'The Role of Multinational Enterprises in the Wage-Gap Debate'. *Review of International Economics* 16: 205–226.

Minten, B., Reardon, T., and Sutradhar, R. (2010). 'Food Prices and Modern Retail: The Case of Delhi'. *World Development* 38 (12): 1775–1787.

Miyamoto, K. (2002). 'Human Capital Formation and Foreign Direct Investment in Developing Countries'. Technical Paper 211, OECD Development Centre, Paris.

Natawidjaja, R.S., Perdana, T., Rasmikayati, E., Insan, T., Bahri, S., Reardon, T., and Hernandez, R. (2006). 'The Effects of Retail and Wholesale Transformation on Horticulture Supply Chains in Indonesia: With Tomato Illustration from West Java'. Draft report for the World Bank by the Center for Agricultural Policy and Agribusiness Studies (CAPAS). Padjadjaran University, Bandung, and Michigan State University, October.

Noorbakhsh, F., Paloni, A., and Youssef, A. (2001). 'Human Capital and FDI to Developing Countries: New Empirical Evidence'. *World Development* 29 (9): 1593–1610.

Nunnenkamp, P. and Spatz, J. (2003) 'Foreign Direct Investment and Economic Growth in Developing Countries: How Relevant Are Host-Country and Industry Characteristics?'. Kiel Working Paper No. 1176.

Olarreaga, M. (1996). 'Tariff Reductions in the Presence of Foreign Direct Investment'. *Review of International Economics* 4 (3): 263–275.

Pavcnik, N. (2003). 'What Explains Skill Upgrading in Less Developed Countries?'. *Journal of Development Economics* 71 (2): 311–328.

Reardon, T. and Hopkins, R. (2006). 'The Supermarket Revolution In Developing Countries: Policies To Address Emerging Tensions Among Supermarkets, Suppliers and Traditional Retailers'. *The European Journal of Development Research* 18 (4): 522–545.

Ritchie, B. K. (2002). 'Foreign Direct Investment and Intellectual Capital Formation in Southeast Asia'. Technical Paper 194, OECD Development Centre, Paris.

Rodríguez, E., Berges, M., Casellas, K., Di Paola, R., Lupín, B., Garrido, L., and Gentile, N. (2002). 'Consumer Behaviour and Supermarkets in Argentina'. *Development Policy Review* 20 (4): 429–439.

Slaughter, M. (2002) 'Skill Upgrading in Developing Countries: Has Inward Foreign Direct Investment Played a Role?'. Technical Paper 192, OECD Development Centre, Paris.

Vernon, R. (1993). *Sovereignty at Bay: Twenty Years After, in Multinationals in the Global Political Economy*, pp. 19–24. New York: St. Martin's Press; London: Macmillan Press.

Xu, B. (2000). 'Multinational Enterprises, Technology Diffusion, and Host Country Productivity Growth'. *Journal of Development Economics* 62 (2): 477–493.

Yu, E. (1982). 'Unemployment and the Theory of Customs Union'. *Economic Journal* 92: 399–404.

Yussof, I. and Ismail, R. (2002). 'Human Resource Competitiveness and Inflow of Foreign Direct Investment to the ASEAN Region'. *Asia-Pacific Development Journal* 9 (1): 89–107.

5 International Labour Mobility and Welfare

5.1 Introduction

Labour flows from the poor to the rich nations have been a crucial component of international economic relations at least to the extent they affect political debate in the developed countries. While international wage differentials should be the major driving force behind such movements, mass migration has also been caused by political violence, oppression, and natural calamities. Although theoretical support for the relation between relative income and mass migration is easy to establish, empirical verification for such a connection has been difficult to find. Total international migration, as of present, is estimated at 100 million, about two percent of world population. Further, about three-quarters of the world population lives in countries whose per capita income is less than one-tenth of the average in the capital rich countries. Yet international migration in aggregate has an extraordinarily low responsiveness (elasticity) to international income and wage differences. Changes in international wage differentials do not necessarily translate into changes in migration.

If one seeks to find the answer to this puzzle exclusively in the domain of economic incentives, frustration is inevitable. A study by the OECD Development Centre (1996) tries to do precisely this, and reflects very little on the political issues that affect international migration. The fact that the capital rich nations have never treated the issues of capital and labour mobility on the same footing seems to bypass a lot of discussions on migration. Since a large part of our analysis will also evolve around economic issues, one should be aware of the limitations of such analyses.

The purpose of this chapter is to provide a broad overview of the literature on international migration, identify the major areas of research, and to reflect on the contemporary policy perspective from the viewpoint of the developing world.

Section 5.2 in this chapter deals with a survey of the conventional results. It mainly focuses on the aggregate welfare implications of factor flows in general, and labour flows in particular. Empirical evidence on trade reform, international mobility of labour, 'migration-hump', and the long run relationship between trade and migration are briefly discussed. In Section 5.3 we discuss, from the source countries' perspectives, how capital inflow may lead to greater outflow of skilled workers. Section 5.4 develops a model to provide a theoretical explanation behind such empirical observations. Section 5.5 concludes. Note that the vastness of international labour mobility demands that adequate attention is devoted to the theoretical models of labour migration. There is a substantive contribution in the area of labour mobility across information-wise distant countries, which we wish to deal with in greater detail in Chapter 6.

The way emigration helps the process of development of a poor economy has to do with the expansion of capital stock, both physical and human. This may entail a process of rising wages and savings. Such a mechanism may fail to operate due to various reasons. Also there is the issue of 'brain drain', which may be detrimental to the process of development. A large outflow of skilled people can promote or hurt local skill or capital formation.

5.2 **Overview**

Bohning (1984) suggests that the effects of international migration depend crucially on the type of movement involved. Every type entails different effects on the receiving as well as the sending country. The typology that follows takes as its starting point the fact that it is the state as an institution rather than the migrant as an actor which determines contemporary patterns of migration, and it is based on the following definitions of regular migrants.

Regular migrants are non-nationals who possess the authorization of the state in whose territory they are, that are required by law in respect of entry, stay, or work (if they are economically active) and who fulfil the conditions to which their entry, stay, or work are subject.

Regular migration is shaped by economic, political, and social forces, primarily those of migrant-receiving countries and looked at from their viewpoints; two broad categories, each having several sub-categories, can be distinguished. The first category relates to a policy that does not subject either the stay or the work of non-nationals to restrictions (except in respect of work that involves the exercise of official authority). Three sub-categories under this type can be identified.

(a) There are free migration policies under which countries abolish substantive entry, residence, and labour market controls for specified nationalities. This holds true in, for instance, the EEC, the Nordic Community Labour Market, the Trans-Tasman Agreement between

Australia and New Zealand, and that for Syrian Arab Republic in respect of Arab Nationals.

(b) Foreigners may be admitted with a view to being granted permanent residence, and in the hope that they would become future citizens. Australia and many English-speaking and Spanish-speaking countries of the Americas are perhaps best known for having pursued such a policy, although this was by no means the only type of policy they adopted at one time or another.

(c) Non-nationals may be permitted to stay indefinitely, in the cases where, after a period of time, the general restrictions on stay and work are lifted, as in many West European countries or where the foreigners who do not qualify for naturalization or who do not wish to change their nationalities are enabled to stay, as in the US.

The other broad category, where regularly admitted migrants are subjected to limitations on stay or work can be divided into at least two sub-categories.

(a) Contract migration, which usually involves only wage and salary earners. It can once again take several forms: individual as opposed to collective contract migration and migration where the workers are employed on ordinary jobs or as project-tied migrants. Contract migration has been given such names as 'workers of distinguished merit and ability', or such labels as 'guest worker'.

(b) Official and business migration is the other sub-category. It covers all economically active persons and comprises, for example, diplomatic or assimilated personnel, transport or media representatives, entertainers or sportsmen, investors, or traders, and the great variety of employees moving under the auspices of MNCs.

This brief excursion into the typology indicates how diverse contemporary migration is. Visibly, this is a shift from the classical theory of labour migration, in which economists tended to make the simplifying assumptions that labour could be regarded as homogenous and in the long run perfectly mobile within one country. Apart from that, there was the tendency to generalize that more attention to capital than labour as a factor of production was bestowed upon by the classical approach, and most models of economic change based on this approach presupposed very similar behaviour of capital and labour insofar as geographical movement was concerned. They also regarded labour as they regarded capital as a supply ready to meet a demand initiated exogenously, and that such supply could vary independently. If the concept of maximization of returns holds good in this connection, it would be observed that a migration model based on the shifting advantages over different geographical locations is well developed. In this classical theory, the advantage was probably thought of as fertile land, later mineral resources, and still later advantages derived from the size of the market. These would primarily attract employers, who would then generate a certain demand for labour and cause to initiate a migratory process.

Nevertheless, even a rigorous classical model would admit that in the short run labour is to be paid higher wages in order to be attracted to a certain country, while such induced, or maybe even autonomous, movements in the long run would cause wages to equalize across nations. This stands out as an equilibrium system in the sense that, except for exogenous shocks, regional wage differentials will tend to be lowered, and the optimum system where each worker receives exactly his marginal product will be continually approached. Models of this kind presuppose that exogenous shocks can be taken care of without forcing the system too far out of equilibrium, and that all migratory patterns might be self-correcting, such that following any shock (for example a change in the export market for a particular industry, or a natural resources discovery such as North Sea gas), the wages in the migrant-sending countries will eventually increase and cause the direction of migration to reverse. However, a situation like this might emerge only with a static population or with a fixed growth in population, the rate of which do not adversely affect the causes and consequences of migration.

Evidently this might sound too simplistic and a variant of the structure is brought forth in another set of models, which are essentially Keynesian, showing that capital was likely to move in the same direction as labour and in effect would intensify and perpetuate the disequilibrium between the gaining and the losing areas. The depressed areas of 1920s, which then had much higher unemployment and much higher emigration rates than the remainder of the country (Great Britain, in this example) were still mainly the depressed areas in the 1930s, in spite of a very large net loss of migration over the 20 years. A solution to this problem was sought in Barlow's Report,[1] demanding government intervention in the form of assisting or persuading firms to move into declining regions so that the continuing process of declining would be halted and then reversed.

These models take it for granted that the level of employment (possibly through its effect on the wage rate) is the determinant of migration. So, the question as to whether migration is self-correcting or cumulative resolves itself into a question of migration's effect on future employment and wages. It may be trivially true that few people wishing to remain in employment move to new areas beyond commuting distance of their existing jobs without having good reasons to believe that they will find employment there. But the models would apply only if employment or wage levels determined net migration

---

[1] Barlow Report: Royal Commission on 'Distribution of the Industrial Population', Cmd. 6153, HMSO (London 1940).

flows, and most country experiences suggest strongly that there is no such simple relationship.

Once it is accepted that the causes of migration patterns are more complex than, and not necessarily related to, employment, it becomes easier to understand why the economic models of the discussed types appear to help so little in evaluating questions about either economic causes or effects of migration and why newer sophisticated analyses are necessitated. In other words, to move towards a more realistic explanation of migration, one has to take into account a number of other economic variables, viz., congestion of the state of an area's infrastructure; geographical factors, viz., the distance from the nearest major population centre; psychological factors, viz., the image of an area and political factors, like new towns or development area policy (Lind, 1969). Naturally, this multiplicity of factors produces a far more complex picture and allows for new approaches to the central question about migration trends— whether they are self-correcting and economically efficient or cumulative and undesirable in terms of present and future policies.

5.2.1 HOST COUNTRY PROBLEM

Gerking and Mutti (1983) are of the opinion that the 'guest worker' programmes initiated by western European nations and the more recent surge of illegal immigration into the US from Latin America are but two examples of movements of predominantly unskilled workers from less developed countries to developed countries. Understandably, such labour movements suggest that the wages paid to unskilled workers in the receiving countries should fall, whereas that paid to their counterparts in the country of emigration should rise. This appears to explain, in a straightforward manner, why proposed liberalization of immigration restrictions in developed countries often meets with strenuous objections from labour groups, while at the same time government officials in LDCs tend to view emigration as a vent for surplus unskilled labour. The authors have established in this paper that, in the context of a static general equilibrium model, when there is a movement of unskilled workers from LDCs to developed countries (DCs):

(a) Wages paid to this type of labour are likely to fall in both countries, while the returns to all capital owners rise.
(b) The developed country accumulates capital at the expense of the LDCs.

They also predict that at that stage, if production technologies differ sufficiently across countries, then the absolute disparity between the wage rates paid to unskilled labour in the two countries may actually increase, which when combined with other results is indicative of the fact that, the then dilemma regarding illegal immigration into the US could be persistent—and in reality it has been because, 'even leaving aside the compounding factor of divergent population growth rates, incentives for entry brought about by international wage rate differences may not tend to disappear when emigration to the USA occurs'. In fact, Bhagwati and Srinivasan (1983) have previously shown that for bilateral mobility of labour and capital between a developed (USA) and a developing (Mexico) country, several policy propositions may lead to substantial gains from factor mobility for the country, which can dictate policies unilaterally.

The Model

Suppose that both the USA and Mexico produces a homogeneous good with the help of two factors of production, namely, capital and labour, that can move about between the USA and Mexico with the USA deciding exclusively on the direction of mobility and Mexico accepting the decision passively. There are at least three possible policies that have significant impact on the level of welfare for the two countries involved.

(i) Free Mobility of Factors
Free mobility of factors allows both countries to attain higher welfare and the distribution would be equitable between both countries. If the capital-rich USA allows capital to move to Mexico, the price of capital rises in the USA and it falls in Mexico by the simple marginal productivity argument. Similarly, if the USA allows labour to flow in from Mexico, where excess supply keeps wages low, resident Mexican workers gain and the USA workers lose by the same productivity argument. A combination of free capital and labour mobility then equalizes wage-rental ratios across countries and allows both to raise GDP by the same level. The worker remittances and rentals on capital transferred across borders in full accounts for the rise in GDP.

(ii) Quotas on factor mobility
If the USA could, as in this structure, dictate the entire policy choice, it would be optimal for the country to allow all Mexican workers in and restrict the export of capital below the level which equates wage rental ratios across countries. The explanation is rather simple. By allowing Mexican labour, the wages in the USA are brought down, while by restricting the outflow of capital, the return to capital at home is also kept low. This should allow growth of business and accrue a larger share of welfare to the USA as compared to Mexico, although the global welfare would remain unchanged. Figures (5.1) and (5.2) help to explain the use of 'quotas' in driving such disproportionate welfare gains.

In Figure 5.1, the capital flows out of the USA to Mexico by an amount, OZ, equalizing cross-country rental on capital. Consequently, the marginal product curve for capital in Mexico is the downward sloping line AVY, while for

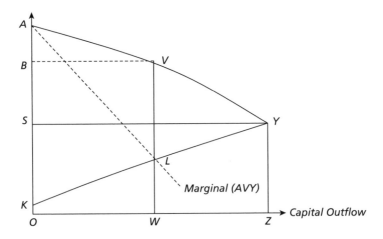

Figure 5.1 Capital Outflow from a Rich to a Poor Country

USA, it is *KLY*. The optimal capital outflow from the USA economy's stand-point should be *OW*, which is derived by taking the marginal curve to *AVY* and the point of intersection with *KLY*. If capital outflow were allowed up to *OZ*, the world welfare gain would be the entire region *AKY*, of which Mexico would gain *ASY* and the USA would gain *SKY*. However, by choosing to export a smaller amount of capital up to *OW*, the USA stands to gain *BVLK*, pushing down Mexico's gain to the region *ABV* only. This disproportionate gain for the USA, despite a smaller overall gain, is still the first best in view of the capital exporter's domestic policy.

Figure 5.2, on the other hand, shows that by allowing in labour from Mexico by the full capacity (at which the cross-country wage rates are equalized) marginal product curve of labour and hence, wages within the USA fall steeply from point *A* to point *N*, marking a welfare gain by *ASN*. The global welfare following free labour mobility is the entire region of *ATN*, of which Mexico's improvement in productivity generates a gain by the amount *TSN*. In this case, an arbitrary imposition of immigration restriction would lead to a greater welfare loss for the USA compared to Mexico. If a quota of *OW* workers for immigration is imposed on Mexico, it reduces the US welfare gain to *AWB* only, and that of Mexico to *TKL*. The global loss of welfare is quite overwhelming and suggests that the optimal combination of policies in this case would be to allow all immigrants while restricting capital outflow to the optimal level.

The host country can raise the level of welfare even further. After allowing the migrant workers, the host country can devise a tax policy to extract the wage earnings of the Mexican workers in the USA. The optimal labour inflow tax rate is obtained by equating the marginal cost of migration from Mexico to the marginal product of labour in the USA. This should unambiguously

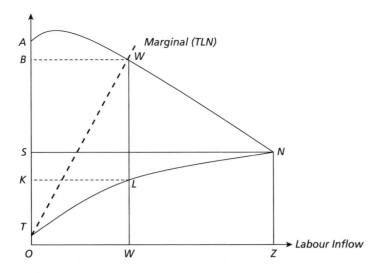

Figure 5.2 Labour Inflow from a Poor to a Rich Country

lower the world gain and transfer the gains disproportionately to the host country. Ramaswami (1968) showed that the labour inflow tax imposed by the USA should generate a greater gain to the host country compared to its tax-cum-restriction policy on capital outflow.

Sapir (1983) also witnesses that during the 1960s and 1970s, employment of foreign labour became an important aspect of western European economies. The fact suggests that western European capitalists in structurally weak sectors might have used immigration policies as a means of remaining competitive. Clearly, one way for industries in the industrialized countries to resist the competition from less-developed, labour-abundant countries, is try to reduce their labour costs, and therefore there has to be a crucial relationship in a capital-abundant economy between trade competition and immigration from labour-abundant countries. He proposes in this regard, that, 'within the Ricardo-Viner (sector-specific) model, a host country protecting its importable sector might experience a welfare gain or loss from an inflow of foreign labour which receives its full (tax-free) marginal product. If workers are paid only in terms of the importable good, there will be a gain; if they are paid only in terms of the exportable good, there might be either a loss or a gain. Moreover, these results hold regardless of whether the host country is labour- or capital-abundant.'

While Sapir's conclusion remains conditional and therefore open-ended, Wong (1983) in his paper rank-orders a set of policies or 'regimes', from the viewpoint of overall welfare impact.

Two possibilities have come up in his paper:

(a) Given a well-behaved social utility function and diversification in production, the more the national factor-price ratio deviates from and on the same side of the autarkic factor-price ratio, the higher welfare level the country will have.

(b) Given a well-behaved social utility function and diversification in production, the more the combined (national and foreign) factor endowment ratio deviates from and on the same side of the national factor endowment ratio, the higher welfare level the country will have.

Schiff (1996) offers three scenarios under which trade and migration are complements rather than substitutes, i.e. when trade liberalization will temporarily lead to more migration, not less, creating the 'migration hump'. Intuitively, trade liberalization by creating new employment in migrant-sending countries provides families with a means to finance international migration, which they could not afford in the past. Secondly, following trade reforms with sectors showing specificity in factor usage, there would be some economic costs involved in switching resources from one sector to another. This would lead to some transitional unemployment and therefore increased migration pressure. Finally, if (and in reality, it is) the most protected import-competing sector is labour intensive, then trade liberalization renders labour unemployed.

It follows from the concept of migration hump, that in the aftermath of a trade reform at time zero, the assumed short run complementarity between trade and migration will cause an increase in migration above the status-quo trajectory line, which is rising at a decreasing rate. On the other hand, the assumed long run substitutability between trade and migration will cause a downslide of the hump much below the trajectory line. So, the migration hump in the short run suggests a net long run 'saving' in unwanted migration as a result of trade reforms.

It is also assumed, in this regard, that the duration and amplitude of the hump are relatively small. Thus, when viewed over a long enough period of time, there is less migration with trade than without it.

If, however, trade and migration are substitutes both in the short and the long run, the migration hump becomes a migration trough. This view is supported by standard trade theory, whereby, specific endowment (L and K) rich countries end up specializing in the commodities they have comparative advantage in. On the other hand, if the standard neoclassical assumptions are relaxed, then even the traditional $2 \times 2 \times 2$ framework might evoke complementarity between trade and migration and henceforth a migration plateau. These are however based on the underlying assumptions that markets are perfect, adjustments are instantaneous, trade is not due to scale economics, and there is no disparity in factor productivity. These features are illustrated in Figure 5.3.

The market imperfection induced migration underlies the 'New Economics of Labour Migration' pioneered by Stark, where migrants are viewed as financial intermediaries who provide their families with liquidity and income

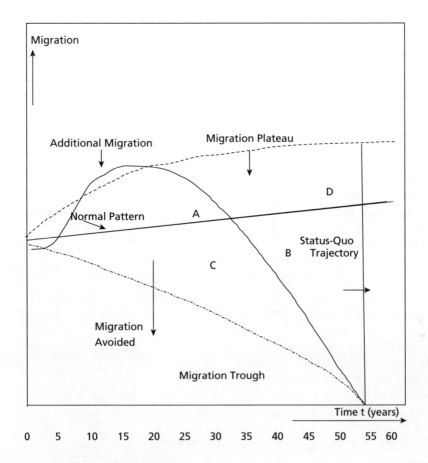

Migration

Additional Migration

Migration Plateau

Normal Pattern

A

D

Status-Quo
B   Trajectory

C

Migration
Avoided

Migration Trough

Time t (years)

0   5   10   15   20   25   30   35   40   45   50   55 60

t = 0 : Time of Trade Reform
A = Migration Hump, Short-run Complementarity between Trade and Migration
B = Migration Avoided, Long-run Substitutability between Trade and Migration.
Area (A + D) = Migration Plateau; Area (B + C) = Migration Trough.

Figure 5.3 Migration Hump, Plateau, and Trough

insurance. Stark (1991)argues that, the desire to overcome the risk and capital
constraints is a primary motivation for migration. Previously, Katz and Stark
(1986) examined the effect of migratory opportunities for children on fertility,
when the decision by the child whether or how much to remit is endogenous
to the analysis. International migration under asymmetric information has
also been extensively dealt with in Katz and Stark (1987), where they introduce a migration model in the absence of costly 'signalling' and in the presence of the time-consuming revelation of the true productivity of the migrant

workers. It shows that asymmetric information will tend to reduce the skill level of migrants, by changing qualitatively as well as quantitatively the distribution of migrant groups in the population. The restoration of informational symmetry reinforces the possibility of migration only by the high-skill and the low-skill groups, with the middle group not migrating. With the same structure, Katz and Stark (1989) also show that when migration is desirable at the lowest skill level, introduction of asymmetric information results in a reduction of the quality and quantity of international migration or has no effect at all. Contrarily, when at the lowest skill level migration is not desirable, introduction of asymmetric information will result in migration by all or by none. This is dealt with in greater detail in Chapter 6.

By another strand of analysis, however, the phenomenon of international migration is the one that is characterized by disincentives rather than incentives. It is also much more institutionally determined than by free economic choices, owing to the existence of immigration quotas sanctioned by developed countries (by national legislation in Great Britain as of 1905, and in the US as of 1921). Conversely, there are also some potentially inefficient restrictions on emigration of nationals mainly in the socialist countries but also in the developing countries (for skilled personnel like doctors and engineers). What appears on the whole, with respect to the institutional question, is that there is virtually no international code of conduct that attends the question of how immigration restrictions ought to be operated. The international governance of the issue is provided only by fragmented attention from various agencies like the International Labour Organization (ILO) for foreign workers, UN High Commission for Refugees (UNHCR), United Nations Educational, Scientific, and Cultural Organization (UNESCO), and United Nations Conference on Trade and Development (UNCTAD) for brain drain etc., and above all there has been a sustained lack of concern in attempting to set up such a supra-national agency (Bhagwati, 1984).

It is further emphasized that institutions showed a 'deliberate' lack of speed in response to migration that occurred in substantial magnitudes in the post-war era. On the question of post-war international migration flows, Bhagwati (1988) classifies the movement between 'poor to poor' countries as essentially refugee movement. The post-war worker movement between 'poor to rich' countries was mainly an outcome of the west European 'gastarbeiter' programme and similar policies adopted by the Organization of the Petroleum Exporting Countries (OPEC) in the late 1970s.

It is also very important to discuss in this light, the long-debated issue of 'brain drain'. As Bhagwati (1988) puts it, 'brain drain' is an 'emotive phrase', and preserves the overtone that outflow of skilled manpower is a problem. The author suggests that a brain drain model and a spill over model can be identically treated and, according to the empirical judgement, it appears that substantial outflows often create difficulties for small source countries with limited educational opportunities. He further points out that for large countries with a wide educational network, emigration of doctors or engineers may not really be a problem, although emigration of 'talented' individuals might stall the domestic institution-building process. However, such emigration can pave the path for improving the productivity of distinguished nationals as part of prestigious foreign institutions, and enhance opportunities for other nationals to train abroad.

The issue of 'return migration' also requires some attention in this context. Piore (1979) notes that contributions by migrants in terms of the regional economics development or as a source of significant industrial skills have been generally elusive for the source countries. For the developing countries on the path of industrialization, it is expected that the technical requirements of the job structure would follow the technical evolution of the labour force. The process is such that increasing levels of education and training are required of the labour force as development proceeds, in order to bridge the gap between the skills of the labour force and the requirements of the technology that the countries are introducing. Return migrants in general have not contributed sufficiently towards overcoming this gap.

To see empirically the issue in question, an explicit link between trade reforms and migration is found in Faini and de Melo (1996), who ran a macro simulation for Morocco, revealing that the removal of import restrictions in Morocco shifted the composition of demand in favour of foreign goods. The total impact on employment in the short run depends critically on the labour-intensity of exports to import-competing goods, and in the Moroccan case, labour intensive exports expanded (because of real exchange rate depreciation) quickly. There was a reduction of total output on account of the now dearer imported inputs and despite all this, no distinct effect on employment is visible. The reason is that the textile, being the major item of trade, provided local employment as an alternative to short run migration.

Lee and Roland-Holst (1996) offers a ten-country, computable general equilibrium model (CGE), to estimate the impact of various trade reform measures on employment in the Pacific Basin. Although the model does not link countries on the labour side through migration, trade-induced changes in employment and wage disparities across countries suggests the direction, if not the magnitude, of changes in migration pressure resulting from trade reform. The remarkable finding of their study is the surprisingly small impact of trade liberalization on total employment in the region, the reason being that for all these countries, imports were more labour-intensive than exports.

Other empirical support for the analysis with respect to the labour market effects of migration and trade comes from Borjas, Freeman, and Katz (1992), in a North American context. They base their analysis on a 1980s finding that the wage and employment-population rate of less-skilled Americans, particularly young men, fell relative to the more-skilled workers. The real earnings of

25–34 year old male high school graduates and dropouts declined = from 1973 and reversed the historic trend. Borjas, Freeman, and Katz empirically support the two suggested causes, (a) inflow of less-skilled immigrants, including illegal migrants and (b) the trade deficit. In a later article, Borjas and Freeman (1997) concluded that 44% of the said decline in wages (1980–1995) resulted from immigration.

The study by Borjas and Freeman (1997) contradicts the findings of Altonji and Card (1991), who computed the correlation between the fractions of immigrants in a city, and the employment and wage outcomes of natives for 120 major SMSAs (Standard Metropolitan Statistical Areas) over 1970 and 1980 censuses. Here, the basic finding was that a 1% increase in the fraction of immigrants in a SMSA reduces less-skilled native wages by roughly 1.2%. The least square estimates showed a wage reduction of 3%. According to Rivera-Batiz (1998), the US economy has absorbed millions of workers during this century and yet earnings and living standards have generally gone up. The explanation is that an increased labour supply tends to generate other mechanisms in the economy that increase the demand for labour and therefore employment. Any influx that significantly reduces wages in a particular labour market also tends to attract industries in that labour market. Given cheaper labour, further reinforced by the continuous process of immigrant inflow, this leads to the setting of competitive prices in these industries. Over time, then, there is a higher demand facing these industries, and the downward pressure on wages exerted by increased stock of labour is subsequently reversed as demand rises.

Lastly, Kuhn, and Wooton (1991) estimated the effect of immigration on the US workers. Based on 430 four-digit manufacturing industries for the years 1960, 1970, 1980, and 1984, the estimate indicates that at least since 1970, factor intensities in US manufacturing show a consistent pattern; unskilled and skilled labour are used intensively in import-competing and export industries respectively. They draw the conclusion that increased immigration of either skilled or unskilled workers to the US will, in the long run, hurt US workers of both types and benefit owners of capital.

5.3 Various Effects of Migration: Source and Destination Interactions

Developing countries undertaking economic reforms during the last two decades have experienced two apparently contradicting phenomena—a significant rise in the inflow of foreign capital, and a simultaneous emigration of labour, both skilled and unskilled. Such evidence seems to defy certain

standard hypotheses that the inflow of foreign capital would generate sufficient employment in the host countries and thus would stem the flow of skilled
and unskilled labour from these countries to their richer counterparts.[2] In fact,
the erstwhile Mexican president Carlos Salinas de Gortari promoted the inclusion of Mexico in the NAFTA (North American Free Trade Agreement), partly
on the grounds that it would restrict emigration of Mexicans mainly to the
USA, once sufficient economic opportunities and jobs were created within the
country through freer trade and greater inflow of US-Canadian investments.

However, Figure 5.A1 in the Appendix shows that the absolute number of
migrants from Mexico to the USA, after falling during 1996–1998, picked up
strongly ever since to exceed the pre-1996 levels. Thus more trade and capital
flows between the USA and Mexico have also been accompanied by increased
labour mobility.[3] This is consistent with the earlier theory on the complementarities between factor mobility and trade in goods, especially in the presence
of external economies of scale (Razin and Sadka, 1992).[4] Moreover, for the
USA-Mexico case, sceptics asserted that NAFTA is unlikely to bring about wage
equality between the two countries, and thus, there would remain enough incentives for both skilled and unskilled workers in Mexico to undertake cross-border
migration (Markusen and Venables, 1995; Markusen and Zahniser, 1999).

This pattern seems to be true for other migrant-sending countries as well.
Generally speaking, over the last decade trade expanded manifold in both
industrial and agricultural goods and services between the North and the
South, and foreign capital in the form of FDI (foreign direct investments) and
FII (foreign institutional investments) from the developed countries remained
concentrated mostly in the industrial, technological, and service sectors of the developing economies.[5] Such capital inflow requires skilled/ highly-skilled workers
as complementary input and can therefore potentially create direct employment
for skilled personnel in the developing countries, with ancillary opportunities for
semi-skilled and unskilled workers. Despite such possibilities, it is interesting to
note that emigration from developing countries has been on the rise and more

---

[2] There are a number of studies which discuss the impact of foreign capital on the demand for skill
in the recipient countries, e.g., Berman et al. (1994, 1997), Head and Ries (2002) Pavcnik (2003). These,
and some of the other studies, suggest that if countries are well-endowed with human capital to start
with, foreign capital flows in to use this stock, eventually bringing about skill-biased adjustments in
sector-wise, capital-labour ratios—an outcome of capital deepening so to say. However, Pavcnik (2003)
finds that for Chile, plant level skill upgrading is not associated with adoption of foreign technology
and may be attributed mostly to unobservable factors.

[3] Mexico is the USA's second largest trading partner after Canada, and Mexico-US trade reached
$232 billion in 2002. Mexico-US trade has increased by over 225% since the North American Free
Trade Agreement of 1994 (Jannol et al. 2003).

[4] See Marjit and Kar (2004), for a discussion on short-term complementarities and long-term substitution between trade and factor mobility.

[5] For general trends in capital inflows to the developed and the developing countries see Figure 5.
A3 and for India see Figure 5.A4.

importantly, outflow of skilled workers as a percentage of total emigrants has risen for most of these countries.[6]

Statistical evidence in support of this claim can also be obtained from a comparison of the rates of skilled and unskilled immigration to a number of migrant-receiving developed countries.[7] Figure 5.A2 (in the Appendix) shows that for most of these developed countries, the rate of skilled immigration has gone up over the years compared to the rate of unskilled immigration, with Australia and New Zealand standing out in particular. In its report (2004, Ch1), The Committee on Migration, Government of Australia, shows that Australia has emerged as an aggressive bidder for immigration of skilled professionals.[8]

5.3.1 IMMIGRATION AND SKILL FORMATION

There is at least one readily available explanation behind such increased international mobility of skilled workers. Although the skilled-unskilled wage differential has widened for both developed and developing countries, the impact is harder in the former due to a number of factors such as freer imports of low-skill, low-technology intensive products from the south, skill biased technological changes in the north and undeterred immigration of unskilled workers. A number of studies have tried to measure the relative importance of each of these causes in the developed countries.[9] For a potential skilled immigrant, this widening wage gap in the north, in addition to the shortage of skilled workers in many OECD countries including the USA, Canada, and Australia, operates as a natural incentive to undertake migration. On the other hand, as unskilled workers have become relatively worse-off in the migrant-receiving countries, there is a natural disincentive for unskilled workers to undertake migration from the developing countries after covering for the initial cost of migration. Furthermore, developed countries have imposed various restrictions

---

[6] See for example, OECD (2001) and Lowell and Findlay (2001).

[7] Most developing countries do not maintain a continuous database for level of out-migration of skilled and unskilled workers. Thus one has to rely on the data supplied by the migrant receiving countries.

[8] Among other European countries, Germany receives a considerable number of immigrants from all over the world (see Sapir, 1975 for a pioneering work on migration to Germany). Although synchronized data as in Figure 5.2 is not available for Germany, granting of job permits is mostly concentrated in the skilled categories. More recently (May, 2004) a new immigration law is being developed so as to offer long-term work permits to IT specialists from India, China, and other countries.

[9] See Davis and Haltiwanger (1991), Berman et al. (1994), Katz and Murphy (1992), Krueger (1993) for technology-based changes in skill intensity at the workplace. Trade-based explanations in support of increasing wage gaps in the developed countries can be found in Borjas and Ramey (1993), Wood (1998), and Deardorff (2000). Discussion of the role of unskilled migration in the increasing skilled-unskilled wage gap may be found in Borjas et al. (1992) and Trefler (1997). For the wage gap debate in the developing countries, see Kar and Beladi (2004), Marjit and Acharyya (2003).

on the mobility of unskilled workers, by, for example, raising the application fees. Cutting down on illegal migration is also an important agenda for many developed countries at present, which has significantly restrained unskilled migrants from entering these countries.

The discussion earlier constitutes the 'pull' factor behind migration of skilled workers. There is also a 'push' factor in operation: skilled workers undertake international migration simply because their home country cannot create sufficient 'opportunities' for them to stay back. This implies that there could be unemployment or other factors within the country such that skilled workers neither get 'proper working conditions and resources' nor 'fair and comparable returns' on their skill levels and thus are compelled to migrate.[10]

We believe that under the present economic conditions in the developing world, there can be additional factors behind the push factor, hitherto unexplored in the literature. In this context, it may be noted that many of these countries have well-developed public and private education systems and despite being deficient in resources, have been producing graduates with skill levels of global standards. Following the recent spate of globalization, the rate of skill formation in many developing countries has increased at rates that far exceed the absorption capacity of skilled workers within these countries. Our model shows that under such conditions, trade reform might increase the rate of emigration of skilled professionals from the developing countries. Despite providing improved working conditions and higher wages, these countries fail to retain a considerable proportion of their skilled and highly skilled population, thereby perpetuating the trend of out-migration of skilled workers. In particular, we show that the rate of skilled emigration from developing countries may increase even if resources, which can create jobs for skilled workers, expand in size. Moreover, we point out that a terms-of-trade improvement for the migrant-sending country through growth of its export sector (using foreign capital and skilled labour) would unambiguously increase emigration of skilled workers—a result contradictory to expectations and yet possible in the presence of a strong skill formation sector.[11]

It should be noted that skill formation is essentially a dynamic concept which involves time, effort, and other costs on the part of the individual

---

[10] For the unskilled workers on the other hand, push factors mostly constitute forced eviction from their homeland due to war and conflict, religious, social or ethnic persecution, and often stark poverty and famine due to natural calamities such as drought. However, these types of emigration take the form of refugee movements or that of asylum seekers, and tend to be essentially cross-border migration. This is categorically different from unskilled workers strategically migrating to a developed country for finding similar and yet higher paid jobs.

[11] In an earlier paper, Djajic (1998) shows that, with foreign capital, effect of emigration on the welfare of those left behind may go up. We do not engage in a welfare analysis in this book, but rather figure what the impact of foreign capital inflow and trade liberalization would be on the rate of skill emigration from the country.

acquiring skill. We consider a static model to observe the mobility of labour across various sectors in a small open economy, subject to parametric adjustments.[12] This simplification allows us to focus exclusively on the impact of external shocks on rate of skill formation and skill emigration in the developing countries.[13]

5.4 **A Model and the Results**

We consider a small open economy without population growth, producing one import-competing good X, an exportable good Y and skill S. The prices of tradable goods are exogenously given, production of commodities follow constant returns to scale, and diminishing returns to factor inputs. Markets are perfectly competitive and factors of production are fully employed. The rate of return per unit of foreign capital is negotiated and set exogenously at r^*. Initially, foreign capital in many developing countries is offered a host of incentives in the form of tax concessions, full repatriation of capital gains, and other similar benefits. Also, foreign banks and other financial institutions are not required to meet social obligations like their domestic counterparts. For example, foreign capital in the power sector in India still commands a 16% post-tax return in dollar terms, while NTPC (National Thermal Power Corporation) does not get any guaranteed rate (Kumar, 1999, page 1002).

The following symbols are used to describe the model incorporating these features.

w_S : Skilled wage;	w : Unskilled wage
r : Return to domestic capital;	r^* : Return to foreign capital
P_j : Commodity price for the jth sector;	$\bar{U}$: Supply of unskilled labour
$\bar{K}$: Supply of domestic capital;	$\bar{K}^*$: Supply of foreign capital
S : Skilled labour;	α : Skilled emigration
a_{ij} : Use of ith input in j^{th} sector;	t : Tariff rate on commodity X
T : Total supply of land;	τ : Return to land

---

[12] Jones and Marjit (2003) use a small open economy model with linear neighbourhood structure to discuss impact of changes in agricultural price on wages when unskilled workers obtain education to join the ranks of skilled workers.

[13] Introducing the dynamics of migration in the model would enrich and not alter any of the results we obtain here.

'∧' represents percentage changes for variables and parameters.
The system of equations is given as:

$$a_{SX}w_S + a_{KX}r = P_X^*(1+t) \tag{5.1}$$

$$a_{SY}w_S + a_{K^*Y}r^* = P_Y^* \tag{5.2}$$

$$a_{US}w + a_{KS}r = w_S \tag{5.3}$$

$$a_{UZ}w + a_{TZ}\tau = P_Z^* \tag{5.4}$$

We assume that for a foreign skilled wage, $w_S^* > w_S$, such that some skilled workers always migrate.[14] This is based on a plausible assumption that a skilled wage in the foreign country is rigid downwards and does not fall, despite an inflow of skilled workers from abroad. Besides, it has been discussed that in reality, a skilled wage has relatively increased in most developed countries for various reasons (see Footnote 6). Thus, there is a leakage of 'α' proportion, determined endogenously, from the pool of skilled workers, S. This pool is generated by converting unskilled workers to skilled workers, with the help of domestic capital.

Therefore,

$$a_{SX}X + a_{SY}Y = S(1-\alpha) \tag{5.5}$$

$$a_{KX}X + a_{US}S = \bar{U}. \tag{5.6}$$

Equation (5.4) provides information about how many skilled workers are available to be used in sectors X and Y, if α proportion migrates from the pool. Equation (5.5) helps determining how many skilled workers can be generated from a fixed resource of unskilled workers given the input-output ratio in this sector.[15] Finally, Equations (5.6) and (5.7) present full-employment conditions

---

[14] As more and more skilled workers migrate, *ceteris paribus* domestic return to skill will rise and will create disincentives for further migration or even promote reverse migration. Thus, the present form of equilibrium is sustained as long as 'some' skilled workers undertake migration, or $\alpha \in [0,1)$.

[15] Use of unskilled labour in other sectors of the economy is not considered to retain our focus exclusively on skill formation and migration in the presence of foreign capital. Including an unskilled sector will extend and not reverse the patterns we obtain. Here, unskilled labour works in sector S only, and some of them become skilled while the rest remains unskilled. See Kar and Beladi (2004) for a more comprehensive model without foreign capital in any of the sectors.

for domestic and foreign capital respectively, such that given input coefficients and skill turnouts, output levels for X and Y can subsequently be determined:

$$a_{KX}X + a_{KS}S = \overline{K} \tag{5.7}$$

$$a_{K^*Y}Y = \overline{K}^* \tag{5.8}$$

$$a_{TZ}Z = \overline{T}. \tag{5.9}$$

Determination of other variables from the set of equations goes as follows. From Equation (5.2), w_S is determined given exogenous price and foreign interest rate. Substituting w_S in (5.1), we obtain domestic interest rate r and from Equation (5.3), unskilled wage, w. Finally, from Equation (5.4), we can solve for the return to land, τ. Again, from (5.8) and (5.9), solve for Y and Z. Substituting Z in (5.7) determine S from the stock of unskilled workers, and from (5.6), determine X once the equilibrium value of S is determined. Equation (5.5) solves for the rate of skill emigration, α.

5.4.1 EFFECTS OF TRADE LIBERALIZATION

We consider two types of liberalization of the external sector of our stylized economy. We first consider a scenario of a tariff cut in the import-competing sector and a simultaneous increase in the stock of foreign capital in the economy, i.e. $\hat{t} < 0$ *and* $\hat{\overline{K}}^* > 0$.[16] Second, a cut in the negotiated foreign interest rate, such that $\hat{r}^* < 0$. The first exercise is justified by the reform experiences of most developing countries, where trade liberalization and entry of foreign capital take place simultaneously. The second exercise is similar in spirit and outcome, as we shall shortly demonstrate, to an increase in the price of the export good Y implying a terms-of-trade improvement for the country. We point out that with greater independent inflow of foreign capital and formation of a stable capacity over time, the government and other host agencies might be able to negotiate a lower interest rate on each unit of foreign capital, such that, $\hat{r}^* < 0$.

The following proposition captures the first set of results.

Proposition 5.1: *Percentage change in skill emigration is positive if the ratio of the 'rate of inflow of foreign capital and rate of tariff cut' is lower than a threshold level 'ϕ' (a positive constant).*

---

[16] Note that tariff cuts and inflow of FDI may be causally related, when the country has undertaken a reform package under bilateral or multilateral negotiations. We, however, treat these as independent and simultaneous occurrences.

Proof: $\hat{\alpha} > 0$, iff, $(-\widehat{\bar{K}}^*/\hat{t}) < \varphi$, where, $\widehat{\bar{K}}^* > 0, \phi > 0$ and $\hat{t} < 0$. Detailed algebraic proof of this condition is provided in the Appendix.

A tariff cut in the import-competing sector reduces return to domestic capital in this sector. This directly follows from Equations (5.1) and (5.2). As the price of the exportable good remains unchanged, the skilled wage does not change and thus a tariff cut would only lower return to domestic capital in sector X. Domestic capital moves to sector S. From Equation (5.3) it can then be shown that unskilled wage increases more than skilled wage and the skilled-unskilled wage gap falls. As far as output is concerned, a tariff cut causes the import competing sector to shrink, releasing both capital and skilled labour. While capital moves to the skill formation sector, skilled labour moves to sector Y.[17] An increase in the stock of foreign capital allows sector Y to absorb the flow of skilled workers from sector X.

In other words, skill formation increases in the economy and skill employment in sector Y increases while that in sector X falls. Thus the impact on skill emigration could be ambiguous. However, the actual impact on skill emigration can be obtained by comparing the rate of tariff cut to the rate of foreign capital inflow, such that,

$$\hat{\alpha} > 0, \ iff, \ (-\frac{\widehat{\bar{K}}^*}{dt}) < \gamma, \ where, \widehat{\bar{K}}^* > 0, \gamma > 0 \ and \ dt < 0.$$

Gamma is defined in the appendix. This result may have an interesting policy implication. A comparison of the rate of foreign capital inflow with the rate of tariff cut would determine the direction and rate of skilled migration. For example, given the value of γ, rate of tariff cut or rate of entry of foreign capital can be appropriately chosen either to promote emigration of skill or to encourage skill inflow into the country. Clearly, some combinations of $\widehat{\bar{K}}^* > 0$ and $dt < 0$ may violate this condition and would imply either reverse migration or inflow of skilled workers from elsewhere. On the other hand, a decline in the stock of foreign capital ($\widehat{\bar{K}}^* < 0$) along with a tariff cut ($dt < 0$) in the import competing sector unambiguously leads to an outflow of skilled workers from the country.

---

[17] In India, for example, availability of bank loans for financing education has increased manifold compared to the decade of the 1980s. Also, the numbers of private primary, secondary, post-secondary schools, and colleges have multiplied in many states, including the establishment of private business and technical schools.

5.4.2 A TERMS-OF-TRADE IMPROVEMENT OR AN INTEREST CUT ON FOREIGN CAPITAL

The following proposition is based on the second comparative static exercise.

Proposition 5.2: *A lower negotiated return to foreign capital or an exogenous increase in the export price, ceteris paribus, will both unambiguously increase the proportion of skilled emigrants.*[18]

Proof: Detailed algebraic proof is provided in the Appendix.

First, we investigate the price effect. A rise in the export price $\hat{P}_Y{}^* > 0$, other things constant, leads to an increase in the skilled wage and a fall in the return to domestic capital. This directly leads to a fall in the skilled-unskilled wage gap, $(\hat{w} / \hat{w}_S > 1)$. When there is a TOT improvement with unchanged foreign interest rate, skilled wage increases more than proportionately to the increase in the price of the export good. In a competitive market, this makes sector Y unviable and it contracts. Intuitively, factor proportions change in the same direction as factor prices such that elasticity of substitution in this industry is greater than zero, $\sigma_Y = (a_{K^*Y} - a_{LY}) / (w - r^*) > 0$. As skilled wage increases, sector Y should uses more capital by factor substitution, but capital is sector-specific and its supply is fixed. Thus contraction in sector Y is unavoidable.

The price effect simultaneously lowers the return to domestic capital invested in sector X (using Equation 5.1). Domestic capital moves out to the skill formation sector and sector X contracts in the process. As skilled wage rises, on the one hand there is incentive to skill formation, and on the other, there is capital inflow into sector S such that overall skill turnout in the economy expands. Thus, greater skill formation in the economy is accompanied by a contraction of sectors that are potential employers of skilled workers. This results in the unambiguous outflow of skilled workers from the country. With a sticky interest rate on capital, a TOT improvement may therefore be immiserizing for the export sector and can contribute to a skill exodus from the country.

Second, as negotiated foreign interest rate is lowered (imposing higher tax or withdrawing subsidies) at unchanged commodity prices, skilled wage increases. As interest rate is lowered, once again there should be capital-biased factor substitution in the sector—a possibility thwarted by sector specificity of capital and fixed supply. This leads to a contraction in output.

Now, a fall in interest rate will lower the skilled-unskilled wage gap if, and only if, the capital-labour ratio in the production of S is greater than that in the

---

[18] The two parametric changes yield results similar in direction, although magnitudes vary. One can then think of a situation, for example, when an exogenous increase in export price or a drop in interest rate could be countered by a policy of allowing more foreign capital to keep the export sector viable and thus minimize the immiserizing effects of a terms-of-trade improvement. We provide detailed explanations in support of this.

production of X. However, from Equation (5.1) this implies a lower interest rate on domestic capital and from Equation (5.3), a higher unskilled wage. Thus, domestic capital moves to the skill formation sector, which expands at the cost of both X and Y. Thus generally, for both cases,

$$\hat{S} > 0; \ \hat{Y} = -\hat{a}_{K \cdot Y} = -\sigma_Y \theta_{SY} (\hat{w}_S - \hat{r}^*) < 0; \ and \ \hat{X} < 0.$$

Contraction of output in both sectors X and Y implies lower employment of skilled workers in the economy who then take to international migration.[19]

5.5 **Conclusion**

This chapter provides a broad overview of the literature on international mobility of factors, of which migration of labour is perhaps the most important element. Starting with several analytical and empirical results concerning international mobility of labour, we also discuss how the host country choices are influenced by gains from such mobility. The comparison of capital and labour mobility across countries with dissimilar capital-labour ratios, reminiscent of the famous HOS (Heckscher-Ohin-Samuelson) structure, as in Bhagwati and Ramaswamy's famous contributions, epitomizes and leads the debate to a measurement of the distribution of global welfare from factor mobility. Fortunately, it does not exhaust the scope of welfare gains, and what we offer as a model in later sections is about skill formation in the source country when opportunities of factor mobility open up.

We construct a simple general equilibrium model to show that emigration of skilled workers from a small open economy *may* increase following trade liberalization and foreign capital inflow in the country. Furthermore, we demonstrate that a terms-of-trade improvement via increase in the price of its export good, which uses foreign capital and skilled labour, would also increase the rate of outflow of skilled workers from the economy. The outcome would be similar, if the country negotiates a lower interest rate on foreign capital (by imposing higher tax or withdrawing subsidy) at unchanged commodity prices.

---

[19] The software industry in India is undergoing similar changes at present, where the wage growth is faster than in similar jobs in the US. To retain earlier profit levels, firms are cutting down on production leading to lay-offs of skilled professionals in the industry. We provide a theoretical explanation of how this in turn might aggravate the pressure of skilled emigration from the country. The general policy relevance of this issue is quite high under anticipations of future skill shortage in many developing countries.

At first sight, Proposition 5.1 may not appear unexpected. Downsizing of the protected skill-using, import-competing sector would render skilled workers unemployed, leading to an eventual exodus of skill from the country. This is the typical 'push' factor. The novelty of our analysis lies in our treatment of simultaneous changes in tariff rate and a more 'open-door' policy towards foreign capital. We show that the relative 'strengths' of these two changes determine the direction and magnitude of possible skill emigration from the country. Particularly, we point out that there would be skill emigration if the ratio of the 'rate of foreign capital inflow' to the 'rate of tariff cut on the importable sector' is lower than a positive constant.

Proposition 5.2 seemingly opposes conventional wisdom. We show that an exogenous increase in the price of the export good which uses foreign capital and skilled labour leads to a contraction of the export sector—an immiserizing effect of TOT improvement. As the rate of skill acquisition increases in the economy, and following a contraction of output and employment in both the import-competing as well as the export sector, skilled workers are unambiguously pushed to undertake international migration. Contraction of the export sector is explained by the fact that factor substitution towards greater use of foreign capital is thwarted by its sector-specificity and fixed stock. Thus a TOT improvement produces an immiserizing impact on the export sector and contributes to skill exodus from the country. On the other hand, lowering of the negotiated foreign interest rate also contracts sector Y, as despite lower interest rate, more foreign capital cannot be employed in sector Y. Therefore, in both of these cases, allowing more foreign capital seems to be the only choice in favour of a possible expansion of sector Y and for retaining skilled workers in the country (footnote 17).

Obviously, these results have strong policy implications central to the skill emigration issue. It follows from the first result that a suitable rate of tariff cut may have to be decided in comparison with the growth rate of foreign capital stock, depending on the importance of the migration (brain drain) agenda in the public domain—whether to allow undeterred emigration of skilled workers or to encourage inflow of skilled workers into the country. Based on similar preferences on the issue of migration of skilled workers, the second proposition should also provoke thoughts on whether more foreign capital should be allowed entry when the economy faces an exogenous improvement in the TOT. Taxing foreign capital or withdrawal of subsidy on returns enjoyed by foreign investors will, however, discourage further investments and thus the outflow of skilled workers may be unavoidable. Chapter 6 addresses a related set of issues under conditions which are deliberately left out presently. All through, we assumed that mobility of factors do not suffer from asymmetry of information between source and destinations. However, a sizable literature, essentially part of the larger discussion in labour and public economics, deals explicitly with cases where such asymmetry of information dictates the direction of factor flows, the magnitude, and the welfare gains associated with it. To the extent that information affects appropriation of welfare gains related to factor mobility, both at the individual as well as the national level, we consider a review of such literature as important for this book.

■ Appendix: Algebraic Proofs and Graphical Analyses

Notations follow Jones (1965).

Proof of Proposition 5.1:

Let $\hat{t} < 0$ and $\widehat{\overline{K}}^* > 0$,

From (5.1), $\theta_{SX}\,\hat{w}_S + \theta_{KX}\,\hat{r} = \pi\hat{t}$, where, $\pi = \dfrac{t}{1+t}$.

From (5.2), $\theta_{SY}\,\hat{w}_S + \theta_{K^*Y}\,\hat{r}^* = 0$.

From (5.3), $\theta_{US}\,\hat{w} + \theta_{KS}\,\hat{r} = \hat{w}_S$.

From (5.4), $\theta_{UZ}\,\hat{w} + \theta_{TZ}\,\hat{\tau} = 0$.

These yield three immediate solutions given, $\hat{r}^* = 0$

$$\hat{w}_S = 0, \hat{w} = -\frac{\theta_{KS}}{\theta_{US}}\frac{\pi\hat{t}}{\theta_{KX}} > 0 \ \ and \ \ \hat{r} = \frac{\pi\hat{t}}{\theta_{KX}} < 0 \ \ and, \ \ \hat{\tau} = \frac{\theta_{UZ}}{\theta_{US}}\frac{\theta_{KZ}}{\theta_{KX}\theta_{TZ}}\pi\hat{t} < 0. \quad (5A.1)$$

As $\hat{w} > 0$ *and* $\hat{w}_s = 0$: $(\hat{w} - \hat{w}_S) > 0$. Thus, wage inequality decreases.

Again, from (5.9),

$$\hat{Z} = (-\hat{a}_{TZ} = -\theta_{UZ}\sigma_Z(\hat{w} - \hat{\tau}) = \frac{\theta_{UZ}}{\theta_{TZ}}\frac{\theta_{KS}}{\theta_{US}\,\theta_{KX}}\sigma_Z\pi\hat{t}) < 0, \ as \ \hat{t} < 0. \quad (5A.2)$$

$$\lambda_{K^*Y}\,\hat{Y} = \widehat{\overline{K}}* - \lambda_{K^*Y}\,\hat{a}_{K^*Y} = \widehat{\overline{K}}* - \lambda_{K^*Y}\left[\theta_{SY}\sigma_Y\left(\hat{w}_S - \hat{r}^*\right)\right]$$

From (5.8), $\ \ \hat{Y} = \dfrac{\widehat{\overline{K}}*}{\lambda_{K^*Y}} > 0$ since, $\left(\hat{w}_S - \hat{r}^*\right) = 0$ and $\widehat{\overline{K}}* > 0$. $\quad (5A.3)$

From (5.7) and using (5A.1) and (5A.2), we solve for $\hat{S}$:

$$\hat{S} = -\frac{\theta_{KS}}{\theta_{KX}\theta_{US}}\pi\hat{t}[\frac{\lambda_{UZ}}{\lambda_{US}\theta_{TZ}}\sigma_Z + \sigma_S] > 0, \ as \ \hat{t} < 0. \quad (5A.4)$$

Next, from Equation (5.6),

$$\lambda_{KX}\widehat{X} = -\lambda_{KS}\hat{S} - \lambda_{KX}\hat{a}_{KX} - \lambda_{KS}\hat{a}_{KS}$$

such that, $\widehat{X} = \dfrac{1}{\theta_{KX}}\pi\hat{t}[\dfrac{\lambda_{KS}}{\lambda_{KX}\theta_{US}}\{\sigma_S + \dfrac{\lambda_{UZ}}{\lambda_{US}}\dfrac{\theta_{KS}}{\theta_{TZ}}\sigma_Z\} + \theta_{SX}\sigma_X] < 0.$ (5A.5)

Finally, using (A.1–A.5) and fully differentiating Equation (5.5), we get

$$\pi\hat{\alpha} = [\hat{S} - \{\lambda_{SX}\theta_{KX}\sigma_X + \lambda_{SY}\theta_{K\cdot Y}\sigma_Y\}\hat{r} - \lambda_{SX}\widehat{X} - \lambda_{SY}\widehat{Y}].$$

Rearranging and substituting, $\hat{\alpha} > 0$ *iff,* $\left(-\dfrac{\widehat{\widehat{K}}^{*}}{\hat{t}}\right) < \varphi$ (5A.6)

$$\varphi = \pi\gamma\dfrac{\lambda_{K\cdot Y}}{\lambda_{SY}}$$

where, *and* $\gamma = \left[\dfrac{\theta_{KS}}{\theta_{US}}\dfrac{\lambda_{UZ}}{\lambda_{UUS}}\dfrac{\sigma_Z}{\theta_{TZ}}(\lambda_{KX} + \lambda_{KS}\lambda_{SX}) + \dfrac{\lambda_{KS}}{\lambda_{US}\lambda_{KX}} + \lambda_{SX}\sigma_X + \lambda_{SY}\theta_{K\cdot Y}\sigma_Y\right]$

Thus, emigration of skilled workers increases if condition (5A.6) holds.

Proof of Proposition 5.2
Using a similar procedure as before and using $\hat{P}_Y^{*} > 0$, we get,

$$\hat{w}_S > 0, \hat{r} < 0, \hat{w} > 0 \quad and \quad \dfrac{\hat{w}}{\hat{w}_S} > 1$$

However, when there is a lowering of interest rate on foreign capital, i.e., $\hat{r}^{*} < 0$, we get, $\hat{w}_S > 0, \hat{r} < 0, \hat{w} > 0$. But, $\hat{w}/\hat{w}_S > 1$, *iff,* $(\theta_{KS}/\theta_{US})/(\theta_{KX}/\theta_{SX}) > 1$. In other words, the skilled-unskilled wage gap falls with a lower foreign interest rate, if and only if, the capital-labour ratio in the production of S is greater than that in sector X, i.e., sector S is more capital-intensive. Now,

$$\widehat{Y} = -\hat{a}_{K\cdot Y} = -\sigma_Y\theta_{SY}(\hat{w}_S - \hat{r}^{*}) < 0 \text{ and,}$$

$$\hat{\alpha} = \dfrac{1}{c}[\hat{S} - \lambda_{SX}\widehat{X} + \lambda_{SX}\sigma_X\dfrac{\hat{P}_Y^{*}}{\theta_{SY}} - \lambda_{SY}\widehat{Y} + \lambda_{SY}\sigma_Y\theta_{K\cdot Y}(\hat{w}_S - \hat{r}^{*})] \text{ where, } c = \dfrac{\alpha}{1-\alpha}.$$

Since all other results hold under both $\widehat{P}_Y^* > 0$ and $\widehat{r}^* < 0$, we get the general conditions: $\widehat{S} > 0$; $\widehat{Y} = -\widehat{a}_{K \cdot Y} = -\sigma_Y \theta_{SY} (\widehat{w}_S - \widehat{r}^*) < 0$; $\widehat{X} < 0$.

Substituting these in Equation (5.4) fully differentiated, we get, $\widehat{\alpha} > 0$.

Migration of skilled workers unambiguously increases if the negotiated foreign interest rate drops or the price of export good Y increases. These effects are magnified in the presence of trade liberalization.

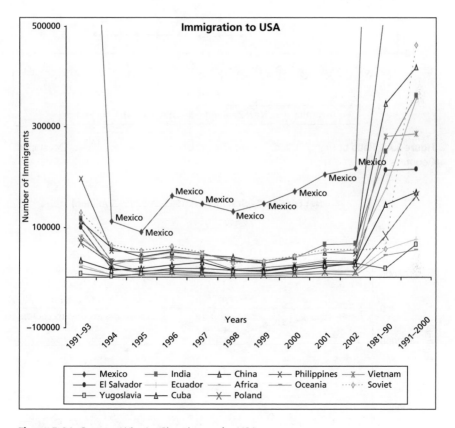

Figure 5.A1 Country-Wise Immigration to the USA

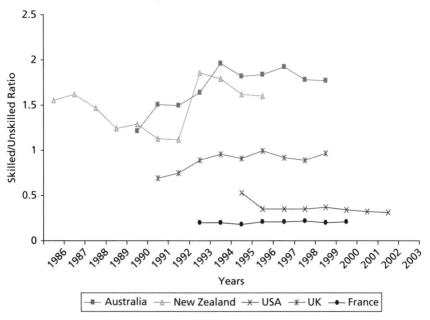

Figure 5.A2 Ratio of Highly Skilled to Relatively Unskilled Immigration in Select Developed Countries

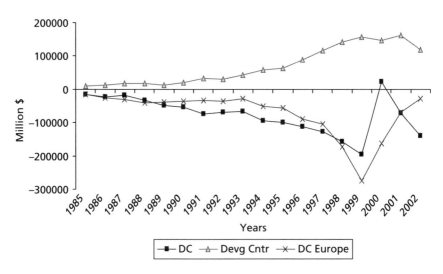

Figure 5.A3 Net Foreign Capital Inflows in Developed and Developing Countries 1985–2002

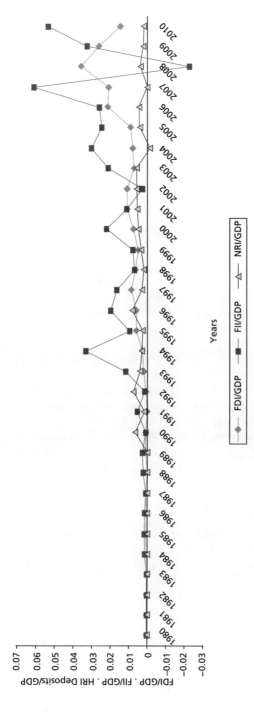

Figure 5.A4 Foreign Capital Inflow in India

■ REFERENCES

Altonji, J. G. and Card, D. (1991). 'The Effects of Immigration on the Labour Market Outcomes of Less-Skilled Natives'. In: J. M. Abowd and R. B. Freeman (eds). *Immigration, Trade and the Labor Market*, pp. 201–234. Chicago: University of Chicago Press.

Berman, E. J., Bound, J., and Grilliches, Z. (1994). 'Changes in the Demand for Skilled Labour Within US Manufacturing'. *Quarterly Journal of Economics* 109: 367–397.

Berman, E., Bound, J., and Machin, S. (1997). 'Implications of skill-biased technological change: International evidence'. Cambridge, MA: National Bureau of Economic Research Working Paper, 6166.

Berman, E., Bound, J., and Machin, S. (1998). 'Implications of Skill-Biased Technological Change: International Evidence'. *Quarterly Journal of Economics* 113 (4): 1245–1280.

Bhagwati, J. N. (1984). 'Incentives and Disincentives: International Migration'. *Weltwirtschaftliches Archiv* 120 (4): 678–700.

Bhagwati, J. N. (1988). 'Global Interdependence and International Migration'. In: J. Cassing and S. Husted (eds) *Capital, Technology and Labour in the New Global Economy*, pp. 149–183. Washington: AEI.

Bhagwati, J. N. and Srinivasan, T. N. (1983). 'On the Choice Between Capital and Labour Mobility'. *Journal of International Economics* 14: 209–221.

Bohning, W. R. (1984). *International Migration: Implications for Development Policies in Population Distribution, Migration and Development*. Department of International Economic and Social Affairs, UN.

Borjas, G. J. and Freeman, R. B. (1997). 'Findings We Never Found'. The *New York Times*, December 10.

Borjas, G. J., Freeman, R. B., and Katz L. F. (1992). 'On the Labour Market Effects of Immigration and Trade'. In: J. M. Abowd and R. B. Freeman (eds). *Immigration, Trade and the Labour Market*. Chicago and London: University of Chicago Press.

Borjas, G. and Ramey, V. A. (1993). 'Foreign Competition, Market Power and Wage Inequality: Theory and Evidence'. NBER Working Paper 4556. NBER: Cambridge, Massachusetts, December.

Davis, S. J. and Haltiwanger, J. (1991). 'Wage Dispersion Between and Within US Manufacturing Plants, 1963–1986'. Brookings Paper on Economic Activity: Microeconomics, 115–180.

Deardorff, A. V. (2000). 'Policy Implications of the Trade and Wage Debate'. *Review of International Economics* 8 (3): 478–496.

Djajic, S. (1998). 'Emigration and Welfare in an Economy with Foreign Capital'. *Journal of Development Economics* 56: 433–445.

Faini, R. de Melo, J. (1996). 'Trade Liberalization, Employment and Migration: Some Simulations for Morocco'. CEPR Discussion Paper 1198, London, UK.

Gerking, S. D. and Mutti, J. H. (1983). 'Factor Rewards and the International Migration of Unskilled Labor: A Model with Capital Mobility'. *Journal of International Economics* 14: 367–380.

Government of Australia (2004). To Make a Contribution: Review of Skilled Labour Migration (Chapter 1). www.aph.gov.au/house/committee/mig/skillmig/report/Chapter1.pdf

Head, K. and Ries, J. (2002). 'Offshore Production and Skill Upgrading by Japanese Manufacturing Firms'. *Journal of International Economics* 58: 81–105.

Jannol, R., Meyers, D., and Jachimowicz, M. (2003). US-Canada-Mexico Fact Sheet on Trade and Migration. Migration Policy Institute, Washington DC.

Jones, R. W. and Marjit, S. (2003). 'Economic Development, Trade and Wages'. *German Economic Review* 4: 1–17.

Jones, R. W. (1965). 'The Structure of Simple General Equilibrium Models'. *Journal of Political Economy* 73: 557–572.

Kar, S. and Beladi, H. (2004). 'Skill Formation and Trade Reform—Welfare Perspective of Developing Countries'. *Japan and the World Economy* 16: 35–54.

Katz, L. F. and Murphy, K. M. (1992). 'Changes in Relative Wages, 1963–1987: Supply and Demand Factors'. *Quarterly Journal of Economics* 107: 35–78.

Katz, E. and Stark, O. (1987). 'International Migration under Asymmetric Information'. *The Economic Journal* 97 (387): 718–726.

Katz, E. and Stark, O. (1989). 'International Labour Migration under Alternative Informational Regimes: A Diagrammatic Analysis'. *European Economic Review* 33: 127–142.

Krueger, A. B. (1993). 'How Computers Have Changed the Wage Structure: Evidence from Micro Data, 1984–1989'. *Quarterly Journal of Economics* 108 (1): 33–60.

Kuhn, P. and Wooton, I. (1991). 'Immigration, International Trade and Wages of National Workers'. In: J. M. Abowd and R. B. Freeman (eds). *Immigration, Trade and the Labor Market*, Chicago: University of Chicago Press.

Kumar, A. (1999). 'Trade, technology and employment generation in India'. *The Indian Journal of Labour Economics* 42 (4): 1001–1007.

Lee, H. and Roland-Holst, D. (1996). 'CGE Modelling of Trade and Employment in Pacific Rim Countries'. In: J. E. Taylor (ed.) Development Strategy, Employment and Migration, OECD Development Centre, Paris, 107–148.

Lind, H. (1969). 'International Migration in Britain'. In: J. A. Jackson (ed.) *Migration: Sociological Studies 2*. London: Cambridge University Press.

Lowell, B. L. and Findlay, A. (2001). 'Migration of Highly Skilled Persons from Developing Countries: Impact and Policy Responses'. Synthesis report for project INT/01/M09/UKM, ILO: Geneva.

Marjit, S. and Acharyya, R. (2003). 'International Trade, Wage Inequality and the Developing Economy: A General Equilibrium Approach'. In: *Contributions to Economics*. Heidelberg and New York: Springer Physica-Verlag.

Marjit, S. and Kar, S. (2004). 'Trade, Wages and Labour Mobility'. In: A. Bhattacharjea and S. Marjit (eds). *Globalization and the Developing Economies*. New Delhi: Manohar.

Markusen, J. R. and Venables, A J. (1997). 'The Role of Multinational Firms in the Wage-gap Debate'. *Review of International Economics* 5(4): 435–451.

Markusen, J. R. and Zahniser, S. (1999). 'Liberalization and incentives for labor migration: theory with applications to NAFTA'. In: R. Faini et al. (eds). *Migration. The Controversies and the Evidence*. Cambridge: Cambridge University Press.

OECD (2001). Trends in International Migration.

OECD Development Centre (1996), *Development Strategy, Employment and Migration*, (ed.) Paris: J. E. Taylor.

Pavcnik, N. (2003). 'What Explains Skill Upgrading in Less Developed Countries?'. *Journal of Development Economics* 71: 311–328.

Piore, M. J. (1979). *Birds of Passage: Migrant Labour and Industrial Societies*. London: Cambridge University Press.

Razin, A. and Sadka, E. (1992). 'International Migration and International Trade'. NBER Working Paper 4230. NBER: Cambridge, MA, December.

Ramaswami, V. K. (1968). 'International factor movements and the national advantage'. *Economica* 35: 309–310.

Rivera-Batiz, F. L. (1998). 'Migration and the Labor Market: Sectoral and Regional Effects in the United States'. In: 'Migration, Free Trade and Regional Integration in North America'. OECD Proceedings, OECD, Paris.

Sapir, A. (1983). 'Foreign Competition, Immigration and Structural Adjustment'. *Journal of International Economics* 14: 381–394.

Sapir, A. (1975). 'A Note on Short-Run Greek Labour Emigration to Germany'. *Weltwirtschaftliches Archiv* 111 (2): 356–361.

Schiff, M. (1996). 'Trade Policy and International Migration: Substitutes or Complements?' In: J. E.Taylor (ed.) *Development Strategy, Employment and Migration*, pp. 23–42. Paris: OECD Development Centre.

Stark, O. (1991). *The Migration of Labour*. Oxford: Basil Blackwell.

Trefler, D. (1997). 'Immigrants and Natives in General Equilibrium Trade Models'. NBER Working Paper 6209. NBER: Cambridge, Massachusetts, October.

Wood, A. (1998). 'Globalization and the Rise in Labour Market Inequalities'. *The Economic Journal* 108: 1463–1482.

Wong, Kar-Yiu (1983). 'On Choosing Among Trade in Goods and International Capital and Labor Mobility—A Theoretical Analysis'. *Journal of International Economics* 14: 223–250.

6 Information, Labour Migration, and Occupation

6.1 Introduction

An important issue that is central to factor mobility, in particular labour mobility given the current trend of South-to-North migration pattern, is how the immigrants perform in the developed world. The question of economic prospects for immigrants in developed countries is strongly driven by the fact that the general information regimes are distinctly different between many source and host countries. When the cross-border labour markets are predominantly characterized by the presence of asymmetric information between employers and immigrant employees, the labour market outcomes, as well as the general economic conditions, are significantly influenced. We review a large literature around this phenomenon to begin with. It follows that the migration patterns and the benefits such as remittances that accompany large labour movements may evolve around such observations. More importantly, the outcomes with regard to occupational choice by migrant labour bear strong implications for the poorer source countries in terms of socio-economic aspirations, choices, and decision-making.

Self-employment among immigrants in richer countries as one aspect of occupational choice, appears to have been a dominant trait for some years now. Particularly for the United States and Canada, as well as for a large number of Western European countries, there exists a vibrant source of empirical estimates, which shows that the self-employment rate among immigrants of first and successive generations exceeds that of native borns (Bates, 1997; Clark and Drinkwater, 2000; Li, 1997; Yuengert, 1995; Fairlie and Meyer, 1996; and also Razin, 1992, a case study on Israel with respect to Asian, African, East European, and North American immigrants; Kidd, 1993 for Australia).[1] Although availability of

---

[1] Fairlie (1996), for example, shows that the Korean American men and women have self-employment rates of 27.9% and 18.9 %, respectively, followed by Lebanese immigrants and so

appropriate data precludes similar studies on developing countries, there is some belief that the occupational behaviour of immigrants to such countries, where the group largely comprises of refugees and asylum seekers, would not be significantly different from that observed in richer countries. In fact, we show that the crucial conditions that may lead to such an outcome in the richer countries are rather universal and might also be tenable for the developing world. However, given the voluminous literature, we need to offer a brief overview of the existing evidence before we delve into the uniqueness of arguments generating such conditions.

The question of occupational choice was preceded by concerns about income assimilation of immigrants with that of natives (see Chiswick, 1978; Carliner, 1980). However, Yuengert (1991) notes that most previous studies of immigrant assimilation either excluded self-employed workers or included them without concern for the economic process generating sector choice and earnings. Interestingly, a study by Lofstrom (2002) shows that self-employed immigrants are found to do substantially better than wage-salary immigrants. Earnings of self-employed immigrants are predicted to converge with natives' wage at the age of 30, and to natives' self-employment earnings at the age of 40. Generally speaking, studies in this area mostly estimate the cross-section earnings functions and have so far reached two main conclusions: (i) the age-earnings profile of immigrants is steeper than that of the native population with the same measured skills; (ii) the age-earnings profile of immigrants crosses that of natives about 10 to 15 years after migration. In particular, Chiswick's (1978) analysis showed that at the time of arrival, the immigrants earned about 17% less than the natives. Because immigrants experience faster wage growth, their earnings overtake native earnings within 15 years after arrival, so much so that, after 30 years in the US, the typical immigrant earns 11% more than a comparable native worker.[2]

Among existing explanations of occupational choice of immigrants, the first type deals mainly with racial and ethnic backgrounds of immigrants (Bates, 1997; Borjas, 1987; Duleep and Regets, 1997; Funkhouser and Trejo, 1995; LaLonde and Topel, 1992; Light, 1984; Yuengert, 1995). The notion of cultural traits observed at the source of immigration is used as crucial information in understanding the choice of occupation and often the entrepreneurial behaviour of immigrants seems to be moulded in the country of origin, or rooted in their cultural background. Alternatively, Waldinger et al. (1990) note that minority self-employment patterns can be better explained by considering constraints and opportunities facing immigrants in the host country, when

---

on. Kidd (1993) shows that among skilled Australian immigrants (collegiate), self-employment rate exceeds that of natives.

[2] Duleep and Regets (1999) provide yet another convincing picture on immigrant-native (and also between immigrants) income assimilation, mainly driven by investment in human capital.

racial characteristics like 'thrift and cooperation' (Bonacich and Modell, 1981, p. 45–47) play a significant role. This modifies earlier findings (for example, by Lucas, 1978) that entrepreneurial ability is an innate trait: some have personal abilities to be an entrepreneur independently of their socio-economic and political history, while others do not.

The second type of explanation, and more akin to our analysis here, is based on the notion that immigrants' choice of occupation is mainly governed by their *attitude* towards risk and uncertainty present in the labour and capital markets (for example, Boadway et al., 1998; Chau and Stark, 1999; Coate and Tennyson, 1992). Other than these, social and economic discrimination in labour markets and in capital markets are also relevant factors in shaping immigrants' choice of occupation (Borjas and Bronars, 1989; Coate and Tennyson, 1992; Moore, 1983). Interestingly, the existence of such constraints may change immigrants' occupational preferences substantially. This group of studies therefore suggests that both the existence of asymmetric information in factor markets and direct discrimination can mould the final choice of occupation by immigrants, although the first of these arguments has not been explored directly.

In contrast, the income assimilation debate seems inconclusive and far from over. According to Borjas (1985), the positive cross-section correlations between the relative wage of immigrants and years since migration 'need not indicate that the wage of immigrants converges to that of natives' (p. 465) and that this assimilationist hypothesis draws inferences about earnings based on a 'single snapshot' (Borjas, 1987, p. 532) of the entire immigrant population. There is the possibility of error in doing that, since immigrant quality over time might have changed and could be responsible for convergence.[3]

In this chapter we argue that one core element in the entire mechanism that can significantly explain both has thus far not received the adequate attention it deserves. We show that the existence of asymmetric information in cross-border labour markets is such an element that strongly influences the choice of occupation among immigrants in favour of self-employment / entrepreneurship, and subsequently acts as a strong catalyst in favour of catching-up economically. The choice of a riskier occupation with more volatile but higher returns provides them with a head start towards faster income assimilation with the natives. In other words, this paper seeks to understand the occupational distribution and income assimilation for the immigrants in the foreign labour market characterized by imperfect information regarding the quality of the immigrant workforce. A key assumption is that screening

---

[3] Also see Duleep and Regets (1997) supporting the entry of lower ability immigrants in the US, and with less transferable skills. Berger and Gabriel (1991) for the USA show that the earnings profile for immigrants before 1970 exceeds that of natives. Those who arrived after 1970 have a lower mean income. This supports Borjas (1985, 1987).

devices are non-existent for such markets or at best inefficient. Our results should be equally tenable in any labour market where the employer has insufficient information about the productivity of a potential job seeker—a situation that is often compelling in many developing countries as well where the urban employer cannot instantaneously ascertain the skill of a worker arriving from a remote village.

It is well known that informational asymmetry in the labour market is an application to a situation where (at least initially) employers do not know the productivity levels of individual employees. It can arise if the markets are isolated such that 'information does not ordinarily flow across them (or does not flow costlessly and freely)' (Katz and Stark, 1987, p. 718). Undoubtedly, informational asymmetries become much more obvious when labour mobility between different countries is considered, with the source country languages,[4] systems, institutions, and cultures differing widely from that of the destination country. Moreover, over the last few decades, migration of labour from poor to rich countries has completely overshadowed the earlier white European migration to the 'New World', as also has intra-Europe migration. The cultural and ethnic distances and consequently the informational gap on an immigrant's true type have thus increased to such an extent, that available screening devices may not be adequate for assessing the true types of this heterogeneous pool.[5] Besides, immigration to developed countries is highly skewed in favour of the relatively unskilled (Kar and Guha-Khasnobis, 2006) and education as a signalling device is often incomprehensible, especially when educational systems are largely different between countries of the North and the South.[6] Recently, Kar and Saha (2009) characterize several menu contracts offered by rich country employers to influence self-selection among immigrants, when screening devices are inefficient.

However, the informational asymmetry that we consider in our model does not go beyond the labour market. Furthermore, inclusion of direct discrimination in both labour and capital markets (or inter-market spill over effects of discrimination as in Coate and Tennyson, 1992) and imperfections in other factor markets should extend the basic model we develop here.

Clearly, the most important question at this point is whether the existence of asymmetric information in the labour market of the migrant-recipient

---

[4] Among many studies along this line, Dustmann and Fabbri (2003) recently measure the importance of the host country (UK) language in the income assimilation profile of an immigrant, such that, lack of fluency in English leads to income losses. Also see Borjas (2000).

[5] Borjas (2000), for example, shows that foreign-born teaching assistants (TAs) (and their communication skills) are often less preferred to native TAs by US undergraduates. It is well known that the US universities do make substantial use of a well-developed screening mechanism while offering admission and financial aid to such foreigners, including a test of English language speaking abilities.

[6] Chau and Stark (1999) note that 'whatever workers may take with them when they migrate, they cannot possibly transfer their home countries' information structure' (p.455).

country is sufficient to drive the results discussed earlier. We establish, as we present the model, that asymmetric information across labour markets which leads to 'statistical discrimination' against the immigrants should be treated as a crucial factor responsible for both high self-employment participation among immigrants and for their eventually higher income levels.

Finally, it is useful to define self-employment in a way that shall be used throughout the study. In a statistical sense, individuals are 'self-employed if they earn no wages or salary, but derive their incomes by exercising their profession or business on their own account and/or for their own risk' (De Wit, 1993, p. 2).

We demonstrate possible migration patterns under symmetric and asymmetric information prevalent in the destination countries. Section 6.3 offers a simple model on the interaction between asymmetric information and choice of occupation with generalized and implicit solutions in favour of the degree of risk aversion for immigrants and natives, with further implications for income convergence between the two groups. Section 6.3.1 uses more specific functional forms to arrive at an explicit solution of the levels of risk aversion between the two groups. Section 6.4 concludes.

6.2 Asymmetric Information and the Decision to Migrate

The present section offers an analytical structure on who should migrate when the host country labour market is characterized by asymmetric information between employers and employees. The available literature offers important contributions on the pervasiveness of asymmetric information, even in regimes of high information flows. In several related papers, Borjas (2000), Chau and Stark (1999), Katz and Stark (1986; 1987; 1989), Stark (1991), and others argue that the lack of information is still a dominant character of the cross-country labour market (see, Chau and Stark, 1999). Therefore, lack of uniformity of country-specific systems and that of standardization would continue to prevent free and full flow of information. Katz and Stark (1987) offer conditions when, with some probability, full information may be reinstated and they show that with a 50-50 chance of discovery, the low skilled types would still find it worthwhile to migrate. However, without getting into these conditions, we can still discuss the migration patterns across skill types from a poor (P) source country to a rich (R) destination or host country.

Katz and Stark (1987) assume that in a given occupation, the wage of a worker with skill level $S \in [0,1]$ is $[W_R(S), W_P(S)]$ in the R and P countries respectively, such that $[W_R'(S) > 0 \ and \ W_P'(S) > 0]$. It is also assumed that

$[W_R(S) > W_P(S) \forall S]$ so that the R-country is labour-scarce and pays more compared to the P-country, where the density function on S is $F(S)$. In addition, it is assumed that the workers intending to migrate from P to R discount their potential wage at the destination with a factor $0 < k < 1$, such that they will consider migrating to a foreign country if and only if, $kW_R(S) > W_P(S)$. The discount factor is held constant across skill types, which in reality might not be the case. It is possible that individuals with higher S have lower k, while those with lower skill level face higher S. k accounts for various factors from culture to customs and from food habits to living away from family and friends. In any case, even with same k for all skill types, it can still be shown that the migration pattern is far from monotonic.

The following relationship: $kW_R(S) - W_P(S) = 0$ suggests that there may be several values of S at which this equality holds. This would be possible if at least one of the wage functions $[W_R(S)\ or\ W_P(S)]$ is non-linear in S. A non-convex $kW_R(S)$ will generate the following figure where several distinct migration groups are plotted in the horizontal axis and the wages in the vertical axis. The non-convex case shall identify which groups find it worthwhile to migrate and those that do not migrate.

Figure 6.1 shows that $W_P(S)$ is linear and increases with S, while $W_R(S)$ is non-convex and intersects the P-country wage at several points, viz. A, B, C, and D. Thus, between $[0, S_1]$ individuals migrate, between $[S_1, S_2]$ individuals do not and so on up to $S=1$. In other words, at points like A, B, C, and D the migration flow from the poor to the rich country displays non-monotonic properties. This has many implications for the source country, where availability of

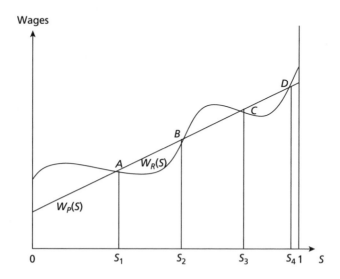

Figure 6.1 Migration Pattern Under Asymmetric Information

skill depends on who migrates under these conditions. This migration pattern, as Katz and Stark (1987) display, undergoes considerable modification when the host country labour market is characterized by asymmetric information between workers and employees.

Let us assume that the productivity of individual workers is known with certainty in the source country, but not in the destination country. In addition, when screening mechanisms are inefficient, as subsequent studies continue to demonstrate and that the signals are quite expensive (see Kar and Saha, 2011), the asymmetric information between potential workers and employers continue to be a dominant characteristic of the labour market in rich countries. Consequently, if employers observe productivity imperfectly, they tend to offer the same wage to a large number of workers about whom they have little or no prior information. This wage is equivalent to the average product of the migrant group and written as:

$$\bar{W} = \frac{\sum\limits_{i=1}^{n} \int\limits_{S_i^L}^{S_i^H} W_R(S)F(S)dS}{\sum\limits_{i=1}^{n} \int\limits_{S_i^L}^{S_i^H} F(S)dS} \tag{6.1}$$

where, (S_i^H, S_i^L) are the highest and lowest skill categories within each group i, $F(S)$ is the density function on S, and $\bar{W}$ is the average wage for all continuous skill groups migrating, and that the skill level rises with i. Given that $(0 < S_i^H < S_i^L < 1)$ for a non-empty migrating set, $\bar{W} < W_R(S_n^H)$, where, n is the highest skill-type migrating. Clearly, the presence of asymmetric information is likely to hurt the more skilled workers in this group in favour of a premium enjoyed by the relatively unskilled. This may lead to searching for opportunities outside the typical labour market as we demonstrate in Section 6.3.

More importantly, however, it is shown that unlike the full information case prevalence of asymmetric information shall lead to a different migration pattern where if a skill type S_n^H migrates, all skill types below it shall also migrate. Notably, this is different from the migration pattern displayed in Figure 6.1. According to this theorem, if the top skill level migrating under asymmetric information is (S_j^H), then any skill level $S^* < S_j^H$ shall also migrate. Intuitively, if the top skill level migrating is (S_j^H), then it must be that $k\bar{W} > W_P(S_j^H)$. It follows that $W_P(S^*) < W_P(S_j^H) < k\bar{W}$, such that, all skill types lower than S_j^H finds the discounted foreign wage higher than the domestic wage for that skill category. For the source country, this implies that if the domestic wage structure is so poor that the higher skill types find it worthwhile to migrate despite the discount rate and the pooled wage across skill types, then most skill types below it will also emigrate creating a shortage of workers at home. Recalling the Romanian evidence (Wesselingh, 2010), the government has revised doctors' pay from €220 to €400 in the wake of emigration wave. This may slow down exodus of large numbers of anaesthetists, cardiologists, urologists, and neurosurgeons compared to the Polish experience. In the present structure, it would imply that if a doctor's pay is so low that it influences out migration in large numbers, for lower skill types it may be even worse and might drive even larger numbers of unskilled or semi-skilled workers from the country.

However, this also suggests that (Theorem 2 in Katz and Stark, 1987) under symmetric information, the highest skill level migrating will never be lower than, and may be higher than, the top skill level migrating under asymmetric information. The proof is quite intuitive. Recalling the previous example, if the top skill level migrating under asymmetric information is (S_j^H), then $k\overline{W} > W_P(S_j^H)$. But, symmetric information about productivity in the labour market manifests itself into $kW_R(S_j^H) > k\overline{W}$. Thus, if (S_j^H) migrated as the top skill type under asymmetric information, then they would most likely migrate when information symmetry is reinstated. Reinstating symmetry, however, can happen either with a costly signal or with screening mechanisms that are quite standardized across countries and individuals. The lack of symmetry might result in various occupational choices at the destination, as we show in Section 6.3.

6.3 Asymmetric Information in the Labour Market

Let the mass of immigrants moving from a poor country to a rich country be unity. Assume that there are two groups of immigrants, skilled and unskilled. The number of skilled immigrants is α, and accordingly, the number of unskilled immigrants is $1 - \alpha$.[7] The proportions of skilled and unskilled individuals in the native born population are the same. The product of a skilled individual in the rich country is x; and the product of an unskilled individual is y, such that, $x > y$. Each individual must decide whether to be employed or self-employed. Employed individuals earn their product with certainty.[8] Thus, an employed skilled immigrant should ideally earn x and an employed unskilled immigrant, y. We assume that the skills possessed by a high-skill individual enable such individuals to be self-employed if they choose to. In

---

[7] We assume that α is exogenously determined.

[8] Of course, the employed workers may also face wage uncertainty, but more often than not it is less than the self-employed individuals are subject to.

contrast, we assume that unskilled workers cannot be self-employed: all unskilled workers are employed.

The income of a self-employed individual is uncertain: each such individual earns his product plus a random component plus a deterministic compensation for being exposed to risk.[9] Thus, the income of a self-employed individual is

$$z = x + \varepsilon + \delta \tag{6.2}$$

where ε is a random variable supported by $(-a, a)$ with a density function $f(\varepsilon)$, such that $E(\varepsilon) = 0$; and $E(\varepsilon^2) = \sigma^2$, and δ is a positive constant. In other words, $f(\varepsilon)$ follows uniform distribution.

All individuals, immigrants, and non-immigrants have a utility function with a constant absolute risk. The utility function is therefore of the form

$$U = -e^{-rw} \tag{6.3}$$

where w is the individual's total income, and r is the individual's absolute risk aversion, such that, $1 > r \geq 0$. Absolute risk aversion, r, varies among individuals according to a density function $g(r)$ supported by $[0, 1)$. We assume that all individuals maximize expected utility.

Employers in the rich country can discern the skill levels of local individuals. However, they cannot discern skill levels of individual immigrants, and immigrants do not engage in any 'signalling' about their skill level.[10] We finally assume that the employers do not have an efficient screening device to ascertain immediately the true skill levels of the migrants originating from such diverse backgrounds. Hence, the wage offered to any employed immigrant equals the average product of the entire employed immigrant cohort.[11]

Denote the proportion of skilled immigrants who are employed (as opposed to being self-employed), by π^*. Since α is the total number of skilled immigrants, this implies that the number of skilled immigrants who are employed is $\alpha\pi$ and the number of skilled immigrants who are self-employed is $(1 - \pi^*)\alpha$. Hence, the wage paid to the employed immigrants is

$$\bar{w} = \frac{\alpha\pi^* x + (1 - \alpha)y}{\alpha\pi^* + 1 - \alpha}. \tag{6.4}$$

---

[9] Given a population of risk-averse individuals, such compensation will always be a feature of the equilibrium.

[10] See Katz and Stark (1987) for international migration patterns under asymmetric information with signalling. However, signalling may be quite expensive for many immigrants originating in poor countries or for several other factors beyond the scope of discussion in this paper (for example, permanent refugee movements). Besides, cross-border refugees, asylum-seekers and illegal migrants cannot signal their skill levels before physically migrating to a different country.

[11] This is a linearity assumption, and fairly common in the related literature. See for example, Chau and Stark (1999).

The higher the proportion of skilled immigrants employed in equilibrium, the higher the average wage for all employed immigrants.

Let r^* be the level of risk aversion at which skilled individuals are indifferent between employment and self-employment. Individuals with $r \geq r^*$ choose employment, while those with $r < r^*$ choose self-employment. Hence, the proportion of skilled immigrants who are employed is $\pi^* = 1 - h(r^*)$, where $h(r^*) \equiv G^{-1}(r^*)$. Hence, substituting for π in (6.4) the average wage paid to immigrants is

$$\bar{w} = \frac{\alpha(1 - h(r^*))x + (1 - \alpha)y}{\alpha(1 - h(r^*)) + 1 - \alpha}. \tag{6.5}$$

If $r^* = 0$, all skilled immigrants are employed, and the wage earned by immigrants is the maximum attainable given x, y, and α. And if $r^* = 1$, all skilled immigrants are self-employed, and unskilled workers receive their true product, y. The higher the degree of risk aversion of the marginal skilled employed immigrant, r^*, the lower the mean wage of employed immigrants. In other words, a high value of r^* implies that more skilled immigrants choose self-employment over employment, thereby depressing the equilibrium wage.

The expected indirect utility of an employed immigrant (EI) with risk aversion r_I is therefore given by (using 6.3)

$$V_{EI} = -e^{-\left(\frac{\alpha(1 - h(r_I^*))x + (1 - \alpha)y}{\alpha(1 - h(r_I^*)) + 1 - \alpha}\right)h(r_I^*)} \tag{6.6}$$

and the expected indirect utility of a self-employed, skilled immigrant (SEI) is given by

$$V_{SEI} = -\int_{-a}^{a} e^{-h(r_I^*)(x + \varepsilon + \delta)} f(\varepsilon) d\varepsilon. \tag{6.7}$$

The 'critical risk' aversion is obtained by equating the indirect utilities from these two sources and it applies to all individuals at the margin who are indifferent between the two choices. All those who are distributed with a risk aversion higher than the critical level would be employed, and those distributed below the critical level would be self-employed. Hence, the critical degree of risk aversion is determined by equating V_{EI} and V_{SEI}. The value of r^* for immigrants, r_I^* is implicit in

$$\int_{-a}^{a} e^{-h(r_I^*)(x + \varepsilon + \delta)} f(\varepsilon) d\varepsilon = \exp(-h(r_I^*)) \left(\frac{\alpha(1 - h(r_I^*))x + (1 - \alpha)y}{\alpha(1 - h(r_I^*)) + 1 - \alpha}\right). \tag{6.8}$$

For the skilled natives, the problem is somewhat different in the sense that their skill levels are *known with certainty*. In other words, under symmetric information the employer does not face a problem with interpreting the true skill levels of the natives and offer them wages as per their true productivities. However, the natives who would be self-employed in equilibrium must also face the same random return as in the case of immigrants. Once again, un-skilled natives are excluded from the choice of self-employment.[12] Thus, the critical r for non-immigrants is found by equating the expected utility of a self-employed skilled native worker (*SEN*)

$$V_{SEN} = -\int_{-a}^{a} e^{-h(r_N^*)(x+\varepsilon+\delta)} f(\varepsilon) d\varepsilon \qquad (6.9)$$

and the utility of an employed, skilled, non-immigrant, (*EN*)

$$V_{EN} = -e^{-xh(r_N^*)}. \qquad (6.10)$$

Thus, r_N^* is implicit in

$$\int_{-a}^{a} e^{-h(r_N^*)(x+\varepsilon+\delta)} f(\varepsilon) d\varepsilon = e^{-xh(r_N^*)}. \qquad (6.11)$$

Proposition 6.1: *The presence of asymmetric information in the labour market of the rich country results in a higher 'critical' risk aversion among the immigrants compared to the natives, i.e., $r_I^* > r_N^*$.*

Proof: Unless $r^* = 0$;

$$\frac{\alpha(1-h(r^*))x+(1-\alpha)y}{\alpha(1-h(r^*))+1-\alpha} < x.$$

Now, in order to achieve certainty, a skilled immigrant must allow for a risk premium

$$P_I = \delta + x - \frac{\alpha(1-h(r_I^*))x+(1-\alpha)y}{\alpha(1-h(r_I^*))+1-\alpha}$$

---

[12] Choice of self-employment among the unskilled may be introduced without any change in the direction of the results, and is offered elsewhere in a related context.

whereas, a skilled native worker bears a risk premium

$$P_N = \delta.$$

Hence,

$$P_I > P_N.$$

But, from the work of Arrow-Pratt it is well known that, everything else being equal, willingness to bear a higher risk premium implies greater risk aversion. Hence, the critical value of r_I exceeds the critical value of r_N, i.e., $r_I^* > r_N^*$

Proposition 6.2: *The average income of the immigrants at a point in time exceeds that of the natives, as long as, $r_I^* > r_N^*$, but with a higher temporal variance of income. But the cross-sectional variance of income may be lower if:*

$$\bar{w} < \frac{1}{2 - \alpha h(r_I^*)} \left[\alpha h(r_I^*)(x + \delta) + \sqrt{\alpha \frac{(1 - \alpha)(x - y)^2 + \alpha h^2(r_N^*)\delta^2}{1 - \alpha h(r_I^*)}} \right].$$

Proof: In order to prove Proposition 6.2, we first compare the *average incomes* of the two groups—the immigrants and the natives, based on the results derived. Since $r_I^* > r_N^*$, the proportion of self-employed immigrants $h(r_I^*)$ exceeds the proportion of self-employed native-born, $h(r_N^*)$. The mean income of an immigrant is, therefore,

$$\mu_I = \alpha h(r_I^*)(x + \delta) + (1 - \alpha + (1 - h(r_I^*))\alpha) \frac{\alpha(1 - h(r_I^*))x + (1 - \alpha)y}{\alpha(1 - h(r_I^*)) + 1 - \alpha}$$
$$= \alpha h(r_I^*)(x + \delta) + \alpha(1 - h(r_I^*))x + (1 - \alpha)y = \alpha h(r_I^*)\delta + \alpha x + (1 - \alpha)y$$

whereas the mean income of a native born is

$$\mu_N = \alpha h(r_N^*)(x + \delta) + \alpha(1 - h(r_N^*))x + (1 - \alpha)y = \alpha h(r_N^*)\delta + \alpha x + (1 - \alpha)y$$

so that,

$$\mu_I - \mu_N = \alpha\delta(h(r_I^*) - h(r_N^*)) > 0.$$

Clearly, mean income of the immigrants exceeds the mean income of the native-born individuals.

Next, we argue that the income variance for both immigrants and natives has two components. One of the components, *cross-sectional* variance, is calculated from the income variance of those who are employed in equilibrium as compared to the mean income of the entire population. The other component, *temporal* variance, is the income variance due to self-employment earnings of immigrants and natives.

Hence, the temporal variance of the income of an immigrant is

$$\sigma_I^2 = \alpha^2 h^2(r_I^*)\sigma^2$$

and the temporal variance of the income of a native born is

$$\sigma_N^2 = \alpha^2 h^2(r_N^*)\sigma^2$$

so that, $\sigma_I^2 > \sigma_N^2$.

In contrast, the relative size of cross-sectional variance of the income of an immigrant and a native born is less unambiguous. However, as we define it here, cross-sectional variance for immigrants is

$$\sigma_{CI}^2 = [1 - \alpha + \alpha(1 - h(r_I^*))][\bar{w} - \mu_I]^2$$

whereas, for natives it is

$$\sigma_{CN}^2 = \alpha[x - \mu_N]^2 + (1 - \alpha)[y - \mu_N]^2$$

such that,

$$\sigma_{CI}^2 < \sigma_{CN}^2, \quad iff, \quad \bar{w} < \frac{1}{2 - \alpha h(r_I^*)} \left[\alpha h(r_I^*)(x + \delta) + \sqrt{\alpha \frac{(1 - \alpha)(x - y)^2 + \alpha h^2(r_N^*)\delta^2}{1 - \alpha h(r_I^*)}} \right]. \tag{6.12}$$

The implications one may draw from these results are straightforward and likely to be valid for a wide range of cases involving immigrants and natives in a migrant-receiving country. If the initial disadvantage pushes more skilled migrants into riskier self-employment relative to their native counterparts, there arises a strong possibility of income convergence between the immigrants and natives. However, this may not be possible unless the immigrants are exposed to a higher income volatility compared to natives. These theoretical results, therefore, can be quite useful in generalizing the large number of empirical studies with regard to the income patterns and associated volatilities facing the immigrants. The value addition of the paper is specific in providing a much-needed microeconomic interpretation of the route to faster income assimilation between immigrants and natives.

6.3.1 AN EXAMPLE

Let us provide a specific example to establish that the results obtained are tenable for a wide range of specifications under the standard *von N-M* type utility functions characterized by degrees of risk aversion. In other words, let us begin by assuming that $h(r_j^*) = \begin{cases} r_j^* & j = I, N \ \forall w \neq x \\ 1 & otherwise \end{cases}$, where, w is the total income earned by skilled natives and immigrants. The implications are simple. In the absence of asymmetric information, the workers are not exposed to risk on their choice of employment and would therefore receive their true product in the labour market. Conversely, if some kind of uncertainty in the total income earned exists, then the workers are exposed to certain degrees of critical risk aversion, $r_j^* \in [-\bar{r}^*, \bar{r}^*]$. This would require that we relax the previous limits on the values of (r_I^*, r_N^*).[13] The scaling up of the limit implies that $(r_I^*, r_N^*) \leq \bar{r}^*$ set as the upper limit. With these prerequisites we can proceed to the explicit solutions of the two critical risk aversion levels.

Retaining Equations (6.2)–(6.4), we rewrite Equation (6.5) as

$$\bar{w} = \frac{\alpha(1-r^*)x + (1-\alpha)y}{\alpha(1-r^*) + 1 - \alpha} \tag{6.13}$$

where $\pi^* = 1 - r^*$ is the equilibrium employment of skilled workers. Then substituting (6.13) in (6.6) and reformulating both (6.6) and (6.7) in terms of $h(r_j^*)$, one can find r_I^* explicitly from equating the expected utility of self-employment to that from employment as in Equation (6.15):

$$\int_{-a}^{a} e^{-r_I^*(x+\varepsilon+\delta)} f(\varepsilon)d\varepsilon = e^{-r_I^*\left(\frac{\alpha(1-r_I^*)x + (1-\alpha)y}{\alpha(1-r_I^*)+1-\alpha}\right)}$$

$$\text{or,} \quad \frac{1}{2a}\int_{-a}^{a} e^{-r_I^*(x+\varepsilon+\delta)} d\varepsilon = e^{-r_I^*\left(\frac{\alpha(1-r_I^*)x + (1-\alpha)y}{\alpha(1-r_I^*)+1-\alpha}\right)}. \tag{6.14}$$

Equation (6.14) shows that r_I^* can have two solutions:

$$(6.a) \ r_I^* = 1; \text{ and } (6.b), r_I^* = \frac{(1-\alpha)(x-y)-\delta}{\alpha\delta}, \text{ such that, } r_I^* > 1 \tag{6.15}$$

---

[13] It has been shown in several empirical and experimental exercises that the observed degrees of risk aversion usually varies between -1.5 to $+1.6$.

Now, while comparing the levels of risk aversions across natives and immigrants, the previous results would equally go through even if $r_I^* = 1$. But for sake of generality, we would establish that for $r_I^* = (1-\alpha)(x-y) - \delta/\alpha\delta$, $(r_I^* - r_N^*) > 0$. We first need to obtain a solution for r_N^* in this connection. Equality of (6.8) and (6.9) from earlier, along with the characterization of $h(r_j^*)$, imply that natives employed in equilibrium face $h(r_j^*) = 1$. Substituting this in (6.10), we get,

$$\frac{1}{2a}\int_{-a}^{a} e^{-r_N^*(x+\varepsilon+\delta)}d\varepsilon = e^{-x} \qquad (6.16)$$

which solves for, $r_N^* = (x/x+\delta) < 1$, since, $\delta > 0$.

However, $r_I^* = [(1-\alpha)(x-y) - \delta]/\alpha\delta > 1 \Rightarrow (x-y+\delta) > 0$, which is always true given the initial assumptions. It follows directly

that $r_I^* \dfrac{(1-\alpha)(x-y) - \delta}{\alpha\delta} > 1 > r_N^* = \dfrac{x}{x+\delta}$

The rest of the results in Section (6.3) automatically carry forward:

$\mu_I - \mu_N = \alpha\delta\left(r_I^* - r_N^*\right) > 0$, and it can be directly argued that a higher critical risk aversion among immigrants leads to higher mean income vis-à-vis natives for similar skill composition across the labour force. Thus, despite no *a priori* assumption about preference of risk among natives and immigrants, it turns out that the presence of asymmetric information in the labour market of the migrant receiving country leads to a higher critical risk aversion among immigrants. Higher critical risk aversion in turn is instrumental in raising the average income of immigrants above that earned by the natives, although with a higher temporal variance of income. Indeed, for most v N-M type utility functions with similar arguments these results should hold, but intractability with algebraic solutions may require numerical support in some cases.

6.4 **Concluding Remarks**

This chapter dealt with asymmetric information in the labour market of a migrant-receiving country and its impact on occupational choice. In this set up, we provided an analysis of how the migration flow between a rich country and a poor country evolves in the absence and presence of information between various agents. Subsequently, we showed that asymmetric information shapes occupational pattern in the host country with implications for the source country. In the later portion we offered a number of explanations for why the immigrants tend to be over-represented in the self-employment/ entrepreneurship in a culturally and information-wise distant migrant recipient country. A large number of empirical studies motivate the fact that in typical North-South trade and factor mobility models, the flow of factors generates significant impact on both host and source countries. The occupational choice facing immigrants, as influenced by the lack of information flow, has not been looked into as part of this expansive literature. However, as we showed, who migrates under information asymmetry and what type of jobs and income profile results from such pattern are important elements in the decision-making process in developing countries. It simultaneously determines the availability of skill and conditions for human capital formation in the poorer source countries. This is also borne out in several empirical studies on the occupational and income patterns of migrants, and its impact in the source country. The explanations towards occupational patterns and income distribution in the host country broadly discuss factors such as, discrimination, ethnicity, and cultural lineage of the immigrants when they arrive in the host country.

The idea of asymmetric information that leads to pooling of workers across the entire cohort of mixed skill types helps to show that the immigrant labour of the skilled variety, owing to its initial disadvantage in the labour market, may actually be excluded from the labour market. In this matter, we have been not used *ex ante* distribution of risk aversion across skill types, which some of the earlier papers use. The *a priori* assumption about attitudes towards risk pre-determines who migrates and who becomes self-employed. We argued that such patterns might undergo changes when the workers are drawn from a pool of workers uniformly distributed on a scale of risk aversion. With this pre-condition, one can establish that prevalence of asymmetric information in the labour market can generate a critical level of risk aversion. Individuals who are more risk averse are distributed in the region above the critical risk aversion and those who are less risk-averse are distributed below it. Consequently, the distribution of individuals over occupations, *ex post* determines the average income and cross-sectional income volatility of all individuals of migrant origin. The wage pooling in rich countries pushes more skilled workers to self-employment, because they stand to lose most if employed. On the other hand, the lower skill types find it rewarding to remain in employment as long as at least one high skilled worker remains in employment. This has clear implications for the average income of all migrant workers. Notably, this is not the case with natives in the rich country. The skilled natives receive their true return from the labour market and will not be pushed into self-employment automatically owing to the prevalence of statistical discrimination. Thus, the proportion of immigrants in self-employment exceeds that of natives leading to a higher average income for all immigrants. However, since the income from self-employment is uncertain, the income volatility facing immigrants is also higher than that of the natives.

Clearly, this is not an end in itself. Although we do not derive the conditions for income convergence explicitly, the result implies that *ceteris paribus*, if the average income of immigrants exceeds that of the natives in a particular year, the two income levels would converge over time with the possibility that the immigrants overtake the income level of the natives after some years of residence in the foreign country. This validates our initial claim that the role of asymmetric information is quite crucial in shaping occupational choice among immigrants and that it may culminate in income convergence with the group (natives) that surely has a more advantageous position, information-wise, at the time when the immigrant first arrives.

The analysis leaves out a number of factors in favour of future attention, that may have potential roles in driving these results, such as, access to credit, the role of asymmetric information across other factor markets, training undertaken by migrants in the foreign country, language ability, etc. These ideas have earlier come up for discussion in some empirical papers, although without drawing any explicit relationship with the issue of asymmetric information in the labour market. Furthermore, this bears important implications for potential migrants from developing countries who use the income and related information about previous migrants to decide whether or not to migrate.

■ REFERENCES

Bates, T. (1997). *Race, Self-Employment and Upward Mobility: An Illusive American Dream.* Baltimore and London: The Woodrow Wilson Center Press, Washington DC, and The Johns Hopkins University Press.

Berger, M. and Gabriel, P. (1991). 'Risk Aversion and the Earnings of US Immigrants and Natives'. *Applied Economics* 23 (2): 311–318.

Boadway, R., Marceau, N., Marchand, M., and Vigneault, V. (1998). 'Entrepreneurship, Asymmetric Information and Unemployment'. *International Tax and Public Finance* 5 (3): 307–327.

Bonacich, E. and Modell, J. (1981). *The Economic Basis of Ethnic Solidarity.* Berkeley: University of California Press.

Borjas, G. (1985). 'Assimilation, Changes in Cohort Quality, and the Earnings of Immigrants'. *Journal of Labor Economics* 3 (4): 463–489.

Borjas, G. (1987). 'Self-Selection and the Earnings of Immigrants'. *The American Economic Review* 77 (4): 531–553.

Borjas, G. (2000). 'The Case for Choosing More Skilled Immigrants'. *American Enterprise* 11 (8): 30–31.

Borjas, G. and Bronars, S. G. (1989). 'Consumer Discrimination and Self-Employment'. *Journal of Political Economy* 97 (4): 581–605.

Carliner, G. (1980). 'Wages, Earnings, and Hours of First, Second, and Third Generation American Males'. *Economic Inquiry* 18 (1): 87–102.

Chau, N. H. and Stark, O. (1999). 'Migration Under Asymmetric Information and Human Capital Formation'. *Review of International Economics* 7 (3): 455–483.

Chiswick, B. (1978). 'The Effect of Americanization on the Earnings of the Foreign-Born Men'. *Journal of Political Economy* 86 (5): 877–921.

Clark, K. and Drinkwater, S. (2000). 'Pushed Out or Pulled In? Self-Employment Among Ethnic Minorities in England and Wales'. *Labour Economics* 7: 603–628.

Coate, S. and Tennyson, S. (1992). 'Labor Market Discrimination, Imperfect Information and Self-Employment'. *Oxford Economic Papers* 44 (2): 272–288.

De Wit, G. (1993). *Determinants of Self-Employment: Studies in Contemporary Economics Series*. Heidelberg: Physica-Verlag.

Duleep, H. O. and Regets, M. (1999). 'Immigrants and Human-Capital Investment'. *The American Economic Review* 89 (2): 186–191.

Duleep, H. O. and Regets, M. (1997). 'The Decline in Immigrant Entry Earnings: Less Transferable Skills or Lower Ability?' *Quarterly Review of Economics and Finance* 37 (Supplement 1): 189–208 (Special Issue).

Dustmann, C. and Fabbri, F. (2003). 'Language Proficiency and Labour Market Performance of Immigrants in the UK'. *Economic Journal* 113 (489): 695–717.

Fairlie, R. W. (1996). *Ethnic and Racial Entrepreneurship: A Study of Historical and Contemporary Differences*. NY and London: Garland Publishing, Inc.

Fairlie, R. and Meyer, B. (1996). 'Ethnic and Racial Self-Employment Differences and Possible Explanations'. *The Journal of Human Resources* 31 (4): 757–793.

Funkhouser, E. and Trejo, S. (1995). 'The Labor Market Skills of Recent Male Immigrants: Evidence From the Current Population Surveys'. *Industrial and Labor Relations Review* 48: 792–811.

Kar, S. (2009). 'International Labor Migration, Asymmetric Information and Occupational Choice'. *Trade and Development Review* 2 (1): 34–48.

Kar, S. and Guha-Khasnobis, B. (2006). 'Foreign Capital, Skill Formation, and Migration of Skilled Workers'. *Journal of Policy Reform* 9 (2): 107–123.

Kar, S. and Saha, B. (2011). 'Asymmetric Information in the Labour Market, Contract Menu and Self-Employment (with Bibhas Saha)'. IZA Discussion Paper 5508, Bonn.

Kar, S. and Saha, B. C. (2011). 'Asymmetric Information in the Labor Market, Immigrants and Contract Menu'. IZA DP No. 5508, Bonn.

Katz, E. and Stark, O. (1984). 'On Migration in the Presence of Asymmetric Information'. *American Economic Review* 74 (3): 533–534.

Katz, E. and Stark, O. (1986). 'Labor Mobility Under Asymmetric Information With Moving and Signalling Costs'. *Economics Letters* 21 (1): 89–94.

Katz, E. and Stark, O. (1987). 'International Migration Under Asymmetric Information'. *Economic Journal* 97 (387): 718–726.

Katz, E. and Stark, O. (1989). 'International Labour Migration Under Alternative Informational Regimes: A Diagrammatic Analysis'. *European Economic Review* 33 (1): 127–142.

Kidd, M. (1993). Immigrant Wage Differentials and the Role of Self-Employment in Australia. *Australian Economic Papers* 32: 92–115.

LaLonde, R. and Topel, R. (1992). 'The Assimilation of Immigrants in the US Labor Market'. In: G. Borjas and R. Freeman (eds). *Immigration and the Work Force: Economic Consequences for the United States and Source Areas*, pp. 55–89. Chicago: University of Chicago Press.

Li, P. (1997). 'Self-Employment Among Visible Minority Immigrants, White Immigrants, and Native Born Persons in Secondary and Tertiary Industries of Canada'. *Canadian Journal of Regional Science* 20 (1–2): 103–117.

Light, I. (1984). 'Immigrant Entrepreneurs in America: Koreans in Los Angeles'. In: *Clamor at the Gates: The New American Immigration*. San Francisco: ICS Press.

Lofstrom, M. (2002). 'Labor Market Assimilation and the Self-Employment Decision of Immigrant Entrepreneurs'. *Journal of Population Economics* 15 (1): 83–114.

Lucas, R. (1978). 'On the Size Distribution of Business Firms'. *Bell Journal of Economics* 9 (2): 508–523.

Moore, R. L. (1983). 'Employer Discrimination: Evidence From Self-Employed Workers'. *The Review of Economics and Statistics* 6 (3): 496–501.

Razin, E. (1992). 'Paths to Ownership of Small Business Among Immigrants in Israeli Cities and Towns'. *The Review of Regional Studies* 22 (3): 277–296.

Stark, O. (1991). *The Migration of Labour*. Oxford: Basil Blackwell.

Waldinger, R., Aldrich, H., Ward, R., and associates (1990). *Ethnic entrepreneurs: Immigrant Business in Industrial Society*. Newbury Park, CA: Sage.

Wesselingh, I. (2010). 'Romania's Doctors Leaving the Country: One in Seven Emigrate for Better Conditions'. *The Gazette*, Montreal, December 26.

Yuengert, A. M. (1991). 'Self-Employment and the Earnings of Male Immigrants in the US'. Federal Reserve Bank of New York Research Paper 9105.

Yuengert, A. M. (1995). 'Testing Hypotheses of Immigrant Self-Employment'. *The Journal of Human Resources* 30 (1): 194–204.

7 Trade, Foreign Aid, and Welfare

7.1 Introduction

The study of international income transfers has received a great deal of attention in the theory of international trade. Several papers by Bhagwati (1970, 1971); Brecher and Bhagwati (1981, 1982); Hatzipanayotou and Michael (1995); Lahiri et al. (2002, 2000) offer a brief glimpse of the expanse of this topic covering a long period of time. The papers provide accounts of the relationship between foreign aid and its implications for both the sending countries and the recipient countries. Not surprisingly, a lion's share of the research on foreign aid concentrates on its empirical relevance and scope in developing countries. A major concern, among a host of other issues it seems, is whether foreign aid has strong implications for growth and development and subsequently for reduction of poverty and inequality. Arguably, an important channel through which the foreign aid affects per capita consumption is improvement in infrastructure that has the potential to affect growth and development of a country translating the same into higher income. Japanese foreign aid, for example, is particularly well known for supporting infrastructure development in many developing countries. However, infrastructure aid is only one aspect in this expansive and complex literature.

The extant literature on income transfers between countries is broadly characterized by three main assumptions or limitations. First, trade policies of both countries are assumed exogenous. Second, the donor and the recipient countries do not behave optimally with respect to the transfer, i.e. the transfer is also exogenous. And third, when transfers are assumed to be part of a contract that tie up the use of aid to some policy variables, details of such contracts are not optimally chosen by the donor country (Lahiri et al., 2002). In other words, the tying rule at the bilateral level is usually exogenous.

Now, in order to lend the proper perspective to the details of the implications of foreign aid, one must begin by comprehending the plethora of reasons why countries give aid. For some donor countries, altruism could be the

Table 7.1 Total Bilateral Aid to All Sectors in Developing Countries [Current Prices, USD millions]

Years	All Donors Total	DAC Countries Total	Non-DAC Countries, Total	Multilateral, Total
2002	62030.04	40999.75	3152.43	17877.86
2003	71742.35	50076.21	3552.15	18113.99
2004	80120.85	54714.61	3123.90	22282.34
2005	108649.80	82979.77	2924.43	22745.64
2006	107338.60	77373.93	4463.50	25501.20
2007	108491.90	73496.76	5551.00	29444.17
2008	127916.70	86958.68	8190.76	32767.27
2009	126977.20	83801.63	5454.05	37721.54
2010	131685.70	90849.22	5409.23	35427.22
2011	141196.80	94183.58	7887.31	39125.94
Percentage change between 2002 and 2011	127.62	129.71	150.19	118.85

Source: OECD: International Development Statistics, Paris.

main motive, and for some others, political alliances and benefits to be received from it may be significant determinants. However, there is also evidence that in many cases, economic self-interest has been a major reason for income transfers, particularly after the end of the cold war. As far as economic self-interest goes, the existing literature is not well equipped for analysing why some countries give aid, why some countries receive aid, and how the amounts of aid and the tying rules are chosen. Apart from these, the well-known paradoxes on welfare related to bilateral transfer of aid require convincing empirical support as well. As aggregate data suggests, the total bilateral aid to all sectors in developing countries from all donors taken together has more than doubled between 2002 and 2011 (Table 7.1), despite serious economic downturns in many OECD countries. The rise in the volume of aid between 2002 and 2011 is symmetrical for the Development Assistance Committee (DAC) (129.71%, DAC, OECD)[1] as well as the non-DAC countries (150.19%). The rise in aid to African countries has also risen by 150% between 2002 and 2011 (Table 7.2). The flow of aid to Asian countries doubled between 2002 and 2008 and then started falling, and for the South American countries the rate of growth has been less than 100% during the same time. It should be interesting to note that between 2002 and 2011, the foreign direct investment (private) flowing from DAC countries to all developing countries has risen by 494.37% (Table 7.3). Countries like Australia and Denmark switched from

[1] The Development Assistance Committee (DAC) is a forum under the Organisation for Economic Cooperation and Development, comprising selected member states to discuss issues surrounding aid, development, and poverty reduction in developing countries.

Table 7.2 Total Bilateral Aid to All Sectors [Current Prices (USD millions)]

Destinations /Years	2002	2003	2004	2005	2006	2007	2008	2009	2010	2011	Average
All Developing Countries	62030.04	71742.35	80120.85	108649.80	107338.60	108491.90	127916.70	126977.20	131685.70	141196.8	106615.00
Africa, Total	21397.28	27444.89	30002.32	35833.29	44568.44	39546.34	45172.63	47807.62	47976.13	51736.67	39148.56
Africa—North of Sahara, Total	2105.32	2239.54	3172.70	2665.12	2854.62	3373.58	4223.83	2992.16	2597.65	4048.37	3027.28
Africa—South of Sahara, Total	18820.23	24694.00	26221.94	32415.46	40869.21	34719.92	39627.43	42465.41	43805.06	45669.62	34930.80
America, Total	5022.91	6128.76	6838.49	6707.94	7340.30	6983.83	9287.90	9021.75	11295.68	11537.74	8016.53
North & Central America, Total	2307.10	2576.20	3437.18	3270.90	3497.16	3483.82	4321.80	4352.15	6871.72	5942.69	4006.07
South America, Total	2371.16	3166.71	2938.28	2854.95	3321.90	2940.24	3754.34	3773.29	3082.47	4270.49	3247.38
Asia, Total	19163.63	20705.27	23249.34	46635.25	33080.37	36883.56	44220.06	38168.74	36734.15	37877.05	33671.70
Middle East, Total	2641.05	6070.03	7620.04	25512.02	14203.38	14517.69	19913.74	10378.09	9488.02	11365.99	12171.01
South & Central Asia, Total	8838.27	8117.88	9340.20	11655.11	11429.96	14089.81	15981.01	18464.19	18636.44	20101.29	13665.42
Far East Asia, Total	6531.73	6266.71	6006.41	8391.40	6526.44	7286.12	7019.23	8248.81	7498.12	5247.66	6902.26
Europe, Total	5064.08	3554.96	3626.87	4061.82	5082.40	4333.86	5376.93	5740.91	5855.28	8866.41	5156.45
Oceania, Total	714.07	817.25	938.52	1160.56	1199.15	1308.86	1533.03	1560.03	2018.20	2222.74	1347.24
Developing Countries, Unspecified	10668.07	13091.22	15465.31	14250.98	16067.97	19435.48	22326.16	24678.17	27805.23	28956.22	19274.48

Source: OECD: International Development Statistics, Paris.

Table 7.3 Total Direct Investments—Private Current Prices (USD Million)

Sources /Years	2002	2003	2004	2005	2006	2007	2008	2009	2010	2011	Average
DAC Countries Total	36705.33	51080.58	79269.87	103947.60	135271.90	185059.30	187013.20	116189.30	179317.00	218169.10	129202.30
Australia	-102.87	239.00	506.00	1588.21	4967.95	2366.97	1673.00	..	4444.40	4218.84	2211.278
Austria	1073.21	764.94	923.59	2711.98	1852.60	15654.12	7061.36	2550.60	5664.44	5174.04	4343.088
Belgium	554.78	..	-169.40	1422.21	3533.33	1487.99	1617.06	3.31	4789.78	-2134.29	1233.863
Canada	828.50	2625.50	3613.25	6647.12	7716.86	7932.03	14872.14	6603.76	11257.16	4554.82	6665.114
Denmark	-63.41	106.44	517.73	33.36	454.32	2241.59	2302.86	598.52	1778.79	-354.45	761.575
Finland	16.02	77.61	600.07	149.14	401.66	10.95	-31.73	790.97	2378.81	-1067.85	332.565
France	2914.90	681.28	1534.35	6855.58	10588.87	14336.76	24608.94	16300.32	6666.53	15717.46	10020.50
Germany	323.60	1908.41	6760.75	14068.85	10794.91	11639.84	12002.11	12941.25	21991.02	29875.11	12230.59
Greece	40.33	33.24	-13.71	324.63	2453.70	2880.36	459.83	241.26	242.53	59.84	672.201
Italy	639.08	505.15	807.77	950.89	1151.42	1353.44	1544.02	128.55	4365.58	7529.65	1897.555
Japan	6361.77	7015.78	9171.12	14472.24	14143.81	18037.03	25709.79	19439.83	21649.81	40315.26	17631.64
Korea	1049.92	1740.16	2368.83	3325.88	4934.29	9826.85	7863.43	5018.03	8711.72	8343.32	5318.243
Netherlands	281.00	3448.14	1986.40	2347.70	6350.59	-1028.06	-24523.30	540.31	8789.40	4787.26	297.945
New Zealand	17.23	21.42	24.82	25.98	23.97	26.23	29.06	24.39	26.43	28.47	24.80
Norway	22.87	1198.50	635.04	1846.81	2514.63	2638.00	-246.46	891.97	1504.01	..	1222.819
Portugal	-359.68	679.64	186.76	555.90	43.54	1549.81	341.00	-2270.72	-1225.05	-705.41	-120.421
Spain	6539.56	4737.08	10502.81	4158.46	7607.76	16625.68	23333.90	6294.48	4703.90	15981.89	10048.55
Sweden	296.43	-337.12	593.78	429.76	333.36	2232.18	-313.65	884.95	69.38	1369.27	555.834
Switzerland	590.88	1592.15	272.55	7451.00	11250.01	4677.50	10754.57	5317.37	20365.94	8724.41	7099.638
United Kingdom	2753.21	9745.26	18092.36	14811.85	7530.36	24978.99	23783.25	11615.12	188.42	33039.44	14653.83
United States	12928.00	14298.00	20355.00	19770.00	36624.00	45591.00	54172.00	28275.00	50954.00	42712.00	32567.90

Source: OECD: International Development Statistics, Paris.

Table 7.4 Percentage of GDP Committed to Foreign Aid in Developed Countries

	Country	Percentage of GDP to Aid
1	Sweden	0.99
2	Norway	0.88
3	Denmark	0.82
4	Netherlands	0.80
5	Belgium	0.50
6	United Kingdom	0.48
7	Ireland	0.43
8	Finland	0.43
9	Spain	0.43
10	Switzerland	0.42
11	Austria	0.42
12	Germany	0.38
13	France	0.38
14	Canada	0.32
15	Australia	0.29
16	New Zealand	0.27
17	Portugal	0.25
18	Italy	0.21
19	Greece	0.20
20	Japan	0.20
21	United States	0.19

Source: OECD: Development Assistance Committee, 2012.

being destinations of FDI to becoming sources, although the latter, similarly as Belgium, Finland, and Portugal, have once again become locations for investment. The other OECD countries have, however, contributed steadily to FDI flows to the developing world in addition to aid. Table 7.4 provides statistics for 2012, showing countries that commit a significant portion of their GDP to aid. We discussed related issues on the role of FDI in Chapter 4.

Table 7.3 offers some interesting phenomena. It shows that the FDI outflow from the UK has generally been through a rollercoaster ride. If isolated time points between 2002 and 2011 are considered, the growth in FDI has been 1100%. But, it does not reflect that the FDI took a nosedive from US$11615.12 million to merely US$188.42 million in 2010 during the peak of the financial crisis. The next year, it went up to US$33039.44 million, recording an astronomical percentage growth for one year. The average between 2002 and 2011 has been US$14653.83 million. On the other hand, the US FDI was at US$50954 million during 2010 and went down in 2011. The aggregate trends, however, do not provide adequate information to look into the relationship between foreign aid and FDI for a particular country. Beladi and Oladi (2007) earlier argued that foreign aid crowds out foreign direct investment if aid is used for purchasing a public consumption good, and that the import-competing sector is more capital-intensive than the public goods sector. This result may find some empirical support in Easterly (2003), which generally suggests that the financing-gap approach of foreign aid would prove to be a failure in the long run. It shows, for example, that Zambia received a total aid of $2 billion, which seemingly should have put Zambia among the industrialized countries of the world with a per capita income of $20,000. Instead, Zambia's per capita income was found to be $600, primarily because Zambia's investment went down as foreign aid flooded the capital market. Similarly, the growth rates in countries like Guinea-Bissau, Guyana, Chad, Mauritius, Mozambique, and Zimbabwe were lower than predicted.

This chapter offers a survey of some of the influential pieces on foreign aid including what we consider as an important analytical framework capable of inciting further research on trade-aid interactions. Section 7.2 deals with various (often anachronous) developments in theory and empirics of foreign aid. In the process, we borrow from rich analytical contributions, as per relevance to the matter at hand. Section 7.3 discusses foreign aid and related issues, in particular aid and governance, in the host country. Section 7.4 concludes.

7.2 **The Analytical Dimensions of Foreign Aid**

The early concept of foreign aid emerged after World War II primarily as a manifestation of the Marshall Plan. Reinstating war-devastated countries back into normalcy and eventually onto the pre-war growth path was an important welfare agenda. Pure income transfers to facilitate production and consumption in Europe as well as in the developing world just freed from centuries of colonial rules seemed a good way during the regime of peace that followed. Note however, that the subject of foreign aid has been studied since the 1920s. The most famous discussion on this topic was the exchange in *The Economic Journal* between Keynes and Ohlin in 1929. But earlier, Hume, Smith, Ricardo, and Mill had already discussed the effects of international transfers. The early debates essentially centred on the war reparation payments, with focus on the analysis of terms of trade effects or exchange rate effects. In fact, following the Keynes-Ohlin debate, the modern literature began focusing on the welfare effects of transfer.

The modern era on the issue of aid began to surface in the nineteenth and twentieth centuries, as the western powers considered income transfers to their colonies and to other poor countries. In Great Britain, the Colonial Development Act 1929 was the result of a long process of moving from a *laissez-faire* type of economic operation to restricted assistance. In the years 1940 and 1945, the Colonial Development and Welfare Acts went further, included education, and allowed recurrent costs to be paid for under the provision of the Acts. The 1948 Overseas Resources Development Act set up the Colonial Development Corporation.

Note that, 'tied aid' was a key feature of the British development assistance. It was also true of the American aid in the 1930s and 1940s, made to the Latin American countries under the 'Good Neighbour Policy' of the Roosevelt administration. In fact, as early as 1812, the Congress passed an Act for the Relief of the Citizens of Venezuela, and from the late nineteenth century onwards, food surpluses began to be deployed for tied aid (Hjertholm and White, 2000). However, the two major events that marked the official beginning of the *foreign aid era* were the Marshall Plan and the setting up of the United Nations, along with the signing of the Bretton Woods agreement that set up the IMF and the World Bank. The Marshall Plan and the World Bank (formerly, the International Bank for Reconstruction and Development) subsequently set up the priority reconstruction of war-ravaged Europe. During this time, the inaugural speech made by the US President Harry S. Truman in 1949 stated, among other things, 'making the benefits of our scientific advances and industrial progress available for the improvement and growth of the underdeveloped countries' (Woolley and Peters, 1999). During the 1950s, the Act of International Development was passed in the US.

7.2.1 TYPES OF FOREIGN AID

The Historical Factors

History has played an important role in determining the savings rate in respective countries, and it is important to discuss it in this context because the emergence of the well-known two-gap models of development depends crucially on the savings patterns of a country. Some economies had always been high savers, such as Japan. Religious, ideological, and cultural factors also played an important role in shaping a thrifty or an extravagant society. On the other hand, the history of inflation and political insurgencies in a country might, as equally potent sources, lead to low savings. The consequently low rate of investment and dependence on foreign aid to sustain consumption, therefore, stands at the core of various possible relationships. Obstfeld (1999) added foreign aid to the Ramsey-Cass-Coopmans optimal growth model and predicted some positive impact of foreign aid on domestic investment. Besides, Gong and Zhou (2000, 2001) discussed the effects of different foreign aid programmes on economic growth and considered an infinitely lived, representative agent model that follows Uzawa's endogenous time preference. The representative agent's subjective discount rate depends negatively on the utility level and the current utility is an increasing function of income. Foreign aid raises the agent's income and increases his/her consumption. This reduces the agent's subjective discount rate and makes him/her less patient, reducing savings and capital stock as a consequence. Thus, a permanent increase in foreign aid leads to a reduction in the long-run capital accumulation, a rise in domestic consumption, and an increase in foreign borrowing.

Cui and Gong (2006), however, offer a theory that is consistent with the positive association between foreign aid and savings and investment, as many recent empirical findings display. An open economy, in which households with a given amount of foreign aid maximize discounted instantaneous utilities over an infinite horizon, faces an increase in long run capital accumulation, a reduction in domestic consumption, and a decrease in foreign borrowing if it anticipates a permanent increase in foreign aid. The analysis is based on the Marshallian agent's subjective rate of time preference—the act of saving could increase utility by increasing the quality of future consumption.

Now, foreign aid is mainly a voluntary transfer of resources from one country to another. There are mainly two broad categories of aid, namely, the *humanitarian aid* and the *development aid*. Humanitarian aid is the aid given in the times of distress, i.e. after wars or natural calamities. Development aid aims at raising the growth level of the economy and alleviates poverty in the long run. The main objective, as claimed by the donors, was to create a thriving economic environment that fosters development and socio-economic improvement in the poorer countries.

However, foreign aid can also have very specific objectives. For example, *project aid* is given for a specific purpose such as, the purchase of building materials for new schools. *Programme aid* is given to a specific sector, say, for funding the education sector of a country. If it is 'tied' aid, it has to be used to purchase products from the donor country or a specified group of countries. On the other hand, the recipients can spend 'untied' aid using their own discretion.

Interestingly, foreign aid may also take the form of soft loans and hard loans. Soft loans are meant to impose lower interest rates or longer repayment periods than would be available in the private international markets. Hard loans, on the other hand, are given on commercial terms. Apart from these, foreign aid also includes outright grants. In fact, certain types of foreign aid given on concessional terms are often called the Official Development Assistance (ODA). Furthermore, bilateral and multilateral aid with country-specific conditions and modalities is also made available to a number of developing and transition countries. Bilateral aid refers to that given directly by one government to another, whereas multilateral aid refers to the funds that flow from the governments to the international agencies such as the United Nations, the World Bank, and the regional development banks.

7.2.2 MACROECONOMIC AND GENERALIZED IMPLICATIONS OF FOREIGN AID

The macroeconomic implications of foreign aid mainly include the effects on savings, investment, and growth rates of an economy. The literature on evaluating the impact of foreign aid on growth, savings, and investment has been available for a long time (White, 1992). The aid-growth literature was mainly connected to the larger development debates of the time, including the savings-investment puzzles of the 1960s and 1970s. White (1992) suggests that the failure of the literature might have been due to the fact that as the aid-development discussion subsided after these decades, and further explorations into various implications of foreign aid was also lost in oblivion.

The major models adopted by the IMF and the World Bank for pursuing the case of foreign aid, however, are still based on the Harrod-Domar and the two-gap model of aid even though the models are outdated in the academic literature (Easterly, 2003). The series of external shocks at the beginning of the 1980s (worsening of the terms of trade faced by most LDCs, partly because of the second oil price shock, higher real interest rates, the slowdown in growth, lower demand from the developed countries, and the onset of the debt crisis) forced the macroeconomic issues back into the heart of development debate. The Harrod-Domar model was based on the view that an increase in one unit of foreign aid will result in an increase of one unit of savings, which will translate into higher growth. Easterly (2003), on the other hand, tested the two-gap model of aid and found some interesting results. The rationale behind the two-gap model was that the developing countries suffer from foreign exchange crisis and fall into a vicious circle. The economy can use the foreign exchange to import either capital or consumer goods, while devoting domestic resources to the production of consumer and capital goods. Hence, foreign exchange is needed to supplement savings. Thus, the dual-gap model of foreign aid led to the well-known debate on savings in LDCs. Colman and Nixon (1994) showed that if savings are also a function of aid and income, then the negative relationship between savings and foreign aid vanishes and thus we have the positive relationship between foreign aid and investment. Studies by Areskoug (1969, 1973), Weisskopf (1972), and Chenery and Eckstein (1970) also confirmed the negative relationship between savings and aid.

As briefly argued earlier, it is empirically substantiated that countries facing falling terms of trade depend on foreign aid to sustain themselves. Smaller countries like Colombia or Ghana, which depended on exports of coffee and cocoa, experienced a reduction in their terms of trade when such exports declined. Thus, they had to increase the foreign inflows, and low savings rates were associated with high foreign inflows. More generally, it seems that the predominantly agrarian economies are in fact more dependent on foreign aid.

In a monsoon dependent economy with 50% of GDP coming from agriculture, two years of bad harvest can reduce savings and subsequently growth rates for the following three or four years. During this time, the foreign exchange reserves are likely to be used, with the foreign borrowing and foreign aid both expected to increase.

Generalized Welfare Impact of Foreign Aid

Kanbur (2003) suggested that the development policy debates regarding foreign aid should focus largely on the unconditional and conditional transfers. The literature based on unconditional transfers is trade-theoretic in nature, vis-à-vis studies on conditional transfers typically using contract theory structures. If the transfer is small, and if it does not perturb the equilibrium prices from the first best competitive framework, then the transfer makes the donor worse off and the recipient better off. However, then the question arises as to why the donor would ever make such a transfer. The donor's utility function might include the well-being of the recipient and there might be economies of scale in transfers.

Based on these classifications, foreign aid and the welfare impacts considered the generalized as well as the non-generalized structures. Keynes had considered the German reparation payments after World War I and found that Germany was not only burdened by the reparation payments but also, due to an indirect decrease in the terms of trade, was establishing an orthodox view suggesting that the donor country's terms of trade deteriorates due to transfer. Samuelson (1952) argued that the orthodox view could also be established when there are trade impediments like tariffs or transportation costs. Jones (1975) on the other hand, suggested a variety of cases where an income transfer might actually improve the donor country's terms of trade, providing the anti-orthodox view.

These results seemingly qualify (or disqualify) results in Leontief (1936), where the transfer was welfare immiserizing for the recipient country and welfare enriching for the donor. Samuelson (1947) argued that the 'paradoxical' welfare effect is consistent only with market instability. Following it, a large number of studies were carried out to show that Leontief's result could also arise in the case of market stability.

In 1960, Johnson discussed the possibility of the immiserizing growth in the context of the two factor income classes (capital and labour) in an open economy, where the donor and the recipient are completely specialized in the ownership of a single different commodity or factor. The departure from the two-agent competitive framework in the presence of no other distortions was later invoked by Gale (1974) analysing a three-agent model using fixed coefficients in consumption and a given endowment of goods. Diamond (1978) considered the welfare impact of the transfers when price distortion exists in the economy with convex technology, and the comparative-static results are consistent with the paradoxes.

With these developments in place, finally, Bhagwati and Brecher (1978) pioneered the three-agent model of aid and thereby started a huge literature discussing the welfare impact of aid. Their paper divides the recipient country into a set of foreign factors and also a set of national factors, and the conditions for immiserizing growth were extremely compatible with market stability. In the same vein, Chichilnisky (1980) commented on the paradoxical theorem and asserted that even when the world equilibrium is Walras-stable, transfer of commodities or aid results in a decline in the welfare of the nations.

Bhagwati, Brecher, and Hatta (1983) later derived precise conditions to show that immiserizing transfers from abroad in the presence of market stability can arise only if there is a distortion characterizing the economy in question. The study is a three-country extension of Brecher and Bhagwati (1982), which argued that transfers can be immiserizing for the recipient in the presence of a production distortion when the recipient's overproduced good is inferior in the donor's consumption. Price distortions driving a wedge between consumption and production prices as in Diamond (1978) and Hatta (1973) could also result in immiserizing effects for the recipient. The richness of the paradoxical results, in fact, demands a more rigorous treatment in this chapter. We borrow from Bhagwati, Brecher, and Hatta (1983) to discuss the welfare impact of transfers for the recipient when one of the three countries entertained in this model does not take part in the transfer process. Assuming that three countries, denoted by A, B, and C, consume and trade two commodities, X and Y, given a relative price q, the country's social utility/welfare level as u^i, $i = A$, B, and C, transfer T of aid (in terms of good Y), expenditure function of country i, $e^i(q, u^i)$; revenue function, $r^i(q)$ and the income compensated import-demand function, $x^i(q, u^i)$. These specifications help to define the overspending function of country i as: $\sigma^i(q, u^i) = e^i(q, u^i) - r^i(q)$. The expression means that a country generating more producers' revenue (compared to its expenditure) at the relative price shall be able to make transfers to other countries. In fact, if country A makes a transfer as donor (valued in terms of good Y) to C, as recipient, while B watches passively (its expenditure equal to revenue), the following set of equations reflect the three-country equilibrium ensuring market clearing conditions in both markets via the satisfaction of Walras Law:

$$\sigma^A(q, u^A) + T = 0 \tag{7.1}$$

$$\sigma^B(q, u^B) = 0 \tag{7.2}$$

$$\sigma^C(q, u^A) - T = 0 \tag{7.3}$$

and
$$x^A(q,u^A)+x^B(q,u^B)+x^C(q,u^C)=0. \tag{7.4}$$

Using (7.1)–(7.4), obtain the impact of a transfer T on (q,u^i). Thus, differentiating the four equations (7.1) to (7.4), under the initial assumption that, $\delta e^A / \delta u^A = \delta e^B / \delta u^B = \delta e^C / \delta u^C = 1$, while $x_q \equiv \delta x^A / \delta q + \delta x^B / \delta q + \delta x^C / \delta q$, and using $(\delta \sigma^i / \delta q = x^i)$ we rearrange to get:

$$\begin{bmatrix} 1 & 0 & 0 & x^A \\ 0 & 1 & 0 & x^B \\ 0 & 0 & 1 & x^C \\ x_U^A & x_U^B & x_U^C & x_q \end{bmatrix} \begin{bmatrix} du^A \\ du^B \\ du^C \\ dq \end{bmatrix} = \begin{bmatrix} -1 \\ 0 \\ 1 \\ 0 \end{bmatrix} dT. \tag{7.5}$$

Application of Cramer's rule and Equation (7.4) solves for the variables in (7.5), where, $\Delta = (x^A x_U^A + x^B x_U^B + x^C x_U^C - x_q)$. Defining $u^A = v^A(q,T)$; $u^B = v^B(q)$ and $u^C = v^C(q,T)$, and rewriting the world uncompensated excess demand function for x as $\tilde{x}(q,T) = x^A(q,v^A(q,T)) + x^B(q,v^B(q)) + x^C(q,v^C(q,T))$, the partial with respect to q is given by $\tilde{x}_q = x_q^A + x_U^A v_q^A + x_q^B + x_U^B v_q^B + x_q^C + x_U^C v_q^C$. This transforms to $\tilde{x}_q = x_q - x_U^A x^A - x_U^B x^B - x_U^C x^C \equiv -\Delta$, or the negative of the world excess demand for commodity x. Therefore,

$$\frac{du^A}{dT} = \frac{\left[x_q - x^B(x_U^B - x_U^C)\right]}{\Delta} \tag{7.6}$$

$$\frac{du^B}{dT} = \frac{\left[x^B(x_U^A - x_U^C)\right]}{\Delta} \tag{7.7}$$

$$\frac{du^C}{dT} = -\frac{\left[x_q - x^B x_U^B - x_U^A(x^C + x^A)\right]}{\Delta} = -\frac{\left[x_q - x^B(x_U^B - x_U^A)\right]}{\Delta} \tag{7.8}$$

and finally,
$$\frac{dq}{dT} = -\frac{\left[(x_U^A - x_U^C)\right]}{\Delta}. \tag{7.9}$$

Since $du^B / dT = -x^B dq / dT$, therefore $du^B / dT > 0$ if and only if $dq / dT < 0$. In other words, if the relative price of the export good rises in the non-participating country, its welfare rises also. Now, we focus specifically on the donor and recipient, wherein, it is shown from (7.6) that, $du^A / dT = x_q / \Delta < 0$, if $x^B = 0$ and / or $(x_U^B - x_U^C) = 0$. Thus, if the net trade in x for country B is zero or if the marginal propensity to consume x in B and C are identical, the donor suffers loss in welfare since $x_q < 0$, $\Delta > 0$. Conversely, $du^C / dT = -x_q / \Delta > 0$ under symmetric conditions such that the recipient's welfare goes up. But, this is not paradoxical, which may however result, if $[x^B(x_U^B - x_U^C)] < 0$ holds as a necessary condition for the donor in (7.6) and $[x^B(x_U^B - x_U^A)] < 0$ for the recipient in (7.8). A transfer from the donor would then improve its welfare and reduce the same in the recipient country, as long as x_q is not sufficiently negative in either case. Bhagwati, Brecher, and Hatta (1983, also see 1985) argue that despite the apparent non-existence of any distortion in the three-country transfer paradox, the absence of optimal tariff essentially allows in foreign distortion as already identified by Bhagwati (1971). The study suggested that the bilateral transfer of aid could be frustrating in the presence of such paradoxes, and that the internal transfers between the rich and poor could also be complicated and lead to paradoxical results if the non-targeted outside group is a net exporter of food while the rich has a lower marginal propensity to consume food than the poor. All of these results are further extended to discuss alternative conditions for the paradox to hold.

Note that, the effect of foreign aid on growth and development of a country could in many other cases lead to perverse outcomes, since the motives behind foreign aid (unlike the well-meaning transfer of Y in the earlier example or food aid to poor countries) do not necessarily correspond to accelerating economic growth. Krueger (1986) observes that aid may be given when donors wish to enhance military prowess in the targeted country, which might pay back commercially through arms and ammunition trade; 'to support a friendly government in power and to acquire goodwill now in the expectation that it will be politically valuable later' (p. 58). Consequently, the welfare impact of aid could be diminished (and may even be perverse) if the motives behind aid are unrelated to growth objectives. For example, if aid influences greater defence-related expenditures—many of the developing countries are perennially in the state of conflict—development expenditures on schooling and health could be the first casualties. The relationship between aid and development in this case, would be very different from the Harrod-Domar type capacity-enhancing models that explained the success of the Marshall Plan in the late 1940s and 1950s. Similarly for poor countries, it was believed, aid shall help investments in physical capital in order to bridge the investment gap. While such altruistic (see Lahiri and Raimondos-Moller, 1997) and 'humanitarian' motives behind foreign aid had their presence in the literature strongly felt, inquiries into narrowly defined self-interest of donors could hardly be subdued. Thus, a natural follow through (see Krueger, 1986) has been to enquire whether official flows (complying or not complying with the terms and conditions of the market) can improve the global, meaning the donor and the recipient, welfare. If aid leads to global efficiency gains, the economic logic behind aid would at least help the transfer process endure other possible criticisms.

Krueger (1986) finds that the answer to this question lies with the imperfections in the international capital market, whereby private capital flows fail to equalize risk-adjusted returns between developed (donor) and developing (recipient) countries. If returns to capital in capital-scarce developing countries are higher, then official flows are expected to raise welfare in both. With the support of the official flows, the recipient would enter a higher income path and also service debt, while the donor may earn more than comparable assets. Of course, it raises the domestic return to capital and if supply responds adequately, then investments and subsequently growth should not be thwarted. The logic is further strengthened when the incapacity of trade to equalize factor returns in the absence of factor mobility is now empirically verified. In fact, it is well known that the Heckscher-Ohlin theorem and subsequently the Stolper-Samuelson and Rybczynski theorem, all require stringent assumptions regarding market structures, production, and consumption specifications that often do not satisfy the requirements for factor price equalization in the real world. Conversely, if aid permits incremental investments with returns at least as high as that in the donor country and that aid does not negatively influence the behaviour in the recipient country, then official flows must improve welfare, globally. In addition, the success of aid in raising welfare everywhere also crucially hinges on policy optimality in recipient countries and that the poor countries are not suffering from 'debt overhang', which dissuades donors from giving aid even to promote projects with potentially high returns for the fear that aid would be diverted to serve existing debt. Thus, realising that rise in global welfare may be difficult without ideal conditions prevailing everywhere, the literature has encouraged varied suggestions for improving the effectiveness of aid. It includes consideration of concessional aid, government-to-government aid, technical assistance as aid, and the tied and untied aid that we have already defined and discussed earlier.

For example, Chao and Yu (2001) show that aid tied to the purchase of an imported capital good from the donor can still be immiserizing if it reduces domestic capital stock. However, this study explores the supply side effects as distinct from the usual demand side treatments of aid via the terms of trade movements that we have pursued earlier (Bhagwati, Brecher, and Hatta, 1983). Chao and Yu (2001) argue that tied aid often finances the import of capital goods from the donor in addition to consumption goods such as food (on average 91% of the tied aid from Germany, 76% from France, and 78% from Japan in the late 1980s were deployed in capital formation projects). This study finds that the tied aid relaxes the quota placed on the import of a capital good from the donor, which then lowers the price of the good in the country. On the other hand, if the capital good is also directly consumed, then a comparison between the demand effect and the supply effect determines the endogenous price of this good. It is shown that if the demand effect is stronger, capital accumulation leads to higher welfare at the cost of the current account.

Next, a generalized formal treatment of the global welfare impact of aid as previously suggested in Krueger (1986) should help to round up the discussion for this sub-section. Djajic, Lahiri, and Raimondos-Moller (1999) establish that in the presence of barriers to capital movements, foreign aid is welfare-enhancing for both donor and recipient via two main channels, namely, the income and TOT effects and the investment-induced TOT effect. They argue that while the income-TOT link still produces the expected results where the donor is worse off and the recipient better off, the aid-induced rise in investment in the recipient country generates more income and in the second period the TOT improvement helps to redistribute income between the two countries. Consider two countries engaged in international trade over two periods, wherein the recipient (S) receives aid (in the absence of borrowing and lending facilities shaping consumption in both) from the donor (N) and invests in period 1 to augment their capital stock in period 2 (in terms of the numeraire good). Using the structure in Dixit and Norman (1980), where $E^i(\cdot)$ denotes expenditure function, $R^i(\cdot)$ denotes revenue, P denotes relative price of the non-numeraire good, U^i utility, I^i investment, K^i one-time inelastic stock of capital, and T is income transfer from donor to recipient, $i = N, S$, the global equilibrium is represented by:

$$E_1^S(1, P, U_1^S) + I^S = R_1^S(1, P, K^S) + T \tag{7.10}$$

$$E_1^N(1, P, U_1^N) + I^N = R_1^N(1, P, K^N) - T \tag{7.11}$$

and $\quad E_{1P}^S(1, P, U_1^S) + E_{1P}^N(1, P, U_1^N) = R_{1P}^S(1, P, K^S) + R_{1P}^N(1, P, K^N). \tag{7.12}$

The *LHS* in (7.10) and (7.11) represent the expenditures of S and N, respectively, while the *RHS* denote the revenue plus (minus) transfers. In other words, these budget constraints help to attain the level of utility, U^i in respective countries. Equation (7.12) on the other hand is the first-period market clearing condition for the *non-numeraire* good, with I^i dropped from the relation as it does not contribute directly to the demand for the *non-numeraire* good. As in Bhagwati et al. (1983), here also, the Walrasian condition ensures equilibrium in both markets. The period 2 expenditure and revenue functions as well as the market clearing condition for the *non-numeraire* good is given by:

$$E_2^S(1, p, U_2^S) = R_2^S(1, p, k^S) \tag{7.13}$$

$$E_2^N(1, p, U_2^N) = R_2^N(1, p, k^N) \tag{7.14}$$

and $\quad E_{2p}^S(1, p, U_2^S) + E_{2p}^N(1, p, U_2^N) = R_{2p}^S(1, p, k^S) + R_{2p}^N(1, p, k^N) \tag{7.15}$

where, $k^S = K^S + I^S$; $k^N = K^N + I^N$; p being the period 2 relative price of the *non-numeraire* good. The second period capital stock is the sum of the first period capital stock and the investment made in respective countries in period 1. The transfer of T was a period 1 phenomenon, and therefore does not appear in (7.13) to (7.15). Given the capital stock and budget constraint, let us elaborate on the demand side of the economy arising from the utility functions in each country, which Djajic et al. (1999) assume to be time separable:

$$W^S(U_1^S, U_2^S) = U_1^S + U_2^S(1+\rho^S)^{-1} \qquad (7.16)$$

$$W^N(U_1^N, U_2^N) = U_1^N + U_2^N(1+\rho^N)^{-1} \qquad (7.17)$$

(ρ^S, ρ^N) are the time-invariant discount rates/pure rates of time preferences for S and N, respectively. The optimal investment decisions in each country lead to:
$\delta[W^S(U_1^S, U_2^S)] / \delta I^S = 0; \delta[W^N(U_1^N, U_2^N)] / \delta I^N = 0$, which can be solved in the following way:

We have, $\qquad \dfrac{\delta W^S(U_1^S, U_2^S)}{\delta I^S} = \dfrac{\delta U_1^S}{\delta I^S} + \dfrac{\delta U_2^S}{\delta I^S}(1+\rho^S)^{-1}. \qquad (7.18)$

Now, from (7.10), $E_1^S(1, P, U_1^S) = R_1^S(1, P, K^S) + T - I^S$, such that,

$$\dfrac{\delta E_1^S}{\delta U_1^S}\dfrac{\delta U_1^S}{\delta I^S} = -1 \text{ or}, \dfrac{\delta U_1^S}{\delta I^S} = -\dfrac{1}{\dfrac{\delta E_1^S}{\delta U_1^S}} = \dfrac{-1}{E_{U_1}^S} = -\tilde{E}_{U_1}^S. \qquad (7.19)$$

Here $\tilde{E}_{U_1}^S$ represents the reciprocal of marginal utility of income in S for period 1 and $\tilde{E}_{U_2}^S$, for that in period 2.

Similarly, from (7.13), $\delta E_2^S / \delta U_2^S \delta U_2^S / \delta I^S = \delta R_2^S / \delta k^S \delta k^S / \delta I^S$, where, $\delta k^S / \delta I^S = 1$ and denote $\delta R_2^S / \delta k^S = R_{k^S}^2$ as the return to capital investment in S, realized in period 2.

Or, $\qquad \dfrac{\delta E_2^S}{\delta U_2^S}\dfrac{\delta U_2^S}{\delta I^S} = \dfrac{\delta R_2^S}{\delta k^S}\dfrac{1}{\dfrac{\delta E_2^S}{\delta U_2^S}} = R_{k^S}^2 \tilde{E}_{U_2}^S. \qquad (7.20)$

Substituting (7.19) and (7.20) in (7.18), we get, $\delta W^S (U_1^{\,S}, U_2^{\,S}) / \delta I^S = 0 \Rightarrow$
$-\tilde{E}_{U^1}^S + (1+\rho^S)^{-1} R_{k^S}^2 \tilde{E}_{U_2}^S = 0$.

Reformulating, $\qquad\qquad \tilde{E}_{U_2}^S (1+\rho^S) = R_{k^S}^2 \tilde{E}_{U_1}^S$. $\qquad\qquad$ (7.21)

By symmetry, $\qquad\qquad \tilde{E}_{U_2}^N (1+\rho^N) = R_{k^N}^2 \tilde{E}_{U_1}^N$. $\qquad\qquad$ (7.22)

Finally, we look into the effects of foreign aid on world welfare, defined as a composite of the welfares of recipient and donor. Thus, we obtain expressions for $(dW^S / dT, dW^N / dT)$ in order to construct the global welfare. Following the earlier procedures, it turns out that the global welfare is composed of the terms of trade effect dp / dT and the difference between the reciprocals of marginal returns to capital between the donor and the recipient.[2] In other words:

$$\frac{E_{U_1}^S}{W_{U_1}^S} \frac{dW^S}{dT} + \frac{E_{U_1}^N}{W_{U_1}^N} \frac{dW^N}{dT} = M_2^S \frac{dp}{dT} \left(\frac{1}{R_{k^N}^2} - \frac{1}{R_{k^S}^2} \right) > 0 \qquad (7.23)$$

where, M_2^S is defined as the compensated import demand function of the recipient country in period 2. Since the rental return in the capital-scarce recipient countries usually exceeds that in the capital-rich donor country, (7.23) may exhibit a positive welfare gain if the transfer-induced TOT effect is positive also, but in the donor country. Generally speaking, the result is conditional:

$$\left[\frac{E_{U_1}^S}{W_{U_1}^S} \frac{dW^S}{dT} + \frac{E_{U_1}^N}{W_{U_1}^N} \frac{dW^N}{dT} \right] > 0 \quad iff \quad M_2^S \frac{dp}{dT} \left(R_{k^S}^2 - R_{k^N}^2 \right) > 0. \qquad (7.24)$$

Intuitively, since the direct income effect of the transfer and the period 1 TOT effect are of equal magnitude in two countries, but of opposite signs, they cancel out and leave the welfare effect to be borne exclusively by the present discounted value of the investment-induced TOT effect in period 2. Additionally, it turns out that if the country which experiences period 2 TOT gain also has a lower real interest rate, then the global welfare following a temporary transfer must increase. Barriers to capital flow serves as a distortion in this model and therefore minimizing the distortion by temporary aid flow can be welfare enhancing, and is reminiscent of the conditions discussed in Krueger (1986).

---

[2] Detailed derivation is available in Djajic et al. (1999).

7.3 **Foreign Aid, Governance, and Policy**

The literature on various other interactions between aid and economic factors also offers a rich set of analysis. We shall discuss a few studies to provide an idea of the expansive literature. Some of these studies offer interesting channels that link aid with international trade and development in general. For example, Hatzipanayotou and Michael (1995) considered the impact of aid on public goods. Using a two-country general equilibrium trade model, the paper shows that foreign aid finances consumption of a public good in the recipient country. Kemp and Kojima (1985) and Kemp (1985) also analysed the welfare impact of foreign aid when there had been investments in the public consumption goods, either privately provided or publicly provided.[3]

Not surprisingly, the extant literature on conditional aid is also vast. For example, Svensson (1999, 2000) enquired into the workings and the problems of conditional aid. According to empirical evidence, the effectiveness of foreign aid depends on the environment in which aid is being disbursed and how good the policies in the recipient countries are. Svensson (1999, 2000) shows that if aid could be given to the countries not on the basis of a pre-determined commitment but on the basis of the policy reform undertaken by the countries, then aid can be more effective. The advantages of this policy according to Svensson are two: firstly, a conflict of interest among the countries will internalise the opportunity cost of aid, and thus will create an impetus among the countries to undertake proper reforms. It also will give adequate incentives to the donor country to send aid to the countries with good policy environments. Secondly, the competition among the countries will force them to reveal their choice of actions, which otherwise remains concealed.

It is widely felt that there are reasons why the macro and the micro level impact of aid on the recipient are quite different. An important paper in this connection is that by Burnside and Dollar (2000) which finds that foreign aid does have an impact on the growth rates of the countries, conditional on the policies which impact growth. If the aid is invested, it is more likely to be effective. However, the incentive to invest and also the productivity of the capital are both sensitive to policy regimes. They also found that bilateral aid increases government consumption. Collier and Dollar (1998) had earlier shown that aid has the maximum effect on poverty if it depends on the recipient country's level of poverty and also the quality of economic institutions and the policies. Alesina and Dollar (2000) found that the political strategy plays a significant role in the allocation of aid. However, studies by Rajan and Subramanian

---

[3] The welfare analysis of tied aid was discussed in Kemp and Kojima (1985) and subsequently in Schweinberger (1990). Beladi (1990) derived the necessary conditions for the occurrence of the paradoxical as well as normal results on employment and welfare.

(2005), Easterly, Levine, and Roodman (2003), Clemens, Radelet, Bhavnani, and Bazzi (2012) show that the relationship between aid and development is often very fragile and ambiguous.

Some of the more contemporary issues, such as those related to flow of aid into developing countries with high levels of corruption have also emerged in recent times. Marjit and Mukherjee (2007), for example, developed a model where corruption associated with redistributive politics provides a new agenda for research in the area of foreign aid. Marjit and Mukherjee (2007) have shown that poorer developing countries have the incentive to adopt bad policies and thus the growth rates of many poor countries have not improved, whereas the richer developing countries tend to misuse the aid money and direct it towards corruption. They show a positive correlation between good policies adopted in the utilization of aid and also the level of corruption.

The empirical studies have shown mixed results of foreign aid for major recipients in Africa and Asia. We refer to a few studies here. Easterly (2006) argued that aid is not associated with growth in Africa, whereas, Collier (2006) argued that in the absence of aid conditions would have been much worse for Africa. Bourguignon and Sundberg (2007) stated that the multidimensionality of aid which includes poverty eradication, spread of education, and access to sanitation, makes the empirical work all the more difficult. They found that the cross-country evidence on aid effectiveness is fragile. But they also said that it does not mean that aid is ineffective. They concluded that aid will be more effective if the former models of aid are reshaped according to the formula of country specificity of development strategy and aid allocations, depending upon the monitoring system of the recipient country.

In 1986, the Ghanaian government embarked on a programme of educational reform. It aimed at reducing the length of the pre-university education from 17 to 12 years, reducing subsidy at the secondary and tertiary levels, increasing the school hours, and removing the unqualified teachers from schools. The results of the programme supported by overseas aid were quite dramatic. Illiteracy and low level of schooling, which was previously 63% compositely (people who had completed grades 3–6 only), got reduced to 19% within a period of 15 years.

Bangladesh started in a dire situation in the 1970s. A war of independence and extreme poverty kept all social indicators among the worst globally. It quickly became a prime destination for development aid. After thirty years, the situation has improved to a large extent. Fertility rates (i.e. ratio of live births to the population, expressed per 1,000 population per year) fell from seven to less than three, and under-five mortality rates fell from over 250 per 1,000 live births to around 80 by 2004. Secondary schooling increased rapidly in the 1990s, especially in rural areas, partly as a result of the stipend paid to all female students in grades 6–10 in rural areas supported by Norwegian aid, the Asian Development Bank, the World Bank, and the government. It is considered as a success story albeit the dependence on aid continues to be high.

In Kenya, a training and visit programme was undertaken to strengthen the skill level and productivity of the workforce. The research was carried out by the World Bank and the data showed that the farmers who knew the improved practices usually put them into operation, hence proving the fact that the lack of knowledge acted as an impediment. But the World Bank's two projects NEP-I and NEP-II did not meet with success in improving the problem of the lack of knowledge, and did not finally affect production.

Arndt, Jones, and Tarp (2007) have discussed the success story of Mozambique, which became possible only because of foreign aid. The study shows that the increase in growth is attributable to the expansion of education. The increase in education accounts for 15.5% of the increase in growth. During 1999 to 2004, the increase in growth rate is attributable to the expansion of education. The socio-economic indicators also have shown huge improvements. The poverty headcount index fell from 69.4% in 1996–1997 to 54.1% in 2002–2003 (which has been calculated on the basis of the nationally representative household survey data). In 2005, the poverty headcount ratio declined to 50%. A review of the other indicators also shows consistent improvements.

7.4 **Concluding Remarks**

The shared world of international trade and foreign aid constitutes a deeply contested space within which the welfare of all nations is evaluated. The literature is fraught with positive and negative impacts of aid on economic development, measured via a large number of indices. Nevertheless, compelling theories and evidence suggest that the large flow of aid has at least conditionally improved the quality of life in poor countries. We discussed a number of theoretical conjectures and empirical observations from the recipient countries to motivate further research in this area. It should be acknowledged that the literature is already well-developed and complex, and has considered many aspects (see Lahiri, 2007) on the possible interactions between trade and aid. It should also be repeated that the multi-dimensionality of the impact of aid on both recipient and donor renders the empirical tests a vexing one. However, it is also expected that the availability of microdata, in particular large sample surveys at the household level, shall be useful in analysing the effects of aid in countries where the flow has been significant. One must realize that available evidence for the cross-country, aggregative levels do not adequately capture optimal adjustments at the household levels that take place following the transfer of conditional and non-conditional aid. The importance of looking deeper into the microeconomic behaviour at the household (or firm) level in the presence of aid and trade is likely to be as enriching as looking into the possible externalities that aid renders on the aggregate economy.

The policy debate about whether aid should promote individual projects or support overall development programmes at the country level (Krueger, 1986) remains unresolved. On the one hand, project aid helps to transfer capital, specific skill, and technology but on the other, since money is fungible, the flow of aid may relax the resource constraint for other projects that are not necessarily most efficient. Besides, if aid helps the improvement of macroeconomic and institutional fundamentals of a country, the positive impact of aid on the performance of specific projects would automatically increase. Aid to specific projects may suffer from limited outreach and uncertain spill over effects to the larger economy. These issues should be subject to empirical verifications in the future.

A large section of research argues that, given the negative relationship between aid and growth, the performance of industrial nations in development burden-sharing must be redefined. The efficacy of unrestricted trade over aid is often the dominating factor behind this view, and suggests that the rich countries would help the poor countries much more by keeping their markets open or by reducing the internal subsidies to farms and firms. Conversely, the poor country governments must correct the institutional weaknesses, address corruption, and promote policies that give due weights to the economic principles alongside political judgements in order to become less dependent on aid, which many argue has large costs.

■ REFERENCES

Alesina, A. and Dollar, D. (2000). 'Who Gives Foreign Aid to Whom and Why?' *Journal of Economic Growth* 5 (1): 33–63.

Areskoug, K. (1969). *External Public Borrowing: Its Role in Economic Development*. NY: Praeger Publishers.

Areskoug, K. (1973). 'Foreign Capital Utilization and Economic Policies in Developing Countries'. *The Review of Economics and Statistics* 55: 182–189.

Arndt, C. Jones, S., and Tarp, F. (2007). 'Aid, Growth and Poverty Reduction: The Mozambican Case'. In: *Theory and Practice of Foreign Aid (Frontiers of Economics and Globalization, Volume 1)*, pp. 235–282. Emerald Group Publishing Limited.

Bhagwati, J. N. (1970). 'Alternative Estimates of the Real Cost of Aid'. In: P. Streeten, (ed). *Unfashionable Economics; Essays in Honour of Lord Balogh*. London: Weidenfeld and Nicolson.

Bhagwati, J. N. (1971). 'The Generalized Theory of Distortion and Welfare'. In: J. N. Bhagwati et al. (eds). *Trade, Balance of Payments and Growth: Papers in International Economics in Honor of Charles P. Kindleberger*. Amsterdam: North-Holland Publishing Company.

Bhagwati, J. and Brecher, R. (1978). 'National Welfare in an Open Economy in the Presence of Foreign Owned Factors of Production'. Working papers 224, Massachusetts Institute of Technology (MIT), Department of Economics.

Brecher, R. and Bhagwati, J. (1981). 'Foreign Ownership and the Theory of Trade and Welfare'. *Journal of Political Economy* 89: 497–511.

Brecher, R. A. and Bhagwati, J. (1982). 'Immiserizing Transfers from Abroad'. *Journal of International Economics* 13: 353–364.

Bhagwati, J. N., Brecher, R. A., and Hatta, T. (1983). 'The Generalized Theory of Transfers and Welfare: Bilateral Transfers in a Multilateral World'. *American Economic Review* 73: 606–618.

Bhagwati, J. N., Brecher, R., and Hatta, T. (1985). 'The Generalized Theory of Transfers and Welfare: Exogenous (Policy-Imposed) and Endogenous (Transfer-Induced) Distortions'. *Quarterly Journal of Economics* 160 (3): 697–714.

Beladi, H. (1990). 'Unemployment and Immiserizing Transfer'. *Journal of Economics* 52 (3): 253–265.

Burnside, C. and Dollar, D. (2000). 'Aid, Policies and Growth'. *American Economic Review* 90: 847–868.

Beladi, H. and Oladi, R. (2007). 'Does Foreign Aid Hinder Foreign Direct Investment?' In: *Theory and Practice of Foreign Aid (Frontiers of Economics and Globalization, Volume 1)*, pp. 55–63. Emerald Group Publishing Limited.

Bourguignon, F. and Sundberg, M. (2007). 'Aid Effectiveness: Opening the Black Box'. *American Economic Review* 97: 316–321.

Chao, C. and Yu, E. (2001). 'Import Quotas, Tied Aid, Capital Accumulation, and Welfare'. *Canadian Journal of Economics* 34 (3): 661–676.

Chenery, H. B. and Eckstein, P. (1970). 'Development Alternatives for Latin America'. *Journal of Political Economy* 78 (4): 966–1006, Part II.

Chichilnisky, G. (1980). 'Basic Goods, the Effects of Commodity Transfers and the International Economic Order'. *Journal of Development Economics* 7: 505–519.

Clemens, M. A., Radelet, S., Bhavnani, R. R., and Bazzi, S. (2012). 'Counting Chickens When They Hatch: Timing and the Effects of Aid on Growth'. *The Economic Journal:* 122 (561): 590–617.

Collier, P. (2006). 'Is Aid Oil? An Analysis Of Whether Africa Can Absorb More Aid'. *World Development* 34 (9): 1482–1497.

Collier, P. and Dollar, D. (1998). Aid Allocation and Poverty Reduction, The World Bank, Development Research Group, Washington, DC. Manuscript.

Collier, P. and Dollar, D. (1999). 'Aid Allocation and Poverty Reduction'. Policy Research Working Paper 2041. The World Bank, Washington DC.

Colman, D. and Nixon, F. (1994). *Economics of change in Less Developed Countries*. 3rd edition. New York and London: Harvester Wheatsheaf.

Cui, X. and Gong, L. (2008). 'Foreign Aid, Domestic Capital Accumulation, and Foreign Borrowing'. *Journal of Macroeconomics* 30 (3): 1269–1284.

Diamond, P. (1978). 'Tax Incidence in a Two Good Model'. *Journal of Public Economics* 9 (3): 283–299.

Dixit, A. K. and Norman, V. (1980). *Theory of International Trade*. Cambridge: Cambridge University Press.

Djajic, S., Lahiri, S., and Raimondos-Moller, P. (1999). 'Foreign Aid, Domestic Investment and Welfare'. *The Economic Journal* 109: 698–707.

Easterly, W. (2001). *The Elusive Quest for Growth: Economist's Adventures and Misadventures in the Tropics*. Massachusetts Institute of Technology.

Easterly, W. (2003). 'Can Foreign Aid Buy Growth?' *Journal of Economic Perspectives* 17 (3): 23–48.

Easterly, W. (2006). 'Planners versus Searchers in Foreign Aid'. *Asian Development Review*, Asian Development Bank, 23 (2): 1–35.

Easterly, W. (2007). 'Was Development Assistance a Mistake?' *American Economic Review* 97 (2): 328–332.

Easterly, W., Levine, R., and Roodman, D. (2003). 'New Data, New Doubts: A Comment on Burnside and Dollar's "Aid, Policies and Growth"' (2000). NBER Working Paper 9846. Cambridge, MA.

Gale, D. (1974). 'Exchange Equilibrium and Coalitions: An Example'. *Journal of Mathematical Economics* 1 (1): 63–66.

Gong, L. and Zou, H. (2000). 'Foreign Aid Reduces Domestic Capital Accumulation and Increases Foreign Borrowing: A Theoretical Analysis'. *Annals of Economics and Finance* 1 (1): 147–163.

Gong, L. and Zou, H. (2001). 'Foreign Aid Reduces Labor Supply and Capital Accumulation'. *Review of Development Economics* 5 (1): 105–118.

Hatta, T. (1973). A Theory of Piecemeal Policy Recommendations. Unpublished doctoral dissertation, Baltimore: The Johns Hopkins University.

Hatzipanayotou, P. and Michael, M. S. (1995). 'Foreign Aid and Public Goods'. *Journal of Development Economics* 47 (2): 455–467.

Hjertholm, P. and White, H. (2000). 'Foreign Aid in Historical Perspective: Background and Trends'. In: F. Tarp (ed). *Foreign Aid and Development*, pp. 80–102. London and New York: Routledge.

Jones, R. W. (1970). 'The Transfer Problem Revisited'. *Economica*, New Series, 37 (146): 178–184.

Jones, R. W. (1975). 'Presumption About the Transfer Problem'. *Journal of International Economics* 5: 263–274.

Johnson, H. G. (1960). 'Income Distribution, the Offer Curves and the Effects of Tariffs'. *Manchester School of Economics* 28: 223–242.

Kanbur, R. (2000). 'Aid, Conditionality and Debt in Africa'. In: F. Tarp (ed). *Foreign Aid and Development*, pp. 409–422. London and New York: Routledge.

Kanbur, R. (2003). 'The Economics of International Aid'. Working Papers 127784, Cornell University, Department of Applied Economics and Management.

Kemp, M. (1985). 'Aid tied to donors exports'. *Pacific Economic Review* 10: 317–322.

Kemp, M. and Kojima, S. (1985). 'Tied aid and the paradoxes of donor-enrichment and recipient-impoverishment'. *International Economic Review* 26: 721–729.

Keynes, J. M. (1929). 'The German Transfer Problem'. *Economic Journal* 39: 1–7.

Krueger, A. O. (1986). 'Aid in the Development Process'. *The World Bank Research Observer* 1 (1): 57–78.

Krueger, A.O. (2009). 'What the Industrial Countries Can Do to Support Developing Countries' Development Goals'. Staff Paper Series, Department of Applied Economics, University of Minnesota.

Leontief, W. (1936). 'Note on the Theory of Pure Capital Transfers'. In: *Explorations in Economics: Notes and Essays Contributed in Honor of F. W. Taussig*. McGraw-Hill: New York.

Lahiri, S. (2007). *Theory and Practice of Foreign Aid, Volume 1 (Frontiers of Economics and Globalization)*, North-Holland: Elsevier.

Lahiri, S. and Raimondos-Moller, P. (1997). 'Competition for Aid and Trade Policy'. *Journal of International Economics* 43: 369–385.

Lahiri, S. and Raimondos-Moller, P. (2000). 'Lobbying by Ethnic Groups and Aid Allocation'. *Economic Journal* 110 (462): 62–79.

Lahiri S., Raimondos-Møller P., Wong, K., and Woodland, A.D. (2002). 'Optimal Foreign Aid and Tariffs'. *Journal of Development Economics* 67 (1): 79–99.

Ohlin, B. (1929). 'The Reparation Problem: A Discussion'. *Economic Journal* 39: 172–178.

Obstfeld, M. (1999). 'Foreign Resource Inflows, Saving, and Growth'. In: K. Schmidt-Hebbel and L. Serven (eds). *The Economics of Saving and Growth: Theory, Evidence, and Implications for Policy*, pp. 107–146. Cambridge: Cambridge University Press.

Marjit, S. and Mukherjee, V. (2006). 'Chapter 2 Poverty, Utilization of Foreign Aid and Corruption: The Role of Redistributive Politics'. In: S. Lahiri (ed). *Theory and Practice of Foreign Aid (Frontiers of Economics and Globalization, Volume 1)*, pp. 17–29. Emerald Group Publishing Limited.

Marjit, S., Mukherjee, V., and Kolmar, M. (2006). 'Poverty, taxation and governance'. *The Journal of International Trade & Development* 15 (3): 325–333.

Rajan, R. and Subramanian, A. (2005). 'Aid and Growth: What Does the Cross-Country Evidence Really Show?' IMF Working Paper, WP/05/127, Washington DC.

Samuelson, P. (1947). *Foundations of Economic Analysis*. Cambridge, MA: Harvard University Press.

Samuelson, P. (1952). 'The Transfer Problem and Transport Costs: The Terms of Trade When Trade-Impediments are Absent'. *Economic Journal* 62: 278–304.

Samuelson, P. (1954). 'The Transfer Problem and Transport Costs, II: Analysis of the Effects of Trade Impediments'. *Economic Journal* 64: 264–289.

Schweinberger, A. G. (1990). 'On the Welfare Effects of Tied Aid'. *International Economic Review* 31 (2): 457–462.

Svensson, J. (1999). 'Aid, Growth and Democracy'. *Economics & Politics* 11 (3): 275–297.

Svensson, J. (2000). 'When is Foreign Aid Policy Credible? Aid Dependence and Conditionality'. *Journal of Development Economics* 61: 61–84.

Truman, H. S. (1949). Inaugural Address, January 20, Online by Gerhard Peters and John T. Woolley, The American Presidency Project, 1999. http://www.presidency.ucsb.edu/ws/?pid=13282.

Weisskopf, T. E. (1972). 'The Impacts of Foreign Capital Inflow on Domestic Savings in Underdeveloped Countries'. *Journal of International Economics* 2 (1): 25–38.

White, H. (1992). 'The Macroeconomic Analysis of Aid Impact'. *Journal of Development Studies* 28 (2): 163–240.

Woolley, J. and Peters. G. (1999). American Presidency Project State of the Union Data, Santa Barbara, University of California.

Xiaoyong, Cui and Gong, Liutang (2006). 'Laplace transform methods for linearizing multidimensional systems'. *Economics Letters* 90 (2): 176–182.

8 Trade, Poverty, and Readjustments

8.1 Introduction

A large number of cross-country and individual country level empirical evidence suggests that trade reforms and openness to international trade increases the growth rate of income and output. Srinivasan and Bhagwati (2001) stated that, 'trade does seem to create, even sustain, higher growth'. The main tenet behind this observation stems from the fact that undistorted price signals from world markets, in combination with the exchange rate, allow resource allocation consistent with comparative advantage of a country, and lead to an increase in productivity. The obvious question this relationship leads into is that of the distribution of gains from trade across economically and socially diverse sections of the population. In fact, since trade reform and trade liberalization are practised largely by the developing and transition countries across the world, a major concern in this literature is how trade affects the income distribution in unequal societies. This has opened up a new dimension in the subject of trade and development, where the impact of trade on poverty captures the interests of a sizeable global audience. This chapter shall try to identify the sources and transmissions of the gains from trade to segments of the population. In this regard, we shall extensively use a survey-cum-analytical paper by Hoekman et al. (2001) to apprise the reader of the several distinct elements in the relationship between trade, growth, and income distribution. The relationships we explore, however, are not without a cautious admission of the subsequent findings and comments, such as that by Rodrik (2000) and Rodriguez and Rodrik (2001). It argues that to straitjacket the success stories as those of trade openness fitting seamlessly into higher growth trajectories all the way down would be quite erroneous. The reasons that are provided in these letters are simple and yet compelling. The countries like China and India that until very recently registered phenomenal growth performances, opened up on the trade front much later than the actual growth ball started rolling. In China's case, Rodrik (2001) argues the high growth started in the late 1970s with the introduction of the household responsibility system in agriculture and the two-tier pricing system. The authorities did not embark on import liberalization in earnest until during the second half of the 1980s and the 1990s. Compared to this, India was a closed-door country even during the early 1980s, when it registered higher growth rate with about a three percentage point rise in the rate. For India, the forced trade reform started with currency devaluation in 1991, and much of the policy propositions took effect in 1993, with further reforms still pending at the aggregate level. In fact, for both China and India, the level of import restrictions are among the highest in the world and yet they are believed to be the successful globalizers according to the definitions used by several multilateral organizations such as the World Bank and the IMF. The exploration and successful expansion of the domestic market for China also helped to sustain the growth impetus longer than expected. In observance of these mutually offsetting and complex relations, it may be possible to shift the entire debate on the subject of international trade and poverty to three important questions as put forth by Winters, McCulloch, and McKay (2004, p. 74): (a) Does liberalization stimulate growth and relieve poverty? (b) Does trade liberalization boost productivity? and (c) Are open economies less stable? In order to answer these questions, which the aforementioned paper deals with using considerable empirical evidence, let us first examine some analytical structures on what is at stake. Section 8.2 offers a concise model of the relationship between trade liberalization, the size and variety of the informal sector characterizing the developing and transition economies around the world, and implications for the incidence of poverty. However, since the change in welfare as largely argued in the related literature is far from symmetric, we develop a political economy model on how a poor country persists on the path of trade liberalization when the concerns about redistribution looms large. This is available in Section 8.3, with 8.4 concluding with an overall discussion on this rich literature.

8.1.1 **How Does Trade Affect the Poor?**

It is expected that the growth in income of the poor is strongly related to overall growth in the economy. The link of overall growth to poverty alleviation has been demonstrated both in cross-country analyses (Dollar and Kraay, 2002), and for individual countries. Trade liberalization can therefore be expected to help the poor overall, given the positive association between openness and growth. However, such assertions are interjected with legitimate fear that in the shorter run, the openness-trade liberalization policy duo may harm poorer agents in the economy. The pattern may even persist in the longer run, whereby the perpetually disadvantaged become the economically excluded population, of course, depending upon the idiosyncratic political-economic structure of the country in question. It should be appreciated in the first place, that liberalization by its nature implies adjustments and cannot bypass strong distributional consequences, the redress to which is considered an integral part of the political-economy debate of a country. In fact, this lies at the core of the model that we present in Section 8.3. It may be important to reiterate that despite strong arguments in favour of the prevalence and strength of the median voter theorem, in practice it is unlikely that the choice of trade policy will be influenced significantly by the share of the poor (median income) people in the country. If it can be assumed (and only if, it is empirically tenable to assume so) that the prevailing trade policies were anti-poor in terms of distributional consequences, then only a possible liberalization attempt shall help more equitable redistribution. Now, the readers with a lot of background information on the characteristics of a typical developing country may already know that the non-traded sectors of such countries are often huge and sustain millions of people under the aegis of the so-called informal or unorganized sector. Consequently, the impact of trade on the informal sector workers in a country could serve as an estimate of the degree to which poverty responds to growth in income following trade reforms.

Since the poor generally have limited financial and other assets, the impact of trade on the price of consumption goods could also offer a strong indication of how trade and poverty are connected.

The effect of trade liberalization on poverty has preponderance of ambiguous relations. The source of the ambiguity owes partly to the plethora of reasons that cause poverty. The spread and depth of poverty, whether structural, whether arising from lack of human capital, from specific types of occupational choice and imperfections in capital market (see for example, Banerjee and Newman, 1993), lack of public investments in infrastructure, owing to food insecurity and nutritional aspects, technological or institutional backwardness, etc. should respond differently to the trade policy measures of a country. It is quite possible then that the effects of trade reforms, empirically speaking, would be minuscule if the connections between such variables are weak. It could also be weak, for example, if the border price shocks do not percolate to those living in geographically isolated regions and are poor. Winters et al. (2004) argue that the extent of transmission may be limited by a number of factors including transport costs and the costs of distribution. It could also be functions of the extent of competition between traders and the type of markets that deal with such products undergoing a tariff cut. In addition, the domestic or regional tax structures, the size of the market, and other regulations could be important determinants if one wishes to trace the link. In large countries such as India, China, or even Australia with a large desert separating the east and the west coast, the withdrawal of border restrictions will have an uneven impact on the poor depending on their location. In fact, the same policy could lead to more inequality among the poor groups of a country. Winters et al. (2004) develop a brief price transmission mechanism for the goods, which had undergone a border price change. If the local price of an import good is given by $P_l^M = P_w \varepsilon (1 + t_M) + \gamma_M$, where P_l^M is the local price of the import good; P_w is the world price; t_M is the tariff rate on the import good, M; and γ_M is the transaction cost. Similarly, for the export good, the relationship is given by $P_l^X = P_w \varepsilon (1 - t_X) - \gamma_X$, which signifies that the country can buy the good at a much lower price when the tariff and transaction cost related expenses are borne by the importing country. Now, allowing for a positive change in the tariff, the included (excluded) border price would mean that the effect would be smaller for the import good, while higher for the export good. Alternatively, if the tariff rates change and the country in question is large or a price-maker in the world market, then the price effect may partially offset the tariff change unlike in the case of small countries. In this structure, change in the exchange rate will have direct impact on local prices, once again depending partly on how it affects the world price. In this case, the world price is unaffected, the price transmission is a function of the tariff rates and the transaction costs. Since these are comparative static results, it may not be difficult to explore further about what happens when the γ_i, $i= M, X$, accompanies tariff reduction. Evidence suggests that changes in the localized transaction costs hurt the consumers in many cases.

Since improved productivity is necessary for sustaining growth in a country, the links between trade liberalization, growth, and poverty need to consider the first's effects on productivity. Coe, Helpman, and Hoffmaister (1997) use quinquennial observations from 77 developing countries over 1971–1990 to show that transmission of knowledge capital in proportion to the import volume helps to raise the total factor productivity. The knowledge capital is measured in terms of accumulated R&D expenditure and interacts with the importing country's trade openness. At the sectorial level, Martin and Mitra (2001) show that the productivity growth is generally higher in agriculture than at the industry level, when most studies available so far concentrate exclusively on the industry. Kar and Sinha (2013) show that the multinational corporations' (MNC) activities in both industrial and service sectors of a country can lead to strong spill over of knowledge to the larger economy. Martin and Mitra (2001) suggest that there is a strong tendency for international convergence of productivity levels. This implies that certain transmission forces are effective at the cross-country level, although it has been generally difficult to identify the source of such transmissions as arising from trade or technology transfer. Overall (while acknowledging the problems with measuring TFP (total factor productivity)), recent empirical evidence seems to suggest that openness and trade liberalization have a strong influence on productivity and its rate of change. The productivity improvement is expected to raise the returns of the factors from respective markets and may in the short run cause retrenchments, because the same factor becomes doubly productive and therefore lowers the overall factor demand. This may have both shortrun poverty alleviating effects and is believed to be a necessary condition for long-run poverty eradication strategies. If the output growth is substantially more, the fall in prices and consequently the access to various goods and services previously unattainable for a large section of the population becomes the dominant outcome.

However, in order to assess the direct poverty impact of price changes, it is necessary to focus on the responses of individual producers, especially small farmers. With greater availability of microdata, the evidence gets stronger whereby one can identify the exact factor that acts either as a facilitator or as a constraint in the process of transmission of the effects from trade openness to household response. Using micro level panel data for farm households in Zambia over the period 1993–1994 to 1994–1995, Deininger and Olinto (2000) show that for many households a major constraint on improvements in agricultural productivity in the aftermath of trade liberalization and openness was the unavailability of key productive assets (such as bullocks, agricultural equipment, etc.). Lopez, Nash, and Stanton (1995) used panel data for firms in rural Mexico to argue that only those firms that had capital inputs above a threshold level responded significantly to price effects following rise in the volume of trade.

To elaborate on these readjustments, let us offer a generalized analytical picture for the aggregative economy where the inter-sector mobility of factors following trade liberalization determines which goods would be produced and consumed in the post-reform equilibrium. Consider a small open economy that takes product prices as exogenously given. It produces three goods M (an import substitute), X (export), and N *(non-traded)*. There are two types of people in the economy, the poor whose only asset is their labour; and the non-poor whose assets are capital. The effects of trade policy reform on the poor depend on the consumption and production of the poor in these three sectors. The effects also differ in the short and long run. In the short run we assume that the factors of production are fixed and immobile, while they are flexible and mobile in the long run. There is full employment in this economy with nominal and real wages flexible in the labour market. Domestic prices of M $(P_M(1+t))$ and X (P_X) depend on their world price and on policy variables such as the exchange rate and import tariffs. On the other hand, the price of N (P_N) is determined from the domestic supply and demand. Allocation of resources depends on these three product prices. In the long run, resource allocation depends on relative prices only, such as ($P_X / P_M(1+t)$) and (P_X / P_N). Trade liberalization resulting from a reduction in tariff on the import good raises [$P_X / P_M(1+t)$] and labour and capital have an incentive to move from M to X. Whether the import price falls or the export price rises makes an enormous difference in the short run and is likely to determine the success of the reform. This is where complementary policies play a crucial role, including exchange rate policy. Suppose the nominal exchange rate (ε) remains unchanged following a tariff reduction. This causes $P_M(1+t)$ to fall while P_X remains unchanged. This hurts both labour and capital in sector M. The groups that are hurt are likely to lobby for a policy reversal.

Also, although in the long run both imports and exports increase with a tariff reduction, imports tend to increase faster than exports, with a likely deficit in the balance of trade that may be unsustainable. Both the pressure from short-run losers and the balance of trade problem may result in a failure of the reform. This outcome can be avoided or its effects are mitigated by depreciation of the domestic currency. This raises the price of import relative to non-traded goods, and helps dampen both the increase in import demand and the decline of labour and capital's nominal income in sector M. On the other hand, labour and capital in sector X benefit from the devaluation since P_X increases.

Thus, a policy package of tariff reduction and currency depreciation should make it easier for the factors of production in sector M in the short run as well as during the transition period, and should dampen the resistance to the reform. In countries with a flexible or floating exchange rate policy, the lower tariff will raise the demand for imports and for foreign exchange. This will raise the price of foreign exchange or lower the value of the domestic currency. In other words, the exchange rate will depreciate (more units of domestic currency per unit of foreign currency). This is similar to currency devaluation except that it is determined by the market and not by the monetary authorities.

The effect of trade reform on the poor should ideally depend on the second relative price, i.e., P_X / P_N. When the value of the nominal exchange rate cannot be changed, a tariff reduction has no impact on P_X but lowers P_M. This leads to a shift in consumption from N and X to M. Consequently, the price of the non-traded good P_N falls directly by the demand-supply interaction. This again implies an increase in P_X / P_N. However, if there is a full devaluation equivalent to the tariff reduction, P_M remains unchanged and P_X rises by the magnitude of the currency depreciation. This should shift consumption from X to M and N, raising P_N due to rise in demand at a given supply. P_X / P_N rises by the exact same amount as in the absence of devaluation. Finally, with flexible exchange rates, the depreciation is less than the reduction in the tariff. This means P_M falls, while P_X rises. Consumption shifts from X to N and M, and from N to M, so the net effect on the demand for N is ambiguous. This is analogous to the effect on P_N. Note, however, that P_X / P_N rises exactly as in the other two cases.

Compared to this generalized result, it may be interesting to observe if trade brings forth different impact for specific sectors, such as the large unorganized sector in developing countries. Section 8.2 offers a result in this direction.

8.2 Trade, Informal Sector, and Poverty

The rapid expansion of the third world metropolis over the last two decades has several interlinked impacts on the economy and society. As in other developing countries, an overwhelmingly large share (approximately 93% and, excluding agriculture, about 78%) of the workforce in India is employed in the so-called unorganized and/or informal sectors. A substantial portion of such employment opportunities is generated in the urban or semi-urban areas and, not surprisingly, a majority of this workforce is economically marginalized. High incidence of poverty among these groups exposed to difficult and hazardous working conditions, non-existent social security or health benefit schemes other than poorly functioning state-provided medical facilities is quite common. Sustained improvements in the living standards of these groups can only be brought about by capital accumulation, productivity gains, and wage increases in this sector; a detailed discussion of the mechanism was discussed in Section 8.1. Undoubtedly this, and similar economies, are persistently deficient in supplementary resources essential for poverty alleviation. More recently there is an effort in India, which provides 100 days of guaranteed jobs in rural areas where agriculture is still characterized by substantial disguised unemployment. In addition, for a populous country like India, the government has enacted a food security policy that expects to bring 69% of its population under the umbrella of food security and provide at least 70 kilograms of rice or wheat at a total cost of US $1.5 per month. The dual policy of the National Rural Employment Guarantee Act and the Food Security is expected to retain the large set of rural migrants back in their place of origin and therefore dry up the source of informal workers in the urban locations. However, it is not clear if the generous policies might turn out to be self-defeating in terms of high inflation (among other distortions) that this huge pressure on the resources might unleash. In fact the double-digit inflation has been identified as one of the reasons why India is slowly losing its ground as a cheaper destination for locating global production and service sectors. It has also lost ground in terms of growing trade deficits with the destinations still in considerable economic turmoil and only slowly recovering from the global financial crisis. A richer India, however, has been importing much more than before (see Section 8.1 for an analogy with the generalized model) and hoarding imported gold at a time when the domestic bond and equity markets churn out poor returns. This leaves the trade-poverty link in a bigger mess compared to what we were trying to unravel earlier. In fact, Edmonds, Pavcnik, and Topalova (2010) have shown that trade liberalization brought down poverty in rural India, although the effect is asymmetric across districts and in particular harmful for those districts where certain labour-intensive industrial units lost the protection. It is, then, not surprising that it hurt the schooling choice among poor households in these districts, with the burden disproportionately borne by the girl child.

This section, therefore, offers another look at the connection between trade liberalization and poverty reduction, focusing on the informal sector workers in urban regions of the developing world. It has been shown elsewhere (Kar and Marjit, 2001) that the informal sector workers are hard pressed to accept low-paid jobs in the cities rather than wait indefinitely for a formal urban employment to open up. This can significantly explain the persistence of urban poverty in many cities of the third world. We offer a generic model to replicate the conditions of the urban informal sector, and in particular, distinguish the urban informal sector as comprising an industrial section that uses some amount of capital as input and another as using raw labour as the only input. In poor countries the overwhelming volume of workers using only physical labour towards menial occupations as domestic help, mainly women and child workers, household cook, drivers, daily wage labour is too large to be clubbed as one indivisible informal unit, transitional in nature and thus denied a space in most policy discussions. Clearly, this set of assumptions is not different from the analytical structure explored in Hoekman et al. (2001). We argue that the impact of trade liberalization should be distinctly felt by such groups and may even be favourable under plausible conditions.

In the existing literature, welfare implications of trade reforms, with the informal sector as an important part of the economy, have recently come up for much discussion (Marjit and Kar, 2011; Marjit *et al.*, 2007; Chaudhuri, 2003; Marjit, 2003; Chaudhuri and Mukhopadhyay, 2002; Chen, 2000; etc). A primary reason, perhaps, is that leaving out the informal sector fails to capture the impact of trade policy reforms on a huge labour force in the LDCs working under arrangements outside the purview of what is typically known as the formal/organized sector. Data from Southeast Asian, East European, African, and Latin American countries show varying rates of urban informal sector employment within the range of 15% to 20% in Turkey and Slovakia to 80% in Zambia, and even more, to approximately 83% in Myanmar. Moreover, considering the state of agricultural and rural activities in these countries, it is quite apparent that the total shares of the informal sector in these countries are quite high (ILO, 1999). This is also corroborated by some of the other studies (for example, Turnham, 1993), which provide evidence that in low-income countries like Nigeria, Bangladesh, Ivory Coast, India, etc. the share of the urban informal sector is at least 51% of the workforce. Alternatively, seen from the point of view of the 'minimum wage' earners, for example only 11% of Tunisia's labour force is subject to minimum wage while in Mexico and Morocco, a substantial number earns less than the minimum wage; in Taiwan, the minimum wage received by many is less than half of the average wage, etc. (Agenor, 1996).

Some evidence suggests that the level of informalization in a country increases as the economic reforms are initiated. A more general concern that follows is that such expansion will reduce informal wages with retrenched workers crowding in from the formal sector. Some of the previously-mentioned studies show that despite contraction of the previously protected or state-run formal sector as a consequence of trade liberalization, and relocation of relatively unskilled and often older workers into the informal segment, informal wages can still rise if capital also relocates into the informal sector.

In order to explain the term 'informal sector', it should be mentioned that it is commonly interpreted (initially coined by ILO, 1972) to mean, 'illicit or illegal activities by individuals operating outside the formal sphere for the purpose of evading taxation or regulatory burden'. Alternatively, informal sector implies, 'very small enterprises that use low-technology models and do not refer to legal status' (Webster and Fidler, 1996). Although generally, the informal sector activity pertains to non-traded commodities and services offered by street vendors and domestic help, in many countries they produce intermediate goods, processed export and import substitutes with subcontracts from the formal sector. In such cases, the formal sector often adds the capital content (like, the brand name) only. In many other cases, informal industries that produce garments, leather goods, small tools, and machinery are known to export directly, often bypassing the formal regulations and procedures made effective through border trade.[1] Apart from that, in all the developing countries, agriculture, poultry, and fisheries are predominantly outside the formal sphere and consumer non-durables such as vegetables, fish, and meat are procured from such agents, processed, and traded. Analysing the impact of industrial trade reform on these activities and on the workers employed therein should offer a wider view in favour of appropriate policy formulations. It is to be noted that given the considerably large share of employment in these sectors, even small positive gains in the real wage can increase the economic attainments of millions in most developing and transition countries.

8.2.1 MODELLING THE INFORMAL SECTOR

Consider a small open economy with two formal sectors, X and Y, that produce traded commodities. X is an import competing commodity manufactured with capital and skilled labour and is protected by an import tariff, t. The skilled wage is fixed at $\bar{w}_S$ by prior negotiations with the labour unions as an outcome of a bargaining process. We do not model this wage fixation explicitly.[2] Commodity Y is an export item produced with skilled labour, capital, and an intermediate commodity I, which in turn is produced in the informal

---

[1] Earlier, De Soto (1989) pointed out that a heavy burden of taxes, bribes, and inflexible bureaucratic regulations in the formal sector drives many producers into the informal sector.

[2] Chaudhuri (2003) provides examples of how the negotiations regarding wage settlements between employers and labour unions may take place in a similar context.

sector. Since Y is traded at exogenously given world prices the price of commodity I, P_I is determined from its fixed-coefficient production relation with Y. The production of I requires use of capital and unskilled labour available in large stock which receives a wage $w < \bar{w}_S$.

We consider I as one of the several intermediate commodities ranging from leather and rubber products to electronic equipment produced under informal arrangements that are often sold by the formal export industries after appropriate value additions. The third commodity we consider is non-traded, uses unskilled labour as the only input, and represents very low-skilled activities such as domestic help or small vendors with little or no use of capital. It may be considered as an informal service sector. The price relations for a competitive market accommodating these commodity types are given by Equations (8.1) to (8.4). All the factors of production are fully employed as shown by Equations (8.5) to (8.8). The typical nature of the urban informal sector allows us to consider a full employment competitive model of this nature, since for all practical purposes the reservation wage for unskilled informal workers in poor countries is quite low. For the relatively unskilled workers who do not succeed in getting formal employment, the informal sector offers the only available alternative compared to involuntary unemployment. Moreover, in this model, while capital is homogeneous and moves freely between all the sectors, labour is heterogeneous and the skilled workers receive a higher premium. The production follows standard neoclassical assumptions of constant returns to scale technology, diminishing marginal productivity for the factor inputs part of the perfectly competitive market.

The model uses the following symbols:

$\bar{w}_S$: Formal skilled wage; w : Informal flexible wage

r_j : Return to capital in sector j; X : Output of formal import competing sector

Y : Output of formal export sector; (P_j^*) : Exogenous price of jth good

I : Output of intermediate good (informal); Z : Output of non-traded good (informal)

$\underline{L}$: Stock of unskilled labour; $\bar{S}$: Stock of skilled labour

$\bar{K}$: Total supply of capital; t : Import tariff rate

(a_{ij}, a_{Kj}) : Per unit labour and capital use in sector $j = X, Y, I, Z$, $i = L, S, I$

'$\wedge$' represents percentage changes for each variable (for example, $\hat{x} = dx / x$) and detailed algebraic derivations of all the results are provided in Appendix 1.

The competitive price conditions are given by,

$$\bar{w}_S a_{SX} + r a_{KX} = P_X^*(1+t) \qquad (8.1)$$

$$\bar{w}_S a_{SY} + r a_{KY} + P_I a_{IY} = P_Y^* \qquad (8.2)$$

$$wa_{LI} + ra_{KY} = P_I \qquad (8.3)$$

$$wa_{LZ} = P_Z \qquad (8.4)$$

and, the full employment conditions imply:

$$a_{SX}X + a_{SY}Y = \bar{S} \qquad (8.5)$$

$$a_{LI}I + a_{LZ}Z = \bar{L} \qquad (8.6)$$

$$a_{KX}X + a_{KY}Y + a_{KI}I = \bar{K} \qquad (8.7)$$

$$a_{IY}Y = I. \qquad (8.8)$$

The determination of four price variables (r, w, P_I, P_Z) and four output variables $(X, Y, I,$ and $Z)$ from the set of eight equations proceeds in the following way. Given the skilled wage and the exogenous price for commodity X, the return to capital is obtained from Equation (8.1). Substituting r in Equation (8.2) we get the price of the intermediate commodity I, and from (8.3) the unskilled wage is directly obtained. Substitution of w in Equation (8.4) generates the price of the non-traded informal service, Z. Similarly, for the factor markets, we substitute the output level of informal intermediate commodity I from Equation (8.8) into Equation (8.7). Equations (8.5) and (8.7) then form a pair of simultaneous equations that solve for equilibrium output levels of X and Y given the endowments of capital K and skilled labour S. Substituting back the equilibrium value of Y in Equation (8.8), we determine the equilibrium output of I in the economy. Finally, from Equation (8.6) we determine the equilibrium value of Z, the output of the informal service sector.

We are principally interested in observing the impact of a tariff reduction in the formal import-competing sector on the level of output and employment in the two informal sectors under consideration. While the detailed algebraic proof is provided in the appendix, let us offer an intuitive explanation of the phenomenon here subsequent to the following proposition.

Proposition 8.1: *A reduction in the import tariff raises product prices and wages in both informal sectors. However, the sector producing the intermediate good expands in output and employment, while the one producing non-traded services, contracts.*

A reduction in the tariff rate lowers the return to capital in sector X alone, since the skilled wage is exogenous and fixed. Consequently, sector X must contract, which suitably captures the experience in most developing and emerging economies where adoption of freer trade policies and removal of tariff and non-tariff barriers have affected the local import competing (many under public sector control) sectors adversely. Employment levels of both labour and capital in sector X must also shrink under the circumstances and relocation in other sectors become necessary. Since skilled labour is used specifically in sectors X and Y, therefore the latter may draw in more skilled workers and its output may grow if the sector is more skill-intensive compared to the former. This is an exemplification of the *Rybczynski* effect (see, 8.A.11 and 8.A.12, in the Appendix). On the other hand, capital may move to sector Y or sector I, or both. As discussed, sector I's output level is completely dependent on that of sector Y since it is the sole user of the intermediate commodity produced informally. If the capital moves into sector Y, the price of the informal intermediate commodity must improve, given the competitive price conditions. However, since by assumption the intermediate commodity must be used in fixed proportions with any other combination of capital and labour, thus its output must also increase. The sequence of events follows the derivations in the Appendix.

A rise in the price of I, and a factor-led growth in sector Y both contribute to an increase in the output of the informal commodity. This is a significant result in itself, because it implies that a contraction of the formal import competing sector leads to an improvement in the export production and given its connection with the informal sector through the intermediate input, the informal production also increases. Once again, empirical analyses for some of the countries do exhibit these patterns in the post-reform phases, where many formal industries survive and grow by subcontracting their production to the informal sector. Even within the bastions of labour union dominated public and other formal sectors, one observes growing tendencies towards informal and contractual employment practices, often without access to many facilities previously enjoyed by the formal workers.

The contraction of the formal import-competing sector also demonstrates that the unskilled wage rises in the process, another impact quite clearly visible in many of the developing economies including India. In fact, Table 8.A1 (Appendix 2) shows that for most of the provinces in India, the average wage for workers in the unorganized non-directory manufacturing sector has risen by at least 8% on an annual basis. The results from this short theoretical representation further reveal that the informal service sector may shrink on account of an expansion in the production of the informal intermediate commodity. This operates through the mobility of the unskilled workers away from the service sector and into the intermediate manufacturing sector, although wages increase in both.

Consequently, one can argue that this is welfare inducing in various ways. First, the direct improvement in wages has a clear impact for poverty reduction in the informal sector. It may not be a restrictive assumption to consider that there is a substantial overlap between workers in the informal sector and the people registered under the Below Poverty Line category. Second, the flow of workers into an industrial sector, albeit informal, and away from menial and highly insecure non-traded service sector jobs may be the direct impact of improvements in other formal sectors owing to trade reform. These jobs covering street side vendors, low-level construction workers, or domestic help may now find (informal) jobs in the industrial or service sector, increasing the visibility of labour use in the economy. This should be an important step towards collective bargaining of various sorts.

If there is a *ceteris paribus* rise in the price of the export good *Y*, the price of the intermediate good increases, and as there has been no change in the return to capital, the informal wage must go up. This in turn raises the price of the informal services. Clearly, the rise in the price of the intermediate good expands its production and draws labour away from the service sector into the industrial base. This is summarized in Proposition 8.2.

Proposition 8.2: *A rise in the price of the export good, Y, shall raise the prices of both the intermediate good and the non-traded good. The informal wage must rise, and labour moves to the intermediate sector thus lowering output and employment in the non-traded sector despite a higher price per unit.*

The following section deals with the impact of trade reform across various groups in the country, and draws on Beladi and Kar (2011).

8.3 The Political Economy of Trade Policy

Hoekman et al. (2004) comment that existing interest groups, often en-trenched elites benefiting from the status quo, may oppose reform. Alternatively, using the political clout and the elite capture of 'democracy' in poor countries, the reforms are often designed to benefit the non-poor, and raise the income gap between the skilled and the unskilled. Clearly, there are cross-currents that a political economy model of trade policy reform can hardly neglect. Thus, by acknowledging the likely environment in which trade reforms are usually proposed, it is extremely important to investigate the impact of reforms on specific groups in a poor country and design complementary programmes to redress. In such a case, the timing of the implementation of trade reforms needs to be closely linked to the establishment of the programmes that deal with their impact on the poor. Let us provide a sequence of how the trade reform policy gradu-ates (Hoekman et al., 2004, p. 34): (a) If a reform is pre-announced to be implemented over a few years and it is a *credible* reform, then normal market adjustment and attrition can be used to eliminate or greatly reduce adjustment costs. However, this may come at the cost of the threat of reversal of the trade reforms, as entrenched interests will be granted time to mobilize opposition. A staged reform that is scheduled to take more than five years is not likely to be credible unless it is anchored in WTO commitments or a far-reaching regional trade agreement. (b) It is important to address non-tariff barriers and high tariff peaks earlier rather than later. (c) It is also important to reduce tariffs across the board during each stage of a gradual reform. If instead, a target is set based on the tariff average, the tendency will be to cut tariffs only where they cause no immediate difficulty and leave all the adjustment to last. (d) Broad trade reforms frequently meet with much less political resistance than cuts in protection to individual sectors. Broad reforms help the winners from reform recognize their potential gains, and tend to reduce the costs even for industries that lose protection on their output. Together, these suggest that alongside the policies of trade reforms, macroeconomic stability and a competitive exchange rate should be in place. The best outcomes for the poor can be expected when, as a result of the overall reform process of which trade reform is a part, growth accelerates in the economy as a whole.

However, the main resistance to trade liberalization in most countries comes from import-competing industries where it directly leads to job losses. Compensation schemes (generally termed as Trade Adjustment Assistance or TAA) for those who lose jobs due to trade liberalization, are available only in a few advanced countries. None of the developing and transition countries practise TAA schemes. Moreover, the majority of developing countries do not functionally offer unemployment benefit or other social security safeguards.[3] However, any intervention such as unemployment benefit creates further distortions, particularly when unemployment is frictional and not structural. The solution is second-best in comparison to a market-driven best outcome. Note that under political economy considerations, the social planner's choice of second-best could well be the optimum.

TAA ironically can help to achieve political objectives from two angles. On the one hand, it may help to ease resistance to import liberalization and attainment of the best free-trade, and on the other, it appeases those who are directly and indirectly affected by trade reform. Presently, we study whether TAA for developing and transition countries is an efficient outcome in view of aggregate welfare. The aggregate result is extended to look into group-specific welfare levels. We will discuss the results shortly.

---

[3] See Tzannatos and Roddis (1998) for a global survey of benefit programmes and the observation that it exists mainly in the industrialized countries (p. 8). A few developing countries use government subsidy to provide meagre social insurance or unemployment assistance. Compulsory insurance exist for a handful of countries like Egypt and Liechtenstein. The cost of voluntary unemployment is therefore restrictively high.

Optimal compensation to workers who lose due to trade liberalization has been raised in Lawrence and Litan (1986), Brander and Spencer (1994)[4], Feenstra and Lewis (1994), and others. But all of these refer to industrialized countries. Scope and implications of TAA subsequent to trade liberalization in developing countries have not been discussed. Since developing countries may gain substantially from trade liberalization, despite various other imperfections, the case for a trade-related support scheme is not automatic. It needs to be duly formulated, especially in view of the labour market characteristics of developing countries. Generally speaking, welfare implications of trade-related adjustments for the poorer countries may turn out to be similar to that of the rich countries. The present study incorporates trade patterns and labour market characteristics representing developing countries, and obtains the optimal level of trade adjustment assistance as the second-best. We use a competitive general equilibrium model of production with capital and labour, and show that the choice of TAA rate is critically dependent on import elasticity of tariff, import elasticity of wage subsidies, and marginal propensity to spend on imports. A reduction in tariff reduces one of the distortions. However, this may not necessarily improve welfare in the presence of another distortion, namely wage rigidity.

Recent studies dealing with developed countries with low-skill intensive import-competing goods highlight that there is inadequate attention to cases of compensation for retrenched, aged, medium-skilled workers (Davidson and Matusz, 2006; Kletzer, 2004; Kletzer and Litan, 2001). Kletzer and Litan (2001) suggest that the policy of 'wage insurance' (actually, wage subsidy) to the workers from the import industry is the best way to redistribute the positive gains of free trade, without the usual unemployment benefit related disincentives in the labour market. Davidson and Matusz (2006), while using a much bigger canvas with dynamic implications and training, show that trade liberalization may hurt both 'movers' and 'stayers' of the import industry and that there may be at least two ways to compensate those who lose due to freer trade. Given an ability/skill-based continuous distribution of labour— the single input in their economy, a wage subsidy generates a higher level of welfare for all.

In developing countries, by contrast, the spread of the formal industrial base (public and private) is usually quite thin. Unless a small percentage of workers still means large masses as in populous countries like China or India, wage subsidy may face stiff political contest. On the other hand, offering wage/employment insurance to a large number of non-formal

---

[4] Brander and Spencer (1994) showed that if wage subsidy is to be used for compensation it must fall with decreasing income difference.

workers is both legally and financially infeasible—workers in the informal sector are generally unregistered and do not possess employment contracts. Consequently, TAA to a small section of formal workers may cause social and political disturbances and reflect on the elite capture of reforms that we discussed before. The argument is based on the following steps. If trade liberalization raises overall welfare by removing distortions, then wage subsidy is useful for compensating a smaller group of disadvantaged workers. According to our model there are four groups of people in an economy—the capitalists; the non-displaced workers in the rigid wage import competing sector; the displaced workers retrenched from this sector and joining the unprotected flexible wage sector; and finally, the workers who were already in the flexible wage sector. Thus wage subsidy to displaced workers should be treated as a political decision and similar support schemes may also be extended to capitalists who may also lose after liberalization. It is well-known that the capitalists often lobby more aggressively and effectively than worker groups. Presently, we study the outcome-related (wage subsidy) welfare issues at the aggregative and group-specific levels.[5]

Finally, a 'wage subsidy' under TAA is conceived as partial payment (say up to 50%, Kletzer, 2004) towards the 'positive' difference between the wage a retrenched worker earns on a new job and that received in the previous job from which unemployment was caused by trade liberalization only. Given conditions for who should qualify, it has been argued that the compensation should come from lump-sum transfer of tariff revenue (Davidson and Matusz, 2006; Mayer, 1984).[6] Section 8.3.1 develops the model. Section 8.3.2 offers the post-subsidy aggregate welfare measures, while Section 8.3.3 provides group-specific welfare calculations. Section 8.4 summarizes the results.

8.3.1 TRADE AND READJUSTMENTS

We use a stylized model to explore the link between wage subsidy and aggregate economic welfare. The two distortions in the model as we develop it are in the form of tariff protection and wage rigidity in the formal/organized sector. The tariff protection is reduced in the presence of wage rigidity, and a wage subsidy is offered to workers displaced due to contraction in this sector. We obtain aggregate and group-specific welfare effects resulting from these two changes. Since wage subsidy is a lump-sum

---

[5] The mechanism (lobbying) that leads to a particular type of political support scheme and its implications for welfare shall be taken up in future.

[6] Feenstra and Lewis (1994) argued that commodity taxes like Dixit and Norman (1986) coupled with TAA, under perfect mobility of factors, helps to attain Pareto optimality.

transfer and does not distort factor prices, we ignore the issue of financing and assume that the budget remains balanced. Consider a small open developing or transition country producing two commodities at exogenous world prices $(P_Z^*, Z = X,Y)$. X is an import competing good and Y, an export commodity. X uses a relatively capital-intensive production technology and is protected by a tariff, t. Commodity Y represents basic goods ranging from agricultural commodities, mining products, semi-skilled manufacturing, etc. The production and trade basket is in direct contrast with developed countries, where the import competing sector is relatively more labour-intensive and the export sector produces high-tech skill/capital-intensive commodities. In addition, developed countries have low shares of unskilled workers and insignificant shares of informal sector compared to developing countries. These are important differences in view of our analysis.

The production functions in X and Y are homogeneous of degree one in inputs, labour (L) and capital (K), both non-specific and mobile across sectors.[7] All workers in sector X are part of a labour union, which fixes their wage at $\bar{w}$ above the market clearing level, w.[8] Owners of capital earn r per unit. Commodity markets are perfectly competitive. In other words, distortions in X lead to large labour participation in the unorganized sector (Y).

The general production functions in Equation (8.9) are reconstructed into corresponding profit functions in Equations (8.8) and (8.11).[9]

$$X = X(L_X, K_X), \quad Y = Y(L_Y, K_Y) \tag{8.9}$$

where, $Z_j > 0, Z_{jj} < 0, \ Z_{js} > 0; \ j,s = (L,K), j \neq s, \quad Z = X,Y, \ H_Z = 0$.

Factor inputs show diminishing returns, and H_Z stands for the Hessian determinant in sector Z. We hold the price of commodity Y as the numeraire, $P_Y^* \equiv 1$ and all other prices are expressed in terms of the numeraire. Thus price of commodity X, with t as the rate of tariff protection, is given by $p^*(1+t)$. Total factor endowments are $(\bar{L} = L_X + L_Y, \bar{K} = K_X + K_Y)$.

$$\pi_X = p^*(1+t)X(L_X, K_X) - \bar{w}L_X - rK_X \tag{8.10}$$

$$\pi_Y = Y(L_Y, K_Y) - wL_Y - rK_Y, \tag{8.11}$$

---

[7] The proposed structure is appropriate for medium to long run, given that TAA can continue for a reasonably long period.

[8] Marjit, Kar, and Maiti (2009) determine the unionized wage endogenously under similar production structures. We bypass this procedure to concentrate on the main theme.

[9] See Batra and Ramachandran (1980) and Batra (1986) for earlier use of this structure.

First-order conditions for profit maximization from (8.8) and (8.11) and full employment conditions yield

$$p^*(1+t)X_L(L_X,K_X)=\bar{w} \tag{8.12}$$

$$p^*(1+t)X_K(L_X,K_X)=r=Y_K(\bar{L}-L_X,\bar{K}-K_X) \tag{8.13}$$

$$Y_L(\bar{L}-L_X,\bar{K}-K_X)=w, \tag{8.14}$$

Equations (8.12)–(8.14) determine (L_X,K_X) and w. These are determined from five parameters, p^*, t, $\bar{L}$, $\bar{K}$, and $\bar{w}$. Substituting equilibrium values of (L_X,K_X) in (8.13) we get the equilibrium value of r.

Suppose there is a reduction in the tariff rate. The sector contracts as the price falls. Demand for both capital and labour falls in X, but wage in this sector is downward rigid. Thus return to capital alone falls. Employment in X goes down. This is usually the case with previously protected industries in developing countries. If capital moves freely into sector Y, r falls in that sector as well and w rises. Both sectors experience an increase in the cost of labour relative to capital. Since Y absorbs labour from X, it expands owing to high labour-intensity in production. The result is counterintuitive. Inflow of labour in Y leads to higher wage and this happens because retrenched capital from X relocates in Y raising the marginal productivity of labour.[10]

The employment and wage esffects are calculated from (8.15). We fully differentiate (8.12)–(8.14) and apply a tariff cut, $dt<0$ as the instrument of trade liberalization. Rearranging:

$$\begin{bmatrix} p^*(1+t)X_{LL} & p^*(1+t)X_{LK} & 0 \\ p^*(1+t)X_{KL}+Y_{KL} & p^*(1+t)X_{KK}+Y_{KK} & 0 \\ -Y_{LL} & -Y_{LK} & -1 \end{bmatrix}\begin{bmatrix} dL_X \\ dK_X \\ dw \end{bmatrix}=\begin{bmatrix} -p^*X_L dt \\ -p^*X_K dt \\ 0 \end{bmatrix} \tag{8.15}$$

where, $|A|=-p^{*2}(1+t)^2(X_{LL}X_{KK}-X_{LK}{}^2)+p^*(1+t)(X_{LK}Y_{KL}-X_{LL}Y_{KK})<0$

with $H_X=(X_{LL}X_{KK}-X_{LK}{}^2)=0$, $|A|\gtrless 0$, iff, $(X_{LK}Y_{KL}-X_{LL}Y_{KK})\gtrless 0$.

From Euler's theorem: $X_L L_X+X_K K_X=X$. Differentiating with respect to L_X, $(X_{LL}L_X+X_{KL}K_X=0)$ and $X_{KL}=X_{LK}\Rightarrow(X_{KL}/X_{LL}=-L_X/K_X)$ (8.15a)

and, similarly for Y.

---

[10] See Marjit and Kar (2009) for theoretical and empirical results where degree of capital mobility is a critical determinant of the change in wage rates.

Together, $|A| = p^*(1+t)X_{LL}Y_{KK}(\dfrac{k_Y - k_X}{k_X}) < 0$

where, $k_Z = (K/L)_Z$ and $(k_Y - k_X) < 0$, implying X is relatively capital-intensive to Y.

Thus, we can find out changes in (L_X, K_X) and w from (8.15). As discussed, (L_X, K_X) both fall with a tariff cut:

$$\frac{dL_X}{dt} = \frac{1}{|A|}\Big[p^{*2}(1+t)(X_L X_{KK} - X_K X_{LK}) + p^* X_L Y_{KK}\Big] > 0. \qquad (8.16)$$

Similarly,

$$\frac{dK_X}{dt} = \frac{1}{|A|}\Big[p^{*2}(1+t)(X_K X_{LL} - X_L X_{KL}) - p^* X_L Y_{KL}\Big] > 0. \qquad (8.17)$$

Using total factor endowments, $dL_X = -dL_Y$ and $dK_X = -dK_Y$. \qquad (8.18)
Finally, wage in sector Y increases as t falls:

$$\frac{dw}{dt} = \frac{p^{*2}(1+t)(k_X - k_Y)}{|A|}\left\{\frac{X_L Y_{LL} X_{KK}}{k_Y} - \frac{X_K X_{LL} Y_{LK}}{k_X}\right\} < 0. \qquad (8.19)$$

We also know that,

$$\frac{dr}{dt} = p^*(1+t)X_{KK}(-\frac{K_X}{L_X}\frac{dL_X}{dt} + \frac{dK_X}{dt}) > 0, \text{if } k_X < \frac{dK_X/dt}{dL_X/dt} \text{ or,}$$

$$\frac{dr}{dt} = p^*(1+t)X_{KK}(-\frac{K_X}{L_X}\frac{dL_X}{dt} + \frac{dK_X}{dt}) > 0, \text{ if } \frac{dk_X}{k_X} > 1. \qquad (8.20)$$

Since $X_{KK} < 0, P^*(1+t) > 0, \dfrac{dr}{dt} > 0, \text{ iff, } -\dfrac{K_X}{L_X}\dfrac{dL_X}{dt} + \dfrac{dK_X}{dt} < 0$

or, $[(dK_X/dt)/(dL_X/dt) < K_X/L_X$. Using (8.15a), $[(dK_X/dt)/(dL_X/dt)] < -X_{LL}/X_{KL}$. Substituting dL_X/dt and dK_X/dt from (8.16) and (8.17) and rearranging:

$$P^{*2}(1+t)[X_{KL}X_{LL}(X_K - X_L) + X_L(X_{LL}X_{KK} - X_{LK}^2)] < p^* X_L(Y_{KL}X_{KL} - X_{LL}Y_{KK})$$

$$(8.21)$$

where, $(X_{LL}X_{KK} - X_{LK}^2) = 0$. Using (8.15a), $(X_{KL}Y_{KL} - X_{LL}Y_{KK}) = [(X_{LL}Y_{KK})]/$ $k_X(k_Y - k_x)$. We have already discussed $(k_Y - k_x) < 0$ and $X_K < X_L$, both because X is relatively capital-intensive compared to Y. Substituting these in (8.21), and rearranging,

$$\left(\frac{X_K}{X_L} - 1\right) < \frac{Y_{KK}}{X_{KL}} \frac{k_Y - k_X}{k_X} \frac{1}{p^*(1+t)}. \tag{8.22}$$

Thus, $(dK_X/dt)/(dL_X/dt) < K_X$ and it implies that $dr/dt > 0$. The fall in tariff lowers per unit return to capital as well.

The market wage therefore rises after trade liberalization and some workers in X lose jobs. Since voluntary unemployment is not an option, these workers join sector Y. Note that the wage in Y has gone up. Let the new wage in Y be $\tilde{w} = w + dw$. However, as long as ($\tilde{w} < \bar{w}$), retrenched workers qualify for TAA.[11] Similarly, $\tilde{r} = r + dr$ and $\tilde{r} < r$. These results are summarized in Proposition 8.3. We measure the welfare impact of TAA in the following subsection.

Proposition 8.3: *The trade liberalization policy raises the wage in the export sector, despite inflow of labour from the contracting import-competing sector. Fall in rental rate and consequent lower average cost attracts more firms to the growing export sector thereby improving marginal product of labour.*

8.3.2 WAGE SUBSIDY

Proposition 8.3 is the basis for formulating the policy. All workers, including the displaced that join sector Y, earn more than sector Y offered in the preliberalization regime. However, for the displaced group, this may still be lower than the formal negotiated wage in sector X. On the same note, owners of capital also earn lower returns uniformly in both sectors in the post liberalization regime.

Presently, let us consider that a support scheme is extended only to displaced workers for purely political reasons and based on arguments offered in the introduction. Given the definition and conditions under which workers qualify for wage subsidy, let us assume that the government offers a fraction $0 < \beta < 1$ to cover the positive difference between $\bar{w}$ and $\tilde{w}$. Therefore, wage subsidy per retrenched worker is given by:

$$S_W = \beta(\bar{w} - \tilde{w}). \tag{8.23}$$

---

[11] Note that $\tilde{w} \geq \bar{w}$ is also feasible. If one assumes that unions revise the formal wage to $\hat{w} > \bar{w}$ readily, then one should compare $\tilde{w}$ to $\hat{w}$. This requires revision of TAA.

Now, the number of workers who lost jobs due to trade liberalization is ($-dL_X$). Hence, the total subsidy bill (S) that the government needs to fund is

$$S = \beta(\bar{w} - \tilde{w})(-dL_x). \tag{8.24}$$

We are interested in finding out how the aggregate and group-specific welfare change after implementation of S (from zero) following trade liberalization. Apparently, trade liberalization and the injection of wage subsidy render opposing impacts on welfare. At the point where these two effects balance, the second-best is achieved. Therefore, the optimum wage subsidy is obtained at the second-best equilibrium that maximizes aggregate welfare in the post-liberalization regime. First, we measure the aggregate welfare impact of trade liberalization.

Let the direct utility function for the group of identical workers in the country be $V = V(D_X, D_Y)$, where the arguments are consumption of X and Y at home. We measure overall change in welfare by:

$$d\Omega = p^*(1+t)dD_X + dD_Y. \tag{8.25}$$

From the condition of balanced trade[12],

$$p^*(1+t)dD_X + dD_Y - tp^* dD_X = p^*(1+t)dX + dY - tp^* dX \tag{8.26}$$

or,
$$d\Omega = p^*(1+t)dX + dY + tp^* dM_X. \tag{8.27}$$

Now, from the RHS of (8.27),

$$p^*(1+t)dX + dY = p^*(1+t)[X_L dL_X + X_K dK_X] + [Y_L dL_Y + Y_K dK_Y]. \tag{8.28}$$

Using (8.26),

$$p^*(1+t)dX + dY = p^*(1+t)[X_L dL_X + X_K dK_X] + [Y_L(-dL_X) + Y_K(-dK_X)]. \tag{8.29}$$

The marginal products after trade liberalization are substituted in (8.29). Using (8.20–8.22): $X_L = \bar{w}/p^*(1+t), X_K = \tilde{r}/p^*(1+t), Y_L = \tilde{w}, Y_K = \tilde{r}$. From (8.29),

$$p^*(1+t)dX + dY = p^*(1+t)\left[\frac{\bar{w}}{p^*(1+t)}dL_X + \frac{\tilde{r}}{p^*(1+t)}dK_X\right]$$
$$+ [\tilde{w}(-dL_X) + \tilde{r}(-dK_X)].$$

---

[12] See Caves, Frankel, and Jones (2006) and Kar and Marjit (2001) for similar formulations.

Rearranging, $\qquad p^*(1+t)dX + dY = [(\bar{w} - \tilde{w})dL_X]$. $\qquad\qquad$ (8.30)

Therefore, from (8.27), $\qquad\qquad d\Omega = (\bar{w} - \tilde{w})dL_X + tp^* dM_X$. $\qquad$ (8.31)

Since, $\quad M_X = M_X(p^*(1+t)/\bar{w}, \Omega)$, $\quad dM_X = S_{XX}dt + \mu_X d\Omega$, $\quad$ where, $S_{XX} = \delta M_X / \delta t < 0$ is the own price effect and $\mu_X = \delta M_X / \delta\Omega > 0$ is the income effect. Substituting these in (8.31), we get

$$d\Omega = (\bar{w} - \tilde{w})dL_X + tp^*[S_{XX}dt + \mu_X d\Omega]$$

such that, $\qquad \dfrac{d\Omega}{dt} = \dfrac{1}{(1 - tp^*\mu_X)}\left[(\bar{w} - \tilde{w})\dfrac{dL_X}{dt} + tp^* S_{XX}\right]$. $\qquad$ (8.32)

Since $\mu_X = m_X / (1+t)p^*$, where m_X represents the marginal propensity to consume import goods, and $0 < (1 - tp^*\mu_X) < 1$, if $t < 1/p^*\mu_X$.

Equation (8.32) shows that welfare may only conditionally improve subject to a tariff cut. Note that, complete free trade entails $d\Omega/dt|_{t=0} > 0$.

On the other hand, from (8.24) $(\bar{w} - \tilde{w})dL_X = -\dfrac{S}{\beta}$. $\qquad\qquad$ (8.33)

Substituting (8.33) in (8.31), $d\Omega = -S/\beta + tp^* dM_X$

$$\text{such that, } \frac{d\Omega}{dS} = -\frac{1}{\beta} + tp^*\frac{dM_X}{dS}$$

$$\text{or, } \frac{d\Omega}{dS} = -\frac{1}{\beta} + tp^*[\frac{dM_X}{dS}\frac{S}{M_X}]\frac{M_X}{S}$$

$$\text{i.e. } \frac{d\Omega}{dS} = -\frac{1}{\beta} + tp^*\eta_s^X\frac{M_X}{S}$$

$$\qquad\qquad (8.34)$$

where, $\eta_s^X = [(dM_X / dS)(S/M_X)]$ is the import elasticity of wage subsidy. This exhibits $\lim\limits_{S\to 0} d\Omega/dS = +\infty$.

Therefore, individual effects of trade liberalization and wage subsidy need to be compared. Equations (8.32) and (8.34) yield the *second-best* and the optimum β^* is chosen at a given t.

$$\frac{d\Omega}{dt} = \frac{d\Omega}{dS} \Rightarrow -\frac{1}{\beta} + tp^*\eta_s^X\frac{M_X}{S} = \frac{1}{(1 - tp^*\mu_X)}\left[(\bar{w} - \tilde{w})\frac{dL_X}{dt} + tp^* S_{XX}\right]$$

$$tp^* \eta_S^x \frac{M_X}{S} = \frac{1}{(1-tp^*\mu_X)}\left[(\bar{w}-\tilde{w})\frac{dL_X}{dt}+tp^*S_{XX}\right]+\frac{1}{\beta}$$

Therefore, $\beta^* = \dfrac{(1-tp^*\mu_X)}{tp^*\left[\eta_S^x \dfrac{M_X}{S}(1-tp^*\mu_X-S_{XX})-(\bar{w}-\tilde{w})\dfrac{dL_X}{dt}\right]}$.　　　(8.35)

But, $0<\beta^*<1$ requires (i)　　$t<\dfrac{1}{p^*\mu_X}$　　　(8.35a)

and, (ii) $(1-tp^*\mu_X)\left[1-tp^*\eta_S^x\dfrac{M_X}{S}\right]+(\bar{w}-\tilde{w})\dfrac{dL_X}{dt}<-tp^*S_{XX}$.　　(8.35b)

Condition (8.35) indicates several possibilities for relating (t^*,β^*) given $[p^*,(M_X/S),\eta_S^x,\mu_X,S_{XX},(\bar{w}-\tilde{w})(dL_X/dt)]$. Interestingly, for a wide range of values of t, β^* is concave in t, ensuring unique maximum for β. In the Appendix, we offer a set of eight cases in four separate diagrams where changes are measured for β^* when, (i) the ratio of M_X/S (import-to-subsidy) changes (Figure 8.A1); (ii) the relative price level (p) changes (Figure 8.A2); (iii) the elasticity and consumption propensity of import change (Figure 8.A3) and (iv) the wage gap and/or the low-skill employment response to tariff changes (Figure 8.A4). In each diagram the changes are noted vis-à-vis the benchmark (*BM*) case (Condition 8.35). In Figure 8.A4 for example, a rise in μ_X raises the (t^*,β^*) combination that achieves the second-best as (8.35) yields. Based on a set of values for the price level, import value-to-total subsidy ratio, import elasticity (to tariff rate and aggregate welfare), etc. (available in Table 8.A2, Appendix 2) we find that the maximum β^* payable is 21% when the tariff rate is 65% (Figure 8.A4 and similarly for other figures). For the benchmark case (from which all changes are measured, see Table 8.A2 in Appendix 2 and subsequent analysis, any tariff rate below approximately 20% sets β at zero. This implies that at the level of free trade, β^* is infeasible and becomes a tax instead. Thus only if trade liberalization is incomplete (and tariff rate maintained at a positive level, say 20%), β as an instrument for redistributing gains from trade attains the second-best. Equation (8.35) shows that if β^* is exogenous and politically determined, then the country may conversely choose the optimal tariff rate, t^*, for achieving the second-best. However, under multilateral trade negotiations, tariff rates are usually chosen first and other adjustments follow.

Measurement of aggregate welfare is based on changes in consumption for the entire population. Thus, albeit the owners of capital lose unambiguously, wage subsidy helps to improve aggregate consumption. Any choice of β slightly higher than β^* and within limits set by (8.35a, b) must improve aggregate welfare.

Proposition 8.4: *The choice of TAA rate is critically dependent on income and price elasticity of import demand, import elasticity of gross subsidy, and the wage-employment effect. The relationship between β and t is concave over a large range and optimal combination of (β^*, t*) attains the second-best welfare level in the economy.*

8.3.3 GROUP-SPECIFIC WELFARE

This section calculates welfare implications for three distinct groups. These are the owners of capital, workers in the protected sector, and workers in the unprotected sector. The last group is composed of displaced workers from group two and those who were already in the third group. Individuals within each group are identical. Therefore, calculation of individual welfare gives group welfare. For a simple case, let us consider that the tastes for X and Y are same for all groups. An individual in group i maximizes the following utility function:

$$\underset{D_X, D_Y}{Max} U^i(X,Y) = D_X^\alpha D_Y^{1-\alpha} \text{ subject to } M^i = p^*(1+t)D_X + D_Y \qquad (8.36)$$

where, D_Z ($Z=X, Y$) is consumption of Zth good; $0 < \alpha < 1$; and M^i is the income of the ith group after trade liberalization and the support scheme are implemented ($i= C, WP, WU$, representing capitalists, protected workers, and unprotected workers respectively).[13] (8.36) yields following three maximization problems:

$$\underset{D_X, D_Y}{Max} U^C(X,Y) = D_X^\alpha D_Y^{1-\alpha} \text{ subject to } M^C = r\overline{K} = p^*(1+t)D_X + D_Y. \qquad (8.36a)$$

Using standard procedures of utility maximization subject to budget constraint we get,
$D_X^* = \alpha r\overline{K} / p^*(1+t)$ and $D_Y^* = (1-\alpha)r\overline{K}$ as equilibrium quantity demand for X and Y, respectively. Totally differentiating the equilibrium consumption levels:

$$dD_X^* = \frac{\alpha\overline{K}[(1+t)dr - rdt]}{p^*(1+t)^2}, \ dD_Y^* = (1-\alpha)\overline{K}dr. \text{ Now}, d\Omega^C = p^*(1+t)dD_X^* + dD_Y^*$$

---

[13] If tastes vary across groups, then α is replaced by α_i but the same result holds.

or, $d\Omega^C = \bar{K}[\alpha dr - \alpha r \dfrac{dt}{1+t} + (1-\alpha)dr]$, such that,

$[(d\Omega^C / dt)(> / < 0)$ iff $(dr/dt) - (\alpha r/1+t)(> / <)0, or(dr/dt)(> / <)(\alpha r/1+t)]$. Intuitively, for owners of capital, if the tariff cut induced change in return from investments is higher than the consumption (of X) weighted ratio of returns from investment and the tariff rate, the welfare must go up. Conversely, the individual and group welfare for capitalists may decrease.

Using similar procedure for members of the *protected* group:

$$\underset{D_X,D_Y}{Max}\, U^{WP}(X,Y) = D_X^\alpha D_Y^{1-\alpha} \text{ subject to } M^{WP} = \bar{w} = p*(1+t)D_X + D_Y \quad (8.36b)$$

yields, $dD_X^* = \alpha \bar{w} dt / p*(1+t)^2$ and $dD_Y^* = 0$. Together, $d\Omega^{WP}/dt = -\alpha\bar{w}/1+t < 0$. The implication is direct. Since the remaining workers in the protected sector continue to earn the rigid wage, fall in import price owing to fall in tariff rate leads to real income gain and consequent improvement in group welfare.

Those workers in the *unprotected sector* who are not eligible for wage subsidy decide on their consumption levels based on w. The maximization problem for such workers is:

$$\underset{D_X,D_Y}{Max}\, U^{WP}(X,Y) = D_X^\alpha D_Y^{1-\alpha} \text{ subject to } M^{WP} = \bar{w} = p*(1+t)D_X + D_Y. \quad (8.36c)$$

Change in wage due to trade liberalization is instrumental in driving welfare level for these workers. Thus, $(d\Omega^{WU}/dt)(> / <)0$ iff $(dw/dt)(> / <)\alpha w/1+t$. Note that from (8.19), $dw/dt < 0$. Hence $d\Omega^{WU}/dt < 0$ since $(dw/dt < \alpha w/1+t)$. Once again, a fall in the tariff rate raises the level of welfare for identical individuals in the unprotected group—the result of a rise in real income among uncompensated workers of the unprotected sector.

Finally, we formulate the maximization problem for *displaced workers* receiving TAA as:

$$\underset{D_X,D_Y}{Max}\, U^{WS}(X,Y) = D_X^\alpha D_Y^{1-\alpha} \text{ subject to } M^{WS} = [\bar{w} + \beta(\bar{w} - w)] = p*(1+t)D_X + D_Y.$$

$$(8.36d)$$

Solving the maximization problem in (8.36d) and substituting changes in equilibrium demand for X and Y, we get $(d\Omega^{WS}/dt)(> / < 0)$ iff $(dw/dt)(> / <)(\alpha w/1+t)[\beta\bar{w} + w(1-\beta)]$. The RHS of this condition is positive, while $dw/dt < 0$. Therefore, not unexpectedly, the group receiving TAA unambiguously benefits in terms of welfare level.

In other words, the owners of capital may or may not benefit from trade liberalization. On the other hand, the workers, whether in the protected sector or in the unprotected sector in addition to the displaced individuals, all gain from trade liberalization and wage subsidy. The aggregate welfare conditions derived in the previous subsections accounts for those group-specific changes. It seems that the results we offer here are crucially dependent on the political choice, where the importance of one factor over another could be the determinant of the policy choice. We hope to model this in a future extension.

8.4 Concluding Remarks

While Bhagwati and Srinivasan (2002) note that practically no country that has been close to autarkic has managed to sustain a high growth performance over a sustained period, and reflects the position of a large number of economists who see trade and factor flows as freedom and wings of growth, the increasing integration with the world order has its cost, as we have already discussed in Chapter 1. According to Bhagwati and Srinivasan (2002), the evidence on growth and poverty is perhaps best approached through detailed focus on the two countries that have huge *comparative advantage* in poverty: China and India. Indeed, a vast majority of the world's poor live in the rural areas of China and India. Both countries achieved significant reductions in poverty during 1980–2000 when they grew rapidly. According to the World Bank (2000, Table 4-2) estimates, real GDP grew at an annual average rate of 8% in China and 6% in India during these two decades. No country in the world had as rapid growth as China whereas fewer than ten countries exceeded the Indian growth rate. The effect on reduction in poverty in both countries was dramatic, which according to the Asian Development Bank (2000, Table 3-1) estimates declined from 28% in 1978 to 9% in 1998 in China. By the Government of India's (2000, Table 5) estimates, poverty incidence fell from 51% in 1977–1978 to 27% in 1999–2000. Obviously, the experience of the two giant economies of China and India in achieving faster growth and reduction in poverty through greater integration into the world economy is exemplary and finds supporting evidence from Vietnam (poverty rate cut down from 75% to 37%) and Uganda (Dollar, 2001) for example. However, as we have discussed all through this chapter, the impact can hardly be symmetric and needs redress of other sorts manoeuvered within the political economy arrangements.

Trade adjustment assistance, as one such instrument of redress, has not received adequate attention in the context of developing countries. In retrospect, however, it appears that such dialogues and opportunities might have lessened the initial resistance free trade policies faced in many of these countries. It also makes a politically correct statement to compensate the affected, by using benefits that comes with free trade. Needless to mention, like any other policy, TAA is also subject to controversies and practical issues with implementation. The task of proving loss of jobs due to trade liberalization is not simple either. For developing countries, added complexity comes from the presence of dual labour markets where a large section of the workforce belongs outside formal regulations.

Withdrawal of import barriers render many import-competing industries non-competitive and cause labour retrenchment. Lump-sum wage subsidy is a means to compensate for the wage loss workers face when joining a new sector. We formalized a technique to attain the second-best welfare level in the context of developing countries. We obtained a combination of tariff rates and wage subsidies (as a form of TAA) to compensate 'movers' from import-competing industries. Interestingly, our model shows that trade liberalization increases the real wage, both within the unionized sector and outside it. However, there is no mechanism to guarantee that the nominal outside wage rises to the level of the unionized sector. This allows for TAA in our model, and we obtain the feasible range of wage subsidy over a large range of tariff rates. The second-best is obtained for a level of TAA where welfare impacts of trade liberalization and wage subsidy in the aggregate balance each other. The wage subsidy is critically dependent on price and income elasticity of import, import elasticity of gross subsidy, relative price of the import competing good, and the tariff rate itself. In the Appendix we showed eight sets of results compared to what we call the benchmark case (for a set of parameter values) to measure variations owing to changes in elasticity, relative price, and wage income. For example, when the relative price is 0.75, a wage subsidy of 15 cents may be offered for every dollar if the tariff rate is 95% on the base price. A reduction in the relative price requires that the tariff rate is at least 145% in order to maintain the same rate of wage subsidy. Lowering of the tariff rate to say 60% (from 95% in the benchmark case) would lower subsidy to 8 cents per dollar, and still the second-best is achieved. If the import elasticity of subsidy rises by 80% the (β^*, t^*) combination should be (0.8, 72%) to obtain the second-best. As a final example, if the wage gap times the employment effect of tariff rises by 50%, the (β^*, t^*) combination settles at (0.12, 116%) to maintain the second-best welfare level.

Finally, with regard to supplementary assistance programmes made available at the country level, we should emphasize that the results of the adjustment assistance is not limited to payments of wage subsidy alone. Alternative policies such as subsidized training of retrenched workers may generate even higher welfare gains due to dynamic elements. Consideration of skill heterogeneity, use of capital as a specific factor, involuntary unemployment, and other forms of TAA may offer possible extensions of this structure.

■ Appendix 1: The Relation between Trade and Informal Wages

A reduction in the tariff rate and the consequent equations of change are given later. Two generic derivations are given here and the rest follows the same procedure.

$$\frac{d\bar{w}_S}{\bar{w}_S}\frac{a_{SX}\bar{w}_S}{P_X^*(1+t)} + \frac{da_{SX}}{a_{SX}}\frac{a_{SX}\bar{w}_S}{P_X^*(1+t)} + \frac{dr}{r}\frac{a_{KX}r}{P_X^*(1+t)} + \frac{da_{kX}}{a_{KX}}\frac{a_{kX}\bar{w}_S}{P_X^*(1+t)}$$

$$= \frac{dP_X^*}{P_X^*(1+t)}P_X^*(1+t) + \frac{dt}{t}\frac{t}{P_X^*(1+t)}P_X^*$$

Since $\bar{w}_S$ and P_X^* do not change, and using the envelope condition $[(da_{SX}/a_{SX})(a_{SX}\bar{w}_S/P_X^*(1+t)) + (da_{kX}/a_{KX})(a_{kX}\bar{w}_S/P_X^*(1+t)) = 0]$, the earlier expression yields:

$$\theta_{KX}\hat{r} = \alpha\hat{t}, \text{where}, \alpha = t/(1+t) \tag{8A.1}$$

where, $\theta_{KX} = a_{KX}r/P_X^*(1+t)$, the income share of capital in sector X, and more generally, all θ_{ij}'s are income shares of factor i in the price of commodity j.

Thus, $\hat{r} = \alpha\hat{t}/\theta_{KX} < 0$, as, $\hat{t} < 0$.

Now using Equation (8.2), $\hat{P}_I = -\dfrac{\theta_{KY}}{\theta_{IY}}\dfrac{\alpha\hat{t}}{\theta_{KX}} > 0$, as, $\hat{t} < 0$. $\tag{8A.2}$

Deriving Equation (8.3) and substituting the earlier information yields:

$$\hat{w} = -\frac{\alpha\hat{t}}{\theta_{KX}}\frac{\theta_{KY}}{\theta_{LI}}\left(1 + \frac{1}{\theta_{IY}}\right) > 0, \quad as, \hat{t} < 0. \tag{8A.3}$$

Finally, from Equation (8.4),

$\theta_{LZ}\hat{w} = \hat{P}_Z$, such that, $\hat{P}_Z = -\alpha(\hat{t}\theta_{LZ}/\theta_{KX})(\theta_{KY}/\theta_{LI})(1+1/\theta_{IY}) > 0.$ $\tag{8A.4}$

This implies that, $(\hat{w} - \hat{r}) > 0$.
Similarly, Equation (8.5) may be derived in the following way:

$$\frac{dX}{X}\frac{a_{SX}X}{\bar{S}} + \frac{da_{SX}}{a_{SX}}\frac{a_{SX}X}{\bar{S}} + \frac{dY}{Y}\frac{a_{SX}Y}{\bar{S}} + \frac{da_{SY}}{a_{SY}}\frac{a_{SX}Y}{\bar{S}} = \frac{d\bar{S}}{\bar{S}}, \text{such that,}$$

$$\lambda_{SX}\hat{X} + \lambda_{SY}\hat{Y} = -\lambda_{SX}\hat{a}_{SX} - \lambda_{SY}\hat{a}_{SY} \tag{8A.5}$$

where, $\lambda_{SX} = a_{SX} X / \bar{S}$, the skill endowment does not change and more generally, all λ_{ij}'s represent ith factor's physical contribution to the production of commodity j. Using factor price changes and the degree of substitution between factors, Equation (8A.5) yields,

$$\lambda_{SX} \widehat{X} + \lambda_{SY} \widehat{Y} = -\left[\lambda_{SX} \theta_{KX} \sigma_X + \lambda_{SY} \theta_{KY} \sigma_Y \right] \hat{r}. \tag{8A.6}$$

Again from Equation (8.7), assuming that the informal intermediate input is used in fixed proportions without any substitution with capital or labour, we get,

$$\lambda_{KX} \widehat{X} + \lambda_{KY} \widehat{Y} = -\lambda_{KX} \hat{a}_{KX} - \lambda_{KY} \hat{a}_{KY} - \lambda_{KI} (\hat{a}_{KI} + \hat{I}). \tag{8A.7}$$

However, from Equation (8.8), $\lambda_{IY} (\hat{a}_{IY} + \widehat{Y}) = \hat{I}$.

Since I is used in fixed proportions in the production of Y, thus, $\hat{a}_{IY} = 0$ and the above relationship becomes, $\lambda_{IY} \widehat{Y} = \hat{I}$. $\tag{8A.8}$

Substituting (8A.8) in (8A.7), we get, $\lambda_{KX} \widehat{X} + \lambda_{KY} \widehat{Y} = -\lambda_{KX} \hat{a}_{KX} - \lambda_{KY} \hat{a}_{KY} - \lambda_{KI} \lambda_{IY} \widehat{Y}$

i.e., $\qquad \lambda_{KX} \widehat{X} + (\lambda_{KY} + \lambda_{KI} \lambda_{IY}) \widehat{Y} = \left[\lambda_{KX} \theta_{SX} \sigma_X + \lambda_{KY} \theta_{SY} \sigma_Y \right] \hat{r}. \tag{8A.9}$

These two equations solve for $\widehat{X}$ and $\widehat{Y}$ simultaneously.

Denote $\tilde{\lambda}_{KY} = (\lambda_{KY} + \lambda_{KI} \lambda_{IY})$, i.e., direct and indirect (via production of I) use of capital in the production of Y.

Thus, $\qquad \begin{bmatrix} \lambda_{SX} & \lambda_{SY} \\ \lambda_{KX} & \tilde{\lambda}_{KY} \end{bmatrix} \begin{bmatrix} \widehat{X} \\ \widehat{Y} \end{bmatrix} = \begin{bmatrix} -(\lambda_{SX} \theta_{KX} \sigma_X + \lambda_{SY} \theta_{KY} \sigma_Y) \hat{r} \\ (\lambda_{KX} \theta_{SX} \sigma_X + \lambda_{KY} \theta_{SY} \sigma_Y) \hat{r} \end{bmatrix}. \tag{8A.10}$

Using Cramer's rule on Equation (8A.8),

$$\widehat{X} = \frac{-\tilde{\lambda}_{KY} (\lambda_{SX} \theta_{KX} \sigma_X + \lambda_{SY} \theta_{KY} \sigma_Y) \hat{r} - \lambda_{SY} (\lambda_{KX} \theta_{SX} \sigma_X + \lambda_{KY} \theta_{SY} \sigma_Y) \hat{r}}{(\lambda_{SX} \tilde{\lambda}_{KY} - \lambda_{KX} \lambda_{SY})}$$

or, $\widehat{X} = -\hat{r} \dfrac{(\tilde{\lambda}_{KY} \lambda_{SX} \theta_{KX} + \lambda_{SY} \lambda_{KX} \theta_{SX}) \sigma_X + (\tilde{\lambda}_{KY} \lambda_{SY} \theta_{KY} + \lambda_{SY} \lambda_{KY} \theta_{SY}) \sigma_Y}{(\lambda_{SX} \tilde{\lambda}_{KY} - \lambda_{KX} \lambda_{SY})}. \tag{8A.11}$

Denote $\Delta = (\lambda_{SX} \tilde{\lambda}_{KY} - \lambda_{KX} \lambda_{SY}) < 0$, which implies that sector X is more capital-intensive compared to sector Y. Consequently, $\widehat{X} < 0$, as, $\hat{r} < 0$ and $\Delta < 0$.

Conversely, $\widehat{Y} = \dfrac{\lambda_{SX} (\lambda_{KX} \theta_{SX} \sigma_X + \lambda_{KY} \theta_{SY} \sigma_Y) \hat{r} + \lambda_{KX} (\lambda_{SX} \theta_{KX} \sigma_X + \lambda_{SY} \theta_{KY} \sigma_Y) \hat{r}}{(\lambda_{SX} \tilde{\lambda}_{KY} - \lambda_{KX} \lambda_{SY})} > 0$

i.e.
$$\hat{Y} = \lambda_{SX}\hat{r}\frac{\left[\lambda_{KX}\sigma_X + \lambda_{KY}(1-\theta_{IY})\sigma_Y\right]}{(\lambda_{SX}\tilde{\lambda}_{KY} - \lambda_{KX}\lambda_{SY})} > 0.$$ (8A.12)

Equation (8.8) then yields: $\hat{I} = \lambda_{IY}\hat{Y}$

$$\text{or, } \hat{I} = \lambda_{IY}\lambda_{SX}\frac{\alpha\hat{t}}{\theta_{KX}}\frac{\left[\lambda_{KX}\sigma_X + \lambda_{KY}(1-\theta_{IY})\sigma_Y\right]}{(\lambda_{SX}\tilde{\lambda}_{KY} - \lambda_{KX}\lambda_{SY})} > 0$$

and finally from Equation (8.6),

$$\hat{Z} > 0, \textit{iff}, \lambda_{IY}\lambda_{SX}\left[\lambda_{KX}\sigma_X + \lambda_{KY}(1-\theta_{IY})\sigma_Y\right] > \sigma_I(\tilde{\theta}_{KY}/\theta_{IY} + \theta_{KY}),$$
where, $\tilde{\theta}_{KY} = (\theta_{KY} + \theta_{KI}\theta_{IY}).$

QED.
Proof of Proposition 8.2 follows similarly.

■ Appendix 2: Trade Adjustment Assistance and Welfare

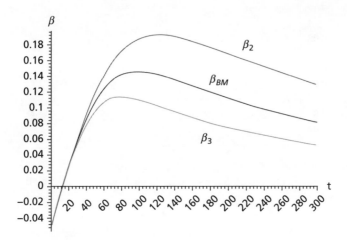

Figure 8.A1 Relationship Between (β, t) for Subsidy-Import Comparison

Note: $\beta_{BM}[p = 0.75, \ \mu_X = 0.1, \ \eta_S^X = 0.05, \ S_{XX} = -0.1, \ S/M_X = 1, \ (\bar{w} - \tilde{w})\,dL_X/dt = 20]$

$\beta_2(\uparrow S/M_X > 1); \beta_3(\downarrow S/M_X < 1)$; BM—Benchmark case.

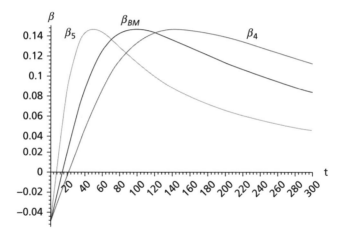

Figure 8.A2 Relationship Between (β, t) for Price Effects
where: $\beta_{BM}[p = 0.75, \mu_x = 0.1, \eta_S^x = 0.05, S_{xx} = -0.1, S/M_x = 1.6, (\bar{w} - \tilde{w})\, dL_x/dt = 20]$
$\beta_4(\downarrow p = 0.5); \beta_5(\uparrow p = 1.5)$; BM—Benchmark case.

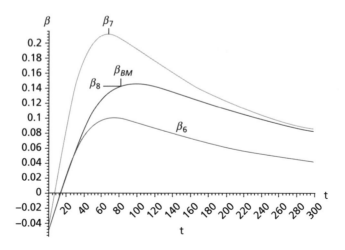

Figure 8.A3 Relationship Between (β, t) for Elasticity Effects
$\beta_{BM}[p = 0.75, \mu_x = 0.1, \eta_S^x = 0.05, S_{xx} = -0.1, S/M_x = 1.6, (\bar{w} - \tilde{w})dL_x/dt = 20]$
$\beta_6(\uparrow \eta_S^x = 0.1); \beta_7(\uparrow \mu_x = 0.2); \beta_8(\downarrow S_{xx} = -0.2)$

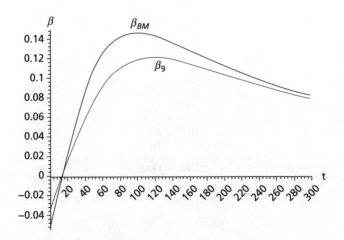

Figure 8.A4 Relationship Between (β, t) for Wage-Elasticity Effect

$\beta_{BM}[p = 0.75, \mu_x = 0.1, \eta_s^x = 0.05, S_{xx} = -0.1, S/M_x = 1.6, (\bar{w} - \tilde{w})dL_x / dt = 20]$

$\beta_9[\uparrow (\bar{w} - \tilde{w})dL_x / dt = 30]$

Source: Figures 8.A1–8.A4, authors' own calculations.

Table 8.A1 Annual Growth Rates of Real Informal Wage for States and Union Territories in India

States	1984–85 to1989–90	1989–90 to1994–95	1994–95 to1999–2000	1999–2000 to2000–01	Post Reform Average
AP	−14.9383	38.37914	0.351421	5.54216	14.75757
AS	−12.5909	9.400387	0.502013	19.94701	9.949804
BH	−12.4796	9.259229	−0.9822	37.41843	15.25582
GJ	−8.01461	5.856186	3.761828	9.471879	6.363298
HY	−15.417	23.39205	−4.11872	33.07289	17.44874
HP	−11.5206	−0.34082	3.509483	24.55454	9.24868
KA	−12.8237	21.54953	7.021524	13.43834	14.00313
KE	−14.8953	12.55645	2.686628	21.20452	12.1492
MP	−12.6123	22.41174	1.455013	13.11878	12.32851
MH	−6.4	9.7482	5.247609	11.28708	8.760962
OR	−13.1553	22.78583	−2.38878	33.1919	17.86298
PN	−15.1443	12.20414	−1.06954	44.061	18.39853
RJ	−15.4959	32.5381	−1.34439	33.03571	21.40744
TN	−8.874	6.406688	14.13201	11.49062	8.67644
TR	−14.3066	14.89337	−5.45877	45.36927	18.26796
UP	−13.2014	18.00436	−1.58454	26.79013	14.40332
WB	−11.2556	11.4885	−7.25447	15.29931	6.485231
AN	NA	14.62978	3.202789	2.98365	6.914311
CH	NA	19.2898	5.496664	12.4677	12.39178
DN	NA	9.8284	−4.01589	37.7676	14.52672
DH	NA	13.26679	20.39249	12.8498	15.25476
LA	NA	−0.21334	9.929694	7.832409	5.849589
PO	NA	20.77112	−3.96475	−18.5548	−0.58281
GO	NA	20.50309	0.947838	23.74566	15.06553
JK	NA	20.71262	2.83883	33.64066	19.06379
MA	NA	24.9116	−4.18481	26.83254	15.85311
ME	NA	18.91503	−5.28746	33.57459	15.73405
MI	NA	19.93168	−6.92451	24.69716	12.56811
NA	NA	15.62657	−1.96228	25.16228	12.94219
SI	NA	28.81384	−0.01264	42.15758	23.65293

Source: NSS Reports on Unorganized Sector in India,v Various Rounds (National Sample Survey Organization) and Own Calculations; NA: Data not available.

List of Abbreviations for States and Union Territories in India

AP—Andhra Pradesh
AS—Assam
BH—Bihar
GJ—Gujarat
HY—Haryana
HP—Himachal Pradesh
KA—Karnataka
KE—Kerala
MP—Madhya Pradesh
MH—Maharastra
OR—Orissa

PN—Punjab
RJ—Rajasthan
TN—Tamil Nadu
TR—Tripura
UP—Uttar Pradesh
WB—West Bengal
AN—Andaman and Nicobar Islands
Ch—Chandigarh
DN—Dadra and Nagar Haveli
DH—Delhi
LA—Lakshadweep
PO—Pondicherry
GO—Goa
JK—Jammu and Kashmir
MA—Manipur
ME—Meghalaya
MI—Mizoram
NA—Nagaland
SI—Sikkim.

Table 8.A2 Sensitivity of $\beta*$ to Parametric Changes

Cases	S/M_x	P^*	η_s^x	μ_x	S_{xx}	$(\bar{w}-\bar{w})dL_x/dt$	t^*	$\beta*$
			Parameters and Variables					
β_{BM}^*	1	0.75	0.05	0.1	-0.1	20	95.70%	0.15
β_2^*	>1 ↑ (60%)	0.75	0.05	0.1	-0.1	20	122.4% ↑ (27%)	0.19 ↑ (27%)
β_3^*	<1 ↓ (40%)	0.75	0.05	0.1	-0.1	20	78.8% ↓ (17%)	0.11 ↓ (27%)
β_4^*	1	0.5 ↓	0.05	0.1	-0.1	20	145.55% ↓ (52%)	0.15(unchanged)
β_5^*	1	1.5 ↑	0.05	0.1	-0.1	20	48.52% ↓ (49%)	0.15(unchanged)
β_6^*	1	0.75	0.1 ↑ (80%)	0.1	-0.1	20	72.55% ↓ (24%)	0.8 ↓ (33%)
β_7^*	1	0.75	0.05	0.2 ↑	-0.1	20	65.43% ↓ (32%)	0.21 ↑ (40%)
β_8^*	1	0.75	0.05	0.1	-0.2 ↓ (80%)	20	96.59% ↑ (.01%)	0.15(unchanged)
β_9^*	1	0.75	0.05	0.1	-0.1	30 ↑ (50%)	116.17% (21%)	0.12 ↓ (20%)

Source: Own Calculations. *Note*: BM—Benchmark case.

■ REFERENCES

Agenor, P. (1996). 'The Labor Market and Economic Adjustment'. *IMF Staff Papers* 32: 261–335.

Asian Development Bank (2000). *Asian Development Outlook*. Manila, Asian Development Bank.

Banerjee, A. V. and Newman, A. (1993). 'Occupational Choice and the Process of Development'. *Journal of Political Economy* 81 (2): 274–298.

Batra, R. N. (1986). 'A General Equilibrium Model of Multinational Corporations in Developing Countries'. *Oxford Economic Papers* 38 (2): 342–353.

Batra, R. N. and Ramachandran, R. (1980). 'Multinational Firms and the Theory of International Trade and Investment'. *American Economic Review* 70 (3): 278–290.

Beladi, H. and Kar, S. (2011). 'Wage Subsidy and Welfare in Developing Countries'. *Economics and Politics* 23 (2): 239–253.

Bhagwati, J. and Srinivasan, T. N. (2002). 'Trade and Poverty in the Poor Countries'. *The American Economic Review* 92 (2), Papers and Proceedings of the One Hundred Fourteenth Annual Meeting of the American Economic Association, pp. 180–183.

Brander, J. and Spencer, B. (1994). 'Trade Adjustment Assistance: Welfare and Incentive Effects of Payments to Displaced Workers'. *Journal of International Economics* 36 (3-4): 239–261.

Caves, R., Frankel, J., and Jones, R. (2006). *World Trade and Payments: An Introduction*, 8th edition. NY: Addison-Wesley.

Chaudhuri, S. (2003). 'How and How Far to Liberalize a Developing Economy with Informal Sector and Factor Market Distortions'. *Journal of International Trade and Economic Development* 12 (4): 403–428.

Chaudhuri, S. and Mukhopadhyay, U. (2002). 'Economic Liberalization and Welfare in a Model with an Informal Sector'. *The Economics of Transition* 8 (1): 143–172.

Chen, M. (2000). 'Women in the Informal Sector: A Global Picture, the Global Movement'. World Bank: Washington DC. http://info.worldbank.org/etools/docs/library/76309/dc2002/proceedings/pdfpaper/module6mc.pdf.

Coe, D. T., Helpman, E., and Hoffmaister, A. W. (1997). 'North-South R&D Spillovers'. *Economic Journal* 87 (440): 134–149.

Davidson, C. and Matusz, S. (2006). 'Trade Liberalization and Compensation'. *International Economic Review* 47 (3): 723–747.

de Soto, H. (1989). *The Other Path: The Invisible Revolution in the Third World*. New York: Harper Row.

De Soto, H. (2000). *The Mystery of Capital*. USA: Basic Books.

Deininger, K. and Olinto, P. (2000). 'Asset Distribution, Inequality, and Growth', World Bank Policy Research WP 2375.

Dixit, A. and Norman, V. (1986). 'Gains from Trade without Lump-Sum Compensation'. *Journal of International Economics* 21 (1-2): 111–122.

Dollar, D. (2001). 'Globalization, Inequality and Poverty Since 1980'. World Bank Washington, DC, http://www.worldbank.org/research/global.

Dollar, D. and Kraay, A. (2002). 'Growth Is Good for the Poor'. *Journal of Economic Growth* 7 (3): 195–225.

Edmonds, E., Pavcnik, N., and Topalova, P. (2010). 'Trade Adjustment and Human Capital Investments: Evidence from Indian Tariff Reform'. *American Economic Journal: Applied Economics* 2: 42–75.

Feenstra, R. and Lewis, T. (1994). 'Trade Adjustment Assistance and Pareto Gains from Trade'. *Journal of International Economics* 36: 201–222.

Government of India (2000). *Economic Survey, 1999–2000*. New Delhi: Government Printing Office.

Hoekman, B., Michalopoulos, C., Schiff, M., and Tarr, D. (2001). 'Trade Policy Reform and Poverty Alleviation, Volume 1. World Bank Policy Research Working Paper 2733.

Hoekman, B., Maskus, K., and Saggi, K. (2004). 'Transfer of Technology to Developing Countries: Unilateral and Multilateral Policy Options'. World Bank Policy Research Working Paper 3332.

International Labour Organisation (1972). *Employment, Incomes and Equality: A Strategy for Increasing Productive Employment in Kenya*. Geneva: ILO.

International Labour Organisation (1999). *Key Indicators of the Labour Market*. Geneva: International Labour Office.

Kar, S. and Marjit, S. (2001). 'Informal Sector in General Equilibrium: Welfare Effects of Trade Policy Reforms'. *International Review of Economics and Finance* 8: 289–300.

Kar, S. and Sinha, C, (2013). 'Sectoral Technical Progress and Aggregate Skill Formation'. *Journal of Industry, Competition and Trade*, DOI 10.1007/s10842-013-0152-2.

Kletzer, L. (2004). 'Trade-Related Job Loss and Wage Insurance: a Synthetic Review'. *Review of International Economics* 12 (5): 724–748.

Kletzer, L. and Litan, R. (2001). *A Prescription to Relieve Worker Anxiety*. Washington DC: Institute for International Economics Policy Brief PB01-2.

Lawrence, R. and Litan, R. (1986). *Saving Free Trade: A Pragmatic Approach*. Washington, DC: Brookings Institution.

Lopez, R., Nash, J., and Stanton, J. (1995). 'Adjustment and Poverty in Mexican Agriculture: How Farmers' Wealth Affects Supply Response'. World Bank Policy Research Working Paper 1494.

Marjit, S. (2003). 'Economic Reform and Informal Wage—A General Equilibrium Analysis'. *Journal of Development Economics* 72 (1): 371–378.

Marjit, S. and Kar, S. (2009). 'Urban Informal Sector and Poverty'. *International Review of Economics and Finance* 18 (4): 631–642.

Marjit, S. and Kar, S. (2011). *The Outsiders: Economic Reform and Informal Labour in a Developing Economy*. New Delhi: Oxford University Press.

Marjit, S., Kar, S., and Beladi, H. (2007). 'Trade Reform and Informal Wage'. *Review of Development Economics* 11: 313–320.

Marjit, S., Kar, S., and Maiti, D. (2009). 'Labour Market Reform and Poverty—The Role of Informal Sector'. In: B. Dutta, T. Ray, and E. Somanathan (eds). *New and Enduring Themes in Development Economics*. NY: World Scientific.

Martin, W. and Mitra, D. (2001). 'Productivity Growth and Convergence in Agriculture and Manufacturing'. *Economic Development and Cultural Change* 49 (2): 403–422.

Mayer, W. (1984). 'Endogenous Tariff Formation'. *American Economic Review* 74 (5): 970–985.

Rodriguez, F. and Rodrik, D. (2001). 'Trade Policy and Economic Growth: A Skeptic's Guide to Cross-National Evidence'. In: B. Bernanke and K.S. Rogoff (eds). *NBER Macroeconomics Annual* 2000. Cambridge, MA: MIT Press.

Rodrik, D. (2000). 'How Far Will International Economic Integration Go? *Journal of Economic Perspectives* 14 (1): Winter 2000.

Rodrik, D. (2001). 'The Global Governance of Trade as if Development Really Mattered', April 2001. A paper prepared for the UNDP, Kennedy School of Government, Harvard University, MA.

Srinivasan, T. N. and Bhagwati, J. (2001). 'Outward Orientation and Development: Are Revisionists Right?' In: D. Lal and R. Shape (eds). *Trade, Development and Political Economy: Essays in Honour of Anne Krueger*. London: Palgrave.

Turnham, D. (1993). *Employment and Development—A New Review of Evidence*. Paris: Development Centre Studies, OECD.

Tzannatos, Z. and Roddis, S. (1998). 'Unemployment Benefits'. Social Protection Discussion Paper Series 9813. Social Protection Unit, World Bank, Washington DC.

Webster, L. and Fidler, P. (1996). 'The Informal Sector and Microfinance in West Africa'. Washington, DC: World Bank Regional and Sectoral Studies, World Bank.

Winters, L. A., McCulloch, N., and McKay, A. (2004). 'Trade Liberalization and Poverty: The Evidence so Far'. *Journal of Economic Literature* 42 (1): 72–115.

World Bank (2000). *World Development Indicators*. Washington, DC: World Bank.

9 Regional Trading Arrangements as Development Strategy

Over the last two decades, there has been an unprecedented proliferation of regional trading arrangements (RTA) and free trade agreements between countries both within and across continents. Bilateral and regional trade agreements had existed even before the World War I period, the most notable of which were the commercial treaty between England and Portugal in 1703 and the Anglo-French treaty in the 1860. The post-World War II period also saw evolution of the European Union, which was motivated in part by the argument that economic cooperation can mitigate conflicts between them and that economic strength is the basis of political and military power. The formation of the European Coal and Steel Community (ECSC) in 1951 and thereafter the European Economic Community (EEC) in 1957 that marked the beginning of today's European Union were also motivated by the success of BENELUX customs union formed in 1948 between Belgium, The Netherlands, and Luxembourg, which later developed into an economic union after the 1958 BENELUX Treaty. In Asia, there was the Association of South East Asian Nations (ASEAN), which came into force in the late 1960s with Indonesia, Malaysia, the Philippines, Singapore, and Thailand as the five founder member countries. There was also the Gulf Cooperation Council (GCC), a political and economic union, formed by Bahrain, Kuwait, Oman, Qatar, Saudi Arabia, and the United Arab Emirates in 1981. The Caribbean Community and Common Market (CARICOM) and the South African Customs Union (SACU) also evolved during the 1960s and 1970s in other parts of the globe.

But these developments of economic and political cooperation amongst a group of countries had been far outstripped by the phenomenal proliferation of new bilateral and regional trading arrangements and trade blocs during the 1990s, particularly in Asia. The number of *active* RTAs had shot up to 230 by the end of 2003 and further increased to 290 in 2010 from a mere 50 in 1992. Ethier (2011) calls this phenomenon *contemporary regionalism*, with features and motivation behind these trade blocs being distinctly different from those that evolved during 1960s and 1970s, termed as old regionalism.

This chapter evaluates this bilateral and regional approach to trade as a development strategy for countries, and examines the conflict and complementarity between this regional approach and the WTO's multilateral approach.

9.1 Types of RTAs

Viner (1950) categorized regional trading arrangements into five stages according to their coverage and intensity of coordination in trade, fiscal, and monetary policies of the member countries. The first stage of trade policy coordination amongst two or more countries is the formation of a Preferential Trading Arrangement (PTA) by which the member countries lower their respective tariff and non-tariff barriers on intra-PTA trade. A Free Trade Area (FTA) is a step forward in trade policy reciprocation in which the member countries abolish their respective tariff and non-tariff barriers on intra-FTA trade. In both a PTA and an FTA, the member countries unilaterally decide about tariff and non-tariff barriers on imports from the non-member countries. These *external* tariff rates and non-tariff barriers are unified by the member countries when they form a Customs Union (CU). This is a higher stage of cooperation than an FTA as they keep intra-CU trade free, like the FTA, but in addition, unify their external tariff rates. The common external tariff is usually set to maximize the aggregate welfare of the union. Sometimes, the tariff setting power is delegated to an aggressive and dominant member of the union, who maximizes its own welfare to set the common external tariff.

The next stage of cooperation amongst the group of countries is achieved when they form a Common Market (CM) whereby, in addition to the trade policy coordination as in CU, the countries allow free movement of capital and labour. Thus, whereas an FTA and a CU aim at making intra-bloc commodity movement free, a CM goes deeper into policy cooperation and coordination by making intra-bloc factor movement free in addition to free commodity movement. The Caribbean Community and Common Market (CARICOM) is a major example of such a regional trade bloc.

Finally, a group of countries is said to have achieved the highest stage of cooperation when in addition to the elements of CU and CM, they coordinate on their monetary and fiscal policy, and most importantly, introduce a common currency for the member countries by forming an Economic and Monetary Union (EMU). The European Monetary Union, with Euro as its common currency, known as the eurozone, is the most important EMU today. This, however, had its precursor in the BENELUX union, formed in 1958.

Though the European Union (EU) had evolved through most of these successive stages, many existing and major trade blocs have either started with forming an FTA or a CU. At the same time, there are trade blocs that have rarely moved into the next higher stage of policy cooperation even after years of cooperation in the form of an FTA. Even a sizeable number of FTAs signed in the 1960s and 1970, mostly among the African countries, has become inactive now. For these countries, the political and military conflict seems to have stood in the way of regional free trade as a development strategy. On the other hand, as Ethier (2011) observes, the contemporary regionalism involves deep integration. The regional trade agreements do not just aim at reduction or elimination of trade barriers, but also at harmonization of other broader economic policies. The most interesting feature of contemporary regionalism is, however, that it often involves one or more small countries linking up with a large country. It is usually the small partner that liberalizes the trade regime more whereas trade concessions on part of the larger partner have been mostly modest.

The FTAs and CUs also vary widely in their scope and coverage. Many of the FTAs exclude trade in agricultural products and most of them exclude service trade. Moreover, according to the WTO Secretariat, of the agreements in force during 1990–1998, only 43 had 100% coverage in industrial products.

9.2 Causes and Consequences of RTAs

9.2.1 STATIC WELFARE GAINS AND OLD REGIONALISM

As discussed in Chapter 2, unilateral free trade policy is not necessarily an optimal development strategy for a country. Unilateral tariff reduction on the part of a country makes it better off in terms of efficiency and resource allocation gains only when its trading partners reciprocate by similar tariff reductions. But, for large countries, there are incentives for unilateral imposition of tariffs on each other's imports. Thus, reciprocation is not ensured through unilateral trade liberalization. Even for the smaller countries, the gain from better allocation of its scarce resources through tariff reductions remains far from realized if its larger trade partner does not reciprocate. This is because, with no increase in market access for its exporters and therefore in the demand for their outputs in these markets, the resources released from the import-competing sectors of the economy cannot be effectively used. Note that for smaller countries, who are price *takers* in the world market, tariff reductions bring in no changes in the TOT. Thus, in absence of reciprocation, unilateral trade liberalization may actually result in a decline in the aggregate value of output and growth of the economy. Here comes the importance of a regional approach to free trade as it ensures reciprocation on mutual market access through regional trading arrangements.

Once reciprocation is ensured through RTAs, substantial gains arise for the member countries, both static and dynamic. Viner (1950) talked about two specific effects of formation of a customs union and welfare consequences thereof. First is the *trade creation effect* resulting in welfare gains for *all* member countries, which in a sense is reassertion of the gains from trade theorem. The second effect of forming a regional trade bloc is trade diversion, which Viner (1950) perceived to be bad for the members. This conclusion was subsequently found to be not a self-enforcing proposition, and led to a controversy between Lipsey (1960) and Bhagwati (1971) over why Jacob Viner thought the trade diversion effect to be bad for member countries of a regional trade bloc.

That trade creation is good can be explained as follows. As tariffs on trade within a regional trading bloc are abolished, the volume of intra-bloc trade increases. For a regional trading bloc amongst countries that are small, such mutual and reciprocated (or regional) tariff reductions do not affect their respective TOT. Hence, all countries experience gain from forming a regional trading bloc, or to be more precise, an FTA through its trade creation effect.

For a trading bloc amongst countries that are large, mutual and reciprocated (or regional) tariff reductions do affect their respective TOT. Thus, there may be gains and losses for member countries from such TOT changes. The region as a whole, however, unambiguously gains because of the distortions being eliminated through abolition of tariffs on intra-bloc imports. Thus, in the case where at the regional free trade equilibrium some of the member countries gain and others lose relative to tariff-restricted regional equilibrium before the formation of the CU, there is scope for compensating the losers through side payments to make the regional trading bloc amongst the large countries (regionally) Pareto optimal and thus beneficial for all. Note that countries may gain individually even if they experience TOT deterioration after the formation of the FTA, provided such deterioration is small enough so that the consequent welfare loss is outweighed by welfare gain from increase in the intra-FTA volume of trade.

Following the illustration of the tariff-retaliation equilibrium by Johnson (1953), Figure 9.1 explains the gain from forming an FTA by two large countries, say the United States (U) and Canada (C). Their offer curves, OU and OC respectively, are drawn non-linear and convex to their respective export axis to reflect the increasing opportunity cost of producing their respective export goods. These also indicate that each country, as it faces the non-linear offer curve of the other, is large enough to influence its TOT by changing its offer of exports (or demand for imports). The FTA equilibrium is at point F where these offer curves intersect each other. The line segment emanating from the origin (or the no-trade point) and passing through this point F is the TOT that prevails after forming the regional (or bilateral) FTA. The convex

Figure 9.1 Welfare Gains from Formation of FTA

curve labelled c_2, which is tangent to the TOT at point F, is the trade indifference curve for Canada showing the utility level achieved by Canada at the regional free trade equilibrium. Similarly, the curve u_2 is the trade indifference curve (TIC) for the United States, showing the utility level achieved by it at the regional free trade equilibrium. The tangency point R_C between a higher TIC for Canada, labelled c_1, and the offer curve of the United States OU represents the unilaterally *optimum* tariff equilibrium for Canada. Thus, given that the United States pursues a free trade policy, an optimum tariff imposed by Canada on imports from the United States maximizes its welfare. Similar unilaterally *optimum* tariff equilibrium for the United States is given by the tangency point R_U between its TIC, labelled u_1, and the offer curve of Canada OC. But these unilaterally optimum tariffs make the trading partners unambiguously worse off, as they are pushed to lower TICs relative to the regionally free trade equilibrium. Thus, a unilaterally optimum tariff imposed by any one country is likely to trigger optimum tariff imposed by its trading partner, resulting in a tariff war or retaliation.

Johnson (1953) has shown that such retaliation will take along the welfare reaction curves (or the best response tariff functions). The backward bending curves labelled OR_C and OR_U represent such welfare reaction curves for Canada and the United States respectively. There are two post-retaliation equilibria—one is at O, which means termination of all trade between Canada and the United States after the tariff war, and the other is at R, where positive trade still exists. Let us suppose that the latter was the pre-FTA situation. Note that although in Figure 9.1, the initial tariff equilibrium point R lies on the same

TIC for Canada as the regional free trade equilibrium point F, this need not be the case. Now, when the two countries sign an FTA whereby they abolish their tariffs on their mutual trade, the region's equilibrium shifts to F from R. In this instance, the welfare of Canada remains the same but the welfare of the United States unambiguously rises as R lies on a lower TIC for it (that passes through R, which is however not drawn to avoid cluttering) than u_2. Thus the region as a whole gains and an FTA is beneficial for both. In case the welfare reaction curve for the United States intersect that of Canada further up along OR_C (so that the initial tariff-equilibrium point R lies above the TIC labelled c_2), forming an FTA makes Canada worse off. But, as is evident from the diagram, TICs of the two countries intersect each other at the tariff-equilibrium (wherever such an equilibrium point lies), which violates the condition for a regional optimum. This means that the region as a whole gains after forming the FTA. This leaves scope for the United States to compensate Canada for its welfare loss and yet retain some of its welfare gain. Thus, again through side payments, both are better off by forming an FTA. Finally, if the initial equilibrium was anywhere in the regions above u_2 but below c_2, both countries individually gain after signing an FTA between them.

On the other hand, the trade diversion following the formation of an FTA (or a CU) may take place because of the discriminating trade policy of a member country vis-à-vis other member trade partners and non-member trade partners. To exemplify, suppose before forming an FTA with the United States, import of software by the Canadian importers was subject to a uniform tariff regardless of the source country. Moreover, suppose, to take an extreme example, all the excess demand for software in Canada was met through imports from a cheaper source such as India rather than the United States. Now abolition of (potential) import tariffs on import of software from the United States after forming an FTA makes it a relatively cheaper source of imports, if the rate of difference in the domestic prices prevailing in India and the United States, p_I and p_U respectively, is smaller than the rate of (uniform) tariff:

$$t > \frac{p_U - p_I}{p_I} \Rightarrow (1+t)p_I > p_U > p_I. \tag{9.1}$$

In such a situation, formation of an FTA between Canada and the United States diverts imports of software by Canada from the non-member source country India, to the member source country, the United States. Viner (1950) perceived that this trade diversion is bad for Canada, because an efficient source of imports is replaced by an inefficient source of imports. This is reflected in the fact that Canada pays a higher price, p_U, to buy its imports than the price, p_I, it was paying before. There is thus a TOT loss for Canada. But what he overlooked is the gains for the Canadian consumers as they now buy imported software at a price lower than the tariff-inclusive price of the Indian software. Thus, trade diversion is bad only if this price (or exchange) gain is small enough. Moreover, tariff abolition shifts domestic production composition in Canada towards its export sector. There will thus be gains from production specialization and consequent efficient reallocation of its scarce domestic resources.

This subsequently led to a controversy between Lipsey (1960) and Bhagwati (1971) over why Viner overlooked these exchange and specialization gains and asserted that trade diversion is bad for importing member countries. Lipsey argued that Viner had in mind a fixed consumption ratio of the two traded goods in the context of complete specialization by Canada in its export good: cloth. Figure 9.2 illustrates Lipsey's argument. Its factor endowment, devoted only in production of cloth, allows it to produce C^* units of cloth. The two goods are consumed at a fixed ratio indicated by the ray Oc through the origin. Since pre-FTA, Canada trades with India at the (relative) price of software p_I, its value of production of cloth must be evaluated at the relative price $1/p_I$. This is shown by the price line $C'I$ with an absolute slope $1/p_I$. For trade to be balanced, the consumption bundle must also lie on this price or budget line. At the same time, the consumption bundle must satisfy the fixed ratio of cloth and software. This requires that the consumption bundle must be E_1 for which the price line $C'I$ cuts the fixed consumption ratio Oc. The flatter tariff-inclusive price line passing through this consumption bundle, however, indicates the higher price that the Canadian consumers pay for software due to import tariff. Post FTA, Canada trades with the member country the United States at the higher relative price of software (or alternatively, at the lower relative price

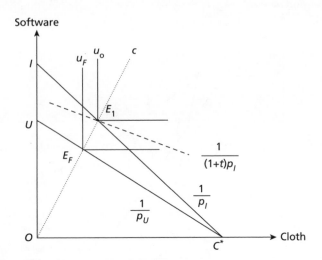

Figure 9.2 Trade Diversion is Bad (Lipsey Case)

of its exports of cloth). This TOT loss results in a fall in the aggregate value of Canada's production of cloth and correspondingly lowers its aggregate value of consumption at bundle E_F. Canada's welfare falls since the post FTA consumption at bundle E_F lies on a lower L-shaped indifference curves labelled u_F. The welfare loss arises purely due to the TOT loss.

Though the domestic consumers pay a lower price for imports of software, consumption of cloth and software at a fixed ratio prohibit them from gaining from such a lower price by substituting the consumption of cloth by the consumption of software. On the other hand, the assumption of complete specialization rules out any possibility of production gain.

A similar result that trade creation is bad can be obtained in an exchange economy with the Lipsey condition that cloth and software are consumed at a fixed ratio. In an exchange economy, there is no production. The endowments of cloth and software are exogenously given. This again rules out the specialization gain (along with exchange gain under the Lipsey condition) so that we are left with only the TOT loss to make the trade diversion effect welfare reducing. Figure 9.3 illustrates this case. Suppose Canada has a fixed endowment of cloth and software as indicated by the bundle E_0. The trade balance condition now requires that its aggregate value of expenditure and aggregate value of *endowment* must match at this price. Thus, the consumption bundle must lie on the price line with an absolute slope $1/p_I$ drawn through the endowment bundle E_0. At the same time, as before, the consumption bundle must satisfy the fixed ratio of cloth and software. Thus, pre-FTA, the consumption was at bundle E_1, with reciprocal of the absolute slope of the flatter line passing through it indicating the tariff-inclusive of software that consumers pay for imports.

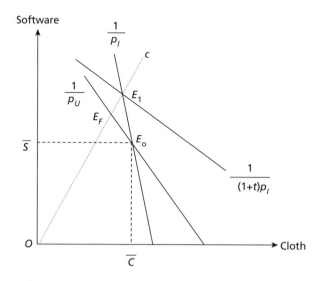

Figure 9.3 Trade Diversion is Bad with No Production

Post FTA, the TOT loss results in a fall in the aggregate value of Canada's endowment of cloth and software and correspondingly lowers its aggregate value of consumption at bundle E_F. If we had drawn L-shaped indifference curves to indicate the welfare levels attained by Canada at the respective pre and post FTA equilibria, it would have been immediate that Canada loses by consuming the post FTA equilibrium bundle E_F. Now, due to fixed endowment of the two goods and no domestic production, the price change cannot bring in any specialization gain.

But, Bhagwati refuted Lipsey's argument on the ground that his assumption of fixed consumption ratio does not conform with the arithmetic example of Viner (1950) to assert that trade creation is bad. Instead, by allowing incomplete specialization in domestic production of cloth and software and substitution in consumption of these two goods, Bhagwati demonstrated that fixed volume of imports by Canada is a sufficient condition for Viner's argument. In Figure 9.4, the downward sloping concave curve AB is Canada's production possibility frontier (PPF) under the assumption of an increasing opportunity cost of producing cloth there. Pre FTA, the composition of domestic production in Canada is given by the production bundle P_o for which the price line $1/(1+t)p_I$ reflecting reciprocal of the tariff inclusive relative price of imported software is tangent to the PPF.

But trade allows it to consume beyond its PPF. The factor that binds such a consumption decision, however, is the trade balance requirement. Thus, Canada must consume along the pre-FTA international price line, $1/p_I$, and its welfare maximizing consumption bundle is c_o. The volume of import

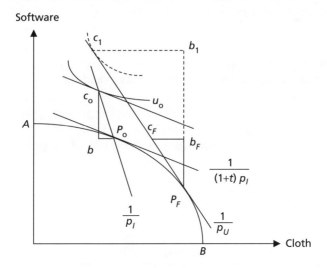

Figure 9.4 Trade Diversion is Bad (Bhagwati Case)

of software from India was $c_o b$ and volume of exports of cloth to India was bP_o. Post FTA with the United States, Canada's production composition shifts in favour of cloth at bundle P_F as a lower relative price of software imports from the member partner the United States contracts domestic production of software in Canada. This shift in production entails a production gain, as domestic resources are now used in the more efficient line of production. If there had been no physical restriction on the consumption of software and corresponding volume of imports, post FTA optimum consumption would have been the bundle c_1, with the volume of imports being $P_F b_1$. Thus, the production gain realized would have been large enough to outweigh the TOT loss that Canada experiences after forming an FTA with the inefficient trade partner the United States. Thus, contrary to Viner's assertion, trade diverting FTA would have been good. But, if the volume of imports is restricted to the pre-FTA level $c_o b = P_F b_F$, then the post FTA consumption bundle would have been restricted to c_F along the price line $1/p_U$ and Canada would experience a net welfare loss despite the production gain. That is, under the Bhagwati-restriction that the volume of imports remains the same, a trade diverting FTA is bad.

While it is understandable now that trade diversion may not be welfare deteriorating, the relevant question that remains is whether a regional trade bloc creates *or* diverts trade. The trivial case where trade is unambiguously created is the one where the cheapest source country of a good is included in the trade bloc. In our example this is the case when Canada (or the United States) and India form an FTA. The possibility of trade diversion is in fact assumed away in this special case. But, when the cheapest source country is excluded from the FTA, then trade may be diverted (given a condition like (9.1)), and it is interesting to examine whether at equilibrium trade is in fact diverted or trade is created. Spraos (1964) provides a simple condition for trade creation in the context of forming a CU by two inefficient producers of a good, say Canada and the United States in our example, leaving out the most efficient producer, India. Suppose pre-union both Canada and the United States were importing software from India at the tariff-inclusive prices. Let Canada be the least efficient producer and thus it required a higher pre-union tariff to ensure some domestic production of software than the United States. Assume that pre-union and before any imports could actually take place, prices and tariffs are such that,

$$(1+t_U)p_I < p_U < (1+t_C)p_I < p_C < (1+t_C^U)p_U \text{ given } t_U < t_C \quad (9.2)$$

where, t_U and t_C are tariffs imposed by the United States and Canada respectively on imports from India and t_C^U is the tariff imposed by Canada on imports from the United States. Note that these price inequalities prohibit any import of software from the United States into Canada (regardless of the latter's tariff on imports from the former) provided of course India can meet all the import requirement of Canada, as well as any import of software into India from either Canada or the United States even if India sets zero tariffs on such imports.

Spraos made two assumptions. First, there are increasing marginal costs of producing software in each country reflected in usual upward sloping supply curves. Second, the world output of software remains constant. After forming a CU, Canada and the United States abolish tariffs on each other's products and set a common external tariff on imports from India. He assumed the usual case where the common external tariff (denoted by $\tilde{t}$) lies between t_U and t_C. These tariff changes alter domestic output levels and by the assumption of increasing costs change the domestic prices in each country. Correspondingly two alternative situations may arise. First is the trade creation where Canada's domestic production of software falls as tariffs are lowered or abolished and the consequent excess demand is met through either increase in imports from India (since $\tilde{t} < t_C$), or imports from the United States (since $t_C^U = 0$) or both. Second is the trade diversion in which part or all of Canada's imports from India is replaced by imports from the United States because now the relative price of software imported from there may fall below the (lower) tariff-inclusive price of software imported from India. But, whether trade will be created or diverted at the end will depend on how the domestic (relative) price of software in India changes. Note that abolition of the tariff on potential imports from the United States equalizes the domestic price of software in Canada and the United States. The pre-union price in Canada falls whereas the pre-union price in the United States rises as imports flow in. The issue then is whether this import from the United States substitutes the import from India. If the price in India rises too as a consequence of these tariff changes, then its excess production of software (or the volume of exports) magnifies, which under the assumption of constant world output of software must mean trade creation at the post-union equilibrium. That is, the excess supply in both India and the United States must be equal to the (increased) excess demand in Canada. To derive then the condition for an increase in the price of software in India, let $S_C(p_C)$, $S_U(p_U)$, and $S_I(p_I)$ denote respectively the supply functions in Canada, the United States, and India. Since the world output of software is assumed to be constant, so supply changes must cancel out each other:

$$\frac{\partial S_C}{\partial p_C} dp_C + \frac{\partial S_U}{\partial p_U} dp_U + \frac{\partial S_I}{\partial p_I} dp_I = 0. \tag{9.3}$$

Pre-union, the domestic prices of software in Canada and the United States are related to that in India in the following way:

$$p_C = (1+t_C)p_I, p_U = (1+t_U)p_I. \tag{9.4}$$

Total differentiation of these price relationships and substitution in (9.3) yields,

$$\frac{\partial S_C}{\partial p_C}\left[(1+t_C)dp_I + p_I dt_C\right] + \frac{\partial S_U}{\partial p_U}\left[(1+t_U)dp_I + p_I dt_U\right] + \frac{\partial S_I}{\partial p_I}dp_I = 0$$

$$\Rightarrow dp_I = \frac{-p_I\left[\dfrac{\partial S_C}{\partial p_C}dt_C + \dfrac{\partial S_U}{\partial p_U}dt_U\right]}{(1+t_C)\dfrac{\partial S_C}{\partial p_C} + (1+t_U)\dfrac{\partial S_U}{\partial p_U} + \dfrac{\partial S_I}{\partial p_I}}. \tag{9.5}$$

Since the denominator in (9.5) is positive by the assumption of increasing marginal costs, $dp_I > 0$ (i.e., trade is created rather than diverted after formation of a Customs Union) if,

$$\frac{\partial S_C}{\partial p_C}dt_C + \frac{\partial S_U}{\partial p_U}dt_U < 0$$

which, using $dt_C = \tilde{t} - t_C < 0$ and $dt_U = \tilde{t} - t_U > 0$ boils down to the following condition,

$$-\frac{\partial S_C}{\partial p_C}(t_C - \tilde{t}) + \frac{\partial S_U}{\partial p_U}(\tilde{t} - t_U) < 0 \Rightarrow \frac{\partial S_C / \partial p_C}{\partial S_U / \partial p_U} > \frac{(\tilde{t} - t_U)}{(t_C - \tilde{t})}. \tag{9.6}$$

Thus, the relative supply response in Canada must be larger than the ratio of change in the United States tariff to the change in the Canadian tariff.

9.2.2 CAUSES OF CONTEMPORARY REGIONALISM

Contemporary regionalism is not so much driven by static welfare gains, rather is often motivated by strategic reasons. One strategic reason is to link non-trade issues like environmental standards, labour standards, and TRIPS (Trade Related Intellectual Property Rights) with trade gains that a regional trading arrangement brings about. Coordination and cooperation among the countries on these non-trade issues are essential, but are often difficult to achieve without attaching any potential economic loss in the event a country defects from the coordinated and cooperative agreement. The regional trading arrangements attach a welfare cost to enforce cooperation on these non-trade issues. For example, the United States now requires a potential FTA partner to commit to TRIPS and certain environmental standards. The EU has linked the FTA gains with patent protection, particularly in health drugs and medicines, in its ongoing negotiation on an FTA with India. MERCOSUR (Mercado Común del Sur), a customs union among Latin American countries, is also working upon linking trade liberalization and environmental issues.

The second strategic reason, particularly in the context of the small Asian countries signing FTAs with larger trade partners in Europe and America, is the competition among these small countries to attract FDI from their larger developed-country trade partners [Ethier (2011)]. The developing countries foresee FDI as a key to success and growth as it brings with it better technology. Investors from the developed countries, however, have many options as there are many reforming countries in Asia, particularly in East Asia, with fairly similar economic characteristics and low-cost supply of skill. Thus, unilateral trade reforms by the similar Asian developing countries per se cannot attract the FDI. Moreover, unilateral trade reforms are uncertain as trade reforms may be reverted if such reforms are not successful. In such a context, a trade agreement between a developing country and a developed country creates a small but significant advantage for the developing country. Through bilateral or regional agreements it *commits* itself to trade and other economic reforms to the advantage of the developed-country partner. The preference and trade concessions granted by the developed-country partner, despite being quite small and marginal in many cases, differentiates the developing-country partner from other similar developing countries in a significant way for the investing firms in the developed-country partner that are looking out for destinations for their foreign investments. Thus, a bilateral or regional agreement attracts all or a large proportion of such investment from the developed-country partner. Thus, growth in regionalism in Asia, according to Ethier (2011), is not to expand exports greatly to their partners and realize static welfare gains, but to compete with other *similar* countries for attracting direct foreign investment.

9.2.3 DYNAMIC GAINS AND FORMATION OF REGIONAL TRADE BLOCS

Apart from the discussed static welfare gains (or losses) through trade creation and trade diversion effects, formation of an FTA or a CU brings in quite a few dynamic gains, which provide further incentives for formation of such bilateral or regional trade blocs. Ghosh and Acharyya (2012) examine the effect of trade bloc formation on product innovation by a multinational firm in the presence of intra-country taste diversity. At the same time they endogenize the decision to form an FTA or a CU and the choice of partners in a three country setting. They consider the three countries as poor (P), middle-income

(M), and rich (R) with respective per-capita income levels denoted by Y_P, Y_M, and Y_R and population sizes denoted by N_P, N_M, and N_R. A patent holder multinational corporation (MNC) belongs to the rich country and produces a vertically differentiated good. The MNC incurs only a sunk cost for innovation which is convex in the quality level innovated:

$$C = \frac{1}{2}s^2 . \tag{9.7}$$

The rich country exports this innovated good to the other two countries and P_j is assumed to be the price of the differentiated good as sold by the MNC in the $\cdot j$ th market. Countries P and M export a homogeneous good, which is taken as the numeraire good, produced under perfectly competitive conditions at constant cost, normalized to one. The good is traded freely around the world with the marginal utility being one.

Ghosh and Acharyya (2012) capture intra-country income diversity by assuming two discrete types in each country. The types are characterized by a taste parameter α_j in each country. More precisely, suppose there are n_{1j} number of buyers with taste parameter α_{1j} and n_{2j} number of buyers with taste parameter α_{2j} in country-j with

$$\alpha_{1j} < \alpha_{2j}, j = \text{P, M, R.} \tag{9.8}$$

Note that $n_{1j} + n_{2j} = N_j$. A consumer of type-i, $i = 1, 2$, buys only one unit of this innovated good or does not buy it at all. The net utility that she derives from consuming one unit of the good of quality s is given by,

$$V_{ij} = \alpha_{ij}s - P_j . \tag{9.9}$$

Given that her reservation utility is zero, she purchases the good only if $V_i \geq 0$. The tie-breaking rule applied here is that if she is indifferent between buying and not buying the good ($V_i = 0$), she actually buys the good. This is also known as the market participation (or individual rationality) constraint.

The MNC, being a monopolist, extracts the entire consumer surplus and sets the price in the j th market such that $V_{1j} = 0$, in case he serves both types (which in the literature on quality choice under consumer heterogeneity is known as *full market coverage*). Such a *full market coverage* pricing means that the MNC sells N_j units of the good in the j th market.[1]

---

[1] An alternative pricing policy of the MNC may be to cater to only the high type in country-j, known as *partial market coverage*, in which case he charges a price such that $V_{2j} = 0$. See Acharyya (1998).

Suppose pre-union, P and M had imposed *ad valorem* tariffs on their imports from R but had free trade (in homogeneous goods) between them. The sequence of events is as follows. In the first stage, P and M choose their respective tariff levels; in the second stage the MNC chooses its innovation level and the price; in the final stage the consumers decide about buying the innovated good. We solve the game by the backward induction method. Given the market participation decision of buyers specified earlier and the price that it sets for full market coverage, on the one hand, and for any rates of tariffs t_P and t_M set by the governments in P and M respectively, on the other hand, the MNC maximizes its profit,

$$\pi_o = [(1-t_P)\alpha_{1P}N_P + (1-t_M)\alpha_{1M}N_m + \alpha_{1R}N_R]s_o - \frac{1}{2}s_o^2 \qquad (9.10)$$

to choose the innovation level:

$$s_o^* = [(1-t_P)\alpha_{1P}N_P + (1-t_M)\alpha_{1M}N_m + \alpha_{1R}N_R]. \qquad (9.11)$$

Given this choice of the innovation level, the governments in P and M choose their respective tariff rates by maximizing national welfare, which comprises of the consumers surplus and the tariff revenue. Note that in this full market coverage case, by charging a uniform price $P_{jo} = \alpha_{1j}s_o^*$ though the MNC extracts are all surplus from the low type buyers in each market, it leaves the high type consumers with a strictly positive surplus:

$$CS_{2j}^o = (\alpha_{2j} - \alpha_{1j})s_o^* \quad \forall \quad j = P, M, R.$$

Hence, national welfare levels equal,

$$W_{jo} = t_{jo}\alpha_{1j}N_j s_o^* + n_{2j}(\alpha_{2j} - \alpha_{1j})s_o^* \quad \forall \quad j = P.M. \qquad (9.12)$$

Substitution of the optimal innovation level specified in (9.11) into (9.12) reveals a strategic interdependence of the unilaterally chosen tariff rates: $W_{jo} = W(t_{Po}, t_{Mo}, x)$, where x is the set of parameters of the model. Welfare maximization yields the (Nash) equilibrium tariffs set by P and M as:

$$t_{Po}^* = \frac{1}{3\alpha_{1P}N_P}[G - 2n_{2P}(\alpha_{2P} - \alpha_{1P}) + n_{2M}(\alpha_{2M} - \alpha_{1M})] \qquad (9.12a)$$

$$t_{Mo}^* = \frac{1}{3\alpha_{1M}N_M}[G - 2n_{2M}(\alpha_{2M} - \alpha_{1M}) + n_{2P}(\alpha_{2P} - \alpha_{1P})] \qquad (9.12b)$$

where, $G = (\Sigma_j N_j \alpha_{1j}); j = P, M, R.$

Substitution of these optimal tariffs in (9.11) yields the optimal level of innovation

$$s_o^* = \frac{1}{3}[G + n_{2M}(\alpha_{2M} - \alpha_{1M}) + n_{2P}(\alpha_{2P} - \alpha_{1P})] \tag{9.12c}$$

and the welfare levels of the countries can be calculated to be

$$W_{jo}^* = (s_f^B)^2 \qquad j = P, M$$

$$W_{Ro}^* = \frac{1}{6} s_f^B [G + n_{2M}(\alpha_{2M} - \alpha_{1M}) + n_{2P}(\alpha_{2P} - \alpha_{1P}) + 6n_{2R}(\alpha_{2R} - \alpha_{1R})].$$

Note that the welfare of the rich country consists of consumers surplus of the high type buyers there and the profit of the MNC.

Given this initial situation, Ghosh and Acharyya (2012) analyse the feasibility of FTA options available to the rich country R with either of the poor and middle-income states, and also the feasibility of formation of a CU by P and M. We start with the case of FTA$_{RP}$ where M imposes an *ad valorem* tariff on the imports from R. Proceeding as before, the optimum tariff levels set by P (or M) and the level of innovation that these tariff levels induce are,

$$t_j^{Fi} = \frac{1}{2N_j \alpha_{1j}}[G - n_{2j}(\alpha_{2j} - \alpha_{1j})] \quad i = P, M; j = P, M; i \neq j \tag{9.13}$$

$$s^{Fi} = \frac{1}{2}[G + n_{2j}(\alpha_{2j} - \alpha_{1j})] \quad i = P, M; j = P, M; i \neq j \tag{9.14}$$

where, t_j^{Fi} is the tariff set by the jth country and s^{Fi} is the optimum level of innovation by the MNC under full market coverage when R forms an FTA with the ith country.

It can be checked that the poor country sets a higher unilateral tariff on imports from R when R negotiates an FTA with M than when there is no trade bloc ($t_P^{FM} > t_{Po}^*$). This is because of the strategic inter-dependence of tariff levels discussed earlier whereby the best-response of the poor country to the abolition of t_M under FTA$_{RM}$ is to raise its own tariff rate. Similar is the case for FTA$_{RP}$. The same condition ensures that the innovation level is higher, that is, $s^{Fi} > s_o^*$. The reason for this is that though P (or M) raises its tariff when an FTA is formed between R and M (or between R and P), since M (or P) removes its tariff, incentives for the MNC rises on the whole to innovate a higher quality good.

Which partner does the rich country prefer to form an FTA with? To examine, compare the levels of the national welfares and innovation under the two alternative FTA regimes under the following simplifying assumption:

$$n_{2P}(\alpha_{2P} - \alpha_{1P}) < n_{2M}(\alpha_{2M} - \alpha_{1M}). \tag{9.15}$$

If we rewrite it as $(\alpha_{2P} - \alpha_{1P}) < (n_{2M}/n_{2P})(\alpha_{2M} - \alpha_{1M})$ then for $n_{2P} \geq n_{2M}$ this condition means that the absolute taste diversity in the poor country must be less than that in the middle-income country.

From (9.12c) and (9.14), it is readily verifiable that

$$s^{FP} > s_o^* \text{ and } s^{FM} > s_o^*. \tag{9.16}$$

Using the assumption made in (9.15), the innovation levels can further be ranked as

$$s^{FP} > s^{FM} > s_o^* \tag{9.17}$$

which, in turn, implies the following welfare ranking for the rich country:

$$W_R^{FP} > W_R^{FM} > W_{Ro}^*. \tag{9.18}$$

This welfare ranking implies that R prefers an FTA. This is obvious because, by forming an FTA, it can ensure a larger market in the non-member country for its MNC and thereby induce it to raise the innovation level. Moreover, under the assumption that taste diversity in the poor country is less than that in the middle-income country, the rich country seems to prefer the poor country as its FTA partner. But, whether this will be the *equilibrium* structure of the FTA or not depends on the gain for the chosen partner and on the *relative* gain for the rich country.

Note that given (9.18), an FTA between the rich country and country-j ($j = P, M$) is feasible and relatively profitable if

$$W_R^{Fj} + W_j^{Fj} > W_{Ro}^* + W_{jo}^*. \tag{9.19}$$

However, this is not guaranteed *a priori*. Ghosh and Acharyya (2012) establish two results. First, under the assumption in (9.15), if an FTA with the poor country is feasible (so that (9.19) holds for $j = P$), an FTA with the middle-income country is also feasible. This follows from the following welfare ranking:

$$W_{Po}^* = W_{Mo}^* = (s_o^*)^2, \ W_P^{FP} - W_M^{FM} = \frac{1}{2}G[n_{2P}(\alpha_{2P} - \alpha_{1P})] - n_{2M}(\alpha_{2M} - \alpha_{1M})] < 0. \tag{9.20}$$

Second, for certain parametric restrictions and the extent of taste diversity, an FTA between the rich and the poor country is feasible and welfare improving for certain parametric restrictions on the extent of taste diversity in the poor and middle-income countries.

Considering this case, that both FTAs are feasible, there are now two cases. The first in which the FTAs are welfare-improving for the partner country as well: $W_j^{Fj} > W_{jo}^*$, $j = P, M$. Then by (9.18), an FTA between the rich and the poor country will be signed. The second case is where side payments are needed: $W_j^{Fj} < W_{jo}^*$, $j = P, M$. Note that the condition (9.19) essentially implies side payments made by R to its FTA partner—that is P in the case of FTA$_{FP}$ and M in the case of FTA$_{FM}$—to enforce the FTA is feasible. This is immediate from rewriting (9.19) as $W_R^{Fj} - W_{Ro}^* > W_{jo}^* - W_j^{Fj}$. The right hand side is the side payments to be made to the trading partner to make it indifferent between accepting the offer of accession vis-à-vis rejecting it. The left hand side, on the other hand, is the welfare gain for R from an FTA with country-j. Hence, side payments are feasible if (9.19) is satisfied. Then by the welfare ranking in (9.20), it is straightforward to check that lower side payments will be required to be paid by the rich country to enforce an FTA with M: $W_{Mo}^* - W_M^{FM} < W_{Po}^* - W_P^{FP}$.

Given the lower side payments to be made by the rich country to the middle-income country, it easy to check that the relative gain for the rich country is larger for an FTA with M than with P: $W_R^{FM} - \left(W_{Mo}^* - W_M^{FM}\right) > W_R^{FM} - \left(W_{Po}^* - W_P^{FP}\right)$.

Therefore, as Ghosh and Acharyya (2012) conclude, if FTAs are feasible, then given the assumption in (9.15), the rich country will prefer the poor country as the FTA partner where no side payments are required to enforce the FTA. Otherwise, the rich country will prefer the middle-income country as its FTA partner.

For poor and middle-income countries, an alternative to FTA formation with the rich country is forming a CU between themselves. In such a case, Ghosh and Acharyya (2012) assume that they set a common external tariff on imports of the innovated good by maximizing their joint welfare, which is lower than the *average* of pre-union tariffs, t_{Po}^* and t_{Mo}^*. A smaller tariff now encourages the MNC to raise its innovation level. Thus, the formation of a CU between poor and middle-income countries has a positive effect on the innovation level. Should this be preferred by these countries over forming an FTA with the rich country? First of all, comparisons of the pre and post union welfare reveal that both P and M have incentives to form a customs union:

$$W_P^{CU} + W_M^{CU} > W_{Po}^* + W_{Mo}^*. \qquad (9.21)$$

Once again, this ensures that even if one of the members stands to lose through CU compared to its pre-union welfare level, it is feasible for the other member to make a side payment to compensate it for the loss, if any. But, since FTAs between R and P and between R and M are possible, the benefit from a CU formation accruing to P (and M as well) is to be weighed against that from the formation of FTAs with the rich country. Ghosh and Acharyya (2012) establish that $W_j^{CU} > W_j^{Fj}$ $\forall j = P, M$. Therefore, a CU will be preferred by *both* P and M.

9.3 **Regionalism and Multilateralism**

It is often argued that global free trade can be achieved through successive enlargement of the regional trade blocs (RTB). Thus, regionalism is seen as a stepping stone to multilateral and global free trade. But the RTBs are inherently discriminatory trade practices and thus in contradiction with the principle of global free trade. The theory of optimal size and enlargement of RTBs also does not suggest that global free trade can be achieved through proliferation and enlargement of RTBs. In the post-war era, the RTBs are formed under the *unanimous regionalism* rule, whereby the member countries must unanimously agree upon the accession of a new member. Under such a rule, Yi (1996) and Bloch (1996) demonstrate that a global trading bloc is not the optimal union structure. On the other hand, Levy (1995) and Krishna (1996) argue that interests of the members confront the enlargement of an RTB, and the member countries are better off only when their trading bloc merges with a larger or equal-sized RTB. Estevadeordal et al. (2008) examine the effect of regionalism on unilateral trade liberalization using industry-level data on applied most-favoured nation (MFN) tariffs and bilateral preferences for ten Latin American countries from 1990 to 2001. It is found that preferential tariff reduction in a given sector leads to a reduction in the external (MFN) tariff in that sector. External liberalization is greater if preferences are granted to important suppliers. However, these 'complementarity effects' of preferential liberalization on external liberalization do not arise in CUs. This is understandable because CUs essentially involve more intense discriminatory trade practices than do the FTAs.

The fallacy of achieving global free trade through regionalism has its root in the European trade history in the late nineteenth century. The Anglo-French treaty in the 1860s was the most important of the treaties at that time which paved the way of multilateral free trade throughout Europe in the late nineteenth century through bilateralism. According to the terms of the Treaty, France abolished all trade prohibitions and imposed specific *ad valorem* duties not exceeding 30% or 25% after 1895. Britain cut the number of dutiable goods from 419 to 48 and reduced the wine tariff. The most important element of the treaty was the unconditional MFN by which either country could extend to any other third country any favour regarding the importation of goods whether mentioned or not in the treaty. This unconditional MFN set the stage for multilateral free trade in Europe. By 1908, Britain had MFN agreements with 46 countries, Germany with 30 countries, and France with more than 20 countries [Irwin (1993)]. Theoretically, the unconditional MFN clause is analogous to *open regionalism*, under which achieving global free trade may be plausible [Yi (1996a)]. But such a rule was hardly followed in practice by the member countries in the post-World War II period. Thus, what the recent proliferation of RTAs means essentially is a spaghetti bowl effect or an entanglement of trade agreements [Bhagwati (1995, 2008)].[2] The same commodity is often subject to different tariffs, tariff reduction trajectories, and Rules of Origin for obtaining preferences [Kawai and Wignaraja (2009)]. Also, different FTAs contain varying modalities and time frames for tariff concessions. More specifically, many FTAs adopt a negative list approach while some adopt a positive list approach with exclusions. With a growing number of overlapping FTAs, the international trading system is likely to become chaotic. Table 9.1 reports the number of regional trade arrangements (RTAs) to which a country is member. These RTAs often overlap with each other and, as Column 3 indicates, often go beyond trade blocs amongst neighbours. The countries reported here are those which are members of at least six RTAs[3] and members of at least one trade blocs amongst cross-continent countries. Thus, the extent of the spaghetti bowl dimension of regional trading arrangements may be much larger than the data reported in Table 9.1 may indicate.

Baldwin (2006) argues that the political economy forces may actually transform spaghetti bowls into building blocks through Juggernaut and Domino effects. The announcement of multilateral trade negotiation based on the principle of reciprocation raises the political cost of protection for a democratic government, because exporting firms resist the policy of trade protection to ensure greater market access in the foreign country under reciprocation. Thus, for each nation it is politically optimum to cut tariffs to some extent. This is the main element of the Juggernaut effect. The key element in the Domino effect, on the other hand, is the relative size of the export sectors. A higher order trade cooperation and coordination amongst members of an existing trade bloc increases the stake of the exporters of non-member countries in joining this trade bloc as they expect trade discrimination against them to a greater extent if their governments decide to stay out. Anti-membership forces, the import competing firms, also get strengthened because joining a more integrated

---

[2] In the context of rise in the incidence of Asian regionalism, the Asian Development Bank president Haruhiko Kuroda referred to this phenomenon as the Asian *noodle bowl* effect of FTAs.

[3] According to the World Bank (2005), the average number of PTAs or FTAs that each country belongs to is six.

Table 9.1 Number of Regional Trade Arrangements Signed by Select Countries Until 2009

Country	Number of RTA	Number of Cross-Continent RTA	Major Partners in Cross-Continent FTA
Chile	10	5	EU, China, Japan
China	17	2	NZ, Chile
Cote d'Ivoire	15	1	EU
Egypt	35	4	EU
EU	24	12	CARICOM, SACU
Iceland	21	16	Chile, Korea, Mexico, Singapore, Canada
Iraq	12	4	Algeria, Morocco
GCC	13	6	USA
Israel	8	8	EU, USA
Jordan	19	11	EU, USA
South Korea	6	4	Chile, Switzerland
Lebanon	17	8	EU
Libya	29	3	GCC
Mexico	15	6	EU, Japan
Morocco	18	9	EU, USA
Norway	19	10	Mexico, Korea, Chile
Peru	6	1	Singapore
Singapore	23	8	Australia, USA
Sudan	24	5	GCC
Switzerland	21	12	Japan, Korea, Mexico
Syria	13	5	EU
Tunisia	17	7	EU

Source: Compiled from the WTO Website (www.wto.org).

RTA means larger market access for foreign firms and thus more competition. If pro-membership forces grow faster than anti-membership forces, it will be politically optimum for the non-member nations to join the trade bloc. This triggers a subsequent domino effect on the remaining outside nations. Their stakes now become even larger. More nations will thus join and there will be successive enlargement of the RTA until global free trade is achieved. While this political economy argument seems appealing, it again is based on open regionalism rule.

Similar to this Domino effect, Saggi and Yildiz (2011) have demonstrated that FTAs can be building blocks for multilateral free trade in an oligopoly model of intra-industry trade. They show that global free trade can emerge as a coalition-proof Nash equilibrium outcome if countries are free to form bilateral FTAs, so that FTAs act as strong building blocks. If bilateral FTAs are infeasible for some reason, and the choice for a country is either to enter into a multilateral free trade agreement or no agreement at all, it will prefer the latter and will not adopt a free trade policy. But, when countries can negotiate bilateral FTAs alongside a multilateral negotiation, a country that does not sign any bilateral FTA is worse off (relative to the situation when no country signs bilateral FTAs) if preferential trade liberalization amongst other countries adversely affects its welfare. The country may then become willing to undertake trade liberalization. Thus, Saggi and Yildiz (2011) conclude that 'the possibility of preferential trade liberalization amongst others can induce a country to participate in multilateral trade liberalization'.

Formally, they analyse the coalition-proof Nash equilibria of two games of trade liberalization between three countries. The game that allows both bilateral and multilateral trade liberalization as options along with no trade liberalization has been termed 'the FTA game' by Saggi and Yildiz (2011). On the other hand, under the 'no FTA game', the countries have only two options: multilateral trade liberalization or no trade liberalization. Moreover, under the FTA game, each country is free to pursue multiple FTAs. The FTA game has three stages. In the first stage, each country announces the set of countries with whom it wants to form a bilateral FTA and abolish tariffs on their mutual trade. An FTA between two countries arises only if they both announce each other's name. Similarly, multilateral trade liberalization and global free trade emerges if all countries call each other's names. In the second stage, firms in each country compete in the product market in a Cournot fashion. In case a country opts not to form a bilateral or multilateral FTA, it retains its existing tariffs on imports from the other two countries. In their analysis, an FTA implies the following trade-off. Forming a bilateral FTA lowers profits of its firm from domestic sales because of the tariff concession it grants to the other member. At the same time, the reciprocal tariff reduction granted by the other member increases export profits of its firm. In this context they show that depending on the extent of cost asymmetry of firms, multilateral free trade may be an equilibrium outcome only if the countries have the option to form FTAs. This they call the *strong building block effect*. But a bilateral FTA can also be a coalition-proof Nash equilibrium of the FTA game, which they call the *weak stumbling block effect*.

Though these theoretical results seem to provide some support to the idea that regional trading arrangements help achieve global free trade, they do not rule out the stumbling block proposition altogether. Moreover, the underlying analytical structure is too specific to offer any generalized conclusion regarding whether regional trade blocs are stepping stones or stumbling blocks to multilateral trade liberalization and global free trade.

■ REFERENCES

Acharyya, R. (1998). 'Monopoly and Product Quality: Separating or Pooling Menu?' *Economics Letters* 61: 187–194.

Baldwin, R. (2006). 'Multilateralizing Regionalism: Spaghetti Bowls as Building Blocks on the Path to Global Free Trade'. *The World Economy* 29 (11): 1451–1518.

Bhagwati, J. N. (1971). 'Trade Diverting Customs Union and Welfare Improvement: A Clarification'. *Economic Journal* 81: 580–587.

Bhagwati, J. N. (1995). 'US Trade Policy: The Infatuation with FTAs'. Columbia University Discussion Paper Series 726. New York: Columbia University.

Bhagwati, J. N. (2008). *Termites in the Trading System: How Preferential Agreements Undermine Free Trade*. Oxford: Oxford University Press.

Bloch, F. (1996). 'Sequential Formation of Coalitions with Fixed Payoff Divisions'. *Games and Economic Behaviour* 14: 90–123.

Estevadeordal, A., Freund, C., and Ornelas, E. (2008). 'Does Regionalism Affect Trade Liberalization Toward Nonmembers?' *The Quarterly Journal of Economics* November 2008: 1531–1574.

Ethier, W. (2011). 'Contemporary Regionalism'. In: M. N. Jovanović, (ed). *International Handbook on the Economics of Integration*, Volume I. Northampton: Edward Elgar.

Ghosh, S. and Acharyya, R. (2012). 'Trading Blocs and Endogenous Product Quality Under a Vertically Differentiated Monopoly'. *Keio Economic Studies* 48: 21–46.

Irwin, D. A. (1993). 'Multilateral and Bilateral Trade Policies in the World Trading System: An Historical Perspective'. In: J. De Melo and A. Panagariya, (eds). *New Dimensions in Regional Integration*, Chapter 4. Cambridge: Cambridge University Press.

Johnson, H. G. (1953). 'Optimum Tariffs and Retaliation'. *Review of Economic Studies* 21: 142–153.

Kawai, M. and Wignaraja, G. (2009). 'The Asian "Noodle Bowl": Is it Serious for Business?' ADBI Working Paper 136. Tokyo: Asian Development Bank Institute.

Krishna, P. (1996). 'Regionalism and Multilateralism: A Political Economy Approach'. Working Paper, Brown University.

Levy, P. (1995). 'A Political Economic Analysis of Free Trade Agreements'. Working Paper, Yale University.

Lipsey, R. G. (1960). 'The Theory of Customs Union: A General Survey'. *Economic Journal* 70: 496–513.

Saggi, K. and Yildiz, H. M. (2011). 'Bilateral Trade Agreements and the Feasibility of Multilateral Free Trade'. *Review of International Economics* 19 (2): 356–373.

Spraos, J. (1964). 'The Condition for a Trade-Diverting Customs Union'. *Economic Journal*, March: 101–108.

Viner, J. (1950). The Customs Union Issue, Carnegie Endowment for Intellectual Peace: NY.

World Bank (2005). *Global Economic Prospects: Trade, Regionalism and Development*. Washington, DC: World Bank.

Yi, S-S. (1996). 'Endogenous Formation of Customs Union Under Imperfect Competition: Open Regionalism is Good'. *Journal of International Economics* 41: 153–177.

Yi, S-S. (1996a). 'Open Regionalism and World Welfare'. *Eastern Economic Journal* 22 (4): 467–475.

10 TRIPS, Product Standards, and the Developing Economies

The success of international trade as a development strategy for the developing countries has been conditioned in recent times by new international rules like Trade Related Intellectual Property Rights (TRIPS) environmental standards for goods exported, and core labour standards including child labour content of goods produced by developing countries. For exports to promote growth for the developing countries, their export products must attain these minimum standards and get access to markets in the developed countries. To the developing countries, these non-tariff barriers are the biggest hurdle of all to cross over in the present era of globalization. The TRIPS have made it virtually impossible to industrialize and emerge as manufacturing exporter through reverse engineering and imitation that many of today's successful countries had adopted at their initial stages of industrialization and growth. On the other hand, environmental standards and pollution abatement costs have eroded much of the comparative advantages that the developing countries may have in production of dirtier goods due to the abundant and cheap labour. Labour standards and prohibition of the use of even cheaper child labour in the production of export goods have the same effect. Of course, the developed countries justify use of such product and labour standards as eroding any unfair comparative advantage that the developing countries enjoy by imitation of new innovations, under-valuation of the environment, and exploitation of labour. This is now the bone of contention between the developing and the developed countries: whereas the developed countries see these standards as creating a level playing field for all, the developing countries see these as non-tariff barriers and as a ploy to protect producers in the developed countries and ensure monopoly rents for their innovators.

This chapter discusses different dimensions of these new rules and institutions of the world trade, and how in many instances these rules are actually creating a new divide in the world trading order. The most important of such instances is the implementation of TRIPS in health care markets that may deprive millions of poor patients all over the world of access to new innovations and drugs, particularly for deadly diseases like HIV/AIDS. Similarly, without properly addressing the problem of child labour, trade sanctions on and boycotts of products produced by child labour may in fact push millions of children into more unethical non-traded activities.

10.1 TRIPS

The TRIPS agreement which is binding for all members of the WTO on and from 1 January 1995, covers a wide range of intellectual property including copyright and related rights—such as the rights of performers, producers of sound recordings, and broadcasting organizations and the like—trademarks, industrial designs, patents, the layout-designs of integrated circuits, undisclosed information including trade secrets, and test data. Article 27(1) of TRIPS specifies that patents will have to be provided for inventions which are 'new, involve an inventive step, and are capable of industrial application'. Article 7 of TRIPS states that the protection and enforcement of TRIPS should contribute to the promotion of technological innovation and be conducive to social and economic welfare. Members, however, are free to determine the appropriate method of implementing the provisions of the TRIPS agreement within their own legal system and practice.

The main argument for protection of Intellectual Property Rights (IPR) is that the innovator must be allowed to extract rents from the buyers to recover the huge amount of research and development costs for its innovation. A weak IPR regime leads to losses from 're-engineered products' for the innovators and discourages them from undertaking research and development (R&D). This would mean a smaller number of innovations and a lower rate of growth. Since most of the innovating MNCs making huge investments in R&D belong to the advanced countries, particularly to the United States, EU, and Japan, these countries have been working towards the global harmonization of IPR regimes over last two decades. The TRIPS is one of the culminations of their efforts. It is often argued that a strong IPR regime will encourage local firms in the developing countries to undertake basic R&D themselves. But, the available evidence suggests that this has not happened so far primarily because developing countries, with a few notable exceptions like China, India, and Brazil, lack the skill and technical know-how required for basic R&D and successful innovation. A World Bank study also observes that the positive impact of a stronger patent protection on domestic R&D activities in the developing countries has not been empirically established [Primo Braga (1990)]. The TRIPS essentially has created a new divide of innovators and non-innovators and contributed to uneven growth of countries, as access to technological knowledge is crucial for economic growth.

While this seems obvious and justified, there are several caveats to this argument. First, to what extent and for how long should the innovator extract rent to recover its R&D costs? The second part of this question is dealt with using the length (or life) of patent protection granted to the innovator, which is fixed at 20 years from the filing date of the patent application in the TRIPS Agreement, but the cost-benefit analysis underlying this number is not clear at all. Second, how far *should* the argument be extended to the market for health care and drugs for deadly diseases like AIDS, malaria, and tuberculosis? We will return to this later.

However, there are certain flexibilities and exceptions within the scope of TRIPS that allow country-specific variations in the implementation of a stronger IPR regime. Article 8, on the other hand, recognizes the rights of members to adopt measures for public health and other public interest reasons, and to prevent the abuse of intellectual property rights, provided that such measures are consistent with the provisions of the TRIPS Agreement. Article 6 of the TRIPS also allows countries to set their own rules of exhaustion of patents and copyrights. This enables countries to allow parallel trade by which a patented product can be bought and imported from a low-priced country once the product is marketed by the patent-holder. Such a parallel import was first endorsed by the European Court of Justice and the Treaty of Rome and is known in the EU as the internal rule of market: the patent-holder's sales right is exhausted EU-wide once the on-patent product is marketed within the EU. Note that a parallel import is different from product piracy. The parallel import contributes to the sales revenue for the intellectual property right owners or the patent-holders, whereas sales of pirated products constitute a loss of revenue for the patent-holder.

But the national rules on parallel imports (or exhaustion of patents, trademarks, and copyrights) vary widely across the globe according to whether a country is an importer or an exporter. Whereas Japan allows international exhaustion, the EU allows regional exhaustion of patented goods. In Japan, an example of parallel importing is the import of low-priced Asian version of Japanese pop music CDs from China, Hong Kong, and Taiwan, which were sold in these markets. In the EU, on the other hand, pharmaceuticals constitute a sizeable proportion of parallel imports. During the 1980s, cosmetics and fragrances, luxury automobiles, and cameras were the most significant items of parallel imports in the United States. But now the United States allows only national exhaustion of patents, trademarks, and copyrights, and even incorporate such clauses (the so-called TRIPS-Plus features) in bilateral trade negotiations to protect the interests of their MNC-exporters [Maskus (2000)]. The Copyright Amendment Act 1998 of New Zealand allows for parallel import of non-infringing copies of work. India and most of the developing countries, on the other hand, allow international exhaustion. Argentina, Thailand, and

South Africa have recently enacted laws permitting international exhaustion of patent rights for drugs and pharmaceuticals.

In Section 10.1.1 we discuss implications of parallel imports on innovation, price convergence, and country welfare.

10.1.1 PARALLEL IMPORTS, INNOVATION, AND WELFARE

Parallel imports restrict the patent-holder's ability to discriminate among different markets on the basis of persisting income differences. If volumes of parallel imports are sufficiently high, the patent-holder firm is forced to charge a uniform price in all markets related through trade. The only difference in prices across markets that might still exist would simply reflect differences in transport costs and different country-specific rates of tariffs. Of course, as Maskus (2001) and Jelovac and Bordoy (2005) argue, there may not be *complete* price convergence, since the consumers in the importing countries may not value the parallel-imports equally (because of different packages or guarantees) as they value the products marketed by the patent-holder. In general, under parallel imports prices tend to converge and if transport costs are negligible and consumers do not value the original and parallel-imported products differently, there will be complete convergence of prices across different country markets. To prevent such parallel imports and arbitrage, and consequent loss of profits, the patent-holder charges a uniform price across all country markets that it covers. Of course, the patent-holder may still keep prices high in the richer countries by not catering to the low-income country markets and thereby prohibiting any scope for allowing parallel imports by the richer countries. This latter possibility, pointed out by Malueg and Schwartz (1994), has larger implications for market access for essential innovations like new drugs for the poor countries. We will return to this issue later.

It is obvious that the richer countries primarily gain from allowing parallel imports and consequent cross-country price convergence because otherwise a patent-holder MNC would charge higher prices for its patented product. Thus, as Richardson (2002) demonstrates, when poorer countries cannot restrict parallel exports, the unique Nash equilibrium will be uniform pricing: The richer countries undo cross-country price discrimination by the patent-holder. On the other hand, poorer countries unambiguously lose from parallel imports allowed by the richer countries, and thus it makes sense for them to prohibit parallel exports. That is, when the poorer countries can restrict parallel exports, market-based (or cross-country) discrimination is the Nash equilibrium pricing [Richardson (2002)]. Moreover, as Malueg and Schwartz (1994) demonstrated, the *aggregate* (or global) welfare under discriminatory pricing would be lower than that under uniform pricing for small cross-country demand dispersions (or for small variations in the country-specific maximum willingness-to-pay), but would be higher for very large dispersions because some markets are *not* served under uniform pricing. Thus, interests of even richer countries may not be the same.

Valetti (2006) adds a new dimension to the debate over a global rule on the exhaustion of patent rights by showing that as the profit of a patent-holder multinational company (MNC) is lower under uniform pricing, parallel imports or international exhaustion of patent rights ex ante lowers the level of innovation of a new drug. The corresponding loss of utility all around thus is to be weighed against the utility gains for those who pay lower prices under parallel imports. Acharyya (2013) and Acharyya and Garcia-Alonso (2008) generalize and extend this result by drawing implications of such under-investment in innovation for national welfare levels and hence for the Richardson result. One interesting result with far reaching implications is that if markets are fully covered under parallel imports (in contrast to Velletti's ex ante restriction on partial coverage of markets), the innovation of a lower quality good than under discrimination must be offered with a lower (uniform) price to induce the buyers to participate in the market. This is in sharp contrast to the conventional theoretical wisdom that the uniform price (resulting from parallel imports) is higher than at least the lowest discriminatory price. Acharyya and Garcia-Alonso (2008), however, demonstrate that despite such a lower price parallel imports unambiguously make all buyers in the poorer or low income countries worse off when intra-country income disparity exists. On the other hand, even discarding the MNC's profit, there will be cases in which the richer country prefers price discrimination as well. That is, in those cases no countries will have any incentive under the welfare criterion to undo price discrimination contrary to Richardson (2002).

To demonstrate these results, Acharyya and Garcia-Alonso (2008) consider a two-country world with a discrete nature of intra-country income disparity similar to that discussed in Chapter 9. This has later been generalized to the continuum of incomes in Acharyya (2013), though the main results remain more or less the same. Let there be only two income levels in each country: $\bar{y}_P$ and y_M in the poor country and, y_M and $\bar{y}_R$ in the rich country, and $\bar{y}_P < y_M < \bar{y}_R$. Essentially this means that the two countries differ both in respect of the minimum and the maximum willingness-to-pay. We shall later discuss the implication of countries differing only in respect of the maximum willingness-to-pay as in Valletti (2006). Let n_{P1}, n_{PM}, n_{RM} and n_{R2} be the number of (potential) buyers in the respective income classes in the two countries. Assume a linear utility function defined in (10.1):

$$u\left(y_j, s\right) = y_j s. \tag{10.1}$$

Each buyer buys only one unit of the innovated product, if at all. Let the reservation utility of a buyer of income y_j be zero. Thus, by the individually rational (IR) constraint, he buys the innovated product if,

$$y_j s \geq P. \tag{10.2}$$

There is a single MNC situated in the rich country that plans to develop a new product of quality s by investing the amount C in R&D. This R&D investment is growing at an increasing rate in the target level of quality of the innovated drug:

$$C = \frac{1}{2}s^2. \tag{10.3}$$

Except for this sunk cost, there is no other cost. Once the drug is developed, the MNC gets a patent that confers it with a monopoly right over its exclusive sales in different markets.

Note that since except for the sunk R&D cost, there are no other costs, quality discrimination is not profitable for the monopolist even if it can effectively segment the two country markets. The MNC will thus develop only *one* quality for all markets. This result may hold even for positive and increasing (marginal) production costs. Given that only one quality is developed, price discrimination in each country market is not feasible either. Perfect price discrimination is not possible because a priori the exact *type* of a buyer in any market is not known to the MNC. For example, for any given choice of the innovated quality s, if in the rich world the MNC charges the poorer buyers with income y_M the price $y_M s$ and the richer buyers with income $\bar{y}_R$ the price $\bar{y}_R s$, the expected revenue $(n_{RM} y_M + n_{R2} \bar{y}_R)s$ is never realized unless the MNC can identify who are the poorer and who are the richer buyers, and accordingly can prohibit the richer buyers from mimicking the poorer buyers. The second degree price discrimination—by which the richer buyer in each country is charged a price according to its self-selection (or incentive compatibility) constraint—is not feasible either since the same quality is provided to both poor and rich buyers in each country. Thus, the MNC charges uniform prices in each country and essentially offers a pooling menu under full market coverage in each country.[1] But prices may differ across these national markets since the patent confers exclusive production rights upon the MNC. Given the income differences across the rich and the poor countries, such monopoly rights create the scope for market-based (price) discrimination (MBD) for the MNC. However, its

---

[1] A formal proof of a monopolist offering a pooling menu, uniform price, and quality, to the heterogeneous set of consumers in a closed economy is provided in Acharyya (1998).

ability to discriminate may be limited by parallel trading allowed by the countries. In such a case, the MNC cannot effectively segment the two national markets and costless arbitrage wipes out price differences.

Under MBD, serving only one market is clearly profit-reducing for the MNC since without parallel trading, there would be no arbitrage across the countries. The choice for the MNC is then whether to cater to all types in each market by charging a low uniform price, to only the richer buyers in the third world but serving all in the rich world, to all in the third world but only the richer buyers in the rich world, and finally, only the richer people in each country. The first one is what we call full market coverage whereas the other three possibilities are the different cases of partial market coverage. These choices of price and the extent of coverage of each market depend on the size of income classes or the pattern of intra-country income disparity in each country. In particular, as Acharyya and Garcia-Alonso demonstrate, with intra-country income disparity, the patent-holder MNC serves all markets with full coverage under MBD if the income distribution pattern in each country satisfies,

$$\frac{n_{P1}}{n_{TM}} > \frac{y_M - \bar{y}_P}{\bar{y}_P} \tag{10.4}$$

$$\frac{n_{RM}}{n_{R2}} > \frac{\bar{y}_R - y_M}{y_M}. \tag{10.5}$$

To check these conditions, Let π_D, $\tilde{\pi}_D$, $\tilde{\tilde{\pi}}_D$, and $\hat{\pi}_D$ denote profits of the MNC when all buyers in all markets are served (i.e., full coverage of all markets), only rich buyers in the third world and all buyers in the rich world are served, all buyers in the third world but only rich buyers in the rich world are served, and only the rich buyers in each country are served respectively. Now consider first the choice in the poor country market given that the rich country market is fully served. If both types of buyers are served in the poor country, then the MNC must charge the price $\bar{y}_P s$ for any given choice of innovated quality s, which results in a revenue of $(n_{P1}\bar{y}_P + n_{PM} y_M)s$ in the poor country market. Since the rich country market is also fully served, the price $y_M s$ is charged there with a revenue of $(n_{RM} + n_{R2}) y_M s$. Thus, the total profit of the MNC from fully covering both markets is $[(n_{T1} + n_{TM})\bar{y}_T + (n_{RM} + n_{R2}) y_M]s - (1/2)s^2$. Profit maximization yields the innovated quality as,

$$\hat{s}_D^e = [(n_{P1} + n_{PM})\bar{y}_P + (n_{RM} + n_{R2}) y_M] \tag{10.6}$$

with a realized profit equal to $\pi_D = \left[(n_{P1} + n_{PM})\bar{y}_P + (n_{RM} + n_{R2}) y_M\right]^2 / 2$.

On the other hand, if the MNC decides to cater to only the richer buyers in the poor country (along with all buyers in the rich country), it charges the price $y_M s$ there and earns a total revenue of $[n_{PM} y_M + (n_{RM} + n_{R2}) y_M]s$. Profit maximization now yields innovated quality as $[n_{PM} y_M + (n_{RM} + n_{R2}) y_M]$ with a realized profit of $\tilde{\pi}_D = \left[n_{PM} y_M + (n_{RM} + n_{R2}) y_M \right]^2 / 2$. Hence, given that the rich country market is fully covered in both these cases, the poor country market is fully covered (i.e., $\pi_D > \tilde{\pi}_D$) if $(n_{P1} \bar{y}_P + n_{PM} y_{PM}) > n_{PM} y_{PM}$, which boils down to condition (10.4). On the other hand, proceeding as before, it can be shown that given full market coverage in the poor country, the MNC will prefer to cater all buyers in rich country if $\pi_D > \tilde{\pi}_D$, which boils down to condition (10.5). In other words, under these income distribution patterns, the MNC would prefer to cater to 'all' buyers than to 'some' buyers in one country and 'all' buyers in the other.

Finally, note that since the richest buyers in the third world and the poorest buyers in the rich world have the same income level y_M, so the same condition (10.5) ensures that $\tilde{\pi}_D > \hat{\pi}_D$. Therefore, if the income distribution patterns in the two countries satisfy these two conditions, then

$$\pi_D > \tilde{\pi}_D$$

$$\pi_D > \tilde{\pi}_D > \tilde{\pi}_D,$$

that is, the MNC serves all buyers everywhere under MBD.

Note that these conditions are consistent with both uniform distribution $(n_{T1} = n_{TM}, n_{RM} = n_{R2})$ and non-uniform distribution. In the rest of our analysis, we confine ourselves to these income distribution patterns that ensure the full market coverage in each country.

Under parallel imports, on the other hand, given (10.5), the relative size of the low-income class in the poor country must be large enough in the following sense to induce the MNC to serve it:

$$\frac{n_{P1}}{n_{PM} + n_{RM} + n_{R2}} > \frac{y_M - \bar{y}_P}{\bar{y}_P}. \tag{10.7}$$

Under these conditions, the MNC charges the global uniform price $\bar{y}_P s$ to *all* consumers everywhere. Proceeding as before, the chosen level of profit-maximizing innovation equals,

$$\hat{s}_{PI}^e = (n_P + n_R) \bar{y}_P \tag{10.8}$$

where, $n_P = n_{P1} + n_{PM}$ and $n_R = n_{RM} + n_{R2}$.

Comparing from (10.6) and (10.8) it is immediate that the innovation level is lower under parallel imports than under MBD under universal full market coverage: $\hat{s}_{PI}^e < \hat{s}_D^e$. This is the under-investment result of Valletti (2006).

Comparing the equilibrium prices, on the other hand, we observe that for the low-income country the price under parallel trading is lower than the discriminatory price charged under MBD:

$$\hat{P}_{PI}^e - \hat{P}_{DP}^e = \overline{y}_p(\hat{s}_{PI}^e - \hat{s}_D^e) < 0 \qquad (10.9)$$

This surprising result is not counter-intuitive though. Since under parallel imports a lower quality of the innovated drug is chosen by the MNC, consumers in the poor country must be charged a lower price than under MBD. Note that this result holds even when, first, the countries have the same lowest marginal willingness-to-pay, $\overline{y}_p$, and second, consumers are continuously distributed over an income range [$\underline{y}, \overline{y}_j$]. This has been demonstrated by Acharyya (2013) where consumers in country-j are distributed continuously over the interval [$\underline{y}, \overline{y}_j$], j = P, R, such that the rich and the poor countries differ only in respect of the levels of personal income earned by their respective richest consumers, $\overline{y}_R > \overline{y}_p$. For such a continuum of consumers and the same lowest income in both countries, the uniform global price under parallel imports is strictly lower than the discriminatory prices charged by the MNC under MBD when it serves all buyers in all markets. This is because the result depends more on the extent of market coverage and the innovation level than on anything else. When the poorest of the buyers in the poor country are served under both MBD and parallel imports (PI), as the MNC innovates a lower quality drug it must charge a lower price as well to induce them to buy the innovated drug. This possibility was overlooked by Valletti (2006) where consumers in each country are continuously and uniformly distributed over different income ranges, because the partial market coverage was implicitly assumed. But as Wauthy (1996) and Acharyya (1998) have demonstrated, the extent of market coverage should be an outcome of profit-maximizing behaviour of the firm(s) rather than an ex ante restriction. It can be easily checked in the simplified framework of Valletti (2006) that the parametric configurations for which the poorest country market is always fully covered, (all) buyers there pay a lower uniform price of the innovated drug under PI than the lowest discriminatory price that they pay in absence of such parallel trading.

What implications does parallel import have for the consumer surplus and welfare? First of all, note that the poorest income group in the poor country has the same net surplus of zero under both the regimes. The poorest buyers in the rich country (those having y_M level of income), on the other hand, gain from parallel imports as they now derive strictly positive net surplus. The richer income group in the poor country (those having y_M level of income), however, unambiguously loses:

$$\left[y_M \hat{s}_{PI}^e - \hat{P}_{PI}^e\right] - \left[y_M \hat{s}_D^e - \hat{P}_{DP}^e\right] = \left(y_M - \bar{y}_P\right)\left[\hat{s}_{PI}^e - \hat{s}_D^e\right] < 0.$$

This is because the under-investment hurts them more than the price decline makes them better off as they value the quality of health care highly. The net gain per capita from parallel imports for the richest in the rich country, on the other hand, equals:

$$[\bar{y}_R \hat{s}_{PI}^e - \hat{P}_{PI}^e] - [\bar{y}_R \hat{s}_D^e - \hat{P}_{DR}^e] = (n_P + n_R)\bar{y}_P + n_R y_M - n_R \bar{y}_R < 0,$$

thus, they gain from parallel trading only when their (per capita) income is smaller in the following sense:

$$\bar{y}_R < y_M + \frac{n_T + n_R}{n_R}\bar{y}_P. \tag{10.10}$$

The intuition is simple. Under parallel imports, the buyers gain from the lower price of the innovated product, but lose from a lower innovation. Under the full market coverage, the price decline does not depend on the income (or marginal valuation) of the richest of buyers (see (10.6), (10.8), and (10.9)). But, the utility loss from a smaller innovation under parallel imports, $\bar{y}_R[\hat{s}_{PI}^e - \hat{s}_D^e]$, increases proportionately with the income level of the richest buyer. Hence, the gain in the price over-compensates the loss from lower health care innovation for them only if their income and marginal valuation for higher innovation is not large in the sense defined in (10.10).

Since the social welfare in the poor country equals only the sum of consumer surpluses, the result implies that parallel trading lowers the welfare of the poor country unambiguously. Note that the parallel exporters there earn zero profit. On the other hand, as established by Acharyya and Garcia-Alonso (2008), despite gains for the buyers in the rich world, the loss of the MNC profit under parallel imports is so large as to lower the welfare of the rich country as well. Therefore, when all buyers in all countries are served, parallel import of the innovated drug from the poor to the rich country *lowers the welfare of both the trading nations*.

What this welfare result means is that when the adverse R&D effect of parallel imports is taken into account, Richardson's (2002) result that rich countries 'undo price discrimination' does not hold. Even if the MNC's profits are not included in the calculation of the rich country's welfare, there may be income distribution patterns in the rich country such that they still prefer price discrimination

Generalizing these results to a continuum of income types, Acharyya (2013) demonstrates that the price and welfare results extend to a three or more country world. Furthermore, he also examines the incentives for low income countries to restrict parallel trading by imposing export tax similar to the analysis of Richardson (2002). The result he establishes is that regardless of the demand dispersion, $\bar{y}_p - y$, the government in the poor country prohibits parallel exports through an export tax. The rich country government's choice is thus inconsequential. Thus, the MBD will be the equilibrium price regime, meaning that the Richardson result extends to the case of vertical product differentiation.

In sub-section 10.1.2, we discuss implications of these effects of parallel imports for TRIPS implemented in markets for health care and pharmaceuticals, and market access for poor patients in the third world.

10.1.2 TRIPS, PARALLEL IMPORTS, AND MARKET ACCESS TO NEW DRUGS

Implementation of TRIPS for the pharmaceutical products by developing countries has been fiercely debated and politically contested. The main argument for TRIPS is again the assertion that product patents will accelerate the innovation of drugs and therefore improve the quality of health care. This in turn will benefit developing and developed countries alike. But innovation of new drugs in the developing world can hardly be expected for two reasons. First, investments in basic R&D and costs of full development of a commercial drug are very high, and second, most of the developing countries lack the technological capability and skill to undertake basic R&D [Lall (2003)]. The exceptions are, of course, China, India, and Brazil. Prohibition of imitation and generic drug production in the developing countries, on the other hand, means loss of market access for the poor patients as a consequence of monopoly pricing of drugs by the patent-holder MNCs from the developed countries. Such loss of market access is not only for the poor patients in these countries, but also those in Asia, Latin America, and sub-Saharan Africa who benefit from cheap imports of generic drugs from India, China, and Brazil.

Interestingly, the possibility of cross-country price discrimination by patent-holder MNCs under TRIPS has raised similar concerns of accessibility to new drugs in the rich world as well. In such a context, parallel imports allowed by the rich countries to ensure market access for their poor patients may worsen market access for poor patients in poor countries. As mentioned, the MNC may not cater to the poor countries at all under parallel imports [Malueg and Schwartz (1994)]. Moreover, parallel imports lower the innovation level and welfare of poor and rich countries alike. There have been, therefore, oppositions to rich countries implementing international exhaustion of patent rights. Thus, benefits of both product patent and flexible clauses and exceptions like parallel imports are neither unequivocal nor uniform across nations. The relevant issue that crops up in these perspectives is: can the inconsistency of co-implementing these two policies be resolved in terms of national welfare levels that incorporate effects of these policies on both the market access for poorer buyers and the innovation of drugs and health care? Acharyya and Garcia-Alonso (2012) address this issue in the context of a policy game where a poor country chooses between strict implementation of TRIPS and using flexible clauses of TRIPS to continue production of generic drugs whereas a rich country chooses between allowing and not allowing parallel imports of an innovated drug.

Though TRIPS is now binding on all members of the WTO, its relevance for pharmaceuticals markets is still questionable. The monopoly power that patent protection under TRIPS confers upon the patent-holder firm has resulted in quite high prices for essential drugs for AIDS in the developing and the poor countries. The cost of individual AIDS-combination therapy in India, Bangladesh, Pakistan, Indonesia, and in other low-income countries has been prohibitively high. Since most of the HIV-infected people live in developing and low-income countries, IPR protection for medicines and drugs may actually deny these patients access to the available drugs and consequently their right to live. In India alone, eight million people are estimated to be HIV-positive, of which five hundred thousand people have already developed AIDS. Thus, consequences of TRIPs in health care are altogether different than in markets for other copyrighted products. There are more critical issues at hand than ensuring profit incentives for the innovators.

10.1.3 TRIPS, INNOVATION, AND GROWTH

As mentioned earlier, a primary argument for patent protection through TRIPS is that it encourages innovation of products by ensuring profits or rents for the innovator and the patent-holder. Development of new products through innovation, which is primarily undertaken by the developed countries (or the North), requires that the market for the innovator be protected through patent protection. But such patent protection is often lacking in the developing countries (or the South). Thus, when the North-South commodity trade opens up under asymmetric implementation of TRIPS, imports of new products developed in the North creates a scope for producers in the South to imitate these products and eventually out-compete the Northern exporters from the market in the South due to cheap labour and low production costs of the imitated products. This loss of monopoly rent for the Northern innovator through international trade discourages innovation in the North and retards its product growth rate. Thus, the rate of innovation and growth in the North is conditioned by the possibility of imitation by the South, necessitating a universal implementation of the Intellectual Property Right (IPR) regime.

But, as demonstrated by Helpman (1993), implementation of TRIPS or an intellectual property right (IPR) regime may not always improve the product growth rate in the developed countries. In fact, contrary to the argument that TRIPS will augment the rate of innovation, a fall in the imitation rate in the developing countries due to tightening of the IPR regime was shown to lower the steady state, long run innovation rate in the South. In the short run, however, the rate of innovation may rise. The idea here is that, whereas a lower rate of imitation raises the return from R&D and thus steps up the rate of product innovation in the developed countries in the short run, in the long run monopoly profit earned for a longer period acts as a disincentive to innovate. The resource constraint also lowers per product output as the rate of innovation augments in the short run, which gradually lowers the profitability of R&D. Conversely, a higher rate of imitation encourages the firms in the developed countries to innovate new products at a faster rate in the long run to compensate for the loss of monopoly rent over the imitated products.

This interesting result was established by Helpman (1993) in the context of new growth theories as developed by Lucas, Romer, and Rebelo during the late 1980s and early 1990s that emphasized upon product differentiation and quality improvement attained through R&D as the sources of growth. Thus, the source of growth is *endogenous* rather than exogenous. In these endogenous or new growth theories, the variable of concern is the product growth rate rather than the output growth rate. For an open economy, these new growth theories imply that faster growth of exports of manufacturing goods per se does not matter for augmenting growth. Rather, a country's ability to produce newer varieties and improve quality of its export products is an important factor behind faster growth.

In the application of the new growth theories in the context of North-South trade and growth, Grossman and Helpman (1991) have demonstrated that international trade augments the product growth rates through larger investment in R&D. On the other hand, a small tariff on traditional manufacturing imports (or an export subsidy to high-technology manufacturing) yields a similar result. Thus, a one shot opening up of international trade from an initial position of autarky and a small reduction in tariff (and consequently only a partial trade liberalization) may have different growth implications. This is analogous to the gains from trade and optimum tariff arguments of static trade theories.

To illustrate Helpman's (1993) result that an IPR regime may actually lower the rate of product innovation, consider a North with two sectors: a production sector, where differentiated varieties of a manufacturing good X are produced; and a R&D sector, where these varieties are developed. Labour is used both in the development of a product in the R&D sector and in production of the developed varieties in the manufacturing production sector. Consumers have identical and homothetic tastes. An infinitely-lived consumer has the following life time utility from consuming the varieties,

$$U(t) = \int_t^\infty e^{-\rho(\tau-t)} \log u(\tau) d\tau \qquad (10.11)$$

where, ρ is the subjective discount factor and $u(\tau)$ is the instantaneous utility that she derives, which has the following Dixit-Stiglitz type love-for-variety specification:

$$u = \left[\int_0^n c(j)^\alpha \, dj \right]^{\frac{1}{\alpha}} 0 < \alpha < 1 \qquad (10.12)$$

Here, n is the number of existing varieties and $c(j)$ is the consumption of the j-th variety.

Note that each variety enters the utility function symmetrically. The homotheticity assumption allows us to derive aggregate demand for each variety directly from the individual preferences. It is easy to check that all such demand functions will have constant (and the same) value of the price elasticity of demand: $\varepsilon = 1/(1-\alpha)$.

Product development requires a_{Ln} / K units of labour per product, where K is the stock of knowledge capital in R&D, which in turn depends on the number of products in existence. If there is learning-by-doing in the sense that the newer varieties developed expand the stock of knowledge capital, then by suitable choice of units, $K = n$. Note that this assumes away any international knowledge spill over. Competition and free entry in the R&D sector equalizes the marginal benefit with the marginal cost of developing a product. Let V denote the return or marginal benefit from developing a product, which is taken as the numeraire. For any given number of products in existence in the North, the marginal cost equals $(a_{Ln} / n) w^N$, where w^N is the real wage in the North measured in terms of the marginal benefit per product. Competition and free entry then implies:

$$1 = \frac{a_{Ln}}{n} w^N \qquad (10.13)$$

Production of any variety of the manufacturing good requires only labour at a fixed labour-output ratio, normalized to unity, and this relation is the same for all varieties developed and produced. Monopoly production of each variety then implies the following (identical) price for each variety, which is a mark-up over the marginal (labour) cost[2]:

$$P^N = \frac{w^N}{\alpha}. \tag{10.14}$$

This follows from the equality of marginal revenue and marginal cost of producing a developed variety.

The full employment of labour means that the total Northern labour force L^N equals the workers engaged in developing additional varieties, $\dot{n}$, and workers engaged in producing x units of output of each of the n number of varieties. If the South successfully imitates n_S number of products out of the n number of total varieties developed until date-t in the North, the Northern firms that were producing these imitated varieties under autarchy will be driven out of the market by the cost advantage of Southern firms in terms of the significantly low wages there. Thus, under international trade and imitation by the South, at any point of time the Northern firms will have the monopoly power in only $n_N = n - n_S$ number of varieties that are not imitated by the Southern firms. Thus, the total output of the manufacturing industry in the North will be $X^N = n_N x$. Accordingly, the labour market equilibrium can be written as,

$$\frac{a_{Ln}}{n} \dot{n} + X^N = L^N. \tag{10.15}$$

Let $g^N = \dot{n}/n$ denote the rate of product development in the North, or the Northern product growth rate, $g^S = \dot{n}_s/n_s$ denote the Southern imitated product growth rate and $\phi = \dot{n}_s/n_N$ denote the instantaneous rate of imitation by the South. Given that under trade and imitation, only n_N number of products are produced in the North, the profit per product (and per Northern firm) there equals,

$$\pi^N(x) = \left(p^N - w^N\right)\frac{X^N}{n_N}$$

which using (10.14) and substituting for X^N from (10.15) can be rewritten as,

$$\pi^N(x) = (1-\alpha)\left[L^N - a_{Ln}g^N\right]\frac{P^N}{n_N} = (1-\alpha)\left[L^N - a_{Ln}g^N\right]\frac{w^N}{\alpha n_N}.$$

---

[2] Following Grossman and Helpman (1991), the monopoly pricing can be justified by an infinitely-lived product patent granted to an innovating firm. Alternatively, we can think of costly imitation, and ex post price competition that prohibits copying of the same variety as that will erode profits from the imitation and the firm will be unable to cover its imitation cost.

But by (10.13), $a_{L_n} w^N = n$, so that

$$\pi^N(x) = \frac{(1-\alpha)}{\alpha} \left[\frac{L^N}{a_{L_n}} - g^N \right] \frac{1}{\psi}$$
(10.16)

where, $\psi = (n_N / n)$ is the proportion of innovated products in the North that are not imitated by the South. The time rate of change in this proportion is given as,

$$\frac{\dot{\psi}}{\psi} = \frac{\dot{n}_N}{n_N} - \frac{\dot{n}}{n} = \frac{\dot{n} - \dot{n}_s}{n_N} - g^N = \frac{\dot{n}}{n_N} - \phi - g^N \Rightarrow$$

$$\dot{\psi} = \left[\frac{\dot{n}}{n_N} - \phi - g^N \right] \psi = g^N - \left(\phi + g^N \right) \psi$$
(10.17)

Thus, at steady state, $\dot{\psi} = 0$, the proportion of innovated products in the North that are not imitated by the South equals,

$$\dot{\psi}^* = \frac{g^N}{\phi + g^N}.$$
(10.18)

Now whether a product will at all be developed or not in the North depends on the arbitrage condition in the asset market at each point of time. Investment in R&D yields profit equal to $\pi^N(x)$ for an owner of a firm in country-j from developing and selling (exporting) a particular variety. But, the probability of a product being imitated by a Southern firm, as captured by the instantaneous rate of imitation of products by Southern firms (ϕ), indicates that there is also a risk involved in innovation. On the other hand, if the owner were to lend the money, they could have earned the interest rate r^N. The arbitrage condition in the asset market then implies that the return from innovating a product must equal the interest foregone on deposits and the risk premium[3]:

$$\pi^N(x) = r^N + \phi.$$
(10.19)

---

[3] This condition can alternatively be derived from the fact that under free entry, the cost of developing a product must be equal to the discounted present value of the expected profit streams.

Finally, define the expenditure by the Northern consumers on innovated product as $E_N = n_N p^N x^N = p^N X^N$.[4] By definition,

$$\frac{\dot{E}_N}{E_N} = \frac{\dot{p}^N}{p^N} - \frac{\dot{X}^N}{X^N}. \tag{10.20}$$

From (10.13), (10.14), and (10.15), we get,

$$\frac{\dot{p}^N}{p^N} = \frac{\dot{w}^N}{w^N} = \frac{\dot{n}}{n} \equiv g^N \text{ and } \frac{\dot{X}^N}{X_N} = \frac{-a_{Ln}\dot{g}^N}{L^N - a_{Ln}g^N}. \tag{10.21}$$

The first relationship tells us that by the exogenously given mark-up pricing, the price of an innovated good rises proportionately with the rise in the Northern wage rate, which in turn is equal to the rate of product innovation itself. The second relationship indicates the trade-off between output expansion and the augmentation of the rate of product innovation due to scarcity of labour. In fact, referring back to (10.15), the exogenously given availability of labour in the North constrains the product growth rate at the maximum $\bar{g}^N = L^N / a_{Ln}$.

On the other hand, maximization of the present discounted value of the stream of utility defined in (10.11) by the consumers subject to the budget constraint that the present discounted value of the stream of expenditures must equal the income (or the wage rate) yields,

$$\frac{\dot{E}_N}{E_N} = r^N - \rho. \tag{10.22}$$

which is in fact the Ramsey rule. Note that r^N is the market interest rate in the North on the consumption loan and ρ is the time preference (or subjective discount factor) of consumers as mentioned earlier.

Combining (10.16), (10.19), (10.20), (10.21), and (10.22) we get,

$$\dot{g}^N = \left[\phi + \rho + g^N - \frac{(1-\alpha)}{\alpha} \left(\frac{L^N}{a_{Ln}} - g^N \right) \frac{1}{\psi} \right] \left(\frac{L^N}{a_{Ln}} - g^N \right). \tag{10.23}$$

---

[4] If the Northern consumers consume both the domestic innovated varieties and the imported imitated varieties, by homothetic taste we can assume that each spends β proportion of total expenditure (or income) on the innovated varieties and $(1 - \beta)$ proportion on the imitated varieties. Hence, $E_N = (1 - \beta)E$.

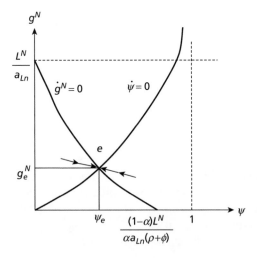

Figure 10.1 Steady State Product Growth Rate of the North

The two steady state conditions $\dot{\psi}=0$ and $\dot{g}^N=0$ define the equilibrium system in this set-up, with ψ being the state variable and g^N being the jump variable (Helpman, 1993). In Figure 10.1, these steady state conditions are plotted in the (ψ, g^N) space. From (10.17) and (10.23) it is easy to check that $\dot{\psi}=0$ and $\dot{g}^N=0$ loci are positively and negatively sloped respectively. The intersection point e represents the steady state long run equilibrium. Helpman (1993) argues that by the values of the parameters of the model 'there exists an upper bound on the instantaneous rate of imitation', $\bar{\phi}$, such that the equilibrium point e is in the feasible region as shown in Figure 10.1. Substitution of value from (10.18) for $\dot{\psi}=0$ in (10.23), and for $g^N < \bar{g}^N$, the steady state, long run equilibrium rate of innovation (or the Northern growth rate) is given by the solution of the following condition:

$$\frac{(1-\alpha)}{\alpha}\left(\frac{L^N}{a_{Ln}}-g^N\right)\frac{\phi+g^N}{g^N}-\phi-\rho-g^N=0. \tag{10.24}$$

The saddle path in Figure 10.1 is shown by the arrow line through this equilibrium point e. Thus, whenever any shock lowers the proportion of products not being imitated below its steady state value, this proportion rises and the growth rate declines over time. In the other case when the proportion rises above its steady state value, it declines and the growth rate increases over time.

There are several interesting conclusions that emerge from this analysis. It is easy to check that the long run Northern growth rate, or the long run rate of product innovation, increases with the increase in the instantaneous rate of imitation of products by the Southern firms (ϕ). An increase in the rate of imitation shifts both the $\dot{\psi}=0$ and $\dot{g}^N=0$ loci to the left, although it shifts the former proportionately *more* than the latter.[5] This results in a rise in the long run equilibrium rate of innovation, $(\partial g_e^N / \partial \phi) > 0$, and a decline in the long run value of the proportions of products not yet imitated.

From this follows two policy implications. First, trade augments the rate of innovation and growth in the North. Under autarchy and hence no threat of innovation ($\phi = 0$), the rate of innovation is least. But as trade opens up, and with it opens up possibility of imitation of an innovated product, the rate of innovation in the North steps up. This is immediate from the comparative static result derived earlier: $(\partial g_e^N)/(\partial \phi) > 0$. The autarchic rate of innovation can be calculated from (10.24) for $\phi = 0$ as,

$$g_a^N = (1-\alpha)\frac{L^N}{a_{Ln}} - \alpha\rho. \tag{10.25}$$

Second, a tightening Intellectual Property Right (IPR) regime that lowers the rate of imitation in the South, lowers the rate of innovation in the North. But as Helpman (1993) shows, in the short run the rate of innovation rises so that tightening of the IPR regime has the usually perceived favourable impact on the rate of innovation in the North. The intuition behind the contrasting short run and long run effects of tightening of the IPR regime is as follows. As the rate of imitation falls, the monopoly rent for an innovated product can now be extracted for a longer period of time. This serves to raise the profitability of the R&D. This augments the rate of innovation in the North in the short run. But as the rate of innovation rises, profit per product as specified in (3.53) falls through, first, a decline in the total and per product output due to resource constraint, and second, a rise in the proportion of products not imitated. These lead to a gradual decline in the profitability of R&D and consequently the rate of innovation itself in the long run.

Likewise, effects of other parametric shifts can be derived with the help of Figure 10.1. For example, a larger North (captured through its larger labour force) shifts only the $\dot{g}^N=0$ curve to the right and consequently raises its long run equilibrium growth rate by relaxing the resource constraint. A similar favourable effect will be realized when the R&D technology improves

---

[5] The lateral shift of the $\dot{g}^N = 0$ curve is the change in ψ for a change in ϕ at the initial value of g^N, which equals $d\psi = -[(\psi d\phi)/(\rho + \phi + g^N)]$. Similarly, the shift of the $\dot{\psi} = 0$ curve equals $d\psi = -[(\psi d\phi)/(\phi + g^N)]$.

(whereby a_{Ln} falls). On the other hand, a rise in the time preference (ρ) or in the demand elasticity (α) shifts only the $\overset{\bullet}{g}^N = 0$ curve to the left and consequently lowers the North's long run equilibrium growth rate. All these can be summarized through the following functional relationship between the long run equilibrium rate of Northern growth and the elasticity of demand, the time preference of consumers, the Northern labour force, and its R&D technology along with the rate of imitation by the South:

$$g_e^N = g^N\left(\underset{+}{\phi}, \underset{-}{\alpha}, \underset{-}{\rho}, \underset{-}{a_{Ln}}, L^N\right). \tag{10.26}$$

Helpman (1993) further derived welfare changes of a tightening of the IPR regime on account of its effects on the terms of trade, production composition, available product, and the inter-temporal allocation of consumption.

10.2 **Environmental Standards**

Like copyright violations in the developing countries and wide variations in the implementation of IPR regimes, cross-country variations in environmental regulations, standards, and the level of pollution abatement have become a bone of contention amongst the developed and the developing nations. The main argument for environmental regulations imposed by the developed countries is that comparative advantage of developing countries in goods that degrade the environment is often based on lax standards in these countries. That is, their comparative advantage is perverse and consequent trade is unfair. There is also the concern of ecological dumping since lax environmental regulations in the developing countries allow their producers to under-value the environment and price their exports at below social marginal cost. On the other hand, many economists like Copeland and Taylor (1994) and Bhagwati and Srinivasan (1996) have justified cross-country variations in environmental regulations as a reflection of variations in per capita incomes and other country-specific parameters that determine the optimal rate of environmental tax or regulation. Moreover, for production pollutions that do not spill over from the source country to the importing countries—cases of national or local pollution—environmental regulations imposed by the developed countries on imports from the developing countries have raised concerns in the developing nations as these measures appear as non-tariff barriers in disguise.

10.2.1 UNFAIR TRADE AND ECOLOGICAL DUMPING

The case of unfair trade and ecological dumping can be explained with the help of a two-good example. Two countries, developed and developing, produce two goods: chemicals and software. Chemicals pollute mostly water bodies and thereby adversely affect the fish population there. This in turn affects the livelihood of fishermen. In this type of negative externality, the social cost of producing chemicals far exceeds the private cost of production. In an unregulated economy, chemical producers do not internalize the adverse effect on the livelihood of fishermen and takes into account only the private costs of production involving labour and material costs and other costs that are being incurred. But if the government there imposes a pollution tax whenever the chemical producers do not take corrective action by abating pollution that such production generates, chemical producers are forced to internalize the costs that they inflict upon the fishermen. Their marginal costs now rise by the extent of the pollution abatement cost (or the pollution tax) and equal the social marginal cost. In such a case, if perfectly competitive conditions prevail in the developed country, the supply price of chemicals will reflect the social marginal cost of producing chemicals (SMC_c) *higher than the private marginal cost* (MC_c) without the pollution abatement cost. Suppose software is a clean good in the sense that it does not pollute the environment. Thus, there will be no divergence between the private and social costs of producing software so that under perfectly competitive conditions, the supply price of computers will reflect both the social and private marginal costs. The relative supply price of chemicals in the developed country (denoted by p) will therefore be the ratio of social marginal costs:

$$p = \frac{SMC_c}{SMC_s} > \frac{MC_c}{MC_s}. \tag{10.27}$$

If the developing country is identical in every respect—has the same market conditions and technology—and the government there takes the same punitive action against polluters as does the government in the developed country, then the relative supply price of chemicals there (denoted by p^*) will also reflect the ratio of social marginal costs and be the same as in the developed country for all levels of the relative supply of chemicals. Finally, if we assume identical and homothetic tastes in both countries, at any relative price, the relative demand for chemicals will be the same in the two countries. All these assumptions together imply that the equilibrium prices in the two countries will be the same before any trade opens up: $p_e = p_e^*$. The identical relative price leaves no scope of arbitrage and thus there will be no scope for international trade between these two countries.

Now consider the following variation in this case. Suppose the government in the developing country does *not* penalize chemical producers. Being unregulated, they do not incur any pollution abatement cost so that the supply price of chemicals will now reflect its private marginal cost of production. Hence, (10.27) now changes to,

$$p = \frac{MC_c}{MC_s} < \frac{SMC_c}{SMC_s}. \tag{10.28}$$

If the government in the developed country strictly enforces the environmental regulation, the supply price there will be the ratio of social marginal costs. Thus, given the assumption of identical costs and demand, the pre-trade equilibrium price will be lower in the developing country than in the developed country: $p_e < p_e^*$.

Lax environmental standards thus encourage producers in the developing country to price the output below the social marginal cost, produce chemicals more than the socially optimum (and more than the developed country producers produce), and establishes a comparative advantage for the developing country in chemical production. Trade between the developing and the developed country thus opens up, which could not have arisen under our assumption if the developing country had also enforced environmental regulation strictly. This type of trade is what the developed world labels as unfair trade. Since this comparative advantage is not based on fundamentals (such as differences in technology or cost, and taste), this is essentially a perverse comparative advantage arising due to undervaluation of the environment. Moreover, exports of chemicals to the developed country are priced below their social marginal cost in the developing country. Hence, this appears to be a case of ecological dumping.

There are a few caveats to these arguments though. First, exports of dirty goods (like chemicals in our example) do not necessarily mean perverse comparative advantage, unfair trade, and ecological dumping. Even when environmental standards are strictly enforced in the developing country, it may have a genuine comparative advantage in the production of chemicals. In many ways that is possible. For example, suppose the demand for chemicals is higher in the developed country than in the developing country. Then, everything else being the same in the two countries, including the environmental regulation, this demand bias will cause the pre-trade relative price of chemicals to be higher in the developed country. Consequently, chemicals will be imported by it. Some of the developed countries like China and India also have the technical knowledge and skill to produce chemicals and chemical products including pharmaceuticals as competitively as many developed

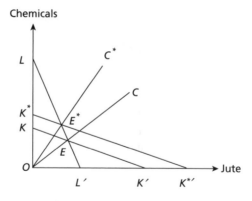

Figure 10.2 Larger Capital Stock and Supply Bias

countries. Thus, exports of dirty goods by developing countries may not reflect lax environmental standards there.

Second, despite lax environmental standards in the developing country, chemicals may actually be exported by the developed country. If the dirty good is relatively capital intensive, then the capital abundance of the richer nations creates a supply bias in the dirty good for them. To illustrate, consider two goods having distinctly different factor intensities: A dirty good, chemicals, which is relatively capital intensive and a cleaner good, jute manufacturing, which is relatively labour intensive. For any given set of prices of the two goods and corresponding rates of returns to labour and capital, the downward sloping lines LL' and KK' in Figure 10.2 represent combinations of the outputs of these two goods for which labour and capital respectively are fully employed in the developing country. The relative supply of chemicals consistent with full employment of both labour and capital in the developing country is indicated by the ray OC emanating from the origin and passing through the point of intersection E between the full employment lines. Suppose the developed country has the same number of workers but a larger capital stock which enables it to produce more of chemicals for any given output of the other good. This is shown by the full employment line $K^*K^{*'}$. Thus, given the same set of commodity prices, the relative supply of chemicals consistent with full employment of both labour and capital in the developed country will be larger, as indicated by the steeper ray, OC^*. Therefore, a larger capital stock in the developed country creates a supply bias in the relatively capital intensive dirty good, chemicals. This supply bias makes the relative price of chemicals lower in the developed country.

On the other hand, a stricter environmental regulation in the developed country and a lax one in the developing country make the relative price of chemicals higher in the former, as spelled out before. If the developed country is too rich in capital, we can expect the supply bias for it in chemicals to be stronger so that its effect on prices outweighs the pollution-abatement cost effect of a stricter regulation. The end result is that, the developed country will have a comparative advantage in chemicals, and will export this to the developing country.

Third, optimal environmental standards and pollution taxes may differ across countries according to their per capita incomes and other relevant parameters. Thus, as Copeland and Taylor (1994) and Bhagwati and Srinivasan (1996) argue, different standards or taxes in the developed and developing world may be a reflection of their structural differences rather than anything else.

10.2.2 TRADE, GROWTH, AND POLLUTION

International trade affects national pollution levels primarily in two ways: First in the short run by changing the composition of the aggregate output, the scale of production, and the technique of producing dirty goods; and second in the long run by augmenting the aggregate output and income and thereby inducing the demand for a better environment.

Whether trade is based on genuine or perverse comparative advantage, the short run impact of international trade on national and aggregate pollution levels depends on the trade pattern itself. When dirty goods are exported by the developing countries, the pollution load shifts from the developed to the developing country. This is because the export of dirty goods by the developing country displaces production of such goods in the developed country. Resources are reallocated towards the cleaner goods in which the developed country has a comparative advantage and production of such goods expand there. On the other hand, higher prices of dirty goods in the developed country (due to its comparative disadvantage in such goods) encourage producers in the developing country to shift resources from sectors producing cleaner goods to sectors producing the dirty goods. The change in pollution level in the two trading nations can be decomposed into three effects: a composition effect, a scale effect, and a technique effect. Following Copeland and Taylor (2003), let Z be the total pollution emission by the dirty good and $e = Z/x$ be emissions per unit of output of the dirty good (X). The aggregate value of the output, $S = pX + Y$, measures the scale of output. On the other hand, the proportion of the output of the dirty good in the aggregate output level, $\beta = X/S$, captures the 'composition' effect. Thus, the total pollution emission by the dirty good production can be written as a combination of the emissions intensity of production, e, the share of the dirty good industry in the economy, β, and the scale of the economy, S:

$$Z = eX = e\beta S. \tag{10.29}$$

Thus, the decomposition of the change in pollution emission can be obtained as:

$$\hat{Z} = \hat{S} + \hat{\beta} + \hat{e} \tag{10.30}$$

where, hat over a variable denotes its proportional change, e.g., $\hat{Z} = (dZ/Z)$. The first term is the scale effect. It measures the increase in pollution that would be generated if the economy were simply scaled up, holding constant the composition of output and production techniques. The second term is the composition effect as captured by the change in the share of the dirty good in aggregate production. The third term is the technique effect.

International trade changes the composition of output towards cleaner goods in the developed country and towards the dirtier goods in the developing country. These composition effects raise the national pollution level in the dirty good-exporting developing country and reduce it in the dirty good-importing developed country. International trade also raises the scale of operation in the exporting country. Note that the change in scale of production equals,

$$dS = pdX + dY + Xdp$$

which by the condition of optimal production under perfect competition, marginal rate of transformation $= -(dY/dX) = p$, boils down to,

$$\hat{S} = \beta \hat{p}. \tag{10.31}$$

International trade raises the domestic price of dirty goods in the developing country ($\hat{p} > 0$) and lowers the same in the developed country, so that by the scale effect, pollution rises in the dirty good-exporting country. Finally, by the technique effect, emission intensity declines in the developing country. This is because as international trade raises the price of the dirty good, the price of the environmental input (in which the dirty good is intensive) rises by the price magnification effect.[6] This induces producers of the dirty good to use less environmental-input per unit of output, which essentially means that the pollution emission per unit declines. Overall, the composition and scale effects dominate so that the pollution emission rises in the dirty good-exporting

---

[6] By the price magnification effect, if the price of one good rises relative to the other good, then the rate of return to the factor used intensively in that good rises more than proportionately and relative to the rate of return to the other factor. Thus, when goods X and Y are produced by labour (L) and capital (K) and good X is relatively labour intensive, then $\hat{w} > \hat{P}_X > \hat{P}_Y > \hat{r}$. See Caves, Frankel, and Jones (1995) for proof.

developing country and declines in the dirty good-importing developed country.

When the comparative advantage of the developing country is perverse in the sense defined earlier, there is an additional welfare loss and pollution emission. Since weaker standards allow the dirty goods to be priced at private marginal cost, which is lower than the social marginal cost, dirty goods are 'over-produced'. International trade further augments such over-production and welfare loss. Moreover, the global pollution rises since dirty good production now shifts to the developed country with weak environmental regulations.

When the developed country has a comparative advantage in dirty goods and exports it to the developing country despite stricter environmental regulation there for reasons spelled out earlier, the pollution load shifts from the developing to the developed country since the dirty goods production is now relocated in the developed country. This *global* composition effect, according to Copeland and Taylor (2003), reduces global pollution because, due to higher standards, dirty industries are forced to adopt cleaner techniques and higher abatement costs than they would have in the developing country.

In addition to these static or short run effects, international trade also affects pollution levels by augmenting per capita income growth of a trading nation. The relationship between per capita income growth and pollution level of a country is, however, non-monotonic. Many cross-country studies have observed that the pollution level first increases with the per capita income of countries and declines afterwards [Grossman and Krueger (1993), Selden and Song (1994)]. This inverted-U relationship is known as the Environmental Kuznets Curve (EKC) hypothesis, which is similar to the relationship between income inequality and per capita income of countries as postulated by Kuznets (1955). The most common explanation of the EKC is that people attach less value to the environmental quality at lower levels of their incomes but increasingly higher value to it when they achieve a sufficiently high standard of living. Copeland and Taylor (2003), for example, argue that at low incomes, pollution rises with growth because increased consumption is valued highly relative to environmental quality. As income rises, the willingness to pay for environmental quality rises. So their argument rests on an income elastic demand for environmental quality: after a particular level of income, the willingness to pay for a clean environment rises by a greater proportion than income.

The other explanation for EKC runs in terms of the composition, scale, and technique effects induced by income growth. These effects are essentially different from the effects that are driven by changes in relative price as discussed earlier. Income growth means greater economic activity, which raises the demand for all inputs including the environment as free input, and hence increases emissions. This is the *scale effect*. The technique effect induced by income growth arises because people increase their demand for a clean environment as their incomes rise, and accordingly will tolerate higher levels of pollution only if the effluent charge is higher. Since higher effluent charges encourage firms to shift toward cleaner production processes, this *technique effect* tends to reduce emissions similar to the technique effect induced by a relative price change. Finally, if clean goods are *relatively* income elastic, income growth lowers the share of pollution-intensive goods in aggregate output. This *composition effect*, which is demand-driven, tends to decrease emissions unlike the composition effect induced by a relative price change. At low levels of per capita income, the scale effect outweighs the composition and technique effects, creating a positive relation between income growth and the environmental damage. At some higher level of income, however, the latter two effects outweigh the former. Hence, we have an inverted-U relationship.

10.2.3 ENVIRONMENTAL REGULATION AS A NON-TARIFF BARRIER

The discussion on the effects of international trade on the pollution level of a country is based on the assumption that pollution emissions and other environmental damages caused by the production of a good are local in nature and do not transmit from one country to the other. In cases of production pollution like in the earlier examples with emission of local pollutants (like NOx, SO_2), trade sanctions or restrictions by developed countries on imports of dirty goods from the developing countries raise domestic production of the dirty goods there. Consequently, the pollution shifts from the developing countries to the developed countries. Thus, imposition of trade restrictions does not appear as a means for protecting the local environment in the developed countries but surfaces as merely non-tariff barriers to protect the local producers, as is often alleged by the developing countries.

There are two specific cases, however, where environmental regulations on imports of dirty goods can be justified. First, economic activities may cause degradation of the global environment, affecting adversely all countries alike, and pollution may transmit from one country to the other. The most common example of global pollution is CO_2 emission by a production activity. On the other hand, a typical example of *trans-boundary* pollution is water pollution transmitted through rivers that flow through more than one country. As a river flows through several countries, water pollution originating in upstream countries transmits to the downstream countries causing health hazards and other environmental problems in the downstream countries. This is the case of *unidirectional* trans-boundary pollution.[7] In these cases of trans-boundary

---

[7] Trans-boundary pollution can also be regional reciprocal in nature, such as degradation of the European atmosphere and acid rain. For a detailed discussion see Acharyya (2013).

and global production pollution, international trade may not actually shift the pollution load from the dirty good importing developed country to the exporting developing country. Trade restrictions in the form of minimum environmental standards then protect the global environment as it forces exporters in the developing country to abate pollution by adopting cleaner technologies. Global pollution also declines because the pollution abatement costs erode some of the comparative advantages of the exporters in the developing country and shifts production of dirty goods to the developed country where stricter environmental regulations apply.

Second, consumption of commodities, rather than or in addition to production pollution, may cause environmental degradation. Again, there can be local pollutants like NO_x, carbon monoxide (CO), and particulate matter (PM), and global pollutants like CO_2. In cases of local pollution by consumption of a dirty good, international trade shifts the pollution load to (instead of from) the dirty good importing developed country. An example is import of tobacco products like cigarettes. In such a case, trade restrictions by developed countries appear justified. In cases of imports of automobiles, on the other hand, environmental norms like European emission standards—the acceptable limits for exhaust emissions—are applied for new vehicles sold in EU member states. Similar emission standards are applied for vehicles in other countries as well. These regulations make economic sense as they target the pollution level in the importing country. However, in many cases of global and trans-boundary pollution, national environmental regulations may not achieve the globally optimum pollution abatement. These are the instances where there are many polluters and many victims and they overlap. Coordinated environmental regulations then appear to be the optimum. Kyoto protocol regarding target reduction of CO_2 emissions by all countries is a most recent example.

However, in either case—trans-boundary pollution or consumption pollution—trade restriction is not an optimal intervention [Bhagwati and Srinivasan (1996)]. Environmental degradation through pollution emission is a typical case of negative externality, production or consumption as the case may be. From the pioneering works of Johnson and Bhagwati, the conventional wisdom that has emerged is that cases of such negative externality require domestic policy interventions rather than trade interventions. Free trade with domestic production (or consumption) taxes is the first best policy.[8] An optimal tax policy forces the producers (or consumers) to *fully* internalize the external costs that they inflict on the local inhabitants, and, in the

---

[8] Pigou (1912) was the first to point out that government should tax those who inflict external costs and subsidize those whose acts generate positive externalities for the society. This policy of tax or subsidy to correct environmental externalities hence is known as Pigouvian policy. The social optimum can also be arrived at through assigning property rights to relevant parties and bargaining amongst them. This purely market solution suggested by Coase (1960) works, however, under certain limiting assumptions regarding size of the contesting agents and complexities of the externality problem.

process, corrects for the over-production (or over-consumption) of the good that would occur at the unregulated equilibrium. Policy instruments other than production tax (or consumption tax) do not work to the extent required to correct the existing distortion. This is because any policy intervention itself creates a distortion in the system. The idea is to counter an existing distortion by introducing another distortion. Thus to be effective and optimal, policy created distortions should be at the exact sphere of economic activity where a distortion exists, and the magnitude of the policy intervention (or the 'rate' of tax) must be just enough to offset the existing distortion, neither more nor less.

10.2.4 CAPITAL FLIGHT AND POLLUTION HAVEN

Apart from influencing international trade or commodity movement across nations, differences in environmental standards seem to motivate capital flows as well. Two hypotheses are put forward to characterize this dimension: capital flight and pollution haven hypotheses. Over the last few decades there has been a noticeable decline in the share of dirty good production in the developed countries and a rise in the same in the developing countries. The basic premise of the capital flight hypothesis is that these compositional shifts have taken place because of the capital flight from the dirty industries in the developed countries to the dirty industries in the developing countries. Due to less political pressure on the local governments in the developing countries to raise the environmental standards (since at low per capita income people have a low preference for better environmental quality), capital finds better returns in dirty industries there than in the developed countries. Thus, the dirty industries seem to have migrated to the developing countries. The pollution havens hypothesis goes even further by arguing that developing countries deliberately keep their standards lower to attract capital inflow from the developed countries. There is often a race-to-the-bottom in the sense that developing countries engage in active competition among themselves in lowering their respective national environmental standards.

While these twin hypotheses seem to be appealing and intuitive, the empirical evidence does not provide much support for either of them. Mixed results are obtained by Xing and Kolstad (2002), Smarzynska and Wei (2004) and Dean, Lovely, and Wang (2004). A more conclusive picture arises for the Asian developing countries, however. It is true that since the mid-1980s, Asian developing countries have emerged as the largest recipient of FDI. It is also undeniable that, particularly since the 1990s, the East Asian countries have competed among themselves to attract FDI under the notion that it is a necessary precondition for faster growth. But such competition has been largely in terms of tariff reductions and signing free trade agreements with larger trade partners rather than in terms of lowering their national environmental standards. Moreover, among the Asian developing countries, the relatively high-income countries attract most of the FDI inflows. Since the demand for a cleaner environment and consequently the demand for stricter environmental regulations are expected to increase with the per capita income level of a country, this piece of evidence does not validate the capital flight hypothesis. Above all, a large part of the capital inflows in East Asian countries has been intra-region in character rather than from the advanced industrialized countries of North America and Western Europe.

10.3 **Labour Standards, Trade Sanctions, and Child Labour**

Labour standards vary from one country to another depending on the stage of development and political, social, and cultural conditions of the countries. But, like TRIPS and uniform environmental standards, the developed countries, particularly the United States, have time and again pressed for implementation of the core labour standards and the use of trade sanctions against the countries that are not complying with such standards. The core labour standards, as agreed upon in the Conventions of the International Labour Organization (ILO), include prohibition of forced labour, freedom of association, the right to organize and bargain collectively, elimination of child labour exploitation, and non-discrimination in employment.

The primary argument for trade measures by the United States and other industrialized countries against the countries with lower labour standards is again to achieve a level playing field. Like lax environmental standards, lower labour standards may also be a source of comparative advantage of a country in relatively labour-intensive goods. It is often contended that low wages in many developing countries are actually a reflection of suppressed wages due to unfair labour practices. In many cases, the use and exploitation of child labour also keeps wage costs low. Trade sanctions to enforce labour standards and a ban on the imports from the developing countries of the commodities containing child labour are thus projected as effective policy instruments to prohibit such unfair trade.

But, whether trade sanctions and boycotts of products using child labour can actually lower the incidence of child labour is a debatable issue. Trade sanctions do not address the problem of child labour appropriately. It is now a general consensus that abject poverty is the root cause of growing incidences of child labour in many developing and poor nations. Poor parents send their children to work because attending schools mean wages foregone, which poor families with large number of dependents can hardly afford. More often in poor nations, children are forced to provide their labour in agriculture in order to pay off the debts of their parents owed to landlord-cum-moneylenders. In Bangladesh, India, and Pakistan, for example, most of the children work under compulsion from their parents. In India alone, at least 15 million among the 70–80 million working children across all age groups work as bonded child labour in order to pay off debts of their parents. In all cases, the creditor-employer offers loans to the destitute parents to secure labour of a child that is even cheaper under bondage. Thus, the incidence of child labour is essentially a supply-side problem whereas trade sanctions and boycotts target the employers of child labour or the demand side of the problem. Consequently, these measures are less likely to be effective. This is also the reason why legislation prohibiting the use of child labour and fines on firms and employers have not worked well, even in containing the incidence of child labour in many developing countries.

Theoretical literature amply demonstrates this. For example, Basu (2004) and Basu and Zarghamee (2005) show that the declining adult and household incomes as a consequence of trade sanctions induce more children to be sent to work by their parents. On the other hand, in a dynamic model of long run wealth distribution, Ranjan (2001) demonstrates that a trade sanction does not necessarily lower the incidence of child labour. Much depends on the access of households to the credit market. The idea is that under *imperfect* credit markets, trade sanctions make the costs of borrowing to smooth out consumption patterns over the period of child education even higher for the parents. This provides further disincentives to send children to school instead of to work. Extending this result, Jafarey and Lahiri (2002) show that although trade sanction is more likely to raise the incidence of child labour in cases where access to credit market is not easy, this perverse result may arise even in the best case of access to world capital markets and the borrowing constraint is binding.

Maskus (1997), on the other hand, demonstrated that a tariff on imports may not lower the incidence of child labour in the exporting country. Grossman and Michaelis (2004), however, observed, in the context of a static general equilibrium framework with exports of a range of differentiated products produced by child labour, that only a firm-specific tariff with the rate varying with the amount of child labour-content can yield the desired result. But a uniform tariff imposed by the developed countries has *no* impact. Edmonds and Pavcnik (2005), on the other hand, find that higher prices of rice exports by Vietnam are associated with declines in child labour. This finding suggests that a trade sanction against rice exports by Vietnam, which would lower the world price, should in fact raise the incidence of child labour there.

Evidence is also growing that in many developing countries, trade sanctions on their exports have instead forced children to move into many non-traded activities in the informal segments of the economy. What is even more disturbing is the fact that such non-traded activities often are not desirable on ethical and moral grounds.

10.3.1 TRADE SANCTIONS, BOYCOTTS, AND PERVERSE EFFECTS ON THE INCIDENCE OF CHILD LABOUR

Basu and Zarghamee (2005) call the possibility that the boycott of products produced by child labour can actually cause the incidence of child labour to worsen as the *backlash proposition*. The intuition behind the backlash result is simple. First of all, product boycotting still being an informal arrangement or at best a social or moral action, not all buyers refrain from buying such products. But there is a guilty feeling from such an act which gets reflected in a lower willingness-to-pay for such products. Under such circumstances, firms will realize that the use of child labour will lower their profits since such products will sell for a lower price. Thus, threat of a boycott and consequently willingness to pay a lower price on the part of the consumers will make child labour a less preferred input than it would have been otherwise. This will lower the child wage. If children were sent to work by their parents because of the state of extreme poverty in which they and their families live, then the lower wage will mean that children will have to work harder and for longer hours. Hence the incidence of child labour worsens.[9]

10.3.2 PRODUCT LABELLING AND CHILD-LABOUR CONTENT TARIFF

Acharyya (2008a) makes a similar argument in the case of product labelling which informs buyers regarding child labour content and causes them to offer lower prices for products with higher child-labour content. Increasingly, a number of products produced and exported by developing countries are now labelled as 'child labour free' in order to distinguish these products from those produced by child labour and to influence the buyers' choice. For example, the certificates for fair labour standards and child-labour free produce is provided by STEP (Sustainable Technology Environments Program™) in Switzerland for manufacturing goods imported from India, Nepal, and Pakistan; by Rugmark and Kaleen for exports of carpets by India to Germany and the USA. These product labels enable the buyers to get product-specific information instead of relying solely upon their country-of-origin perception when they buy such goods.[10] But if labels are also used to provide information regarding the intensity of child labour employment and the willingness-to-pay varies with

---

[9] This result is similar to that of Davies (2005) who has demonstrated that under Bertrand competition among firms producing goods with and without child labour, social labelling is unlikely to drive out child-labour products even when consumers prefer child-labour free products.

[10] Basu, Chau, and Grote (2006), however, raise the issue of false labelling and the associated moral hazard problem.

the child labour content per unit of output, it may do more harm than helping the cause. In the context of a small open economy exporting child-labour produced goods, Acharyya (2008a) demonstrates that if a worldwide trade sanction lowers the world demand and consequently the world price of the export good by a greater margin when it is relatively more intensive in child labour than when it is relatively less intensive in child labour, the parents send their children to work for longer hours. Consequently, the incidence of child labour rises in the exporting country. Thus, the perverse effect of a trade sanction may arise even without any inter-linkage of credit market (imperfect or perfect) and labour market (as in Ranjan (2001)), or the backward bending supply curve for child labour (as in Basu and Van (1998)). To fix the idea, consider a small open economy producing an export good, which uses child labour along with adult labour,[11] and an import-competing good, which uses adult labour and domestic capital. There are K number of capitalists each endowed with one unit of physical capital stock (K) and n number of adult workers (L). Each adult worker or a parent has only one child. The children are assumed to work part-time. A child and an adult (or parent) are each endowed with one unit of time. Whereas each parent as an adult worker works full-time for a wage W (measured in terms of good Y) per unit of time, i.e., inelastically supplies its labour as in Basu and Van (1998), a child's time is allocated over schooling (Z) and work ($1 - Z$). Thus, each child in this economy works for ($1 - Z$) unit of time $T = 1$ and earns a wage W_C (once again measured in terms of good Y) per unit of time, where $Z \in [0, 1]$. At an interior equilibrium, each child works part-time. An adult worker and a child worker are imperfect substitutes in production and their wages are determined separately by competitive forces. The decision for the children to work is taken by their parents, who do so by optimal allocation of the available time unit over schooling and work for their children. All parents are identical, and so the optimal allocation will also be the same. For any such choice of work time for a child, the aggregate child labour (time) is endogenously determined:

$$C = (1 - Z)n. \tag{10.32}$$

Each representative parent derives utility from his child's schooling and household consumption of the two goods:

$$U = C_X^\alpha C_Y^{1-\alpha} Z^\rho, \quad 0 < \alpha < 1, \; \rho > 0 \tag{10.33}$$

---

[11] Family farming in many developing countries, carpet production in India, production of soccer balls in Pakistan, and gem mining and wood furniture production in Indonesia are some examples of child labour working together with adult workers.

where C_X and C_Y are consumption of export good X and import good Y respectively by the child's family. Thus, parents are altruist in the sense that they derive utility not only from the household consumption levels, but also from a child's school time (Z). With full appropriation of a child's income by his parent, each parent has the following budget constraint:

$$P_X^* C_X + C_Y = W + (1 - Z) W_C \qquad (10.34)$$

where, P_X^* is the (relative) world price of the export good X, W is the adult wage rate and W_C is the child wage rate. The optimal time allocation of a child, along with the levels of the household consumption of the two goods, is arrived at by maximizing the household utility (10.27), defined over all non-negative consumption levels and for all $Z \in [0, 1]$, subject to the budget constraint (10.28). It is easy to check that a parent's optimal choice of school time is given as,

$$Z = \frac{\rho}{1+\rho} \left[\frac{1}{\mu_X} + 1 \right]. \qquad (10.35)$$

Thus, the *optimal* schooling time varies inversely with the relative wage $\mu_X \equiv (W_C / W)$ as shown by the downward sloping, convex to the origin curve labelled $Z(\mu_X)$ in Figure 10.3. For any given relative wage, the supply of child labour time $(1 - Z)$ is correspondingly determined. The curvature property of the $Z(\mu_X)$ locus, which is due to the specific form of the utility function defined in (10.33), implies two things. First, at any *equilibrium*, (all) children will always be sent to school for some positive time fraction. That is, *full-time work can never be an equilibrium outcome for a child in this model*. Second, when the relative adult wage $1/\mu_X$ is sufficiently high (i.e., $\mu_X \leq \rho$), children are not sent to work. This is similar to that shown by Basu and Van (1998) and Basu (2004) under the subsistence-income motive of parents in sending their children to work.

Let us now turn to the production side and the demand for child labour. For any given allocation of a child's unit time over schooling and work, the factor and product market equilibrium conditions determine the market clearing wages along with the (real) rate of return to capital. Clearly, any change in the schooling time (Z), and consequently the supply of child labour (time) as defined in (10.32), should change the market-clearing relative wage, μ_X, for any given world relative price of the traded goods. Thus,

$$\mu_X = \mu_X (Z). \qquad (10.36)$$

The nature of such a relationship between the market-clearing relative wage and the schooling time can be traced out as follows. Suppose a child is more

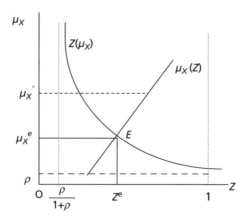

Figure 10.3 Equilibrium School Time

productive when he spends more time in school. Thus, for any given set of wages, per unit production of the export good requires less child labour. Consider now a *ceteris paribus* increase in Z. By (10.32) this means a decline in the aggregate supply of child labour. At initial wages, and hence at the initial choice of technique and scale of operations in the two sectors, this should result in an excess demand for child labour, thereby pushing up the child wage, W_C. On the other hand, by the productivity effect of an increase in schooling time, the demand for child labour (time) declines because now the child workers can complete their jobs in a lesser time. This lowers the child wage. Thus, if the productivity effect is sufficiently weak, the child wage should increase as a consequence of children going to school for longer hours.

The change in the adult wage is also ambiguous. However, again a weaker productivity effect ensures that the adult wage declines. An increase in schooling time lowers the production of good X if its adverse effect on the endowment of child labour is larger than its productivity effect. This releases adult workers from the export sectors and is absorbed in the import-competing sector through a decline in the adult wage. Thus, given that the productivity effect is weaker than the endowment effect, the relative child wage rises with an increase in school time for each (and all) child.[12] This is shown by the positively sloped $\mu_x(Z)$ locus in Figure 10.3.

Suppose the same export good is also produced and exported using child labour by other *similar* small open economies. The export good is labelled to

---

[12] The endowment effect being stronger than the productivity effect ($\gamma > \varepsilon$) is only a sufficient condition for the relative wage, μ_X, to rise, which also ensures that the equilibrium allocation of a child's time in Figure 10.3 is unique and stable.

reveal the information regarding the intensity in which child workers have been used in the production processes. The foreign buyers have thus perfect information while buying the good imported from this small economy as well as other economies. Now consider a worldwide trade sanction against the child labour *content* of the good imported by developed nations regardless of the country-of-origin. All the informed foreign buyers pay increasingly less for products that use more child labour intensive production techniques.[13] Given the assumption of a fixed-coefficient production function for good X, for any given schooling time (Z), and a decline in the child labour intensity of the good with the increase in the time spent by a child in school, the world price of exports under such a worldwide trade sanction against child labour content can be specified as:

$$P_{XS}^* = PZ^\delta, \delta \geq 0. \tag{10.37}$$

Note that as long as $\delta > 0, P_{XS}^* < P_X^* \; \forall \, 0 < Z < 1$. Thus a trade sanction lowers the world price of exports regardless of the child labour content, although the rate of decline in the price, $\delta P Z^{\delta-1}$, increases with the child labour content. The world price schedule is shown in Figure 10.4. A trade sanction against child labour content means the foreign buyers pay for their imports according to the OP' schedule. Thus, if initially $Z = Z_0$, after the trade sanction, the world price of good X falls from aZ_0 to bZ_0, with such declines being higher for smaller values of Z.

Such a trade sanction, however, unfavourably alters the parental choice of the allocation of a child's time over schooling and work. More work for a child now means a fall in the world price of the good, since by the consequent (adverse) productivity effect more child labour time per unit of output is needed, making the product relatively more child labour intensive. But this means that as a consumer, a parent pays less for the good and thus has a utility gain. Thus, a worldwide trade sanction against child labour content paradoxically raises the marginal benefit for a parent from sending his child to work for a higher fraction of the time unit, and this raises the supply of child labour. The demand for child labour, on the other hand, declines as expected, but the magnitude of such a decline varies inversely with the pre-sanction school time. If initially the parents send their children to school for a sufficiently high time fraction, the favourable demand effect is small and is outweighed by the perverse supply effect. A trade sanction against child labour content, in such a case, raises the incidence of child labour at the new equilibrium.

---

[13] This demand behaviour can be interpreted as a generalization of the guilt factor that Basu and Zarghamee (2005) talked about.

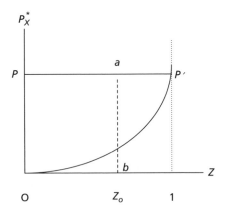

Figure 10.4 The World Price Schedule

Two comments are warranted at this point. First, this result is in contrast to Basu, Chau, and Grote (2006) who demonstrate in a North-South trade framework with price premium for the products with social labels over those without labels that a trade sanction against unlabelled products has no effect on the child labour employment. The difference arises due to the perverse response of parents to the trade sanction against the magnitude of the child labour content in our case.

Second, the perverse effect may hold even when parents have pecuniary, instead of altruistic, motives to send their children to work; we get a similar perverse effect of a trade sanction imposed by our informed buyers. In fact, the perverse effect demonstrated by Basu and Zarghamee (2005) under such a motive extends more strongly to the case of trade sanction against child labour content by the informed buyers.

Let I denote the income level (measured in terms of the import good Y) of a household that is required for bare subsistence. Following Basu and Van (1998) and Basu and Zarghamee (2005), suppose if the adult wage W is at least equal to this subsistence-income, a child is not sent to work at all. But for all $W < I$, the child is sent to work for hours just sufficient to cover the income shortfall. This means that the child's work time, $(1 - Z)$, now varies inversely with the child wage, W_C. Formally, the child labour supply function can be specified as follows:

$$(1-Z) = \begin{cases} 0 & \forall \ W \geq I \\ \min\left(1, \dfrac{I-W}{W_C}\right) & \forall \ W < I \end{cases}. \tag{10.38}$$

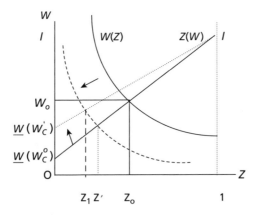

Figure 10.5 Subsistence-Income and Child Labour

Let $\underline{W}$ denote the adult wage for which the income shortfall, for any given W_C, can be covered only if the child works full time, i.e., $Z = 0$. From (10.38) it is immediate that this critical adult wage should equal,

$$\underline{W} = I - W_C. \tag{10.39}$$

Given these specifications, the supply of child labour time is shown in Figure 10.5 by the upward sloping curve labelled $Z(W)$ in (Z, W)-space with slope equal to $1/W_C$. This curve rotates upward along the wage-axis if the child wage falls, because by (10.38), for any given $W < I$, the work time for a child, $(1 - Z)$, increases as W_C falls. The downward sloping curve labelled $W(Z)$, on the other hand, is the locus of different combinations of the adult wage and the supply of child labour time for which the domestic markets clear. The negative slope of this curve follows from the assumption that the endowment effect of an increase in schooling time (or decrease in work time), γ, is larger than its productivity effect, ε. Let the pre-trade sanction equilibrium allocation be Z_o corresponding to the intersection point of the bold $Z(W)$ and $W(Z)$ curves.

For any given Z, a trade sanction in the sense defined earlier lowers both the adult and child wage by the price-magnification effect. Parents, therefore, make their children work harder to compensate for the loss of household income. In Figure 10.5, the $W(Z)$ curve shifts down whereas the $Z(W)$ curve rotates upward. This lowers the equilibrium school time Z. This increase in child labour time in turn affects the wages. On the assumption that the supply (or endowment) effect is stronger than the productivity effect, both the adult and the child wages should fall as argued earlier. That is, the initial declines in wages get magnified, reinforcing the increase in child labour time under these assumptions.

To sum up, a trade sanction against child labour content of a good exported by a developing country may induce the parents, regardless of whether they are altruist or not, to send their children to work for a larger fraction of time. This perverse effect of trade sanctions by the informed buyers works through a fall in the marginal benefit for a parent of an additional time spent in school by a child, relative to that of an additional fraction of work time. Thus, if the product labels, which have already been used in the developed countries to distinguish products produced by child labour, contain more information regarding the extent to which child labour has been used in a product to further influence the buyers' choice, it may not help the cause.

■ REFERENCES

Acharyya, R. (1998). 'Monopoly and Product Quality: Separating or Pooling Menu?'. *Economics Letters* 61: 187–194.

Acharyya, R. (2008). 'Trade Sanction Against Child Labour Content: Does it Work?' In: S. Marjit and E. Yu, (eds). *Contemporary and Emerging Issues in Trade Theory and Policy (Frontiers of Economics and Globalization, Volume 4)*. UK: Emerald.

Acharyya, R. (2008a) 'Trade sanction against child labour content: Does it work?' In: S. Marjit, and E. Yu (eds) *Contemporary and Emerging Issues in Trade Theory and Policy (Frontiers of Economics and Globalization, Volume 4)*: UK: Emerald.

Acharyya, R. (2013), 'Market Coverage, Price and National Welfare Under International Exhaustion of Patents'. *Trade and Development Review* 6 (1-2): 29–63.

Acharyya, R. (2013a). *Trade and Environment*. Oxford India Short Introduction Series (General Editor: Anindya Sen). India: Oxford University Press.

Acharyya, R. and Garcia-Alonso, M. D. C. (2008). 'Parallel Imports, Innovations and National Welfare: Role of the Sizes of the Income Classes and National Markets for Health Care'. Co-authored with *The Singapore Economic Review*, Special Issue on Health Economics, 53 (1): 1–23.

Acharyya, R. and Garcia-Alonso, M. D. C. (2012). 'Parallel Imports, Drug Innovation and International Patent Protection: A Policy Game'. *Journal of International Trade and Economic Development* 21 (6): 865–894.

Basu, A., Chau, N. H., and Grote, U. (2006). 'Guaranteed Manufactured Without Child Labour: The Economics of Consumer Boycotts, Social Labelling and Trade Sanctions'. *Review of Development Economics* 10 (3): 466–491.

Basu, K. (2004). 'Child Labour and the Law: Notes on Possible Pathologies'. Discussion Paper 2052. Harvard Institute of Economic Research, Harvard University, Cambridge, MA.

Basu, K. and Van, P. H. (1998). 'The Economics of Child Labour'. *American Economic Review* 88: 412–427.

Basu, K. and Zarghamee, H. (2005). 'Is Product Boycott a Good Idea for Controlling Child Labour?'. Mimeo, Cornell University.

Bhagwati, J. N. and Srinivasan, T. N. (1996). 'Trade and the Environment: Does Environmental Diversity Detract from the Case for Free Trade?'. In: J. Bhagwati and R.E. Hudec (eds). *Fair Trade and Harmonization: Economic Analysis*, Volume 1, pp. 159–224. Cambridge, MA: MIT Press.

Caves, R.E., Frankel, J., and Jones, R. W. (1995). *World Trade and Payments*. 5th edition. NY: HarperCollins College Publishers.

Coase, R., 1960. 'The Problem of Social Cost'. *Journal of Law and Economics* 3: 1–44.

Copeland, B.R. and Taylor, M. S. (1994). 'North-South Trade and the Environment'. *Quarterly Journal of Economics* 109: 755–787.

Copeland, B.R. and Taylor, M. S. (2003). 'Trade, Growth and the Environment'. NBER Working Paper No. 9823, National Bureau of Economic Research, Cambridge, MA.

Davies, R.B. (2005). 'Abstinence from Child Labour and Profit Seeking'. *Journal of Development Economics* 76: 251–263.

Dean, J., Lovely, E. M., and Wang, H. (2004). 'Foreign Direct Investment and Pollution Havens: Evaluating the Evidence from China'. US International Trade Commission Working Paper # 2004-01-B.

Edmonds, E. V. and Pavcnik, N. (2005). 'The Effect of Trade Liberalization on Child Labour'. *Journal of International Economics* 65: 401–419.

Grossman, G. and Krueger, A. (1993). 'Environmental Impacts of a North American Free Trade Agreement'. In: P. Garber, (ed). *The US-Mexico Free Trade Agreement*. Cambridge: MIT Press.

Grossman, H. and Michaelis, J. (2004). 'Trade Sanctions and the Incidence of Child Labour'. University of Kassel, Discussion Paper No. 54/04.

Helpman, E. (1993). 'Innovation, Imitation, and Intellectual Property Rights'. *Econometrica* 61 (6): 1247–1280.

Jafarey, S. and Lahiri, S. (2002). 'Will Trade Sanctions Reduce Child Labour? The Role of Credit Markets'. *Journal of Development Economics* 68: 137–156.

Jelovac, I. and Bordoy, C. (2005). 'Pricing and Welfare Implications of Parallel Imports in the Pharmaceutical Industry'. International *Journal of Health Care Finance and Economics* 5: 5–21.

Kuznets, S. (1955). 'Economic Growth and Income Inequality'. *American Economic Review* 45: 1–28.

Lall, S. (2003), 'Indicators of Relative Importance of IPRs in Developing Countries'. *Research Policy* 32: 1657–1680.

Malueg, D. A. and Schwartz, M. (1994). 'Parallel Imports, Demand Dispersion and International Price Discrimination'. *Journal of International Economics* 37: 167–196.

Maskus, K. (1997). 'Core Labour Standards: Trade Impacts and Implications of International Trade Policy'. Mimeo, World Bank International Trade Division.

Maskus, K. (2000). 'Parallel Imports'. The World Economy: Global Trade Policy 2000, 23: 1269–1284.

Maskus, K. (2001). 'Parallel Imports in Pharmaceuticals: Implications for Competition and Prices in Developing Countries'. Final Report to World Intellectual Property Organization.

Pigou, A. C. (1912). *Wealth and Welfare*. London: Macmillan.

Primo Braga, C. (1990), 'The Developing Country Case for and Against Intellectual Property Protection'. In: W. E. Siebeck (ed). *Strengthening Protection of Intellectual Property in Developing Countries: A Survey of the Literature*. Washington, DC: World Bank.

Ranjan, P. (2001). 'Credit Constraint and the Phenomenon of Child Labour'. *Journal of Development Economics* 64: 81–102.

Richardson, M. (2002). 'An Elementary Proposition Concerning Parallel Imports'. *Journal of International Economics* 56: 233–245.

Selden, T.M. and Song, D. (1994). 'Environmental Quality and Development: Is There a Kuznets Curve for Air Pollution Emissions?'. *Journal of Environmental Economics and Management* 27: 147–162.

Smarzynska, B. and Shang-Jin, W. (2004). 'Pollution Havens and Foreign Direct Investment: Dirty Secret or Popular Myth?'. *Contributions to Economic Analysis & Policy* 3 (2): 1–34.

Valletti, T. M. (2006). 'Differential Pricing, Parallel Imports and the Incentive to Invest'. *Journal of International Economics* 70: 314–324.

Wauthy, X. (1996). 'Quality Choice in Models of Vertical Differentiation'. *Journal of Industrial Economics* 65: 345–353.

Xing, Y. and Kolstad, C. (2002). 'Do Lax Environmental Regulations Attract Foreign Investment?'. *Environmental and Resource Economics* 21 (1): 1–22.

11 International Outsourcing, Offshoring, and Industrialization Strategies

Fragmentation of production technology and (international) outsourcing of low skill-intensive stages of production to the low-wage, low-skill abundant developing countries by the multinational companies of the developed countries now represents the most important dimension of contemporary globalization [Arndt and Kierzkowski (2001)]. The technological advancement has made it possible to fragment production processes in different stages and spatially separate those production stages. This enables an MNC to locate fragmented and spatially separable production stages in different countries according to their respective patterns of comparative advantage and vertical specialization. Of course, fragmentation and spatial separation of production processes depend on the technological properties of the product and production process itself. On the whole, with the advent of information technology, most of the services can be fragmented. Fragmentation is also quite common in the manufacturing industry but almost impossible in agriculture.

Such organization and location of different stages of production are done either through foreign direct investment (which is often termed as vertical FDI), outsourcing, offshoring, or through international sub-contracting. These business and production strategies adopted by the multinational companies of the developed countries distinguish the present era from the earlier efforts of globalization and development. The developing countries, on the other hand, have often encouraged these vertical FDI and outsourcing of production processes by the multinational companies by establishing export processing zones (EPZs) or special economic zones (SEZs). While this development strategy of attracting foreign capital and encouraging processing activities has certainly conferred some benefits and helped the development process of the low-wage, low-skill abundant developing countries, it also has some associated costs.

The increasing degree of fragmentation of production technologies and the growth of international production networks have changed the nature and dimension of the pattern of trade between developed and developing countries. Vertical production specialization by countries and consequent vertical intra-industry international trade of components and unfinished or semi-finished products now constitute an increasingly larger share of trade.

This chapter discusses these dimensions of trade and development strategy in the present era of globalization.

11.1 **Concepts, Measurement, and Magnitude of Outsourcing and Offshoring**

Though outsourcing and offshoring may simultaneously take place, the two differ in terms of location and worker selection. When offshoring occurs, a business moves all or some of its activities to another country, with the target of re-import of those goods and services produced in that country at a lower cost into the home country, or to export to other markets from this new plant abroad. Thus, offshoring is a process of closing a manufacturing plant by an MNC in its home country to replace it by a new plant located in a host country.

Outsourcing, on the other hand, is the process of utilizing third party workers for traditionally in-house business tasks; this may take place either inside or outside the company's home country. Thus, as Krugman (2011) comments, offshoring is 'moving jobs abroad', and outsourcing means 'having an external contractor (*not necessarily foreign*) perform services that could have been performed in-house'. By definition, outsourcing pertains to supplying raw materials, tools, spare parts, components, equipment, and semi-finished products. Some value must be added to these outsourced supplies, through further development or assembly in a plant to convert them into a final product or service. When the external contractor is in a different country location, it is sometimes called international (or offshore) outsourcing. As Andreff (2009) observes, offshore outsourcing is a relatively more recent phenomenon emerging with the spread and dominant role of MNCs. Of course, such outsourcing of production processes may well be to a subsidiary of the MNC itself in a foreign country location.[1] In this regard, Bhagwati, Panagariya, and Srinivasan (2004) offer an incisive analysis of the scope and outreach of this topic.

Sometimes an MNC opts for international subcontracting, which is essentially outsourcing of the entire production process instead of the vertical production specialization and the assembly line. For example, Jones and Kierzkowski (2001) observe that Nike is the most fragmented firm, which

---

[1] If we consider property rights, when a supply source abroad is simply owned by as a firm's (MNC's) subsidiary, it is sometime labelled as international *in*sourcing.

subcontracts all the manufacturing and engages itself only in design and marketing.

Measuring the magnitudes of offshoring and outsourcing is not easy. It involves data on a host of factors including data on firm-level production, employment, exports, imports, and foreign direct investment. Two main problems may emerge when one looks at the firm-level employment change for a measure of offshoring or outsourcing. First, new jobs for foreign workers without any commensurate decline in domestic economic activity and employment thereof cannot be considered as a measure of offshoring. Second, jobs lost in a firm or in a sector due to domestic outsourcing are necessarily jobs created in another firm or sector of the economy. Thus, this type of job loss cannot be considered as a measure of outsourcing either. Intra and inter firm trade may not also be a good indicator or measure of offshoring activity for several reasons. The most important is that an increase in such imports may not necessarily mean offshoring by a firm. For example, as Agnese and Ricart (2009) point out, if an exporting firm in a country shifts part of its production in a foreign country and exports to its earlier export markets from the new plant in that foreign country, then, instead of its import falling, its exports will fall in consequence of such international relocation or offshoring of export production.[2]

There are quite a few indirect measures or indices of offshoring that intend to take up these problems. These measures or indices of offshoring (and international outsourcing) consider either the share of imported inputs in total non-energy input consumption, or the index of vertical specialization or the share of imported input in gross output [Agnese and Ricart (2009)]. The import-share measure of offshoring was proposed by Feenstra and Hanson (1996) in their pioneering work in this regard. The idea here is that use of imported input displaces domestic input production and corresponding employment and thus is taken as an estimate for offshoring or international outsourcing. Their measure can be algebraically expressed as:

$$O_i = \sum_{j=1}^{n} \left(\frac{I_{ij}}{I_i} \right) \left(\frac{M_j}{D_j} \right) \tag{11.1}$$

where, I_{ij} is the purchase of non-energy input by industry i from industry j, I_i is the total non-energy inputs used by industry i, M_j is the total imports of intermediate goods by industry j and D_j is the domestic demand of intermediate goods by industry j. What Feenstra and Hanson (1996) argue is that the composition of trade and share of intermediate goods matter for measuring

---

[2] More on this debate is available in Blinder (2009).

the effect of wages and employment in the country from where production activities are outsourced (as well as in the host foreign country) and thus should be a better proxy for offshoring activities. We will return to their theoretical argument of how offshoring or international outsourcing may affect wages and factor prices later in this chapter.

The narrow measure of international outsourcing is calculated as imported materials from the same industry. There are, on the other hand, two alternative measures of vertical specialization by countries used to reflect the magnitude of international outsourcing. The first was put forward by Campa and Goldberg (1997), which tries to capture the extent to which semi-finished products of different production stages are traded between countries. Algebraically, their measure is given as,

$$VS_i^{CG} = \sum_{j=1}^{n} \frac{m_j p_{ij} q_{ij}}{Y_i} \qquad (11.2)$$

where, m_j is the share of imports in use of an intermediate good in industry j, $p_{ij}q_{ij}$ is the value of intermediate goods used in production of industry i and Y_i is the value of production of industry i.

The other measure of vertical specialization was put forward by Hummels et al. (2001) in which they account for the imported input content of exports of a country:

$$VS_i^H = \sum_{j=1}^{n} \frac{m_{ij}}{Y_i} X_i \qquad (11.3)$$

where, m_{ij} is the imports of input j used by industry i, X_i is the total exports of industry i and Y_i is the value of production of industry i. There will be no vertical specialization (and hence offshoring or international outsourcing) if industry i does not use any imported input or does not export its output.

Between 1995 and 2000, activities outsourced to the low wage countries by the European Union countries grew by an average rate of 9% per annum. The major host countries of most of international outsourcing are the Asian countries: the Newly Industrialized Countries (China, Hong Kong, South Korea, Malaysia, Singapore, Taiwan, Thailand), and the East and South-East Asian countries (Indonesia, India, and the Philippines).

In China, for example, outsourcing constitutes approximately 20% of Chinese industrial value added and more than 60% value added by foreign companies operating in China. More than 50% of Chinese manufacturing exports in 2005 were actually the assembling of imported manufacturing components and semi-finished products. A large proportion of such exports were actually done by subsidiaries of foreign MNCs located in China.

On the other hand, advances in telecommunications over the last three decades have enabled many services not only to be disembodied and traded but also to be fragmented and performed anywhere in the world through international outsourcing. According to Bardhan and Kroll (2003), services or occupations that can be outsourced are the ones that have no face-to-face customer servicing requirement, high information content, a telecommunicable work process, low setup barriers, and a low social networking requirement. Three types of services are usually outsourced in the world. First are IT services including software design, code writing, and network or software maintenance. Second are engineering services like R&D and structural design and testing, primarily in sectors like automotive, naval, aerospace, telecommunication, utilities, and construction. Third are business processes, which include basic data entry, document completion, call centres, telemarketing, customer relations management, back-office accounting, procurement, and billing services.

However, despite increasing incidences of offshoring or international outsourcing of services, it still accounts for only a small share of the global outsourcing market. India is the top services outsourcing destination followed by China, Ireland, Singapore, Malaysia, Mexico, the Czech Republic, Poland, the Philippines, and Canada. The time zone advantage that India enjoys vis-à-vis the United States, together with a large pool of skilled manpower at a relatively lower cost makes it a major outsourced country for the United States. However, more than 50% of offshore business in India is carried out by the Indian subsidiaries of the US and Europe based MNCs. The business process outsourcing (BPO) segment, including the call centres, on the other hand, generated 1% of India's GDP in 2005.

11.2 Costs and Benefits of Offshoring and International Outsourcing

Offshoring and international outsourcing both incurs costs and generate benefits for the country from where stages of production are shifted. The gains primarily consist of gains from vertical production specialization according to the comparative advantages of outsourcing and the outsourced countries. This makes average production costs of different stages decline. Though there are additional costs that are incurred by the outsourcing MNCs due to what Jones and Kierzkowski (2001) call service links—costs of communication and coordination—between different production blocs located in different countries, overall economies of scale can be achieved when large quantities of the final

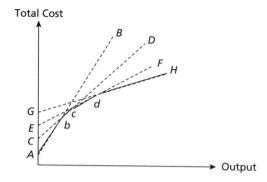

Figure 11.1 International Outsourcing and Economies of Scale

product are produced. Moreover, improvement in telecommunication and information technology has considerably reduced the cost of these service links. This has caused fragmentation of production processes and international outsourcing of less skill-intensive production activities to even the furthest low-wage country locations more cost-effective than ever before. Their argument is illustrated in Figure 11.1.

Lines *AB*, *CD*, *EF*, and *GH* in Figure 11.1 represent total costs incurred by an outsourcing MNC for different degrees of fragmentation and international outsourcing of production activities. Even when the marginal cost for the *entire* production activity is constant (as reflected in the constant slopes of these lines), a higher degree of fragmentation should bring down the (constant) marginal cost because of better allocation of production activities across different locations on the basis of the comparative cost advantage of these locations. Thus, the line *GH* representing the highest degree of fragmentation will be the flattest of all. But fragmentation requires service links in the form of communication and coordination among different production blocks. These costs may be invariant with respect to the scale of operation, but are expected to increase with the degree of fragmentation of the production technology. Thus, the most fragmented production technology indicated by the line *GH* has the largest fixed cost reflected by its vertical intercept. As the scale of production increases, more fragmented production technologies become cost minimizing. Of course, the total cost increases with the larger scale of operation and output, but at a decreasing rate along the lower envelope of these total cost curves, *AbcdH*. Thus, increasing returns arise for the MNCs through the increasing order of fragmentation and international outsourcing of production technologies. This is the major reason why MNCs are increasingly outsourcing low-skill production activities to low-wage countries that have comparative advantages in these stages of production.

But international outsourcing and offshoring shifts employment of skilled labour to the outsourced countries, which is a major cost for the outsourcing or offshoring country if the workers, mostly unskilled and semi-skilled, cannot be absorbed in other sectors of the economy. For the host country, outsourcing is a boon for its unemployed unskilled and semi-skilled labour force as it generates direct as well as indirect employment opportunities. However, it is difficult to quantify jobs lost *in aggregate* in one country and gained in the other. Moreover, these may not be one-to-one either, since labour intensities may differ across outsourcing and outsourced countries for the production processes offshored or outsourced due to the cross-country wage differential. There have been some estimates, though, of direct job losses and jobs at risk in occupations or sectors that have been and may have been offshored. In 2004, for example, Goldman Sachs estimated that actual job losses could be between 300,000 and 500,000 jobs in the United States, whereas the projected job losses over the next ten years would be six million. On the other hand, a study by the University of California, Berkeley, estimated that 14.1 million jobs are at risk. The loss of US jobs to off-shoring has led researchers to study jobs or occupations at risk of being offshored in the future. Bardhan and Kroll (2003) estimated that more than 14 million jobs, which is about 11% of aggregate employment in the United States in 2001, have attributes that could allow them to be sent overseas. According to estimates of Jensen and Kletzer (2005), 13.7% of employment in professional services and 11.4% of employment in the manufacturing industries might be vulnerable to offshoring. However, fears of job losses are increasing not only in the United States but also in many high-wage European countries as technological advances in the coming years is expected to make more occupations offshored.

Contrary to the contrasting employment changes in the outsourcing and outsourced countries, outsourcing may lead to a symmetric rise in wage inequality in both these countries.[3] This possibility was demonstrated by Feenstra and Hanson (1996) in a Ricardian model with continuum of stages of production in a manufacturing industry. The intermediate goods produced at successively higher stages of production are assumed to use skilled labour with higher intensities compared to unskilled labour. Physical capital is assumed to have the same degree of substitution with either type of labour at all stages of production. This production structure resembles the extension of Ricardian continuum goods model of Dornbusch, Fisher, and Samuelson (1977) by Sanyal (1983). Feenstra and Hanson (1996, 1996a) constructed a trade equilibrium without factor price equalization such that all lower stages of production up to

---

[3] The symmetric rise in wage inequality in almost every part of the globe and in the developed and developing countries alike had been observed since the 1980s. The explanation by Feenstra and Hanson (1996a) has been one among the few plausible theoretical explanations of this phenomenon that have been put forward by trade theorists. See Marjit and Acharyya (2003) for an early documentation of rising wage inequality observed by many researchers and plausible alternative theoretical explanations offered by trade theorist and other researchers.

a critical stage, say stage S, were cost efficient in the developing country whereas all production stages higher than stage-S, including the final production stage, were cost efficient in the developed country. Thus, post-trade, the developing country exports the range of relatively low skill-intensive intermediate goods produced in those lower stages of production. The developed country, on the other hand, produces the rest of the intermediate goods which are relatively skill-intensive and produced at the higher stages of production. It also produces the final good, which is exported to the developing country. By the property of the continuum of stages, both the countries produce the intermediate good at stage-S, which is the most skilled-labour intensive intermediate good that the developing country produces but the least skilled-labour intensive intermediate good that the developed country produces. That is, the *local factor intensity* of this commonly produced good differs in the two countries.

Now suppose that the developed country outsources or offshores the production of intermediate good S and a few more finished intermediate goods corresponding to production stages in the interval $[S, S']$. These intermediate goods being more skill intensive compared to the intermediate goods that the developing country were earlier producing, outsourcing of production raises the relative demand for skilled labour there. The wage inequality thus rises in the developing or the outsourced country. In the developed country, on the other hand, the relative demand for unskilled workers declines because the production of the intermediate goods that are now outsourced in the developing country were the least skill-intensive or most unskilled-labour intensive in the developed country. Hence, wage inequality rises in the developed or the outsourcing country as well.

This is in contrast to standard trade impact on the demand for skilled-labour. In a Heckscher-Ohlin-Samuelson kind of model, import competition from low-wage countries changes the composition of domestic production in a high-wage country towards more skill-intensive goods and consequently raises the demand for skilled labour by shifting resources *across* industries. In contrast, if import competition from low-wage countries induces firms in the high-wage countries to outsource non-skill-intensive production stages abroad, then trade raises the demand for skilled workers *within* industries. In the context of the United States, Feenstra and Hanson (1996b) find evidence of this within-industry effect during 1979–1994. Outsourcing of production stages to Mexico by the US firms had indeed caused the relative demand for skilled labour in the United States to rise, which in turn, had contributed to the growing wage inequality there.

Offshoring may also have a growth effect. Mbiekop (2010) examines this growth effect in a general equilibrium model of endogenous growth in a North-South framework, where the North is endowed with more of both human and physical capital than the South. This factor endowment difference results in price differences for intermediate goods unfavorable to the

North and generates incentives for offshoring for the firms in the North. The final consumption good and human capital are obtained by packaging together a continuum of differentiated intermediate goods. Firms in the North, while deciding about carrying out the packaging task abroad, take into account both international transportation costs and the price-wedge for intermediate goods between the two countries. For the host Southern country, the extent of extra demand for intermediate goods generated by offshore activities is of prime importance, especially as backward and forward linkages generally ensure that soaring activities in one sector spill over to other sectors. Of course, with perfectly competitive markets for final goods, if the price-wedge for intermediate goods falls short of transportation costs, the only viable option for the Northern firms to compete in the Southern market is to produce final goods locally using locally-acquired intermediate goods. As a result, the demand for intermediate goods in the South increases in proportion to the price gap between both countries. Clearly, the higher the price differential between intermediate goods from the two economies, the larger are the North–South offshoring flows. Whether the final product is also shipped North or not clearly depends on whether the price-wedge is worth transportation costs between the two economies. In such a set up, Mbiekop (2010) shows that offshoring fosters human and physical capital accumulation while altering the factor content of exports. The result is driven by the factor-augmenting technological progress in the *host* country that offshoring brings in.

Grossman and Rossi-Hansberg (2008) investigate how falling costs of offshoring affect factor prices and growth in the *source* country. They identify a productivity effect, a relative-price effect, and a labour-supply effect. These authors show that improvements in the technology for offshoring tasks amount to a labour-augmenting technological progress that improves the real wages in the source country. Egger and Falkinger (2003) also develop a general equilibrium model to examine the assumptions under which international offshoring can be treated as technical progress in the source country. In their analysis of the distributional effects they distinguish between two driving forces in a substitution and a cost-saving effect.

11.3 Export Processing Zones (EPZs) as a Development Strategy

Export processing zones (EPZs) or Special Economic Zones (SEZs) are industrial zones in a country that aim at attracting export-oriented firms by offering them special concessions on taxes, tariffs, and regulations. The special concessions and incentives include exemption from some or all export taxes, from duties on imports of raw materials or intermediate goods, from taxes like profits taxes, municipal, property taxes, and value added taxes, from profit repatriation for foreign firms. The government also ensures free provision of enhanced physical infrastructure for production and transport. For example, Ireland, Malaysia, Mexico, the Dominican Republic, Mauritius, and Kenya offer a 15-year tax exemption, relief from exchange controls, free profit repatriation. In many countries, particularly the East Asian countries like China, South Korea, Malaysia, and Thailand, EPZs are instruments of a shift in policy of inward to outward orientation. China initiated its open-door policy and ongoing economic reforms by introducing Special Economic Zones (SEZ) in 1979. Initially, China promoted investment in a few carefully selected areas in the SEZs without promoting linkages with its domestic economy. With the initial success and development of infrastructure in SEZs, the level of involvement of foreign investment caused further development of SEZs in China. In other countries like Singapore, the EPZs were originally meant to attract investment to a strategically located economy already free of import and export regulations.

The growth and development of EPZs in China, Korea, Hong Kong, and Taiwan, had shown an interesting dimension. The domestic companies operating in these EPZs had progressed from what Moran (2002) calls original equipment manufacturing (OEM) units to original design manufacturing (ODM) units and finally to own brand manufacturing (OBM) units. Working with foreign capital and technology, they learnt, adopted, and later developed their own technology to become less dependent on foreign suppliers.

During the last decade, EPZs have grown in terms of their number (see Table 11.1), both within and across countries, and in terms of their size and the scope of industries they comprise. The largest growth of EPZs can be observed in China, particularly after the Agreement on Textiles and Clothing, which ended the global quota system for apparel. This growth resulted in manifold increases in China's share of the global apparel exports.

The evolution and growth of EPZs are often modelled along the lifecycle approach, which focuses on the dynamic nature of the EPZs. Basile and Germidis (1984) were the foremost to offer this class of theory of EPZ development.

Table 11.1 Growth of Export Processing Zones

	1975	1986	1995	1997	2002	2006
Number of countries having EPZs	25	47	73	93	116	130
Number of EPZs	79	176	500	845	3000	3500

Source: Estimates by International Labour Organization (www.ilo.org).

They identified four phases of development. First is the provision of basic infrastructure and facilities that prompts an inflow of FDI. The second stage is the expansion of exports through the EPZs, though the rate of FDI inflow begins to slow down. In the third stage, the growth in exports slows down and the small marginal businesses shut down. Finally, there is disinvestment by foreign enterprises. A slightly different argument on the life span of EPZs was put forward by Madani (1999) which suggests that the EPZs lose their significance as countries undertake and implement systematic economic reforms.

EPZs contribute to economic development of a country directly as well as indirectly. The direct channel is the backward linkages generated when EPZ firms raise demand for output in the rest of the economy. There can also be technological spill over when skills attained by local labour trained to work with foreign capital and technology in EPZs are passed on to the rest of the economy. The indirect channel is the contribution of EPZs in promoting exports and earning scarce foreign exchange for developing economies. This relaxes fiscal constraints of the developing country governments and promotes their development expenditures. But in countries where EPZs are enclaves in nature with no or very little link with the main economy, and the low-skilled production process is organized in such enclaves, the EPZs cannot promote technology transfers. Domestic sales from EPZ firms are usually prohibited. Thus, the 'enclave' nature of the EPZ does not promote forward linkages in most cases either. The host economy benefits only to the extent that the EPZs draw on unutilized local resources and in that case it is the backward linkage which is relevant. There may still be positive externalities such as learning-by-doing and on-the-job accumulation of human capital. But, in the enclave model of SEZ development, such externalities hardly percolate to the rest of the host economy. Thus, Warr (1989) argues that the flow of goods and services and the financial flows between the rest of the world and EPZs are irrelevant in evaluating the welfare impact on the host country. These transfers are taking place within the 'enclave' of the zones but not within the rest of the host economy.

Johansson (1994) observed two interrelated reasons as to how and why EPZs can contribute to the industrial development of a developing country. First, since domestic firms in the developing countries often lack technical, marketing, and managerial know-how needed to export and successfully compete in the world market with firms from the advanced countries, the FDI within the EPZs fills this gap. Second, domestic firms seldom have access to international distribution channels and need support from international or joint venture companies.

Empirical evidence does not suggest a very strong direct effect of the EPZs in achieving development goals of countries except for China, Korea, Taiwan, and Mauritius. Even for these countries, it was the combination of economic, demographic, and political factors rather than EPZs per se that contributed to their growth and development.

The other perceived benefit of EPZ is promotion of exports and consequently growth of economies. Rhee and Belot (1990) argued that EPZs help developing countries to increase non-traditional exports. Radelet (1999) also strongly opined that in their early years of industrialization, manufactured exports did not expand rapidly in any of the four Newly Industrialized Economies of Asia except through EPZs. In contrast, many have found EPZs ineffective for promoting economic development. Kaplinsky (1993), for example, argued that by promoting unskilled labour-intensive export processing in EPZs, the Dominican Republic had actually experienced immiserizing growth. Jayanthakumaran (2003) had also observed that EPZs generated only a limited number of backward linkages to the host country. There are also almost no success stories in Africa other than Mauritius. Johansson and Nilsson (1997) tested the catalytic effect of EPZs on ten countries and found that the export-generating effect of the EPZs was large only in case of Malaysia. Foreign affiliates attracted to the EPZs stimulated local firms to begin to export by showing them how to produce, market, and distribute manufactured goods internationally. As reported in ILO (2007), the share of EPZ in total manufacturing exports in fact declined in the Philippines, Mexico, and Mauritius, and was stagnant for Malaysia during 2002–2006 (see Table 11.2). For Sri Lanka, though there had been a marginal increase in the share of EPZ, it was still lower than 44% in 1990 [Jayanthakumaran (2003)]. Significant increase in export share, on the other hand, has been achieved by the Maldives and Colombia. EPZ exports in most of these countries are concentrated in textiles and clothing (as in Mauritius and Sri Lanka) and in electronics (as in Malaysia and Mexico).

Despite significant contribution of EPZs in total manufacturing exports in many countries, their contribution to total employment has not been very large. For example, only about 2.5% of total employment in Asia was generated by the EPZs in this region in the last decade. In countries like India, as well as in China, Mexico, and Russia, EPZs are intended to attract foreign investment and outsourcing activities in business services, information technology (IT),

Table 11.2 Share of EPZs in Manufacturing Exports

	2002	2006
Philippines	87	60
Malaysia	83	83
Mexico	83	47
Vietnam	80	80
Mauritius	77	42
Bangladesh	60	75.6
Sri Lanka	33	38
Maldives	13.2	47.7
Colombia	9.3	40

Source: ILO (2007).

and IT-enabled services (ITeS). But these high-tech EPZs do not generate significant employment and to some extent are insulated enclaves in the economy (see Engman et al. (2007)).[4]

In many countries, however, EPZs have been an experimentation of economic and trade liberalization policies. This has been particularly the case for China and Mauritius. Tekere (2000) observes that if EPZs are successful in promoting the growth of exports, employment, and technology transfer, these 'would signal the desirability and explosion of the trade liberalization program to cover the whole domestic economy, while non-successful EPZs may signal the reverse policy direction' (p. 37).

11.4 EPZs and Welfare in Developing Countries

Does the expansion of EPZs lead to welfare gains in developing countries? Beladi and Marjit (1992) discuss related work available in Brecher and Findlay (1983), Hamilton and Svensson (1982, 1983), Jones and Marjit (1992) and Yu (1985), deploying both Ricardo-Viner and Heckscher-Ohlin structures to argue that growth in the EPZ should benefit countries that import labour-intensive goods. In light of this, one could further argue that since most developing countries import capital-intensive goods and export labour-intensive goods, the expansion of EPZs might be welfare-reducing for them. However, this needs to be established firmly with the help of a model, at least for the short run. Let us assume that a country deficient in capital and technology sets up an EPZ for producing X_1 with the help of foreign capital, K_1 (foreign owners of capital earn a return r_1 with full repatriation of the capital income); and two other sectors outside the EPZ producing X_2 and X_3 which uses domestic capital K_2 (earns a return r_2). All sectors use homogeneous labour and take prices as given. Using standard production functions of CRS types, competitive product and factor markets and diminishing returns to inputs, we frame the economy as follows:

$$a_{L1}w + a_{K_1 1}r_1 = P_1 \tag{11.4}$$

$$a_{L2}w + a_{K_2 2}r_2 = P_2 \tag{11.5}$$

$$a_{L3}w + a_{K_2 3}r_2 = P_3 \tag{11.6}$$

---

[4] EPZs in India also account for a large share of production and exports in apparels, leather goods, and food.

$$a_{K_1}X_1 = \bar{K}_1 \tag{11.7}$$

$$a_{K_2}X_2 + a_{K_2 3}X_3 = \bar{K}_2 \tag{11.8}$$

$$a_{L1}X_1 + a_{L2}X_2 + a_{L3}X_3 = \bar{L}. \tag{11.9}$$

Equations (11.7) to (11.9) represent the full employment conditions in this economy. Suppose now the expansion of the EPZ is driven by more foreign capital being invested in the sector. With no other change in the resource base of this economy, one would expect that a rise in K_1 lowers production in X_3 and raises that in X_2, the latter being more capital-intensive compared to the former. Intuitively, since X_2 is labour-intensive, an expansion in the EPZ draws labour away from the two other sector, of which the labour-intensive sector is adversely affected in terms of output. The capital-intensive sector also receives capital flowing in from Sector 3, owing to a contraction of output there. In order to measure the welfare change, assume that the change in welfare (Ω) is a sum of the changes in demand for goods (D_1, D_2, and D_3) given the respective prices. Since the total change in demand as a measure of welfare is equivalent to the change in output (price of Sector 3 held as numeraire) minus the incremental repatriation of foreign earnings, Equation (11.10) provides the basis for these adjustments.

$$P_1 dD_1 + P_2^*(1+t)dD_2 + dD_3 = P_1 dX_1 + P_2^*(1+t) + dX_3 - r_1 dK_1 \tag{11.10}$$

where, $P_2 = P_2^*(1+t)$. Equation (11.10) becomes the ground for arguing that a rise in X_2 must lower overall welfare in the country. Since there is neither a change in any factor prices nor in the resource base, from (11.10) we can show that, $d\Omega = tP_2^*(dD_2 - dX_2)$, where, $D_2 = D_2(P_1, P_2, \Omega)$. It is evident that without any change in the prices, D_2 can change only with a change in Ω. Consequently, we can represent this change as $(\delta D_2/\delta\Omega)d\Omega = dD_2$. Since, it has been shown earlier (Jones, 1965, pp 526–527) that $(\delta D_j/\delta\Omega)P_j = m_j$, the right hand side being the marginal propensity to consume commodity j, $d\Omega = tP_2^*(dD_2 - dX_2)$ can be rewritten as

$$d\Omega = \frac{tP_2^* m_2}{P_2^*(1+t)}d\Omega - tP_2^* dX_2. \tag{11.11}$$

Rearranging and differentiating with respect to K_1, we get,

$$\frac{d\Omega}{dK_1} = \left[\frac{-tP_2^* m_2}{\left(1 - \dfrac{tm_2}{(1+t)}\right)} \cdot \frac{dX_2}{dK_1}\right] < 0.$$

Since $dX_2/dK_1 > 0$, the fall in welfare due to an expansion of the EPZ is unavoidable. However, if the protected sector were labour-intensive, there would have been welfare gain. The result is reminiscent of Johnson (1967) where growth in the protected sector leads to welfare loss for the home country as the value of the domestic output falls at the world prices. The results obtained according to the present model shows that growth occurred in two sectors: both in the EPZ and also in the protected import-competing sector, with the value of the domestic output net of repatriation cost going down for the country. It should be apparent that the results are symmetric for possible variations in the structure of the model given that the EPZ sector is not dependent on intensity assumptions and as long as some transactions (through factor relocation) between the EPZ and other sectors of the economy are recorded. The policy implications of setting up EPZ in many developing countries bear direct relevance to the results explored in this chapter.

■ REFERENCES

Agnese, P. and Ricart, J. E. (2009). 'Offshoring: Facts and Figures at the Country Level'. Working Paper 792, IESE Business School, Universidad de Navarra.

Andreff, W. (2009). 'Outsourcing in the New Strategy of Multinational Companies: Foreign Investment, International Subcontracting and Production Relocation'. *Papeles de Europa* 18: 5–34.

Arndt S.W. and Kierzkowski, H. (2001). (eds). *Fragmentation: New Production Patterns in the World Economy*. Oxford: Oxford University Press.

Bardhan, A.D. and Kroll, C. A. (2003). 'The New Wave of Outsourcing'. Fisher Center Research Report, University of California-Berkeley.

Basile. A. and Germidis, D. (1984). *Investing in Free Export Processing Zones*. Paris: OECD.

Beladi, H. and Marjit, S. (1992). 'Foreign Capital and Protectionism'. *Canadian Journal of Economics* 25 (1): 233–238.

Bhagwati, J., Panagariya, A., and Srinivasan, T. N. (2004). 'The Muddles Over Outsourcing'. *Journal of Economic Perspectives* 18: 93–114.

Blinder, A.S. (2009). 'Offshoring: Big Deal, or Business as Usual?'. In: J. N. Bhagwati and A. S. Blinder, (eds). *Offshoring of American Jobs: What Response From US Economic Policy?*, pp. 19–59. Cambridge, MA: MIT Press.

Brecher, R. and Findlay, R. (1983). 'Tariffs, Foreign Capital and National Welfare'. *Journal of International Economics* 14: 277–288.

Campa, J. and Goldberg, L. (1997). 'The Evolving External Orientation of Manufacturing Industries: Evidence From Four Countries'. *Federal Reserve Bank of New York Economic Policy Review* 4: 79–99.

Dornbusch, R., Fischer, S., and Samuelson, P. A. (1977). 'Comparative Advantage, Trade, and Payments in a Ricardian Model with a Continuum of Goods'. *The American Economic Review* 67 (5): 823–839.

Egger, H. and Falkinger, J. (2003). 'The Distributional Effects of International Outsourcing in a 2x2 Production Model'. *North American Journal of Economics and Finance* 14: 189–206.

Engman, M., Onodera, O., and Pinali, E. (2007). 'Export Processing Zones: Past and Future Role in Trade and Development'. OECD Trade Committee (May).

Feenstra, R. and Hanson, G. (1996a). 'Globalization, Outsourcing and Wage Inequality'. *The American Economic Review* 86 (2): 240–245.

Feenstra, R. and Hanson, G. (1996b). 'Foreign Investment, Outsourcing and Relative Wages'. In: R. Feenstra, G. Grossman, and D. Irwin (eds). *Political Economy of Trade Policies. Essays in Honour of J.N. Bhagwati*, pp. 89–127. Cambridge, MA: MIT Press.

Grossman, G. and Rossi-Hansberg, E. (2008). 'Trading Tasks: A Simple Theory of Offshoring'. *American Economic Review* 95: 1978–1997.

Hamilton, C. and Svensson, L. (1982). 'On the Welfare Effects of a Duty-Free Zone'. *Journal of International Economics* 4: 225–241.

Hamilton, C. and Svensson, L. (1983). 'On the Choice Between Capital Import and Labor Export'. *European Economic Review* 20 (1-3): 167–192.

Hummels D., Ishii, J., and Yi, K. M. (2001). 'The Nature and Growth of Vertical Specialization in World Trade'. *Journal of International Economics* 54 (1): 75–96.

International Labour Organization, (2002). ILO database on export processing zones, Sectoral Activities Programme, Working Paper 251, ILO, Geneva, Revised April 2007.

Jayanthakumaran, K. (2003). 'Benefit-Cost Appraisal of Export Processing Zones: A Survey of Literature'. *Development Policy Review* 21 (10): 51–65.

Jensen, J. B., and Kletzer, L. G. (2005). 'Tradable Services: Understanding the Scope and Impact of Services Offshoring'. In: L. B. and S. M. Collins, (eds). *Offshoring White-Collar Work—Issues and Implications*, pp. 75–116.Washington, DC: The Brookings Institution.

Johansson, H. (1994). 'The Economics of Export Processing Zones Revisited'. *Development Policy Review* 11 (4): 387–402.

Johansson, H. and Nilsson, L. (1997). 'Export Processing Zones as Catalysts'. *World Development* 25 (11): 2115–2128.

Johnson, H. (1967). 'The Possibility of Income Losses from Increased Efficiency or Factor Accumulation in the Presence of Tariffs'. *Economic Journal* 77: 151–154.

Jones, R. (1965). 'The Structure of Simple General Equilibrium Models'. *Journal of Political Economy*, 73: 557–572.

Jones R.W. and Kierzkowski, H. (2001). 'A Framework for Fragmentation'. In: S. W. Arndt and H. Kierzkowski, (eds). *Fragmentation: New Production Patterns in the World Economy*, pp. 17–34. Oxford: Oxford University Press.

Jones R.W. and Marjit, S. (1992). 'International Trade and Endogenous Production Structure'. In: W. Neuefeind and R. Reizman (eds). *Economic Theory and International Trade: Essays in Honor of J. Trout Rader*, pp. 173–196. Berlin: Springer-Verlag.

Kaplinsky, R. (1993). 'Export Processing Zones in the Dominican Republic: Transforming Manufactures into Commodities'. *World Development* 21 (11): 1851–1865.

Krugman, P. (2011). 'Offshoring vs Outsourcing: One Exports Jobs, Both Pick the Pockets of American Workers'. *Pittsburg Post-Gazette*, July 7 (www.post-gazette.com).

Madani, D. (1999). 'A Review of the Role and Impact of Export Processing Zones'. Washington, DC: World Bank.

Marjit, S. and Acharyya, R. (2003). *International Trade, Wage Inequality and the Developing Countries: A General Equilibrium Approach*. Heidelberg: Physica/Springer Verlag.

Mbiekop, F. (2010). 'A General Equilibrium Perspective on Offshoring and Economic Growth'. *Trade and Development Review* 3 (2): 80–110.

Moran, T. (2002). *Beyond Sweatshops: Foreign Direct Investment and Globalization in Developing Countries*. Washington DC: Brookings Institution Press.

Radelet, S. (1999). 'Manufactured Exports, Export Platforms and Economic Growth'. Discussion Paper 43, Cambridge, MA: Harvard/CAERII.

Rhee, Y. W. and Belot, T. (1990). 'Export Catalysts in Low Income Countries: A Review of Eleven Success Stories', World Bank Discussion Paper 72, Washington DC: World Bank.

Sanyal, K. K. (1983). 'Vertical Specialization in a Ricardian Model with a Continuum of Stages of Production'. *Economica* 50 (197): 71–78.

Tekere, M. (2000). 'Export Development and Export-Led Growth Strategies: Export Processing Zones and the Strengthening of Sustainable Human Development'. Paper presented at the Conference on ICTSD Globalization Dialogue—Africa, Windhoek, 10–11 May.

Warr, P. (1989). 'Export Processing Zones: The Economics of Enclave Manufacturing'. *World Bank Research Observer* 4 (1): 65–88.

Yu, E. (1985). 'Toward a Theory of Customs Unions with Foreign Investment'. *Economia Internazionale* 38: 222–235.

12 Contagion of Crisis and Concluding Remarks

All of us know that graduate students have to impress potential employers with their analytic skills. But I wish we had some way to insist that they acquire command of the facts before choosing the stylized facts they want to explain. To do that, of course, they must read the relevant descriptive literature, which means that we must assign it, even if we have to read some of that dull stuff ourselves.

Peter B. Kenen (2002)

12.1 Introduction

Financial crisis, of which currency crisis is one of the dominant drivers, has been dealt with by some of the most distinguished economists of our times including Peter B. Kenen (viz. 2002), and has been turned into anything but a dull subject. According to Allen and Gale (2000) the prevalence of financial crisis, generally speaking, often sends a signal that the financial sector is unusually susceptible to shocks. In fairly recent times, the spread of shocks from one sector to another and then as a wildfire to the rest of the world is a testimonial to the well-known contagion effects discussed in these studies. Bordo et al. (2001) define financial crises as episodes of financial market volatility marked by significant problems of illiquidity and insolvency among financial market participants and/or by official intervention to contain such consequences. Out of this general description, they further note that a banking crisis would qualify as financial distress resulting in the erosion of most or all of aggregate banking system capital (see, Caprio and Klingebiel, 1996). On the other hand, the currency crisis as we are dealing with in this chapter shall be defined as a forced change in parity, abandonment of a pegged exchange rate, or an international rescue. Bordo et al. (2001) comment that crises often come in waves, with a new one breaking out before the recovery from its predecessor is complete. The analogy is largely influenced by the series of crisis involving the European exchange rate crisis of 1992–3, the Tequila crisis of 1994–5, the Asian crisis of 1997–8, the Brazilian crisis of 1998–9, and the Russia-LTCM affair (see Kaminsky and Reinhart, 1998 for an explanation on banking and balance of payment crises).

However, the currency crisis that at times precedes other forms of financial crisis has strong historical antecedents. In fact, the first quarter of the seventeenth century, up to and through the beginnings of the Thirty Years' War in Germany with the defenestration at Prague in 1618, has been widely described as a period of crisis (Kindleberger, 1991). Gould (1954) and Supple (1957) among others discuss that the crisis was particularly acute between 1619 and 1623 and, despite localized impact in some cases, it was generally described as a commercial crisis. Importantly, the term currency crisis had already been coined around this time and seems to have been set within a deeper structural crisis covering 100 to 150 years of transition from medieval to modern times. It is largely argued that the debasing of currency in a number of European countries had been mainly owing to rapidly changing relative supplies of gold, silver, and copper. The transition, as Kindleberger (1991) puts it, turned into a clear practice of Gresham's Law, i.e., bad currency driving out good currency from a system. At the same time, it would have been impossible to have anything except metallic money. Gold was needed for large international transactions, after clearing as many payments as possible through bills of exchange. Silver was used for purchases in the Baltic, the Far and Middle East, and for large payments in domestic trade. 'There was virtually no problem with the larger gold and silver coins at this time. The trouble lay in the subsidiary coinage, starting out as silver-gulden, groschen, kreuzer, batzen, and even pennies. It also included vellon or billon, silver with varying amounts of copper up to 99%, and pure copper, sometimes weakly whitened' (p. 151). Germany was de facto on copper standard between 1621 and 1623. Since jargons and 'modern' treatments in economics has long provided us the requisite ability to recount these events as students of economics, we can safely attribute the debasing of currency between 1618–23 as an outcome of a negative (positive) supply shock in precious (semi-precious) minerals alongside the mounting trade and fiscal deficits faced by the larger European countries such as Spain, Russia, and Sweden. Kindleberger (1991) suggests that while there was no dearth of supply of looted South American gold once the New World was discovered in 1492 and of silver when around 1540 the silver mountain Potosi in Peru was discovered, the payments made by Spanish traders turned out to be costly for the reserve in (Western) Europe as a whole. Much, perhaps most, of the silver arriving in Spain was spent on trade settlement with the Baltic countries, with Russia and Poland, the eastern Mediterranean, and largely with India and China going around the Cape of Good Hope. The documents further report that in 1612 at the peak of the Kalmar War, and only 19 at the time, King Gustavus Adolphus of Sweden wanted to strike a peace accord with Christian IV of Denmark. The Danes under Christian IV had attacked Sweden as Charles IX, father of Gustavus, had bypassed the Sound Toll in the Baltic Sea previously imposed by the Danes and rerouted merchandise via Lapland in Norway, which too was under Danish occupancy at the time. The Danes captured two sea-fortresses near present day Gothenburg in Sweden with the help of a large number of hired mercenaries, who they did not ultimately pay up. As mercenaries deserted the troop and with Christian IV falling short on war funds, a truce was not unexpected. Further, as England and Holland, with interest in the Baltic-North Sea trade route, were wondering about the consequences if Stockholm fell to Danes, intervened without further delay. Consequently, the Treaty of Knared was signed in early 1613. However, Gustavus had to pay a huge ransom to get Alvsborg free from the Danes, although he was exempted from paying the Sound Toll further on. Now, in order to pay the ransom, Gustavus had begun to increase production of and export copper from the Stora Kopperberg in Sweden. The Swedes pledged the copper stock in Amsterdam and borrowed to pay up the ransom. However, they also started marketing new supplies through Hamburg and Amsterdam rather than Lubeck. At the same time, more copper was imported from Japan, and the price fell almost by one-half. In Germany, on the other hand, copper came to be in short supply as German mints used more and more copper melted down from all sources including church bells, kettles, and musical instruments. Overall, the sharp readjustments in the supply of precious and semi-precious metals effectively changed their relative prices and were heavily responsible for the debasing of currency. The drying up of the gold supplies from the south and the spurt of silver imports ruined the silver mines in central Europe. The excess supply of copper provoked Spain, financially exhausted by the war and drained of silver, to quickly change its currency standard. 'From 1599 to 1606, the Spanish monarchy coined 22 million ducats in vellon, a copper alloy. The bankruptcy of the Spanish treasury in 1607, which destroyed its credit and led to the failure of the Fuggers and a number of Genoan bankers, elicited a royal promise to the Cortes to coin no more copper. Between 1617 and 1619, the monarchy obtained permission of the Cortes to resume and coined five million ducats in copper. Two years later another 14 million were added' (Kindleberger, 1991, p. 152). If there was a time machine, one could possibly go back and forth to also find that the spill over of crisis then and now is hardly limited to the public sector alone. The trans-European private sector at that time felt continuous contraction on what it could use as resources. While there were 50 to 60 operators in Europe importing silver ingots during 1550s, by 1615 the number had come down to eight. Soon after, four of them had gone bankrupt and by 1620, only three remained. The currency debasing and changing patterns of trade clearly had its impact felt on product and factor markets across the countries.

But surely, the drive to revive the shining and precious metallic standards is far too modern for the world economic history to consider that the cross-country debasing (or, the intrinsic devaluation) of currencies in the seventeenth century had taught a serious lesson. Ohlin (1927, p. 151) states that, 'In 1920 the fate of the gold standard was still in the balance. Advocates of some kind of managed currency without the aid of gold were numerous or at least, made their voices heard as if they were.' The irony, as it might seem in view of the chronicle presented earlier, is that Sweden was the first European country to revert back to the gold standard. However, unlike Great Britain and some other countries, Sweden did not introduce any restrictions on the right to obtain gold coins for paper currencies, but simply reintroduced the old gold standard. It nevertheless adopted some modern day central banking features by allowing the Bank of Sweden to import gold without having to pay duties, while the private agencies were required to buy import licences. The Bank of Sweden had then realized that the flooding of gold by the USA in the European market would lead to a sharp fall in its value causing undesirable inflation in all gold standard countries. Nonetheless, Ohlin (1927, p. 151) notes, 'there was never any chance at all of a radical change in the monetary systems of Europe. After six years' experience of the blessings of managed and mismanaged currencies on a paper basis, few people were anxious to have more of it. The faults of the gold standard of pre-war days were forgotten and it was seldom realized how unfair a comparison was made, when a gold standard of peace was put up against a paper standard of war. These were psychological factors which must be taken into account, giving the "managed currency" advocates no chance of success. Was there ever a more ill-timed propaganda for a good cause?'

The world has without a doubt been exposed to international currency crisis for a very long time.

12.2 Analytical Categories of Currency Crisis

Theories on currency crises have been sensitive to the changes in the nature of the crisis. Like most other analytical approaches, this literature too has evolved from a focus on the fundamental causes of currency crises to emphasizing the scope for multiple equilibria and the role of financial variables. With reference to Krugman (2000), from the edited volume of the NBER conference proceedings held in 1998 right after the East Asian crisis shook up a large number of countries in Asia, it stands that the three main questions in this topic are: (1) What drives crises?; (2) How should government behaviour be modelled?; and (3) What are the effects of a crisis? Of these, the first question evidently commands greatest authority given that the adoption of policies to restrain the occurrence and the spread of crisis is among the top

priorities of a social planner. The social planner needs to evaluate a considerable number of factors before pointing to the depletion of foreign exchange
reserve as the sole reason for departure from the fixed exchange rate. Ozcan
and Sutherland (1995) suggest that the available models of currency crises
preoccupied with loss of reserves causing devaluation do not adequately explain the collapse of the European Exchange Rate Mechanism (ERM). They
argue that the collapse was an outcome of (a) some governments making a
conscious decision to leave the ERM; (b) credibility of the policy commitment, prevailing interest rates and the incentive to leave the ERM interacted
in ways that existing models do not explain; and (c) high interest rates in
Germany played an important role in precipitating the crisis by causing recession for other ERM members. In fact, this study suggests that measures such
as the capital controls, raising the cost of switching regime, raising the maturity of debt contracts, and lowering the discount rate of the policy-maker
could be used to minimize the possibility of currency crises. At the level of
the specific policies, capital control raises the expected survival time of the
fixed exchange rate regime when the gap between the high and low values of a
random interest rate shock (that which spread from Germany) also rises. The
extension of the average maturity of private debt replicates this result because
the regime switch is not expected to affect the long run interest rate. In other
words, high values of foreign interest rate will have little impact on the domestic interest rate if the maturity time of private debt is longer such that the
fixed exchange rate regime will have greater sustainability. The logic is also
straightforward. The high interest rate in Germany precipitated recession in
other ERM countries forcing an exchange rate crisis. If the domestic interest
rate is not sensitive to such shocks, then extreme foreign interest rates will be
tolerated and the fixed exchange rate shall continue. Thirdly, the conflict between the discount rate of a policy-maker (usually determined by the tenure
in power) and the monetary policy of the central bank of a country often takes
serious proportions. The 2013 currency crisis in India seems to have been a
result of the conflicting interests of the ruling federal government's urge to
attain higher growth (by keeping low interest rates) and high redistribution
vis-à-vis the Reserve Bank of India's effort to curb high inflation culminating
in low growth and trade deficits (by raising interest rates). The ruling government's discount rate is usually high; in this case they would need to win and
retain power at the centre for the general election in 2014. Thus, an obvious
way, Ozcan and Sutherland (1995) comment, to reduce the discount rate of
the policy-maker is to delegate monetary policy-making to an independent
central bank (without the interference of the government in power). Such an
apolitical institution does not face the electorate at fixed intervals and will
therefore be more farsighted in its monetary policy-making. Obviously, in
hardly any country (including the Federal Reserve or the Bank of England)
the Central Bank is totally free to manoeuvre its policy responses according

to the internal and external signals. The existing models of currency crisis, at least, need to construct political economy models of interdependence between governments and the central banks in making important policies work (for a discussion, see Sen, 2004).

However, so far, three generations of models have typically been used to explain currency crises during the last forty years. The *first generation* models (see Claessens, 1991), were largely motivated by the collapse of the gold price and referred mainly to the currency devaluations in Latin America and other developing countries in the 1970s. Krugman's (1979) seminal paper along with the theory by Flood and Garber (1984) showed that a sudden speculative attack on a fixed or pegged currency can result from rational behaviour by investors who correctly foresee that a government has been running excessive deficits financed with central bank credit. Investors continue to hold the currency as long as they expect the exchange rate regime to remain intact, but they start dumping it when they anticipate that the peg is about to end. This frenzy leads the central bank to quickly lose its liquid assets or hard foreign currency supporting the exchange rate. The currency then collapses. Interestingly, the behavioural aspect of this type of currency crisis may find a strong basis in the 'herd behaviour' among investors.

Banerjee (1992) sets up a model in which 'herd behaviour' arises from an individual replicating or mimicking the actions of others by assuming that they have information to which the individual under consideration is not privy. In other words, the behaviour reflects a situation where everyone does what everyone else is doing, despite the possibility that the individuals' private information suggests doing something quite different. In the process, the individual seems to push her own information under the carpet leading to an absolute convergence to one particular choice or decision in the system. It also follows that an individual being less responsive to her own information will shrink the information set to an extent that it is socially welfare-reducing. In fact, Banerjee (1992) suggests that in equilibrium, the society may gain by forcing some people to follow their own information rather than following what others follow. A common outcome of such information convergence is the creation of a monopoly situation in the market, where for example, herd behaviour drives everybody to a particular restaurant in town despite availability of private information that the other restaurant in town is probably better. If some people standing ahead in a queue choose to enter one restaurant, those who stand behind them in the line are influenced by that decision and overrule their private information, which should have sent them to the other restaurant. The 'herd (and negative) externality' that similar information blackouts generates for the followers strips the system of alternative information and imparts cost even to the extent of a financial crisis, as that experienced by the East Asian countries in 1997 and the Mexican Peso crisis in 1994 (see, Calvo and Mendoza, 2000 and also 1996). The literature on herding behaviour and its relation to financial crisis starts from a premise whereby the acquisition of information is costly for each firm. Consequently, the information frictions lead many of the firms to observe the actions of other firms instead of the costly verification of the fundamentals of the country they have invested in for the short run and the long run. Note that the level of cross-border investments in each period, as an important driver of international financial linkages, and the extraction of signals about the state of the economy are closely connected. Rigobon (1999) for example, suggests that the investors being imperfectly aware of the level of productivity of domestic capital derive poor signals about the state of the economy in which they plan to invest. Moreover, as the level of investment rises, the quality of good signals falls. Intuitively, it implies that at the onset of a boom, the signals might have been good not because the country-level fundamentals were good but because the investors were driving it. Thus, as the investment matures, the signal picks up a lot of noise from both investments and fundamentals and loses its signalling efficiency. Similarly, bad signals at the onset of a recession are informative, but it ceases to remain so as the recession develops. The herd behaviour among international investors is usually a consequence of constricted information of the nature discussed. In fact, information asymmetry of particular types could also be of serious consequence for the financial contagion of crisis. Kodres and Pritsker (1998) suggest that information asymmetries and the ability to cross-hedge across other asset markets and often across national borders could be the fundamental driver of global crisis. Recently, the financial innovations that led to the global crisis of 2007 were typically based on transfer of assets (mortgages of real estates) between investors and across countries. Kaminsky, Lizondo, and Reinhart (1998) discuss that the international market co-movements occurred in the absence of relevant information and despite idiosyncratic country characteristics. In this environment, a negative shock to one country can lead informed investors to sell that country's assets and buy assets of another country, increasing their exposure to the idiosyncratic factors of the second country. Investors can hedge this new position by selling the assets of a third country, completing the chain of contagion from the first country to the third country. Intuitively, it seems that the uninformed investors do not know whether the demand changes that they observe within a market following a shock are due to the hedging of macroeconomic risk across markets, or due to informed investors trading on private information within the market.

12.2.1 TRADE LINKS OF CONTAGION

Dornbusch, Park, and Claessens (2000) discuss at length the role of international trade in crisis contagion. It is argued that the local shocks, such as a crisis in one economy, can affect the economic fundamentals of other countries through trade links and currency devaluations. By contagion, a major trading partner of a country that has been exposed to financial crisis could also experience declining asset prices and large capital outflows. It could also become the target of speculative attacks as investors anticipate a decline in exports to the crisis country and hence deterioration in the trade account. Crises may spread further through competitive devaluations whereby countries competing for the same third country export market are forced to devalue their respective currencies following a devaluation in the country of first crisis (see Corsetti et al. 1999 for devaluation games). The non-cooperative nature of the currency devaluation games between countries could result in still greater depreciation compared with what could have been attained in a cooperative equilibrium. During the East Asian crisis in 1997, exchange rates depreciated substantially even in economies such as Singapore, Taiwan, and China that were not exposed to the same factors causing the crises in south Korea, the Philippines, and Thailand. While we provide another explanation behind the crisis shortly, the international trade link could hardly be ignored. With investors exposed to a potential game of competitive devaluation, short-sell of security holdings of other countries is a common reaction along with refusal to roll over short-term loans and rationing of credit.

They further comment that the contagion by its very nature is an international phenomenon; particularly since the cross-country financial and trade flows reached epic proportions. Both the Mexican crisis and the East Asian crisis involved many countries in South America and Asia, respectively, with both having far reaching effects as well. Therefore, 'contagion is best defined as a significant increase in cross-market linkages after a shock to an individual country (or group of countries), as measured by the degree to which asset prices or financial flows move together across markets relative to this co-movement in tranquil times' (Dornbusch et al. 2000, p. 178). However, note that an increase in co-movements need not reflect irrational behaviour on the part of investors. When one country is hit by a shock, firms encounter losses and the consequent liquidity constraints can force investors to withdraw funds from *other* countries. Importantly, financial transactions being conducted by agents rather than by principals also lends the issue to incentive problems triggering volatility. Besides, the herd behaviour is already known for creating excess volatility. Finally, since there is very little coordination between investors—unless they are part of a multinational financial group—country-specific liquidity problems spill over to other countries quite easily.

The *second generation* of models, on the other hand, stresses the importance of multiple equilibria. These models show that doubts about whether a government is willing to maintain its exchange rate peg could lead to multiple equilibria and currency crises (Obstfeld, 1986; Obstfeld and Rogoff, 1996). The models also suggest existence of self-fulfilling prophecies wherein the speculative attack becomes an outcome of the belief that the currency would be attacked by others. Flood and Marion (1997) also explain that while macroeconomic policies prior to the attack in the first generation models become the main source of crisis, for the second generation models, changes in policies in response to a possible attack can lead to an attack and be the trigger of a crisis. The second generation models are therefore, largely motivated by episodes like the European Exchange Rate Mechanism crisis. For the ERM crisis, countries like the UK came under pressure in 1992 and ended up devaluing, despite possible alternatives as discussed in Eichengreen, Rose, and Wyplosz (1996) and Frankel and Rose (1996).

Finally, models discussing the *third generation* crisis are driven by trade deficits leading to asset price shocks and via exchange rate fluctuations leading to currency crises as exemplified by the East Asian financial crisis. A number of studies, in particular those by McKinnon and Pill (1997), Krugman (1999), and Corsetti, Pesenti, and Roubini (1998) suggest that excessive government intervention and bail-out policies (such as subsidies and nationalization) could make financial institutions and banks take riskier decisions including the holding of large foreign currency denominated debts (see, Chang and Velasco, 2000). Consequently, over-borrowing or imprudent lending practices could trigger general as well as currency crises via the routes we have discussed so far. Radelet and Sachs (1998) argue more generally that self-fulfilling panics hitting financial intermediaries can force liquidation of assets, which then confirms the panic and leads to a currency crisis.

12.2.2 THE EAST ASIAN CRISIS

Towards the end of the 1990s, the miracle growth countries of East Asia, namely, South Korea, Taiwan, the Philippines, Thailand, and Indonesia, all went into a deep financial crisis. All of these countries were deemed the Newly Industrialized Countries (NICS) and were the major economic success stories in Asia apart from Japan. As it has been discussed through the previous chapters, trade openness, economic and financial liberalization, and alignment with the global capital market were at the forefront of strategic policy decisions adopted by most of these countries aiming to land themselves on a higher growth path. It is not surprising that one of the crucial restraining factors for the developing countries continues to be the lack of investible capital.

Low growth, low per capita income, low savings, and low investments are atypical of developing countries necessitating dependence on foreign capital (for the well-known two-gap model, see Basu (1998). For a long time, high transaction costs associated with cross-country investments and asymmetric information about the risk factors at individual country levels created specific patterns of investments worldwide, of which the colonial connections played an important role. Besides, capital also got invested in relatively high growth developed countries, where expansion of industrial and service sectors was the predominant outcome. However, despite the low risk factors involved in investments in the developed countries, and the returns to capital that is expected of 2.5% to 3% per annum growth rates in such countries, the point of interest slowly shifted to the developing countries. The shortage of capital and technical know-how in poor countries naturally raised the premium on every dollar invested much above what the capital-rich countries would be willing to offer. Indeed, the potentially higher returns needed to be evaluated against the added risk factors in politically and economically unstable developing countries. For a venture capitalist, it was a comparison of this real (risk-adjusted) return across countries alongside the period over which capital would be ideally invested. In fact, the choice between short run investments and long run investments became important, with crucial policy changes adopted in the developing countries around this time.

One such policy change, as Marjit and Kar (1998) considers as an important factor behind potential currency crisis, is the level of capital account convertibility in developing countries. At the time, India had not shifted into full convertibility of its capital account, which essentially would mean that a foreign investor could not take back the entire domestic currency denominated investments at any point by converting it into a choice of foreign currency. Technically, currency convertibility refers to the freedom to convert the domestic currency into other internationally accepted currencies and vice versa. Convertibility in that sense is the obverse of controls or restrictions on currency transactions. While current account convertibility refers to freedom in respect of 'payments and transfers for current international transactions', capital account convertibility (CAC) would mean freedom of currency conversion in relation to capital transactions in terms of inflows and outflows. The IMF provides elaborate rules on the matter of current and capital account transactions at the country level.

Article VIII of the International Monetary Fund, provides in Sections 2 and 3 (IMF: *Decision No. 1034-(60/27), June 1, 1960*) that members shall not impose or engage in certain measures, namely restrictions on the making of payments and transfers for current international transactions, discriminatory currency arrangements, or multiple currency practices, without the approval of the Fund. The guiding principle in ascertaining whether a measure is a restriction on payments and transfers for current transactions under Article

VIII, Section 2, is whether it involves a direct governmental limitation on the availability or use of exchange as such. Members in doubt as to whether any of their measures do or do not fall under Article VIII may wish to consult the Fund thereon. Further, in accordance with Article XIV, Section 3, members may at any time notify the Fund that they accept the obligations of Article VIII, Sections 2, 3, and 4, and no longer avail themselves of the transitional provisions of Article XIV. If members, for balance of payments reasons, propose to maintain or introduce measures, which require approval under Article VIII, the Fund will grant approval only where it is satisfied that the measures are necessary and that their use will be temporary while the member is seeking to eliminate the need for them. As regards measures requiring approval under Article VIII and maintained or introduced for non-balance of payments reasons, the Fund believes that the use of exchange systems for non-balance of payments reasons should be avoided to the greatest possible extent, and is prepared to consider with members the ways and means of achieving the elimination of such measures as soon as possible.

Countries obviously manoeuvre within the given framework of rules and regulations and in this regard individual country experiences seem to be the additional sources of information on what level of convertibility stands optimal for the country in question. Sen (2004), for example, suggests that the Mundell-Fleming interest rate parity would no longer offer a meaningful basis to comprehend the state of the international capital market if India and other countries yet to liberate their capital account were to liberate it. Sen (2004) further suggests that since the bigger firms tend to be less capital constrained in developing countries, their share prices are less volatile than those of credit constrained smaller firms. However, for Argentina in the 1990s, the larger firms faced higher volatility in the index of their share prices. In fact, the larger firms in Argentina could access the international capital markets adding to their volatility (Caballero, 2000). It was also found that for Chile the important macroeconomic time series indicators were strongly and positively responsive to the global price of copper, which Chile exported as their main item. Now, Chile is regarded as a major success story for liberalizing its financial sector. And yet, access to international markets does not seem to allow it to smooth its consumption, perhaps owing to the underdeveloped nature of the domestic asset markets. On the same note, Sen (2004) argues that just before the 1994 crisis in Mexico there had been a major privatization drive for the state-owned banks. As it is commonplace in developing countries, the quality of risk appraisal after factoring in the glaring moral hazard problems generic to pervasive informality in an economy, is naturally quite poor. While the private banks followed the path of a rational individual lending against real estate, etc., independently they were not the best evaluators of future turmoil. Loans against real estate (or against company shares, as in Japan) are fine for idiosyncratic shocks, unless of course the prices of such assets nosedive at the wake of a crisis. The sub-prime mortgage crisis that we have discussed was not entirely different from this. Overall, the problem in Mexico was compounded by a sudden depreciation of the peso following the crisis and closely resembles later examples from countries rocked by the East Asian crisis.

Thus, when the entire of South-East Asia, in particular Thailand and Malaysia, was seriously affected by a speculative attack in the currency markets, questions regarding the relationship between economic 'fundamentals' and financial stability under free mobility of capital became crucial. Several studies by Claessens and Glaessner (1997), Claessens and Hindley (1997), Glaessner and Oks (1994), and the G-10 (1997) report of the working party pointed towards the problem of financial openness in emerging markets. The Thai crisis had emerged at a time when the Thai economy, as had been noted in stray discussions, was not doing 'up to the mark'. However, the general macroeconomic indicators in Thailand were still impressive notwithstanding the fact that the country's banking sector was not doing too well at the time. Annual GDP growth had been around 9% over 1990–95, exceeded only by China, Singapore, and Malaysia; the gross domestic saving as a percentage of GDP stood at more than 35%, a formidable statistic, and there was even a fiscal surplus (1993–95) of around 2% of GDP. On the other hand, Malaysia too had a sound track record as far as these macro-indicators were concerned at the cross-country level. And yet it happened in South-East Asia. The IMF-World Bank and Japan had to pledge their support to stabilize the dwindling currencies in the region. Malaysian authorities could not help but blame openly the currency traders and multinationals for pushing the regional economies into unexpected turmoil. Even Singapore, Hong Kong, and China were not totally exempt, mainly owing to the contagion effects we have previously discussed. Now, the 'fundamentals' are often textbook concepts needed to negotiate loans from the world institutions, to woo foreign investors into making long-term commitments, to project something concrete and tangible in a world plagued by monumental uncertainties. In reality, however, when a run on currency starts off, people seldom look at the fundamentals and breathe a sigh of relief. Everyone at that instant believes that those selling the currency know something one does not know and eventually the herd behaviour effect sets in. Even with substantial foreign currency reserves one may not hold up against the onslaught if the short-term commitments are severe. Currency movements are essentially movements of assets with the 'shortest maturity'. Capital flight on the other hand is flight of assets, which constitute the relatively 'short-term' debts of a nation. While a currency trader can sell off 'rupees' within seconds to acquire 'dollars', an NRI short-term deposit-holder will have to wait for some time, if they do not want to lose interest for premature withdrawal. But the burden of short-term obligations is the first approximation of the potential payment problems a country faces at any point of time. The backdrop and the causes and consequences of full convertibility for the Indian economy have been nicely summarized in Bhaumik (1997). In the literature on external debt, on the other hand, the 'external debt burden' of an economy has been the prime focus of attention. Following the Mexican peso crisis in 1982, several authors have tried to analyse the issue of default on international payments, capital flight, consequent depreciation of currencies, loan pushing, and the burden of external adjustments (also see Basu, 1997). While the ratio of total external debt to GNP or GDP constitutes the most popular indicator of the debt burden, the compositional aspects of debt burden, i.e. the pattern of maturity, is of no less significance. Bhagwati and Srinivasan (1993) earlier mentioned that the country's debt composition and the degree of external indebtedness is better reflected by the proportion of long-term debt to total debt burden than by the simple proportion between total external debt and GNP.

In this connection, Marjit and Kar (1998) constructed an index to capture both the extent of the external debt as well as the short-term vulnerability of the debt structure. It is obvious that as far as financial management of the debt burden is concerned, one must look at the proportion of short-term debt to total debt and some other parameters, attach proper weights to these indicators, and construct an appropriate index. Apart from being anxious regarding a proper measure of volatility, one needs to check whether countries with very sound macroeconomic fundamentals continue to have a significant percentage of debt held in terms of short-term obligations, because this would in turn make the impact of any unanticipated shock that induces a capital flight much more severe than under normal circumstances. The reason for the capital flight may lie somewhere else, but the adjustment tends to be quite painful as through a slump in the value of the local currency and the local stocks as also through an imminent economic depression at an unusually rapid pace. In a world with relatively free movement of international capital, short-term disturbances may turn out to be unmanageable.

The index captures the financial vulnerability of 21 developing countries in Asia, Africa, Latin America, and east Europe and includes India, Thailand, and Malaysia for the purpose of observing if capital account convertibility has anything to do with the currency crisis. The information on the external debt of these nations was collected from the 1997 editions of the World Debt Tables and World Tables and involved ranking those countries according to their total debt burdens, i.e., total outstanding debt divided by GNP (EDT/GNP), and also by the proportion of short-term debt in total debt (SDT/EDT). The study also looked at the short-term debt coverage of foreign exchange reserve and the proportion of current account deficit that can be financed through FDI inflow.

Using the standard EDT/GNP ratio, African countries such as Kenya, Ethiopia, and Ghana steal the show with a very high burden. India, Thailand, and Malaysia were in the middle, while the top ranks characterized by lower ratios, were captured by South Korea, Romania, and China. The story, however, appears strikingly different if one looks at the ranking according to SDT/EDT. The rank correlations between the two sets of variables are (–0.46 in 1993, –0.40 in 1994, and –0.29 in 1995; the negativity falls). Seen individually in terms of SDT/EDT only, Thailand, Malaysia, and South Korea had very high percentages of short-term obligations over the period under consideration. Conversely, India, Bangladesh, and some of the African countries remain fairly well placed by this rank over the same period. In the composite rank thus constructed, India was on the top of the chart with the Russian Federation following, at least for 1993. In other words, India was least burdened and shared the joint top rank with Argentina in 1994 and with Poland in 1995. In 1993, Kenya, Mexico, Malaysia, and Thailand turned out to be the worst four in that order. Thailand, however, became the worst performer in 1994 with Malaysia ranking close. For 1995, both Thailand and Malaysia were ranked at par (15th out of 20 countries).

The simple methodology followed in creating the composite rank or the index is as follows. Let a country be ranked at the 'i^{th}' position according to the EDT/GNP in an increasing order, $i = 1, 2,\ldots, n; n = 21$. The same country is ranked' 'j^{th}' according to its SDT/EDT ratio in the same order. Subsequently, a country is assigned a number on the basis of the following index, $b_{ij} = (i + j)/2$, and a corresponding rank R_{ij} in the composite column. India for example (in 1993) was 9th by best performances on EDT/GNP, while 3rd by SDT/EDT, such that it scored (6.0) on b_{ij}, the index, and it turns out to be the best (lowest) score, implying that it is least debt-burdened in terms of external debt and short-term debt to GDP ratios with a 0.5 weight on each of these ratios. For 1993, however, Thailand gets a score of 17 and occupies the 21st (last) rank in the composite index. The African countries remain so much burdened with aggregate debt that for some of them, low short-term obligations during this period did not help to improve their overall rank in the composite case. Next, the reserve position in foreign currency denominated assets, in particular foreign currency reserves (RES) in relation to SDT, was used as a separate measure. With the two variables X_i (EDT/GNP) and X_j (SDT/EDT) already in use, the third (X_k) ratio in the form of a short-term debt (SDT) to foreign exchange reserve (RES) ratio as defined earlier was introduced in the 0.33 weighted index of ratios. The ratio is so constructed that the countries with greater debt covers (lower ratios) in terms of the reserve positions of these 21 countries and ranked near the top, over the 1993–95 period. According to this specific rank-order, Bangladesh continued to stay at the top (1993–94) with its low GNP and low debt burdens; India closely followed during the same period. Thailand, with its relatively huge stock of foreign exchange reserve, was better placed compared to the previous weighted index and ranked at the top. Some divergences poured in, as soon as the three-factor weighted index was tested for the 21 countries under consideration. In 1993, while the South Asian countries like India, Bangladesh, and Sri Lanka captured the top three positions, China was way behind at the 9th. Thailand was jointly 15th with Pakistan, and Malaysia stood marginally better. The African countries were placed lower down the rank order, and the East European countries exhibited a mixed bag, though close to the better group. In subsequent years, i.e., in 1994 and 1995, similar features were repeated with partial improvements or deteriorations for the countries concerned. Thailand, however, continued to be in the rough spot. Using a fourth variable, namely the ratio of the current account balance (CB) and the net FDI for the three years the index with 0.25 as the variable weight was run for 15 countries in total for some years due to unavailability of data. Interestingly, this particular variable assigned top rank to a country with the value approached from the negative end. It is so because all the countries in this group reported deficits in their CB and experienced net inflow of FDI. China, for example, in 1993 had a CB of $ -11,609 million, but a net FDI of $ 27,515 million, such that its CB/FDI was (-0.4), helping it to rank at the top. While Ethiopia faced the worst rank, Thailand was ranked 9th among the set of 15 countries, with a CB/FDI of (-3.9). Following the methodology just discussed, the countries are once again ranked in the ith (EDT/GNP), j^{th} (SDT/EDT), k^{th} (SDT/ RES) and l^{th} (CB/FDI) columns according to their individual ratios. Repeating the procedure, this paper further showed that for the year 1993, India was at the top. Thailand is positioned 11th out of the 15 countries that faced current account deficit in 1993. In 1994, China, the Russian Federation, and Kenya showed current account surplus, and consequently, between the remaining 18 countries, Poland stood on the top, followed by India, Egypt, and Romania in the next three places. Thailand languished at 18th. In 1995, Poland, India, and Egypt retained their positions from the previous year, while Thailand improved to a joint 12th spot with Pakistan, among a set of 16 countries. Finally, with the three-factor and four-factor indices at hand, a tied rank-correlation was run between b_{ijk} and b_{ijkl} for 1994. The year was so chosen that the maximum number of countries (18 here) could be incorporated in the study. The value of the rank correlations coefficient turned out to be 0.86, implying that a country close to the top (better performer) in both ranks was better capable of withstanding a financial crisis. However, since there is strong correlation between the three indices, one can have strong first hand approximations, and also the essential inferences, by considering b_{ij} only. Later indices only add refinements to this index. Despite the fact that the Asian Tigers have reaped benefits of a more or less free movement of financial capital and leading to rapid economic expansion, it also exposed them to volatility, which at the time of the crisis was unmanageable. For each and every nation, sound financial management involves an efficient contingency plan. With huge short-term debt relative to total external commitments, any nation, rich or poor, exposes itself to a potentially disturbing financial environment. Strong economic fundamentals reduce the zone of uncertainty, but do not eliminate it completely. Strong fundamentals, on the other hand, attract foreign investments and so having weak macroeconomic indicators despite a low effective debt burden does not help. At the same time, if unanticipated shocks affect an economy adversely, strong fundamentals by themselves do not take care of the short run crisis. A significant trade surplus is an important prerequisite for convertibility in countries such as India, which fail to generate substantial private capital inflow in the face of huge current account deficits. If a country pursues a policy to maintain the value of its currency it has to generate substantial demand for its own currency-denominated goods and assets. One has to understand that keeping up the value of one's currency is as foolish an action as prescribing continuous devaluation for raising exports. But in case of sudden flight of capital, ability to stop the run on reserves depends crucially on the international purchasing power of the currency, which in turn depends on the demand elasticity for national goods.

12.3 **Concluding Remarks**

We have tried to provide the detailed theoretical passage for each topic in this book. In Chapter 3 for example, the antecedents in the analysis of immiserizing growth, the implications of factor mobility on growth, and the structuralist theories have been suitably combined with newer developments. The terms of trade effects following north-south trade and the large body of literature that developed subsequently form integral topics of discussion in this chapter as a continuation of the problems of trade in primary commodities and a redux of the Singer-Prebisch hypothesis. The unmistakable connection between growth and poverty is given due importance in Chapter 3, suggesting that trade serves as an engine of economic growth for the southern countries, globally. We have also been mindful of the importance of the new growth theories and their synergies with trade in goods. The economic frameworks available in Chapters 1, 2, and 3 provided us with sufficient foundation to look into the implications of sector specific trade and factor mobility in atypical developing and transition countries. Chapter 4 dealt with the foreign capital inflow and multinational activities in countries of the south, where choice of location for the entry of foreign institutional investments and direct investments are treated with adequate importance in view of the delicate welfare implications. The political economy issues built into the choice of the type of investments, whether in the retail sector or in the traditional manufacturing sector, have found renewed interest when some of the late liberalizing countries including India are found to be struggling with ways to convince its nationals about retail FDI. Thus, a brief introduction to the question of FDI in retail is available in Chapter 4 to apprise the reader of the theoretical and empirical research questions that may be linked to it. We emphasized among other things, that asymmetric information may also have an important role to play in the measurement of welfare associated with retail FDI. Furthermore, this chapter discussed the role of foreign capital in promoting skill in the host country. This is reiterated in Chapter 5, where emigration leads to skill formation. Chapter 5 also offers a detailed morphology of the north-south migration patterns that draws on seminal works of Bhagwati, Ramaswamy, and many others. Chapter 6, on the other hand, calls upon the role of asymmetric information in the cross-country labour markets, which shapes the pattern of migration and occupational choices largely facing southern labour in northern countries.

Chapter 7 brings back the well-known debates between trade, foreign aid, and welfare. Despite falling dependence on foreign aid in many developing countries, the theoretical conjectures and empirical observations on the implications of aid on welfare in poor countries are indisputably strong and must feature in a book on trade and development. The link between international trade and poverty on a similar note has lent itself to rigorous analytical treatments for a long time now, and to the best of our understanding needed an evaluation based on how the political forces within a country shapes itself when confronted with the choice between growth and redistribution in a much more open environment. Consequently, we have read and reflected upon a large set of studies that discuss the trade-poverty link and then rounded it up with a model of how trade and redistribution could function well in a political-economy model. Some of the results we discussed in this chapter support the theories of the second-best. Chapter 9 deals with the issue of where the south countries could improve upon the persistent second-best by resorting to regionalism. The tensions between regionalism and multilateralism and also free trade are well-known to the audience. We resorted to established theoretical formulations in order to allow us to manoeuvre in this rather difficult domain where domino and juggernaut effects associated with reciprocal multilateralism are no less compelling than arguments in favour of free trade. The political economy models also serve a useful purpose to resolve some of these puzzles. In the same spirit, Chapter 10 discussed the questions of global standards in production, of intellectual property rights, of the politics of using 'comparative disadvantage' to retain global competitiveness and most importantly, the environmental questions connected directly to international trade in final and intermediate goods. Many of the findings that we accommodated in this chapter are new entries in the time-scale that we have been able to cover and provide elements of continued interest among researchers. In fact, Chapter 11 entertains even newer elements in the subject, where outsourcing, offshoring, and production re-organization at the firm level dominate the scope in the same manner as the 'new-new trade theory' offers in a larger context. Nonetheless, this chapter also deals with the welfare implications of export processing zones in poor countries, mainly because the EPZs are construed, perhaps erroneously, as the driver of production re-organization in poor countries where low productivity is still rampant. The trade-labour inter-action in the behest of large unorganized sector in poor countries, for this very reason, had earlier received due attention in Chapter 8. Finally, Chapter 12, talks about the financial contagion of crisis across national borders.

Overall, this book was intended to traverse a considerable amount of time and space in the subject of International Trade and Economic Development. Beginning with where it all begins, namely, the negative terms of trade shock against the south, we made an attempt to accommodate issues that are glob-ally deemed as important in view of both the graduate course contents and the research agendas involving trade and development. Needless to men-tion, trying to comprehend a subject that has been enriched by contributions from many of the most authoritative masters, including Nobel Laureates, could be an extremely vexing task within the limited sphere of a postgrad-uate textbook. At the same time however, our experience with writing this book turned itself into a reward wherein we collected more pebbles from the seashore than we normally would have done. Indeed, the wealth of contri-butions in topics such as trade and inequality, trade, poverty, and welfare, foreign direct investment, foreign aid, trade and factor mobility, etc. leaves one with difficult choices regarding what not to accommodate in a modern anthology.

Nevertheless, we have made a conscious effort to bring together estab-lished theories and evidence with newer research in order to provoke fur-ther interest in many of these topics. Several interesting questions in trade and inequality; impact of international trade on land, labour, and capital; trade and entrepreneurship, international trade, labour standards and patent rights; trade and re-distribution, etc. currently remain as vibrant subjects of research. Active interest in attending to these and related ques-tions should continue to enrich our understanding.

■ REFERENCES

Allen, F. and Gale, D. (2000). 'Financial Contagion'. *Journal of Political Economy* 108 (1): 1–33.

Banerjee, A. V. (1992). 'A Simple Model of Herd Behavior'. *The Quarterly Journal of Economics* 107(3): 797–817.

Basu, K. (1997) *Analytical Development Economics. The Less Developed Economy Revisited.* MIT Press.

Basu, K. (1998). *Analytical Development Economics.* MIT Press.

Bhagwati, J. N. and Srinivasan. T. N. (1993). 'India's Economic Reform'. Ministry of Finance, Government of India, Working Paper.

Bhaumik, S. K. (1997). 'Capital Account Convertibility and Financial Reforms: The Rationale and the Missing Link'. *Money and Finance* 3, ICRA, September.

Bordo, M., Eichengreen, B., Klingebiel, D., Soledad Martinez-Peria, M., and Rose, A. K. (2001). 'Crisis Problem Growing More Severe?'. *Economic Policy* 16: 32, 51, and 53–82.

Caballero, R. (2000). 'Macroeconomic Volatility in Latin America: A View and Three Case Studies'. National Bureau of Economic Research Working Paper 77782, Cambridge, MA: NBER.

Chang, R. and Velasco, A. (2000). 'Banks, Debt Maturity and Financial Crises'. *Journal of International Economics* 51 (1): 169–194.

Calvo, G. A. and Mendoza, E. G. (2000). 'Rational Contagion and the Globalization of Securities Markets'. *Journal of International Economics* 51 (1), 79–113.

Calvo, G. A. and Mendoza, E. G. (1996). 'Mexico's Balance-of-Payments Crisis: A Chronicle of a Death Foretold'. *Journal of International Economics* 41 (3-4): 235–264.

Caprio, G., Jr and Klingebiel, D. (1996). 'Bank Insolvencies: Cross-Country Experience'. Policy Research Working Paper 1620, The World Bank, Washington, DC.

Claessens, S. (1991). 'Balance of Payments Crises in an Optimal Portfolio Model'. *European Economic Review* 35 (1): 81–101.

Claessens, S. and Glaessner, T. (1997). 'Interationalisation of Financial Services in East Asia'. World Bank, East Asia, and the Pacific Regional Office, Washington, DC.

Claessens, S. and Hindley, B. (1997). 'Internationalisation of Financial Services: Issues for Developing Countries'. World Bank, East Asia, and the Pacific Regional Office, Washington, DC.

Corsetti, G., Pesenti, P., Roubini, N., and Till. C. (1999). 'Competitive Devaluations: A Welfare-Based Approach'. NBER Working Paper 6889, Cambridge, MA: NBER.

Corsetti, G., Pesenti, P., and Roubini, N. (1998). 'What Caused the Asian Currency and Financial Crises? Part I: A Macroeconomic Overview'. NBER Working Paper 6833, Cambridge, MA: NBER.

Dornbusch, R., Park, Y. C., and Claessens, S. (2000). 'Contagion: Understanding How it Spreads'. *The World Bank Research Observer* 15 (2): 177–197.

Eichengreen, B., Rose, A., and Wyplosz, C. (1996). 'Contagious Currency Crises'. NBER Working Paper 5681, Cambridge, MA: NBER.

Flood, R. and Garber, P. (1984). 'Gold Monetization and Gold Discipline'. *Journal of Political Economy* 92 (1): 90–107.

Flood, R. P. and Marion, N. P. (1997). 'Policy Implications of "Second-Generation" Crisis Models'. IMF Working Paper 97/16, Washington DC, International Monetary Fund.

Frankel, J. A. and Rose, A. K. (1996). 'Currency Crashes in Emerging Markets: An Empirical Treatment'. *Journal of International Economics* 41: 351–366.

Glaessner, T. and Oks, D. (1994). 'NAFTA, Capital Mobility, and Mexico's Financial System'. World Bank, East Asia, and the Pacific Regional Office, Washington, DC.

G-10 (Group of 10) (1997). 'Financial Stability in Emerging Market Economies'. Report of the Working Party, Basel, Switzerland.

Gould, J. S. (1954). 'The Trade Depression of the Early 1620s'. *Economic History Review*, 2nd series, 7: 81–90.

International Monetary Fund (1960). Decision No. 1034-(60/27), June 1, 1960.

Kaminsky, G., Lizondo, S., and Reinhart, C. M. (1998). 'Leading Indicators of Currency Crises'. IMF Staff Papers 45 (1): 1–48.

Kaminsky, G. and Reinhart, C. M. (1998). 'The Twin Crises: The Causes of Banking and Balance-of-Payments Problems'. *American Economic Review* 89 (3): 473–500.

Kenen, P. B. (2002). 'Currencies, Crises, and Crashes'. *Eastern Economic Journal* 28 (1): 1–12.

Kindleberger, C. P. (1991). 'The Economic Crisis of 1619 to 1623'. *The Journal of Economic History* 51 (1): 149–175.

Kodres, L. and Pritsker, M. (1998). 'A Rational Expectations Model of Financial Contagion'. Finance and Economics Discussion Paper 9848, Board of Governors of the Federal Reserve System, Washington, DC.

Krugman, P. (1979). 'A Model of Balance-of-Payment Crises'. *Journal of Money, Credit and Banking* 11: 311–325.

Krugman, P. (1999). 'Balance Sheets, the Transfer Problem, and Financial Crises'. *International Tax and Public Finance* 6 (4): 459–472.

Krugman, P. (2000) (ed). *Currency Crises*. Chicago: University of Chicago Press.

Marjit, S. and Kar, S. (1998). '*Financial Volatility and Convertibility: Some Methodological Issues*'. *Economic and Political Weekly*, February 21: 401–406.

McKinnon, R. I. and Pill, H. (1997). 'Credible Economic Liberalizations and Overborrowing'. *American Economic Review* 87 (2): 189–193.

Obstfeld, M. (1986). 'Rational and Self-Fulfilling Balance of Payments Crises'. *American Economic Review* 76: 72–81.

Obstfeld, M. and Rogoff, K. (1996). *Foundations of International Macroeconomics*. Cambridge, MA: MIT Press.

Ohlin, B. (1927). 'The European Currency Situation'. Annals of the American Academy of Political and Social Science, 134, Europe in 1927, An Economic Survey, 151–159.

Ozcan, F. G. and Sutherland, A. (1995). 'Policy Measures to Avoid a Currency Crisis'. *The Economic Journal* 105 (429): 510–519.

Radelet, S. and Sachs, J. (1998). 'The East Asian Financial Crisis: Diagnosis, Remedies, Prospects'. *Brookings Papers on Economic Activity* 1: 1–90.

Rigobon, R. (1999). 'On the Measurement of the International Propagation of Shocks'. NBER Working Paper 7354, Cambridge, MA: NBER.

Sen, P. (2004). 'The Real Exchange Rate, Fiscal Deficits, and Capital Account Liberalisation: Some Sceptical Observation'. *Economic and Political Weekly* 39 (6): 598–600.

Supple, B. E. (1957). 'Currency and Commerce in the Early Seventeenth Century'. *Economic History Review*, 2nd series, 10: 239–255.

Tarapore Committee Report (1996). 'Report on Rupee Convertibility'. Committee appointed by Reserve Bank of India, under S. S. Tarapore, ex-deputy governor, RBI.

World Debt Tables (1996). Volumes 1 and 2, Developing Countries Stock of External Debt (1988–1995), World Bank, Washington, DC.

■ NAME INDEX

■ SUBJECT INDEX